FIRE FROM HEAVEN

Also by David Underdown

FIRE FROM HEAVEN

*Life in an English Town
in the Seventeenth Century*

DAVID UNDERDOWN

YALE UNIVERSITY PRESS
NEW HAVEN AND LONDON

To the memory of my father

Contents

PREFACE

THIS BOOK is about people who tried to build a better world. They failed, as idealistic reformers all too often seem to do, but for a few brief decades they transformed the hitherto not very remarkable west-country town of Dorchester into the most 'puritan' place in England (I leave the term 'puritan' for later definition). The catalyst was a great fire in August 1613 which devastated the town and persuaded the inhabitants to listen more intently to the preaching of their minister, John White. White's intention was to make Dorchester a reformed, godly community, a 'city on a hill', a new Jerusalem. The book explains who the reformers were, whom they were reforming, how and why they did it, and why in the end they failed. It explores a seventeenth-century English community and describes how it was affected by the great conflict that convulsed the country during that period.

I have wanted to write about Dorchester for several reasons. One, I may as well admit at the outset, is because it has given me a good excuse to spend much time in Dorset, with its marvellous countryside and even more marvellous people. But it has also provided me with one more opportunity of trying to understand England's seventeenth-century revolution, that elusive bit of history that some scholars nowadays seem to downplay almost to the point of denying that it ever happened, but which has always seemed to me important enough to justify writing books about it. And Dorchester's records for the years leading up to the civil war of the 1640s are extraordinarily rich. Through them we can, for a few years at least, observe the daily lives of ordinary townspeople, from the top of society to the bottom: from high-minded reformers like John White and his friends all the way down to the hard-drinking, turbulent, rebellious Pouncey family.

Historians have told us a good deal about John White and his articulate counterparts in other places. But they have told us all too little about the Pounceys and their like, except when they appear as faceless entries in a parish register, a rating list, or a calendar of prisoners. Dorchester's remarkable 'offenders' book' brings them to life in all their diversity, their contentious, flesh-and-blood reality, in a way that cannot be done (or at any rate has not yet been done) for any other English town of this period. So writing this book has enabled me to rescue from oblivion some of the ordinary men and women often buried behind the familiar events we know as history, and to give them their historical due. There are critics who will say that they do not matter, because everything of importance in seventeenth-century England happened 'from the top down', with the common people always obediently following the lead of their betters. The reader will have to judge whether those critics are right.

I grew up in a small town. Living in the shadow of the cathedral in twentieth-century Wells was obviously very different from living in the shadow of the Puritans in seventeenth-century Dorchester. But small towns are small towns in any time and place, and my own experience has made it just a little bit easier, I think, for me to understand the outlook of people in all other respects so far removed from us. I also grew up at a time – the 1940s – when to many people it seemed possible that we might be able to build a better world, and that there was something else to life beyond the mere pursuit of our own self-interest. Once again, the differences between seventeenth-century Puritans and twentieth-century democratic socialists are too obvious to be worth mentioning. But having shared something of that vision of a better society makes it more possible for me to appreciate how others with a very different vision may have been motivated.

This book is not written principally for scholars or specialists in the Stuart period, though I naturally hope that they will find something in it to interest them. It is written for readers with an intelligent interest in history, and with sufficient curiosity about the past to be willing to make the mental leap that is required if we are to profit from exploring it. The past, we have often been told, is 'a foreign country', and foreign countries are always stimulating, if also occasionally difficult and baffling. That, I hope is how the reader will approach Stuart Dorchester: Casterbridge two centuries before Thomas Hardy.

As always when a book is finished at last, its author looks back on the long years of research and writing, and realises with gratitude how many people have helped in its composition. Some of them are friends in Dorset, who regularly provided hospitality and good conversation to visitors from New England: I particularly thank Michael and Phyllida Horniman for so many years of friendship, and Anthony and Daphne Crook. Without them it would have been harder for a Somerset native to understand Dorset and Dorset people. Others who have made important, sometimes unconscious, contributions to the book include many friends and fellow scholars on both sides of the Atlantic. I thank especially those at Princeton in 1988–9 who put up with a no doubt excessive series of stories about seventeenth-century Dorchester people, yet were still kind enough to read and discuss an early draft of one of the chapters. And I must add my gratitude to the many students at Brown and Yale Universities, who politely listened to anecdotes about an obscure English town, and often asked challenging questions that made me think harder about its relevance.

Richard Ollard read the entire manuscript, and John Demos, Tim Harris, Maija Jansson, Paul Slack, and Harold Underdown read chapters at various stages of composition and made many helpful suggestions; any errors that remain should not embarrass them, but are entirely the author's responsibility. I am also grateful to Tim Wales for help with Dorchester wills, to Paul Bushkovitch for checking Latin translations, and to Molly McClain for pursuing references at Cambridge. Part of Chapter Two is in the Introduction to *William Whiteway of Dorchester: His Diary 1618 to 1635*, and appears with the permission of the Dorset Record Society. It was also given as a paper at the Mid-Atlantic Conference on British Studies in New York in March 1989. Material from other chapters has been included in papers given at the conference on 'England's Wars of Religion' at the Folger Library, Washington, in March 1990, and at the New England Conference on British Studies meeting at Worcester, Massachusetts, in April 1991. I am grateful to all those who made comments and suggestions on those occasions.

The staffs of the British Library, the Public Record Office, and the libraries of Brown, Princeton, and Yale Universities were, as always, unfailingly efficient and helpful. The staff of the Dorset County Record Office deserve special thanks for always meeting, and sometimes anticipating, my needs. My research in Dorchester was undertaken while first Margaret Holmes and then Hugh Jaques were County Archivists: both always made me feel welcome, and I thank them particularly for introducing me to other scholars working on Dorset history, from whose conversation I derived much benefit. I look back with particular pleasure on discussions with Adrian Moon, who taught me a great deal about Sherborne, and with Brian Bates, who generously shared so much of his knowledge of William Whiteway.

The early stages of research were assisted by a grant-in-aid from the American Philosophical Society, which I acknowledge with gratitude. The respite from teaching during which much of the first draft of the book was written was made possible by the award of a Senior Faculty Fellowship by Yale University, and of a Visiting Mellon Professorship at the Institute for Advanced Study at Princeton, in 1988–9. I am especially grateful to the Institute for providing so stimulating and congenial a setting for research and writing, and to the Mellon Foundation for the grant which made this possible.

Caradoc King's faith in the book, from an early stage of its composition, has been of crucial importance to getting it finished, and Stuart Proffitt has been a marvellous editor, a source of exactly the kind of criticism that an academic author needs when writing for a wider audience. Finally, and above all else, I wish once more to thank my wife, Susan Amussen, for her constant support, challenging criticism, and stimulating ideas, both about the subject of this book and about many wider aspects of history. She has shown in countless ways how it is still possible for someone growing up in a great modern city (New York) to show sympathy and understanding for English country people, of both the seventeenth and twentieth centuries. Without her the book might never have happened at all.

Throughout the book spellings in quotations have been modernised, Dates given are according to the old style calendar, except that the year has been taken to begin on 1 January instead of 25 March.

PROLOGUE
THE GREAT FIRE

TO A TRAVELLER passing through the county of Dorset on 6 August 1613 it would have seemed a reassuringly familiar scene. Riding from the west, let us imagine, along the old Roman road that ran arrow-straight across the great sweep of downland that rises from the vale at Eggardon, he would have observed that harvest time was beginning. Great flocks of sheep grazed the springy downland turf, just as they did on all the rolling chalk hills of southern England. But nowhere were they as plentiful as in Dorset: 'no place in England affordeth more sheep in so small a compass as this county about Dorchester', the rector of Broadwindsor, the great Thomas Fuller, observed.[1] When the road ran near enough to the edge of the plateau for him to look into the valley below, the traveller would have noted the reapers already at work in the huge cornfields that surrounded villages like Compton Valence, a mile down the hill to his left, or on the slopes below the massive earthwork of Maiden Castle, just visible through the noontide haze to his right.

Ahead, as he approached the town, the towers of Dorchester's three churches would have seemed to huddle together, for all three stood on the High Street that ran from west to east, on the same axis as the traveller. Around them rose the tiled or thatched roofs of the houses – a few large and imposing, like the great George Inn, most little better than hovels – tightly packed against each other. But it was a pleasant scene, for the buildings were set in gardens and green fields that covered much of the area even within the town walls – the crumbling, but still visible ramparts built more than a thousand years before to protect Roman Durnovaria.

By twentieth-century standards Dorchester was tiny, with a population of about two thousand, scarcely more than a village. But in its own time it was a proud and important community: the county and assize town, a parliamentary borough, by now the richest place in Dorset. For the hot and weary traveller the most alluring attractions would have been its inns and taverns – the George on High West Street, next to St Peter's church, the Antelope round the corner in South Street, a dozen others – with their promise of rest and cool refreshment.

On that early afternoon of 6 August 1613, Dorchester would not have seemed much different from a hundred other towns that dotted the English landscape. As he entered by the West Gate (open in the daytime, but still closed at night), the traveller would have found the streets almost deserted, for this was after all harvest time. Many of the more affluent inhabitants farmed lands on the edge of the town – at Frome Whitfield, perhaps, or in Fordington fields. There were still fields within the town's boundaries, as well as great stretches of gardens and smallholdings in the areas appropriately known as the East, South, and West Walls. The poorer people would certainly have been at the harvest, women as well as men seizing the annual opportunity to earn a few extra pennies, or to go gleaning when the reapers had finished. As he made his way down the sloping High Street towards the George the traveller would have noticed nothing to disturb him.

But soon after two o'clock on that August afternoon disaster struck, a disaster that was to transform the history of Dorchester. A chandler named Baker was melting tallow in his shop, just across from St Peter's church. Some said that he made 'too great a fire under his kettle'; the tallow blazed up and soon the whole house was in flames.[2] Fanned by a brisk wind, the fire spread rapidly among the closely packed buildings, their thatch and woodwork tinder-dry after a spell of hot weather. With so many people out in the fields, it was some time before enough hands could be found to man the primitive backyard pumps and pass the buckets that were the only fire-fighting equipment available. No detailed description of the fire survives – nothing to match Samuel Pepys's graphic account of the great London fire of 1666 – but it is clear that panic quickly set in among the townspeople as they rushed back from the fields and gardens. 'Man, woman and child ran amazedly up and down the streets', a contemporary pamphlet tells us, 'calling for water, water'. The most terrifying possibility was that the powder magazine in the Shire Hall, where the county's forty barrels of gunpowder were stored, might explode. Someone must have stayed calm enough to take charge – perhaps the two bailiffs, John Spicer and Nicholas Vawter, though the local diarist William Whiteway had a poor opinion of them a few years later. The barrels were hastily wrapped in wet sheets and rolled to safety upwind into the fields.[3]

The high priority given to removing the gunpowder is no doubt one reason why the fire so quickly got out of control – some of the people returning from the fields were probably diverted to the Shire Hall. Another reason may have been people's natural tendency to try to rescue possessions from their own doomed houses before fighting the flames further along the street. William Clarke later complained that the tenant to whom he had sublet the George Inn, Margaret Toomes, was very diligent about getting her own goods out, but made no effort to preserve the building; she complained that in fact she lost property worth at least a thousand marks in 'wines, wheat, oats, hay, linen, bedding, timber, wood and other goods and household stuff'.[4] The wind must have driven the flames eastward, downhill towards All Saints parish. There was fearful destruction in the other two, more westerly parishes, but All Saints, the poorest of the three, suffered worst.[5] At the town's eastern end stood the County Gaol. Excited prisoners were soon being released to fight the flames; several, women as well as men, later received royal pardons for their efforts, and for not taking advantage of the opportunity to escape. The gaol, it seems, was saved, though several houses just across the parish boundary in Fordington were consumed.[6]

At last sanity returned. Perhaps the fire was beaten by sheer numbers, for the throng of townspeople and prisoners was joined by increasing numbers of country folk from nearby villages, drawn to burning Dorchester by the combination of curiosity and fellow-feeling that such disasters produce. Many villagers would of course have had close friends and relatives in the town. The pamphlet account says that only 'a few dwellinghouses that stood about the church' escaped the flames, but does not tell us which church, and must have exaggerated the extent of the devastation. According to a more reliable estimate the 170 houses burned down amounted to about half the total number of buildings in the town.[7] The church that escaped must have been Holy Trinity, the only one of the three whose accounts for the year survive. There was great damage to other property in the parish: fifty-nine houses were consumed. But the church itself required no extensive renovations and the church-wardens received only four pounds from the relief fund, 'for our church losses'. Repairs to a door are noted in the 1614 accounts, and some new seats were installed in the following year, though some of the 'old seats' had also survived and were rearranged. Solid stone walls and slate roofs made the churches far more resistant to fire than the combustible houses that surrounded them. Almost next door to Trinity church, between it and St Peter's, was the George Inn, which was completely gutted. The other two churches may have suffered more damage than Trinity, but both were soon in use again, and when a visiting parson preached at All Saints at Christmas 1613 he made no mention of the disaster.[8]

Miraculously, only one person, an old woman named Cicely Bingham, a shoemaker's wife, died in the fire. But in a period bereft of any kind of insurance, the impact of the disaster was still profound. Although rebuilding quickly began, the town must have presented a dismal appearance during the following autumn and winter. Dorchester, the 1613 pamphlet lamented, 'was a famous town, now a heap of ashes for travellers to sigh at'. When he made his will a month after the fire, an obliging townsman left the rector, John White, two pounds 'towards the re-edifying of his house', but most people were not so lucky and many properties remained in ruins for years. The old Queen's Arms in Durngate was empty for at least a year before it was rebuilt as the Green Dragon, and a 1621 will mentions a still vacant plot of land 'on which there was a house burnt down by the late fire'.[9] An early estimate of total property damage went as high as £200,000, but as the hysteria subsided more modest figures appeared. One wealthy townsman, Denis Bond, put the total losses at £80,000, presumably including business stocks and furnishings in that sum. His kinsman, the younger William Whiteway, suggests £40,000 for houses only, and rector White speaks of something just above that figure, 'at an under value'.[10] In the absence of any proper accounting for the relief fund that was launched shortly after the fire, this is probably as close to an accurate estimate as we are likely to get.

Individual losses must have varied enormously. Bond put his own at £350, which is exactly what he spent on rebuilding the house in South Street which he rented from Sir John Williams, though he must surely also have had losses in business stocks and household goods.[11] Robert Short needed only £40 to rebuild the Queen's Arms (another Williams property), but the recently widowed Joan Gould said that she spent £400 on rebuilding, and suffered total losses of around £1,000. John Watts, a hitherto prosperous merchant and member of the Corporation, was 'much impoverished' by the fire, and his house behind South Street, adjoining 'the Antelope yard or backside', was in ruins for two years before he eventually sold it to a lawyer named Humphrey Joliffe. Joliffe claims to have spent the improbable sum of £1,000 on rebuilding it.[12]

The physical and financial impact of the great fire was, however, far less striking than its emotional and spiritual impact. People who lived through it never forgot the fire. More than sixty years later old James Gould still treasured the two gold pieces he had rescued from the ruins, and passed them on to his son.[13] The local economy recovered with remarkable speed. Still, things could never be the same again. The younger William Whiteway could recall the dismal sight of 'great buildings turned into heaps of stones, into dust and ashes' (he was fourteen, a schoolboy at the Free School, at the time of the fire), and of 'the great miseries of many families that were in an instant harbourless'.[14] The result was a sort of spiritual mass conversion. After the great crisis of the fire came the recognition that what was needed was a total reformation of the town. Fanned by the eloquent preaching of John White, the new civic spirit was to turn Dorchester from a run-of-the-mill provincial backwater into the most 'puritan' town in England, a godly community akin to Calvin's Geneva, or the 'city on a hill' that John Winthrop was soon to be creating at Boston in New England. That, at any rate, is how the reformers perceived it. In the process, Dorchester was projected into the very heart of the great religious and political controversies that were to divide England and much of Europe during the next three quarters of a century. Its history during the years after the fire enables us to examine the impact of puritan reformation on an English community, as no other town makes it possible to do, from top to bottom.

I

DORCHESTER BEFORE
THE FIRE

THE DORCHESTER thus devastated by fire had been until only a few years earlier a small and not very distinguished place. It had a long history going back to Roman times, but even in the fourteenth century it was still behind Bridport and Shaftesbury in wealth, and in 1535 the inhabitants complained that it was 'outrageously decayed', blaming this on the temporary loss of the county Assizes to Shaftesbury. A few years later the traveller John Leland scarcely bothered to mention it in his description of Dorset, and in Elizabeth's reign William Camden dismissed it as 'poor and little'.[1]

In spite of all this, the inhabitants were proud of their history: when someone vandalised the ruins of the Roman walls in Charles II's reign a townsman protested that 'it was pity that part of so ancient a monument of the town should be demolished'. The three churches demonstrated the medieval recovery from the destruction inflicted at the Norman Conquest; the solid town houses told of a more recent, though intermittent, prosperity. There had once been a castle, but that had long vanished, remembered only by the name of an open space. Since at least the early fourteenth century Dorchester had been the shire town, the site of the county gaol and (usually) the Assizes. In 1324 Edward II had granted it some limited rights of self-government: two bailiffs elected annually by twenty-four 'lawful men'.[2] By the seventeenth century the twenty-four had been reduced in number: to 'the Fifteen', the 'Capital Burgesses' who governed the town. Dorchester was not yet a fully incorporated borough, though it sent two representatives to Parliament.

Dorchester's prosperity depended less on its being the centre of county government than on its role as a regional market town. Whatever its earlier vicissitudes, by the time of the 1613 fire it was certainly the richest place in Dorset. For centuries there had been three big summer fairs – on the day after Trinity Sunday, St John's Day at midsummer, and St James's Day in July – and a winter fair at Candlemas in February was added early in Elizabeth's reign.[3] The fairs lured traders and buyers from miles around, and the town also had its regular weekly markets. Dorchester had its butchers, bakers, chandlers, shoemakers, and tradesmen of all the varieties to be found in an early modern market town, their shops strung out along the bustling streets, the stalls in the market, the butchers' shambles (the meat-market and slaughterhouse), and along South Street. The butchers' 'standings' were rented from the town. In 1593 William Fooke took over one in the shambles, on the north side of the stairs leading from High East Street into St Peter's churchyard, 'under some part of the Town Hall'; in 1618 John Standish acquired one on the north side of High East Street, adjoining 'a pillar of stone which beareth part of the house called the Bow'. Equally coveted were the glovers' standings in South Street, and the ones occupied by various hosiers, chandlers, blacksmiths and cutlers in all the main streets of the town.[4]

Much of the town's wealth depended on the cloth industry. Dorchester contained large numbers of weavers and other craftsmen connected with the trade, and the master clothiers were important men in the life of the town. Through the nearby port of Weymouth, Dorchester's merchants traded busily with France and other parts of the continent; the town, the pamphlet describing the fire noted, was 'one of the principal places of traffic for western merchants'. Its shops and warehouses were packed with woollen cloth, fine linens and other luxury goods, as well as the more humdrum shoes, pewter, grocery wares, and the thousand and one other necessities that drew the country people to its fairs and markets.[5]

A century or so earlier, a few merchant families had begun to rise above the general run of those who made up the town oligarchy. The most notable were the Williamses. John Williams was bailiff of Dorchester four times between 1479 and 1503, and by the time he died in 1515 he had acquired much property in the town. His son, another John Williams, born around 1480, did even better. He amassed immense wealth – in 1524 his tax assessment was the highest in the county – and he used it to buy land at several places in Dorset and establish a major county family. His principal estate was at Herringstone, a few miles south of Dorchester, which he bought for £360 early in Henry VIII's reign. The Williamses had moved out of the confines of a small town into the more exalted circles of the county gentry, but they did not forget their Dorchester origins. They contributed to local charities, their splendid tombs adorned St Peter's church, and they retained much of their property in the borough. The fortunes of the family were to remain entwined, sometimes tragically, with those of Dorchester, throughout the Tudor and Stuart centuries.[6]

Another family to prosper in the sixteenth century was the Churchills, who did well out of former church lands after the Reformation. John Churchill, a clothier, was an established figure in the town during Henry VIII's reign, bailiff in 1525 and again in 1540. In 1549 he acquired part of the property of the dissolved Hospital of St John; some of it he sold, but on part of it he built a fine house at Colleton, on the edge of the town. Colleton and the nearby cottages in Colleton Row were eventually to be within the parish of Holy Trinity, but not within the borough, an anomaly that was to cause endless litigation. The Churchills were less affluent than the Williamses, but they too made the transition to county society while still maintaining a foothold in Dorchester.[7]

The Churchills and the Williamses were unusual in crossing the great divide between burgess and gentleman. Most of the men who ran Tudor Dorchester were content with the more restricted horizons of the town. Families like the Adyns and Palmers occupied civic offices more or less in rotation, and took little part in the affairs of the county or the kingdom. Dorchester in this period was politically under the thumb of the neighbouring gentry and their courtly or aristocratic patrons, great men like Lord Russell, Henry VIII's principal agent in the western counties in the 1540s, who became Earl of Bedford under Edward VI. The Russells controlled the election of Dorchester's MPs, using their patronage to find seats for reliably protestant Dorset gentlemen like John Leweston of Leweston, and court officials like Robert Beale, Clerk to the Privy Council. After the second Earl's death in 1585 the process continued under different patrons. Dorchester obediently elected Exchequer officials like Nowell Sotherton, and various clients of the Marquis of Winchester. Before 1601 only two local men – William Holman in 1559 and William Adyn in 1571 – represented Dorchester in Elizabethan parliaments.[8]

The Russells were a remote and barely visible influence. A more immediate presence was that of the neighbouring gentry families. Besides the newly rich Williamses and Churchills, these included the powerful Trenchards of Wolveton, just north of the town. Sir Thomas Trenchard was High Steward in Henry VIII's reign: his son George was MP for Dorchester in 1572, and Recorder for a year or two in James I's reign. They too owned property in the town. So did the Scropes, from whom the Corporation bought the rectory of nearby Frome Whitfield in 1585, and the Brownes of Frampton.[9]

The sixteenth century was not a good period for English provincial towns. By the middle of the century a good many of them faced stagnation or decay. Two long centuries of under-population beginning with the Black Death were followed by an economic dislocation in which more and more of the country's trade was gobbled up by London. Population began to recover after 1500, but there were further set-backs, including the awful decade of the 1550s when disease wiped out as much as a fifth of the inhabitants in some places.[10] There were more bad years towards the end of Elizabeth's reign, especially in the bleak 1590s. After a run of bad harvests had pushed up food prices to famine levels, the mortality of 1597 was the worst of the century. By this time, though, most places were worrying about the opposite problem: over-population. During the sixteenth century the population of England grew by over fifty per cent – from well under three million to over four million – and for the towns most of the increase was concentrated in the last quarter of the century. That this rapid growth in population was not accompanied by a corresponding increase in food production meant inevitably that a massive increase in food prices followed. The demographic explosion and the problems that stemmed from it – inflation, land shortage, unemployment, declining living standards for the ever-increasing numbers of the poor – determined much of the character of the century. The splendours of the age of Gloriana, of Drake and Spenser and Shakespeare, concealed even more misery and privation than was the common fate of ordinary English men and women throughout the country's history.

The fire of 1613 destroyed most of the records from which we might have been able to reconstruct the conditions of life in sixteenth-century Dorchester. From what little remains, we can be certain that the place had experienced the typical depression and under-population that had recently beset most English towns. By the beginning of Elizabeth's reign Dorchester's population had fallen below one thousand – less than it had been in the middle ages. But between the 1570s and the second decade of the seventeenth century it doubled in size to over two thousand, and fairly rapid growth continued for more than another twenty years. By 1642 the town contained over two thousand five hundred inhabitants.[11] From the dramatic rise in the number of births in the 1580s and 1590s, it looks as if during these years there was a considerable influx of young people from the countryside. After 1600, on the other hand, population growth was almost entirely spurred by natural increase, an excess of births over deaths. There were some temporary set-backs to the generally upward population curve. The plague year of 1563 witnessed twenty-four burials in Trinity parish, more than twice the annual average for the decade. The worst year of that grim final decade of the century, 1597, was even more lethal, with forty burials of local people, as well as of four 'strangers' who died in the parish. Years like this reminded the pious that in the midst of life they were in death, but they did not materially affect the underlying trend of population growth. At the start of Elizabeth's reign Dorchester must have seemed a decayed and stagnant place; by the time the Queen died it was a much more vibrant and expanding one.

Population growth brought problems for Dorchester, as it did for the rest of the country. One such problem was poverty and the associated threat of disorder that came with it. A crescendo of anxious voices lamented the proliferation of the poor and unproductive in the towns and villages of England. Moralists constantly complained about the swarms of idle and dissipated young people who were not being contained within the system of household discipline – the system on which, most people believed, social stability depended.

Stability in the state, Tudor preachers never tired of reminding their congregations, rested on stability in the family. The authority of the monarch corresponded with that of the patriarchal father over his household: undermine discipline and obedience in one sphere, and it would inevitably collapse in the other. And the family might include others besides those related by blood or marriage: it also contained the servants and apprentices for whose moral and spiritual welfare the father (master) was also responsible. Everyone was supposed to be under the tutelage of a parent or master until, on marrying, they became either the head of a new family or the wife of one. Those who escaped from the system became that much feared phenomenon, the masterless person, of which the most dangerous variety was the sturdy beggar or vagrant.

So in the course of Elizabeth's reign there were constant thunderings against the perceived, but little understood, evils associated with poverty and masterlessness. The sprawling numbers of the idle and undisciplined, moralists like John Northbrooke and Philip Stubbes proclaimed, threatened the very foundations of order and religion. As so often is the case, poverty was blamed on its victims. They hung about in alehouses, it was said, when they ought to have been working or worshipping, and preferred the traditional sports and festive pastimes to the disciplined sobriety which the Stubbeses and the Northbrookes thought they ought to pursue. The weakening of household discipline affected other dependent people besides servants and apprentices: women, for example. There were complaints that they were becoming dangerously and immodestly assertive, sinfully inclined to rebel against the quiet submissiveness which the preachers and other (male) opinion-formers proclaimed as the lot that God had ordained for them. The 'scold' (the disorderly woman who publicly abused her neighbours), and the witch (almost invariably a woman, of course), were two characteristic targets of people who were worried about social stability. By the time of the great fire, Dorchester, like virtually all other English towns, was caught up in what modern historians have called a 'crisis of order'.[12]

There were many efforts to deal with the underlying problems. There was the new poor law, the series of measures that culminated in the great consolidating statute of 1601. Parishes were now required to elect overseers of the poor, collect a poor rate, distribute relief to the deserving, and maintain stocks of hemp and suchlike products with which the idle and undeserving (the unemployed, in other words) could be set to work. The poor law did not preclude private charity, which was indeed still the source of more money for the poor than the public rates generated. So there were still many bequests for the relief of the poor and afflicted, and for the promotion of sobriety and industriousness. Such philanthropy was not unique to English Protestants – it was common in many continental cities, Catholic as well as Protestant – but Protestants, as we shall see, were particularly attracted to it.[13] There are signs of this kind of philanthropy in Dorchester long before 1600. The Williams family had given money for a leper hospital, and had contributed to an almshouse for destitute widows, whose original endowment remains obscure. A major bequest towards the end of Elizabeth's reign exemplifies the protestant encouragement of thrift and hard work. In 1598 one of the Churchills of Colleton established a fund from which loans were to be made to deserving 'poor artificers', a type of endowment that was becoming common in other English towns at about this time.[14]

Bequests of this kind are signs that by the end of the century the problem of poverty was beginning to be better understood: that lack of work was not necessarily the result of sin and idleness, but that even virtuous and well-intentioned working people might need assistance in the conditions of over-population and high food prices that now prevailed. The town's governors were also beginning to recognise that some people could not look after themselves through no fault of their own, and that parish funds and private charity were not always available for them. In the 1580s they made occasional special payments for the benefit of sick people: eight shillings to a certain Robert Hall, for example, 'for curing of a poor boy's leg'. But this was not done in any systematic way, and there was a good deal of favouritism in it. Thomas Galton received ten shillings 'for his painful attendance' on sick persons, which had been 'chargeable to him, and hindersome'; and two payments were made for treating one of Roger Pouncey's family. Both Galton and Pouncey were clients of Matthew Chubb, by this time the most powerful member of the Dorchester Corporation.[15]

❖

The population explosion was one source of the transformation that occurred in sixteenth-century Dorchester. The other was the Reformation. Before the Reformation – and indeed, in very different ways, after it – the whole intellectual and cultural, as well as the religious, life of Dorchester revolved around the churches. Since time immemorial there had been three of them: Holy Trinity to the west, St Peter's in the centre, and All Saints down the hill to the east. We have no first-hand descriptions, but we can assume that like most other medieval churches they were vividly decorated. Stained glass, painted screens and murals, statues and reliefs would have portrayed biblical scenes and the lives of saints, imparting the truths of Christianity to the congregation. The clergy wore rich and colourful vestments, and on feast days and holy days there were elaborate processions, with banners and streamers held aloft. Even after several years of Protestantism, in 1552 Holy Trinity still owned 'a canopy of silk, a cope of white silk, a banner of red silk, a streamer, and six banners of canvas painted'. St Peter's had similar vestments, as well as a 'streamer of sarcenet' and four banners of painted canvas.[16]

One peculiarity of Dorchester's parochial structure was that Trinity and St Peter's had only one rector between them. The rectory was that of Holy Trinity, St Peter's being served by an assistant curate, though in fact the rector often officiated there too. By the end of the sixteenth century St Peter's was distinctly the most affluent and least crowded parish. There were rich and poor in all three parishes, but St Peter's had more of the rich and fewer of the poor, All Saints more of the poor and fewer of the rich; Trinity lay somewhere in between.[17]

The parish churches were by no means the only religious foundations in Dorchester. The most prominent of the others was the community of Franciscans, or Friars Minor, the site of whose house is recalled by the modern Friary Lane; it had once housed over thirty friars, but there were probably many fewer by the sixteenth century. There was also a Hospital dedicated to St John the Baptist, with its attached chapel, in which relief was provided for the poor and the sick, and which until the Reformation also supported a scholar at Oxford. A good deal of the town was owned by these and other religious bodies: the Knights of St John of Jerusalem, the abbeys of Milton, Abbotsbury, and Bindon.[18]

Much of Dorchester's religious life before the Reformation was conducted in the numerous church guilds, or fraternities. A fraternity, as a recent historian explains, was 'an association of layfolk who, under the patronage of a particular saint . . . undertook to provide the individual member of the brotherhood with a good funeral', along with subsequent masses for the benefit of the member's soul.[19] But the fraternities did more than this. They had their special fasts and feast days, they organised schemes for the welfare of their poorer members, and some of the richer ones built schools and almshouses. They competed in putting on colourful processions, pageants, and plays, and the services in their chapels (which were usually within their parish churches) were richly adorned with incense, bells, and music. Some fraternities were associated with specific trades, others brought together the leading men of their town's governing oligarchy and have thus been described as 'the local corporation at prayer'. They were opulent, self-confident, highly visible; apparently permanent fixtures in any late medieval English town.

The most notable of Dorchester's fraternities was one in St Peter's parish, dedicated to the Blessed Virgin Mary. It owned houses and other property all over the town, and its officers were among the most powerful members of the civic hierarchy: John Williams, for example, was warden in 1526. This parish also contained the fraternities of the Holy Cross and of Corpus Christi. In Trinity parish there were two fraternities, one of them being, naturally enough, that of the Holy Trinity. People left them money and other goods; in 1473 the mercer John Pascowe gave the fraternity of the Holy Cross two sheep. Through the fraternities people could establish chantries, with priests to pray for their souls and those of their families; Pascowe did this, as did another wealthy burgess, John Seward, early in the fifteenth century. We have no direct evidence of the plays and processions which they almost certainly organised, but there are hints that suggest the importance of their continuing contributions to the religious and cultural identity of late medieval Dorchester. Even in 1535, at a time when Henry VIII had already broken with Rome and the attack on the monasteries had begun, a Dorchester widow, Margaret Auden, could still leave money to the wardens of All Saints so that masses could be said for her soul, 'and the souls of all faithful departed', for twenty years to come. How could she have foreseen that the mass, the tapers, the tolling bells,

and the doctrine of purgatory which underlay them would so soon
be swept away? [20]

But swept away they were. The Franciscans reluctantly surrendered to the King in 1538; within a year or so people were speaking
of the house 'late of the Friars Minors'. Among the goods sold off
were the Friary's bells, organs, vestments, and three 'great alabaster
images'. Henry VIII's church was not yet a truly protestant one, but
great and violent changes were convulsing it. In 1543 the Friary was
bought by one of Henry's courtiers, and early in the next century it
became the town house of the Recorder, Sir Francis Ashley. During
that time, like so many of the monasteries that were converted into
private residences, it was extensively rebuilt. [21] The fraternities and
their chantries survived into Edward VI's reign, but then they too
were dissolved and their revenues confiscated. The Dorchester Corporation acquired much of the property of the fraternity of the
Blessed Virgin. Some of the revenue was used for the maintenance
of St Peter's church, and former tenants got a share of it, but as in
other places, most of the plunder of the church ended in the hands
of the nobility and gentry: the Earl of Bedford, for example, or more
locally, the Churchills. [22]

Nostalgic reminders of the old religion gradually vanished from
the town. The cross 'before Mr Brent's door' (evidently a survival
from the Friary) was demolished about the year 1571, though there
still remained another town cross, sometimes called the 'pig cross'
in the market-place. A building known as the 'chantry house' still
existed in 1633, though whether it got the name because it housed a
chantry chapel, or merely because it belonged to one of the chantries,
is unknown. [23] The destruction of records in the 1613 fire means that
much of Dorchester's experience during the thirty years of unsettling
religious changes that began in 1529 remains shrouded in mystery.
How did the townspeople react to Catholicism without the Pope
under Henry; to the lurch to Protestantism in Edward's reign; the
return to Rome under Mary; and the second establishment of Protestantism after Elizabeth's accession? If they were like people in other
English towns and villages, a handful of enthusiasts at the two
extremes of the religious spectrum presumably grieved or rejoiced,
as appropriate, while the majority stoically accepted whatever was
decreed from on high, and at least outwardly conformed. The clergy
who served the three parishes during these years are shadowy figures:

Nicholas Knewstub and Richard Hunt in the 1540s; William Wood-man in the first part of Elizabeth's reign, Richard Johnson and Richard Everard in the latter.[24]

How quickly Protestantism took root in Dorchester we can only guess. In the sixteenth century the town had no great reputation as a centre of reformation; it was Poole that was said to have contained 'the first that in that part of England were called Protestants'. When the former Marian exile William Kethe settled in Dorset in the 1560s he found the county still infected with the festive culture that he associated with the bad old days of Popery.[25] There were still Catholics in Dorchester at the end of the century; the older ones would have been able to remember the mass being celebrated in the three churches during Mary's reign. But by this time persecution had thinned their numbers. One Dorchester man fled to the continent in the 1580s to escape the repression and because, he said, 'he could not resolve to frequent the preaching'. He was picked up in the Netherlands a few years later, suspected of being a spy for the Spaniards.[26]

There were even more Catholics in the Dorset countryside: Dorchester came to think of itself as a besieged protestant island surrounded by a sea of Papists and people who sympathised with and shielded them. The eastern part of the county, it was reported in 1602, was still 'much infected with recusancy'. Zealous protestant JPs like Sir George Trenchard might round up local recusants, but as he and one of his colleagues told the Council, they still lived comfortably in gaol and had their meetings, 'in despite of the Justices, do what they can'. Some of them, it was alleged, were protected by powerful people. At the Quarter Sessions in 1591 the grand jury were instructed, as usual, to prosecute Catholics, but a 'secret warning and intelligence' was given them by some mysterious county dignitary, 'to forbear to meddle with the said recusants'. Priests and the people who had sheltered them in the Arundells' house at Chideock (a well-known nest of Catholics) were hunted down, and several were executed as traitors at Dorchester in 1587 and 1594. Public executions, particularly those involving the fiendish penalties of hanging, drawing and quartering that were inflicted on traitors, were always great theatrical occasions, conveying awesome messages of power and authority. The memory of the dismemberment of the most celebrated of the 1594 victims, Father Cornelius, was kept alive for years by the sight of his head displayed atop one of the town gates. Pious Catholics believed that the heavy mortality of 1597 was God's punishment on the town for this act.[27]

Such events helped to harden the tepid, half-hearted Protestantism of the majority of the English people in the 1560s into the militant, nationalistic Protestantism that defined so much of the identity of late Elizabethan England. The belief that the nation was specially predestined by God to defend His cause against Antichrist (the Pope, of course) was spread in countless sermons and books. One of them, John Foxe's *Acts and Monuments of the Reformation* (the famous *Book of Martyrs*), was to become, after the Bible, the central text of English Protestantism. As religious conflict ignited in continental Europe, the habit of seeing the world as divided into two irreconcilable camps became more and more common. On one side stood the forces of good: England; the German Lutheran states; the militant adherents of John Calvin in Geneva; the commercially vibrant cities of the Netherlands; and the French Huguenot towns. On the other stood the forces of evil: the Pope, the King of Spain and their allies, especially the new Jesuit order and other militants inspired by the spirit of Catholic revivalism in the Counter-Reformation, all bent on eradicating the reformed religion. In their way stood England, God's 'elect nation', beset, so Elizabethan zealots believed, by enemies at home and abroad, its liberties, religion, and independence all threatened by the popish kingdom of darkness.[28]

Dorchester was no remote rustic backwater, isolated from the great affairs of the kingdom and of Christendom. The bells of the three churches no longer rang out on the feast days of the outlawed Catholic saints, but they clanged jubilantly every 17 November, the anniversary of the Queen's accession, a day that was becoming a great annual celebration of loyalty, national pride, and protestant virtue.[29] The town sent four men to the army that went to France to assist the Huguenots in 1562. Twenty years later, as the great conflict with Spain drew closer, money was spent on weapons: 12s. for 'new muster arrows' and for re-feathering the stock of arrows. In 1586 one of the town's cannon was repaired, and there were further outlays for powder and arrows in subsequent years. It is unlikely that they would have availed much against Parma's veterans if invasion had come, and Dorchester people must have waited anxiously in the summer days of 1588 as the great Armada made its way up Channel. The richer 'men of ability' had been required to contribute to the cost of equipping a Weymouth ship that sailed with the Queen's navy. No doubt some of them rode down to Portland to watch the Spanish fleet pass by on its way to Gravelines and disaster. There was rejoicing at the victory, but we should not exaggerate popular enthusiasm for the war, especially when it turned to disappointing anti-climax in the 1590s. Before the decade was out there was much discontent in Dorset about the way conscripts were being levied; the 'beggarly and rascally sort', it was said, looked to profit from the resentment, and had great 'hope of novelties' and political upheaval. But 1588 remained one of the great dates in England's protestant calendar, a permanent reminder of God's mercies to his elect nation.[30]

The return to Protestantism in Elizabeth's reign thus meant that the nation was involved in a great international conflict against Rome and its allies. But it had other meanings. For many Englishmen it also meant dedication to those typically protestant virtues of spiritual self-reliance, of moral vigilance, of rigorous personal discipline, none of which could be achieved without the ability to read and understand the scriptures. This was one reason for the growing concern for education in Elizabethan England; another was the perceived need to train a class of educated laymen to serve crown and commonwealth. Many monastic and other kinds of church schools had vanished at the Reformation, but by the end of the century they had more than been replaced. Among the new schools founded in this period was the Free School in Dorchester, established by a group of townsmen early in the Queen's reign. A site was acquired in South Street and by 1567 building operations were proceeding; stone was brought from the famous Ham Hill quarries and timber from an earlier schoolhouse which was now demolished. The school's early history is obscure, but in 1579 it was rescued and re-endowed by Thomas Hardy of Melcombe Regis (a later document says that the town 'bestowed' the school on him). Dorchester people also contributed to the endowment, as did country gentlemen like Sir Robert Napper, and by the end of the century the school was gaining a solid reputation for the classical education it provided for the sons of the wealthier townsmen and the neighbouring gentry. Robert Cheeke, who came as Master in 1595, was to be a man of some importance in the town.[31]

Everyone could agree on the importance of educating young men of respectable backgrounds for the service of church and commonwealth. But not everyone agreed on what the precise nature of that church, that commonwealth, ought to be. The Church of England established by the Elizabethan Acts of Supremacy and Uniformity was a protestant church, fervent in its repudiation of Rome. It retained a traditional form of church government – bishops and clergy appointed and ordained by authority, rather than called from below by the congregations – but its theology was largely Calvinist, including the doctrines of election and predestination. There were blurred edges, and not everyone accepted the Calvinists' ultimate conclusion that an all-powerful deity had predestined for salvation only a tiny handful, the elect, leaving the reprobate majority to eternal damnation, and that nothing could alter this. Many who did accept this conclusion also believed that the Elizabethan church still needed further reformation, in that both its doctrines and its liturgical practices retained far too many vestiges of Popery. They objected to such 'popish' survivals as the required wearing of the surplice by the clergy, to empty ceremonies like the use of the sign of the cross in baptism, bowing at the name of Jesus, or kneeling to receive communion. They also tended to profess higher standards of personal morality than their fellow Christians, and to feel that they had a special mission to stamp out the ungodly depravity that surrounded them: they were particularly upset by violations of the sanctity of the sabbath, and by 'heathenish' pastimes like dancing round the maypole or the many other kinds of merrymaking beloved by the common folk.

By the end of Elizabeth's reign such people were often called 'precisians' (because they were thought to be over-precise in matters of conduct and doctrine), or 'Puritans'. As the much debated term 'Puritan' will be a constant presence throughout this book, it is important to understand what is meant by it. First, it should be stressed that the word was a term of abuse, hurled at enemies: people we call Puritans were more likely to think of themselves as 'the godly' or 'God's people'. As for the word 'Puritanism', it is of course a modern abstraction, and there are historians who would like to jettison it, though nobody has been able to think of a usable alternative. 'Puritan' remains a convenient shorthand term, and if there are still people who are doubtful of its historical validity, I invite them to read the rest of this book and think again.

Puritans were people within the Church of England who wished to reform it further, not people criticising the church from without. We can distinguish between Puritans and non-Puritans within the Anglican church; but we cannot correctly speak of Puritans and Anglicans, because Puritans *were* Anglicans. The Puritans were those who wished to press on with the reformation of the Church of England, towards an ideal of protestant perfection that for many of them was represented by Calvin's Geneva. Preferably this would be done by the actions of godly princes and magistrates, but if those authorities proved to be backsliding or temporising, they would if necessary do it 'without tarrying for the magistrate'. Apart from this somewhat less than absolute acceptance of the duty of obedience, Puritans differed from other members of the church not in kind but in degree – in the intensity of their convictions.

There was no single great divide separating Puritans from other members of the church, but a spectrum on which beliefs shaded off with different emphases, one into another. Some uncompromising souls might reject all ceremonies as popish superstitions; others might see it as their duty to obey the hierarchy's least offensive directives, so that they might continue to serve God and their flocks. At one time some might work to establish a new kind of 'presbyterian' discipline (imposed by parish clergy and lay elders rather than bishops) within the church; at another to accept that royal and episcopal hostility made this impossible. Some might emphasise the separate, distinctive identity of the godly; others the unity of the whole church. On all these and many other issues there were moderates and extremists, but on all, too, there was a large middle ground. Sympathy for the moderate puritan call for further reformation could be found even among bishops and archbishops, though the Queen did not share it, as Elizabeth's Archbishop Grindal found to his cost when he was suspended.

But although we should not exaggerate the contrast between Puritans and other members of the Church of England, we should be wrong to deny that some sort of contrast existed. Moderate Puritans usually managed to conform if they were not pushed too hard, but

there were sporadic eruptions of a less compromising attitude, sometimes provoked by bouts of official harshness – in the presbyterian
movement of the 1570s and 1580s, the bitter pamphleteering campaign against the bishops by the pseudonymous 'Martin Marprelate',
and the resistance to the canons of 1604 – which led to widespread
suspensions and ejections.[32] And the Puritan as censorious (and no
doubt hypocritical) moralist was fast becoming familiar – a stock
comic figure, immortalised as Shakespeare's Malvolio and carica-
tured by Ben Jonson and countless later authors.

So Puritans were people who thought of themselves as orthodox
members of a protestant Church of England, and were indeed the
most inclined to emphasise the protestant traditions of that church.
We can identify some characteristic beliefs that most of them shared,
while always remembering that they did not form a monolithic
movement, and that there were many differences and shades of
opinion among them. They put preaching and the study of scripture
above the repetition of sacramental rituals, though they did not deny
the importance of communion as a commemorative act which
fortified the faith of 'God's people'. They set high standards for
themselves and others, engaging in regular and often obsessive self-
examination to assure themselves that they were indeed among the
elect and that they were doing the Lord's work. Their beliefs
demanded a constant striving after salvation, a refusal to compromise
with sin and human fallibility, and required them to press on with
building the new Jerusalem, the task that God had marked out, above
all others, as their destiny. Theirs was the duty to fight God's battles
– against Popery, against superstition and sin – even if those set in
authority over them (and they did not question the lawfulness of that
authority) were tepid and half-hearted. Confronted by the epidemic
of immorality and disorder that was ultimately traceable to the population explosion, Puritans became the most vigorous exponents of
policies of reforming and disciplining the lawless, of stamping out
sin and even youthful frivolity. Theirs was a world in which the
individual Christian was always engaged, however apparently trivial
and insignificant the action, in the eternal struggle between Christ
and Antichrist.

❖

Little of this kind of militant Protestantism can be detected in Dorchester before the end of Elizabeth's reign. The Earl of Bedford earlier, and the Trenchards later, were sympathetic to the protestant vanguard, and the schoolmaster Robert Cheeke had something of a puritan reputation. By 1600 a few people of similar views were moving into the town, and some members of the old elite had been, or were soon to be, supporters of further reformation.[33] But they were the exceptions. Few, if any, of the governors of late Elizabethan Dorchester seem to have had any vision of an alternative to the way their community, with all its problems, was run. As we have seen, they gave some unsystematic hand-outs to the needy, but they also played fast and loose with poor relief funds, borrowing forty pounds from the three parishes in 1600 when the town ran into debt because of some expensive building operations at the Town Hall.[34] There were still a few Catholic sympathisers among them – William Anthony, bailiff in 1597, was expelled for recusancy a few years later.[35] For the most part, though, the Elizabethan Corporation was made up of men who superficially accepted the religious changes that had been imposed on them but who had not yet internalised the protestant message of salvation, and certainly not its Calvinist version of election, predestination, and constant moral struggle. They showed no interest in the kind of philanthropy which distinguished their successors. The vintner Ralph Palmer, several times bailiff, left nothing to charity, and several of his colleagues – Joseph Eyres, Richard Barker, and Nicholas Vawter, for example – did little better. Perhaps they had given generously during their lifetimes, but if so, there is no evidence for it in the surviving records.[36] They were no doubt becoming more conscious of their civic identity and anxious to strengthen their own authority: they got a new charter in 1610, under which Dorchester became for the first time a fully incorporated borough.[37] But very few of them wished to use their new powers to reform the town in any dramatic way.

The most influential member of the borough oligarchy in the early years of James I's reign was Matthew Chubb. His father, John Chubb, came from Misterton near Crewkerne, just over the Somerset border, married a Dorchester woman, and around 1548, soon after Matthew's birth, moved into the town. John Chubb must have prospered, as he soon became a member of the Corporation – he was town steward in 1555 – but his son quickly surpassed him.

Matthew set up a school when he was a young man in the 1560s, but abandoned it when the Free School came into existence. He then became a scrivener, drawing up wills and conveyances, and married in turn two conveniently wealthy wives. Along with this he regularly lent money to his neighbours, and eventually became a goldsmith and the richest man in Dorchester.[38]

Matthew Chubb was a member of the Corporation by 1583, when he became town steward. He was already being entrusted with important public business: he was sent to Exeter to lobby the judges when there was a danger that Dorchester might lose the Assizes. He was bailiff for the first of several times in 1588, and in the next twenty years he held that and every other possible town office with great regularity. In 1601 he became the first townsman to represent Dorchester in Parliament since William Adyn thirty years before, and he was again returned in 1604. This time he tried to get out of it, protesting both before and at the election 'the disability of his body to endure that service'. When his fellow burgesses ignored his objections he simply refused to go to Westminster and got them to join him in unsuccessfully petitioning the Commons to let him resign. Chubb was in reasonable health during the next few years, so it looks as if he simply wanted to avoid the trouble and expense of the journey to London. To him it was a straightforward cash matter: he offered five pounds 'to some others to be chosen' at the election. Nowhere is there any sign that Chubb saw membership in Parliament – or any other public office – as anything more than a matter of self-interest.[39]

Such was the condition of Dorchester when on 11 November 1605 – less than a week after the discovery at Westminster of Guy Fawkes's plot to blow up King and Parliament – a new rector was presented by the crown to the living of Holy Trinity, Dorchester. The previous incumbent, Richard Johnson, had died some years earlier, and although the curate, Richard Everard, had filled the gap, the towns-people must have looked forward eagerly to their minister's arrival from Oxford. John White was a fellow of New College and this was his first parish. About thirty years old, he was descended from a prolific Hampshire family from whose other branches had come men of some consequence: a Lord Mayor of London, a Warden of New College, a Bishop of Winchester. Family connections helped White's father to get from New College a lease of the manor of Stanton St John, near Oxford, where John was born in 1575, and also eased the boy's entry first to school at Winchester and then to New College itself.[40]

The Oxford in which John White came to intellectual maturity was vigorously involved in the conflicts and controversies of the kingdom: it was no tranquil ivory tower. A trickle of recent student conversions back to Rome had caused alarm, and the outlook of convinced Protestants was correspondingly militant. The two universities were supposed to train an educated clergy, to provide the 'preaching ministry' that reformers had found sadly lacking at the beginning of Elizabeth's reign, and this had been done more successfully, many thought, at Cambridge. But although Oxford's reputation for producing puritan clergy was less impressive, it contained a number of colleges of distinctly Calvinist inclinations. One of them was New College, where there had been a particularly thorough purge of Catholic Fellows after the Reformation; even a generation after White's time, as Archbishop Laud noted disgustedly, Calvin's *Institutes* were still studied there with more than usual intensity.[41]

Calvin's teachings made their mark on others besides John White. Among his contemporaries at New College was Arthur Lake, destined for a bishopric but a strong Calvinist just the same; White's friend Richard Bernard described him as 'a blessed bishop, a very man of God'. They were later to work together in the Massachusetts Bay Company, and Lake confided in White that he himself would have liked to go to New England. Another of White's New College acquaintances was William Twisse, afterwards chaplain to Elizabeth of Bohemia, and in the 1640s chairman of the presbyterian Westminster Assembly. Besides Bernard (who was to follow White to the west country in 1613, to the Somerset village of Batcombe), White's friends included another Cambridge man, John Burges, whose sister White married soon after he came to Dorchester. Burges was a stormy petrel, ejected from one parish for refusing to wear the surplice and from another for opposing the anti-puritan 1604 canons, imprisoned for audaciously preaching against ceremonies before the King himself. Burges went further than most Jacobean

Puritans in his nonconformity; White was of a more moderate disposition. The 'religion of Protestants' which characterised the church in James's reign could accommodate both, as well as many clerics with less Calvinist fervour, within its comfortable bounds.[42] John White, committed Calvinist and determined servant of the Lord, was no revolutionary. But he came to Dorchester with a mission.

2

DORCHESTER'S GOVERNORS

WHITE'S sermons were soon provoking argument. There had been no recent shortage of sermons in the town: the Elizabethan campaign for a 'preaching ministry' had seen to that. We know almost nothing about the preaching of White's predecessors at St Peter's and Holy Trinity, or of his colleague at All Saints, the amiable William Cheeke. But since at least 1600 the town had had a lecturer, or 'stipendiary preacher', a certain Mr Lougher, and there had also been sermons by visiting clergy from the parishes round about. None of them had had anything like the impact of the newly-arrived reformer from Oxford. It was his uncompromising Calvinism that set the town talking. White preached, one of his listeners complained, 'that Christ was not the Saviour of the whole world, but of his elected and chosen people only': Christ's 'fatherly care' extended no further than to the elect. Calvinist teachings on grace had been part of the official doctrine of the English church ever since the completion of the Elizabethan settlement, and in many parishes by 1606 predestination would not have aroused controversy. But it was still a live issue in Dorchester.[1]

Within a few months of White's arrival anonymous 'libels' began appearing in the town – some were found lying in the streets, others thrown into shop doorways. The circulation of scurrilous verse satires, often with a strong sexual content, was a common way of conducting public arguments in the early seventeenth century, and Dorchester had its share of them. The first 'libel', which began 'To all sturdy puritan knaves', was picked up in late June 1606 by a butcher's boy, who gave it to Gervase Scrope, a young gentleman at the Free School. Scrope took it home with him (he boarded at the house of the bailiff, Matthew Chubb), and soon it was all over the town. White was not explicitly named, but the libel contained references to an attempted 'beating down' of stage plays, a policy which Puritans were well known to favour, and to restrictions on the ringing of church bells, which some Puritans (though not White) had also proposed. There were sneers at the poverty of many Puritans and their corresponding greed and dishonesty:

> Thy mind is high, thy purse is small,
> God knows it to be true,
> For were it not for other men's goods,
> thy state were of bad hue.

And there were accusations of other kinds of hypocrisy, particularly in sexual matters, including a gleeful story of an affair involving one of the brethren, a minister from the Isle of Purbeck, and the wife of John Conduit, a pious tailor of Dorchester who specialised, his enemies sneered, in 'women's apparel'. The minister had previously 'most willing been to lead a quiet life', but now 'the devil urged him to lie with Conduit's wife', and apparently she was willing to oblige. The moral was obvious:

> Is this the Puritans' life that all of you do profess?
> Then all your pure lives be nothing but dissembling, as I
>   guess.

Six weeks later a second libel appeared. Thomas Foy, a shoemaker, found it in the street near the Cross, and seeing Matthew Chubb chatting with his fellow bailiff, Richard Blachford, on Blachford's porch, he took it to these surely law-abiding officials, who would naturally investigate and punish the libeller. One of the constables, Richard Barker, happened to be passing, so Chubb read out the scandalous verses for his information – in low tones, Chubb later maintained, though others thought he deliberately raised his voice so that idle bystanders could enjoy them. This one began 'You Puritans all, wheresoever you dwell', and like its predecessor was a mixture of general invective against puritan hypocrisy and attacks on particular individuals. The libel followed what was by now becoming a familiar line in anti-puritan controversial writing:

> You carry your bible God's word to expound
> And yet in all knavery you daily abound . . .
> Yea, covetousness, lechery and lying for gain
> Amongst you Puritans is not counted vain.

It then launched into an indignant denunciation of the doctrines of the eminent Cambridge divine William Perkins, who had died a few years before. Again, White was not named, but the doctrine of Perkins that most aroused the libeller's rage – that all but the elect were predestined to eternal damnation – was one that he was preaching in Dorchester. If Perkins had been 'a schismatic dog and imp of the devil', and his friends rebels against the King for refusing absolute ceremonial conformity, then the same charges could also be made against White.

In October a third libel, addressed to 'the Counterfeit Company and pack of Puritans', was found in the entry-way to Matthew Chubb's house. Chubb was at dinner with his cousin, the butcher Hugh Haggard, and after finishing their meal they took the paper to the town's new bailiff, James Gould, where Chubb read it aloud to the company. This time the libeller attacked White directly:

> Having myself heard a sermon now of late
> preached in the church by a puritan prelate . . .
> The Saviour of the world, Christ Jesus in person
> of his famed death was brought in question,
> How that he was not the saviour of us all,
> but of the elected which can never fall.[2]

Secrets never last long in a small town, and gossip soon identified the author: one of Dorchester's few Catholic recusants, a cranky individual named Robert Adyn. His family had been prominent in the town for over a century; both his father and brother had held high civic office. Robert, however, had remained of the old religion, and had often been in trouble for it. When the news of Queen Elizabeth's death reached Dorchester he said openly that she had 'used the recusants tyrannously', and had offered Chubb a horse, to be paid for only when mass was again said in St Peter's church – which Adyn obviously expected to happen very soon. For these and other indiscretions he was convicted at the Assizes, and spent the rest of his life in and out of Dorchester Gaol. He was still there in 1631, arguing with visitors and fellow prisoners about White's sermons.[3] Adyn was an isolated figure, though not as isolated as he would have been a generation later, for a good many people in the town shared his opinion of White's preaching. One of them, it seems, was Matthew Chubb.

Everything we know about these events is derived from a libel suit brought in the Court of Star Chamber by John Conduit, the allegedly cuckolded tailor. Conduit charged Adyn with having written the verses, and Chubb with having instigated and distributed them. Court testimony, obviously, should never be taken at face value. But in the Dorchester case all the evidence points to Matthew Chubb as the central figure. The first libel is brought to his house by the schoolboy lodger, and he then finds an excuse to read it aloud at a meeting of the leading townsmen, ostensibly called to discuss a parliamentary subsidy. He happens to be sitting on Blachford's porch when the shoemaker Foy picks up the second one, and again he promptly finds a pretext to read it out in public. The third is in a letter addressed to him, thrown into his entry-way while he is at dinner; having read it out to his guest, Haggard, he then does so again at the house of Bailiff Gould, claiming that Gould was unable to read it himself.[4]

Opinions differed on whether Chubb was trying to give the libels the maximum possible publicity, or whether he merely read them in the execution of his duty. But he was on bad terms with White, while on reasonably friendly ones with Adyn, so we are entitled to our suspicions. Adyn was often at Chubb's house, ostensibly because both of them were trustees of the estate of Robert's recently deceased brother; Robert also had suits pending in the town court, over which Chubb presided as steward. Conduit's friends thought that the relationship went far beyond business. Adyn, they noted, sometimes went to the Chubbs' house to play cards; his hosts conceded that there was conversation on other matters than business during these visits. One of Adyn's seditious comments about the Queen's death was spoken in their house, and Chubb admitted that he had often 'intreated' Adyn, in friendly fashion, to conform and go to church.

Chubb's attitude to White, on the other hand, was one of undisguised hostility. We should of course treat the statements of Conduit and his friends with appropriate scepticism. According to them, Chubb was an enemy of all who 'profess the truth of doctrine authorised by the Church of England' (Calvinist doctrine, in other words), or who 'endeavour to live religiously and without scandal' (Puritans, in other words). He was said to uphold the 'popish' doctrine of salvation by merit (thus, like Adyn, rejecting predestination), to have 'scoffed and jested' at the local clergy, and to have threatened to drive White, the schoolmaster Robert Cheeke, and other godly people out of the town. Naturally Chubb denied holding popish views on salvation or anything else. Still, it is interesting that when a visiting minister, William Jones, preached an unmistakably anti-Calvinist sermon at All Saints on Christmas Day 1613 he dedicated the published version to Chubb, his friends Richard and Thomas Blachford, and other 'gentlemen of Dorsetshire'. Jones insisted that Christ died 'for the sins of *all* the world', and his sermon contained adulation of the Virgin Mary, along with traditional nativity stories, and praise of Christmas as a legitimate time for feasting, all doctrines that were anathema to Puritans.[5]

There is much other evidence to show that Chubb disliked White's sermons. A puritan tailor named Benjamin Derby had certainly heard as much; Chubb had said that he would give one hundred pounds to get White away from Dorchester, and he and his wife had refused to receive communion from the rector. 'When the bell hath been rung to the sermon at Dorchester', another witness observed, the Chubbs were wont to cross the fields into nearby Fordington for prayers and the sermon there. Francis Kirton, a Somerset gentleman, dined at the Chubbs' in 1608. Compromise was in the air and White was invited too, though he seems to have come only reluctantly when the lecturer, Lougher, went to fetch him. After some of the now familiar 'speeches of unkindness', Chubb and White agreed to a formal reconciliation, which was drawn up and sealed, with Kirton and others signing as witnesses. The situation must have been serious indeed if so formal a procedure was needed to end a feud between the rector and the town's leading burgess.

Further acrimony had been aroused by that old target of puritan militancy, stage plays. If ever Dorchester had had a native theatrical tradition it had died with the Reformation, but in the later years of

Elizabeth's reign travelling companies had occasionally performed there. Adyn's first libel implies that White had made his dislike of these ungodly spectacles clear immediately after his arrival in Dorchester. In April 1607 there was a major conflict when Lord Berkeley's men, a popular company in the west country, came to town.[6] They were allowed to play in the 'Common Hall', but not on the sabbath. Not satisfied with this, they announced a Sunday performance and asked the new bailiffs for the key to the hall. When this was refused they went to Chubb, who was now constable. Chubb, on his own admission, told them that 'he for his part was contented they should play', but was unable to overcome the objections of the other magistrates, with whom he had some angry exchanges. Sir Adrian Scrope, father of the schoolboy lodger, was dining with the Chubbs and offered to let the players perform in his chamber at the inn. This was done, with both Scrope and Chubb among the audience. So Matthew Chubb promoted and attended a play in Dorchester . . . on a Sunday.

Conduit's Star Chamber suit tells us a lot about Matthew Chubb and his circle. It shows that Chubb was at the centre of a group which had a very different vision of the ideal community from the one espoused by the puritan White and his allies. Chubb stood for an old conception of neighbourliness, of community harmony, of a social order held together by an interlocking network of mutual obligations joining people of all ranks and conditions.[7] At the top, the rich – wealthy burgesses in the towns, prosperous gentry in the countryside – would provide hospitality and charity to whomsoever they chose, in the mythical good old way, not simply to those who were deserving because they were godly and well connected. Society was all very well as it was, and did not need the attention of self-righteous reformers. Of course the laws had to be enforced, malefactors punished, but there was no need to be too censorious about it; indeed a tolerant attitude to the sort of human frailty that found its outlet in alehouses and popular recreations was all to the good. As long as people went to church first, public festivities (including theatrical performances) could be allowed even on the sabbath, for they gave people relief from toil and a sense of participating, albeit as spectators, in a collective ritual that affirmed the identity of their community. To Chubb and his friends, Puritans, with their emphasis on the gulf between the elect and the reprobate, were uncharitable and divisive.

Many of these ideas can be detected in Chubb's response to Conduit's lawsuit, and in the wills that he and his wife made a few years later. Margaret Chubb's will, made in 1625, urged her heirs 'to maintain that hospitality, for the entertainment of my said husband's friends and mine, which [he] in his lifetime and myself after his death have used'.[8] Chubb's witnesses against Conduit were asked questions designed to construct an image of him as 'a good town's man', always ready to punish offenders and uphold the King's laws, but also generous and hospitable to rich and poor alike. The contrasting stereotype of the Puritan – plebeian, stingy, sanctimonious, and probably disloyal – can easily be read between the lines. Matthew was 'of very good estimation' among the knights and gentlemen of the county, the shoemaker Foy was prompted to say, and for the previous twenty years or so had been 'the best housekeeper in the town'. Margaret Chubb, the draper Joseph Eyres agreed, was 'an absolute kind woman and very beneficial to the poor'. Other evidence was cleverly deployed to reinforce this impression. Matthew was on good terms with Sir John Williams of Herringstone, and when Sir John's son came to the house a number of other Dorset gentlemen were also present. The fact that Sir Adrian Scrope was Chubb's landlord and his son a lodger in his house might suggest that Chubb was Sir Adrian's client, but the relationship was a good deal closer than that, for the two were on sufficiently familiar terms to dine and go to the play together.

No doubt properly respectful to such people, Matthew Chubb had no need to abase himself before them, for he was richer and probably more powerful than many of them: certainly the richest man in Dorchester. There were those who thought he had made his fortune by exploiting his less fortunate neighbours, 'lending out money upon usury', as Conduit's interrogatories put it. One poor man, Thomas Galton, seems to have fallen completely into his power and had to leave him his entire estate, debts and all, when he died in 1603. And there had been trouble over the interest Chubb was demanding on a loan of one hundred pounds to the town a few years earlier. When he died in 1617 a fellow townsman caustically recorded the passing of 'Matthew Chubb the usurer'.[9]

This reputation was widespread enough to suggest that there was a darker side to him. But Matthew Chubb constructed a plausible image of himself as the virtuous, hospitable townsman. It may be that having no children of his own made him the more inclined to emphasise his ties to a wider family circle.[10] His will asked Margaret to be 'loving and kind' to 'such of my kindred as shall be dutiful unto her', and he left an unusual number of small legacies to kinsfolk then living in his house, including other Chubbs, Bucklers (his wife's kin), and his cousin Haggard the butcher. He also left five pounds to another Dorchester butcher, Roger Pouncey, one of a family later to be belligerently at odds with the reformers. Chubb's circle embraced a wide cross-section of Dorchester society.

The Chubbs were not greatly interested in reforming society, and their attitude to charity reflects this. They cultivated the reputation of being generous to the clergy and hospitable to the poor, and so they were, in their way. But that way was not the selective philanthropy, directed towards improving people, that the Puritans favoured. Matthew made a great show of entertaining visiting preachers, and of providing a house for the lecturer, Lougher. But when the reformers, in one of their first moves, proposed to increase the income of Trinity parish by annexing to it the decayed parish of Frome Whitfield, Chubb made a long speech against the necessary legislation in the House of Commons. During his lifetime he spent lavishly on building almshouses at Crewkerne and Shaftesbury, but his will did little for Dorchester: a token five shillings for each of the three churches, and nothing for the poor. He did leave the Corporation a nominal £500 for unspecified charitable purposes, and he may have had some intention of using this for the benefit of the 'Old', or Women's, Almshouse. But the £500 was to come from money owed him by the King that, as we shall see, he knew was unlikely ever to be paid. In 1620, after Matthew's death, his widow was more generous: she gave £200 to the Almshouse (it was later renamed Chubb's Almshouse) and another £200 to the new Hospital for poor children. But she too seems to have identified as much with other places she had lived in as she did with Dorchester. Her will left five pounds to All Saints church, where she and her husband were buried, but a much more substantial twenty pounds to the church at Bubdown, her birthplace.[11]

Matthew Chubb cultivated the image of the jovial, generous,

hospitable town dignitary. His whole style of living, and even what little we can discover about his vocabulary, gives the impression of a man comfortably at home in both elite and plebeian circles: with Sir Adrian Scrope as much as Hugh Haggard the butcher. He went to plays – not as often as he used to, he said in the Star Chamber suit, and he had not 'favoured players any more than some others of his place' had done – but still in 1607 he had no scruples about going to one on a Sunday. He was ready, he said, to spend 'cartloads of money' to defeat Conduit and his puritan friends; he would 'play Hunckes the great bear and would break their backs' before the libel suit was over. He had the reputation of driving a hard bargain and even of engaging in usury, yet he was also capable of lavish, though not entirely indiscriminate, hospitality.

He was indeed a formidable enemy, as John Conduit discovered. Shortly before the row over the libels, Conduit had bought some hay from Chubb, paying him with coins that included a gold French crown. Chubb refused to accept it and sued Conduit for the six shillings at which it was valued. While the suit was pending and after the one over the libels had begun, Chubb, by this time constable, received a warrant ordering him to requisition horses to carry provisions to James I's Court, which was then at Salisbury. One of the first horses to be honoured for this service was John Conduit's. When the town serjeant arrived without warning to collect the horse Conduit thought that he was illegally distraining it for the six-shilling debt. There was a scuffle in which Conduit's wife and servants also joined, which ended only when Conduit discovered that the serjeant was taking the horse not for Chubb, but for the King. New roles were instantly adopted. Conduit the indignant protector of his property became Conduit the loyal subject, 'very willingly' handing over his horse even though he knew he had been unfairly singled out – the beast was tired after a long day's journey, whereas a fresh one owned by one of Chubb's aristocratic friends had been exempted. Conduit's Star Chamber suit over the libels in April 1608 was followed a month later by Chubb's counter-suit in the same court, accusing the tailor of riot and resistance to lawful authority.[12]

Chubb's methods are strikingly illustrated by the way he ran the relief fund after the great fire. As was customary after such disasters, the Privy Council authorised a general collection throughout the kingdom for the relief of the victims. Briefs were distributed to the

parishes, and a few fragmentary glimpses of the process have survived: collectors appointed in Lancashire, an official of the ecclesiastical courts receiving money raised in London. But the whole business,
the diarist William Whiteway complained, 'was by Mr Matthew
Chubb's solicitation committed to himself and to Mr Richard Blachford both for collection and distribution, no one burgess besides . . .
allowed to have any hand therein'.[13] Chubb subscribed £1,000 to the
fund, the magnitude of his generosity being marred only slightly by
the fact that he had already got a royal promise of repayment out of
the proceeds of the next parliamentary subsidy. Given the chaotic
nature of early Stuart finances the likelihood of such repayment was
never very great, and it disappeared completely when the ensuing
Parliament of 1614 was dissolved without any subsidies being
voted.[14]

   Chubb had still not been paid when he made his will in 1617. As
we have seen, he left a nominal £500 for charitable uses from the
£1,000 owed him by the King, but this obviously did not mean very
much. There were many complaints about the management of the
fund. Richard Barker claimed that Chubb promised him eighty
pounds for his losses, which had reduced his income by thirty pounds
a year, but that he never saw a penny of it. The most interesting case
concerns the George Inn, the finest hostelry in Dorchester, which
was owned by the town. The Corporation had let it to George
Clarke; he in turn sublet it to the widow Margaret Toomes. Ruined
by the fire, she could neither rebuild nor pay the rent, so Clarke took
possession. He estimated his losses at £500, but Chubb would allow
him only forty-five pounds from the fund; he too got behind with
the rent and forfeited his lease. The Corporation promptly granted
another lease to a new tenant, who rebuilt the inn 'very fair'. The
new tenant was Matthew Chubb.[15]

   The affair is an interesting example of Chubb's style. He turned
fire relief into an exercise in patronage, rewarding friends and punishing enemies, picking up a good bargain for himself in the process.
At the end of it all he emerged with his reputation for generosity
further enhanced, and if the King ever repaid the £1,000 he might
even escape without suffering any significant financial losses. What
happened to the money collected in other parts of the kingdom is
not clear, but the choice of Blachford as Chubb's fellow trustee does

not inspire confidence, for he was one of a family notorious for greed and double dealing.

In 1623 there was another fire in Dorchester, serious, but not as devastating as the earlier one. It broke out on 30 January in a malthouse belonging to John Adyn (nephew of the Catholic libeller), 'the straw taking fire that lay something near to the oast mouth'. Adyn had been warned about his 'dangerous making of fire', but had taken no precautions. About thirty houses were destroyed, all in Trinity parish, the damage amounting to some £3,500. Once again there was only one fatality, a tiler named Edmund Benvenewe. 'Running home all black and deformed by the fire', William Whiteway tells us, Benvenewe was chased by anxious neighbours who wanted to help him have his burns dressed. In the panic and confusion, a bystander thought he was a looter being pursued by an angry crowd, and beat him so severely that he died a few days later.[16]

Relief for the survivors was quickly organised, and it was managed very differently from the way Chubb had run things in 1613. Some of the homeless were immediately given beer, cheese, and other victuals, and small sums of money were already being doled out on the day after the fire. On Sunday 1 February there was a collection at St Peter's which realised nearly fifty-eight pounds, and donations were soon coming in from neighbouring country gentlemen like Sir Walter Erle. A wealthy draper named William Joliffe was appointed treasurer of the fund, and from his businesslike accounts we know that altogether nearly £556 was received. The elder Whiteway got the brief issued for a general collection, and to tide the victims over while the proceeds were coming in Joliffe borrowed £100 from an Axminster gentleman.

Most of the contributions came from the southern counties, though as far away as Morton, Derbyshire, 8d. was collected 'for the borough of Dorchester, being burnt with fire'. Conduit and other townsmen made long journeys to deliver the briefs. Robert Crabb went to Gloucester and then on to Ledbury; Nicholas Stone visited Exeter, Plymouth, and other western towns. John White's clerical friends, including his wife's kinsman Cornelius Burges in Hertfordshire, were also enlisted in the appeal. Exeter, where many Dorchester families had kinsfolk, was especially generous. Money was still dribbling in years later, but by the time the account was closed in 1630 all but 17s. 1d. had been distributed. That sum, kept 'in my chest at shop in a leather bag', Joliffe reported, was then doled out to the poor of Trinity parish.[17]

New men had come to the fore in Dorchester during the previous ten years. The way the 1623 fund was run is typical of their methods: brisk, efficient, meticulously accounted, and with a less obvious tincture of self-interest behind the veneer of philanthropy. Most of them, like John White, wished to reform their town. Religion, to an extent that most of us today find it difficult to imagine, really was at the centre of their world. But so it was too, in a different way, for Matthew Chubb and the many other inhabitants of Dorchester who shared his suspicions of the Puritans. The conflict between Chubb and the reformers was one for the town's very soul: for its entire moral and spiritual character. Yet people of both persuasions belonged to the same church: the conflict was in part one for control of its rituals and perhaps even (as in the debate over predestination which Adyn's libels reflected) its doctrines. The church was far more than the physical building in which people worshipped. But Dorchester's three churches encompassed much that was important in the life of every inhabitant of the town. In them were performed all those rites of passage that marked their lives and those of their parents and neighbours. In them they too were married, and their children were baptised and buried. In them they absorbed, week after week, whatever their own views, the messages conveyed by the preachers and by the liturgy, as well as the subliminal messages transmitted by the sacred space surrounding them.

All three churches were feeling the strain of the recent population growth. Trinity had been enlarged just before the fire, and its seating capacity was further increased in 1617, when a gallery was built; new seats were crammed into every available space. All Saints was enlarged, too, during the winter of 1626–7. There was more room at St Peter's, and in 1633 the Corporation told a prospective assistant minister that although Trinity and St Peter's each had congregations of at least a thousand, the churches were big enough to accommodate them.[18] At Trinity, and no doubt at the other churches, the leading male parishioners sat in rows in the middle aisle, with eminent men like Richard Bushrod at the front, poorer men towards the back. Their wives sat separately in the side aisles, but again in rows which reflected the parish hierarchy: John Parkins's wife had the front pew on the north side. In the south aisle, however, several wealthy parishioners actually shared pews with their wives. Benches at the back accommodated the daughters of the respectable, but in a 1617 seating plan no provision was made for their sons or servants, and the humbler members of the parish are also nowhere to be seen in the plan. Presumably they had to find places on benches wherever they could. Subsequent churchwardens took care of this, and the purchase of life-interests in seats became the rule for even the poorest, and an important source of parish revenue.[19]

How happy Trinity's parishioners were with these arrangements we do not know. Conflicts over church seats – symbolic struggles for precedence – were common in early seventeenth-century England, but there are only a few traces of them in Dorchester. The most significant was one at Holy Trinity in 1617 involving the powerful Churchills of Colleton. The Churchills had customarily occupied the front pew in the centre aisle, but John White wanted to assign it to the borough's bailiff and Recorder. The Churchills were seconded by one of the churchwardens, but at a parish meeting they were overwhelmed by White's supporters. By 1621 the 'bailiff's seat' was well established at Trinity, and although the Churchills still had a prominent pew it was no longer in the place of honour. As the Corporation members made their stately processions into the church they were now ritually proclaiming their independence of the neighbouring gentry.[20] The Churchills were not the only local family to resent their virtual exclusion from the town.

Trinity is the only one of Dorchester's three churches about whose physical condition we have much information. During these years it must have appeared plain and unadorned, and by 1640, with the new gallery and seats overflowing into the chancel, distinctly crowded. The chancel was not railed off, and the communion table stood where most people thought it belonged – in the nave, not turned altar-wise in the popish fashion. The church was not completely without colour, though. In obedience to royal proclamation, the

King's arms were installed in 1616–17, and four years later the Ten Commandments were set up for all to read. The pulpit, always the centrepiece in a religion in which the word took precedence over the sacraments, was given a canopy in 1625–6; a few years later it had to be moved to make room for more seating. Money was spent on 'colouring the casements', and in 1627–8 the pillars in the nave were painted. They must have been a striking exception to an otherwise drab scene. For the churchwardens the never-ending struggle to preserve the fabric was more important than any kind of adornment. The roof was regularly repaired, yet for years there was a place in the gallery where, despairing churchwardens noted, 'it did always rain in'.[21]

The three churches were in constant use. Besides morning and evening prayer there was catechising on Sunday afternoons, as well as weekday services on Fast Days and other special occasions. At Trinity and St Peter's these were the orthodox services of the Church of England. Unlike some earlier, more uncompromising reformers, John White always wore the required surplice (a new one was bought for him in 1640) and conducted services according to law. Trinity church owned its 'Great Bible', Book of Homilies, and Book of Common Prayer; in 1621–2 the Bible was exchanged for the new King James version and another Prayer Book bought. White's inclinations were puritan, but he was still an orthodox, conforming minister of the protestant Church of England. His colleague at All Saints, William Benn, may have been less punctilious. According to one disgruntled parishioner, he did not always read Common Prayer, and often omitted the Epistle and Gospel at communion. No such charges were made against John White.[22]

The small number of White's sermons to have survived show that however rigid his Calvinism, his preaching, too, was in the protestant mainstream. A sermon preached at the Assizes in March 1633 was a set-piece affair for a great public occasion, scarcely typical of his normal output, but it shows that he had conventional views on authority and government.[23] After the great row with Chubb was over few people in Dorchester openly questioned his teachings. One who did was a tailor named Philip Nichols, who was shocked to hear White describe Jesus as 'an innocent and simple man'. Not, one would have thought, a very controversial idea, but Nichols fancied himself as an amateur theologian, consulting Kellison's *Survey of*

Religion in the town library, and often going up to the Gaol to argue doctrine with 'old seminary', the ageing Catholic, Robert Adyn. White's parishioners certainly followed his sermons intently. Many took notes for subsequent review and discussion; William Paty's apprentice used a form of shorthand. Note-taking was part of the education of young people, but adults did it as well: one parishioner paid for 'a place to stand and write in the south gallery' at Trinity church. Not everyone was enthralled by the interminable sermons, when the hour-glass was turned and perhaps turned again. Joseph Whittle 'pinged' another boy, Peter Keysar, in the leg after Keysar had repeatedly 'blotted his book' during the sermon. But this was at All Saints, where there were adults too who thought William Benn somewhat long-winded. In 1634 Trinity bought a half-hour glass. Perhaps White's advancing years and the 'infirmities . . . lately fallen upon him' had reduced his stamina and he could no longer preach for a full hour.[24]

The younger sort might be inattentive, but many of their elders were totally absorbed by religion. Biblical texts were freely swapped in everyday debate, and a scribe practising penmanship in a parish account book turned naturally to scripture: 'God spake these words and said, I am the Lord thy God, thou shalt have none other gods but me'.[25] Portents of God's intentions were always available for those who could read them: the comet of 1618, the aurora borealis in January 1630. Apparent accidents were also full of meaning. When the normally godly Sir Thomas Trenchard entertained Archbishop Laud's Vicar-General during the 1634 Visitation he was appropriately chastised for it by falling downstairs and nearly breaking his neck. The more pious townsmen collected stories recounting the punishment of revellers and sabbath-breakers: a Glastonbury boy killed by a falling maypole, a young man knifed at Beaminster after 'sporting and drinking' on a Sunday, a man beating his companion's brains out during a sabbath game of bowls at Bridport.[26]

Much in the religious life of Dorchester was shared by Puritan and non-Puritan alike. But the leaders of the reform movement were always conscious of their distinct identity. Several of them were men of puritan sympathies who had migrated to Dorchester only a few years before John White's arrival, or very shortly afterwards. Dorchester was a prosperous trading community, a good place for a young man with a bit of capital to make his way in the world, so they were not necessarily attracted by the religious complexion of the town, which in Chubb's heyday was not noticeably more pious than that of many other places. They did not come to Dorchester because it was a haven for Puritans. But they were soon to make it into one.

The newcomers quickly became prominent in the town. Edmund Dashwood, born at nearby West Stafford, was in Dorchester by 1599; the haberdasher Richard Bushrod, who came from Sherborne, married a daughter of the already established Watts family sometime before 1605; John Parkins, soon to be a powerful member of the Corporation, had also arrived by this time. Denis Bond came in 1610, to marry the daughter of another recent arrival, John Gould. The Bonds had had a small estate at Lutton in the Isle of Purbeck for several generations, and Denis's father was a prosperous Weymouth merchant, of which town he was four times mayor.[27]

There had been Goulds in Dorchester as far back as the early fifteenth century, but the two cousins from Devon who became part of the reform group arrived only in the 1590s. James Gould was born into a large family at Dartington in Devon so he had no prospects in the village. Being 'very industrious in his calling', his admiring widow recalled, he came to Dorchester and made a fortune in the cloth trade: in the 1610 subsidy he and his cousin John were rated only slightly below Matthew Chubb himself. Strongly solicitous for his kinsfolk, James nevertheless made a clear distinction between the godly and industrious on the one hand, and those like the nephew whom he accused of 'living idly and wasting his estate', on the other. His cousin John was also a Devonian, from Staverton near Exeter, and he retained close ties with friends and kinsfolk in that city. John did almost as well in business as his cousin. He died in 1630, the same year as James's widow; both were major benefactors to Dorchester charities.[28]

The Goulds were not the only migrants from Devon. Another was William Whiteway, who was born at Denbury in 1570, son of a small farmer who had married one of the Goulds of Staverton. Apprenticed to a merchant, he was sent to France and in 1590 was captured by Catholic forces during the Wars of Religion; he spent a year in prison before being ransomed. In 1600, a year after the birth of his eldest son (another William), he followed his Gould cousins to Dorchester, and within ten years had become a member of the Corporation. His treatment in France gave him a fervent hatred of Catholicism and a correspondingly intense protestant piety. The Bonds had a similar history. Denis Bond's father, fourteen years older than Whiteway, had gone to France as a young apprentice and was at Rouen in 1572 at the time of the St Bartholomew massacre. Fearing for their lives, the English merchants took as hostages the wife and children of one of the leading citizens. As Denis recalled hearing the story from his father, they marched them up to the roof of the house in which they were besieged, telling the mob 'that if they did meddle with the English' the hostages would be killed. Such experiences, and the tales woven around them, remind us how deeply embedded Protestantism had become in the national mythology.[29]

Related by ties of blood, marriage and friendship, the newcomers formed a close-knit group that even by 1613 was challenging Chubb's ascendancy.[30] By the time of the second fire the old guard had been almost swept away. When the 1610 charter was obtained only six of the Capital Burgesses – the 'Fifteen' who governed the town – were puritan reformers. This soon changed. When reformers died they were succeeded by men of similar outlook: Bushrod, Joliffe, Dashwood, Bond and others of their kind. When 'Elizabethans' died their places were taken by Puritans. By 1623 only three of Chubb's old allies were left. Soon two of those were gone: John Spicer died, having been for many years, according to Whiteway, 'in decay of his understanding'; and Nicholas Vawter, brother-in-law to the libeller, Robert Adyn, was expelled for persistent absenteeism. Only old Richard Blachford was left, though he did manage to have his son John elected in 1623. The Blachfords were the only exceptions to what was otherwise a puritan monopoly.[31]

The new men were godly reformers. But in income and status they were not very different from their predecessors. What little evidence we have about their relative wealth suggests that somewhat more of the reformers in the Corporation were in the highest tax bracket – nine out of twenty-two whose assessments are known, compared with three out of thirteen of the 'old guard' – though two other reformers appear to have been poorer than any of the earlier

Capital Burgesses. But the assessments are too uncertain a guide to real wealth for them to be taken very seriously.[32]

What can be said about the leading reformers is that they were by Dorchester standards prosperous, well connected, and well educated. The clothier John Allambridge was the only Capital Burgess during this period who could not sign his name when he was elected, and he soon learned how to do it. In every other respect Allambridge's career paralleled those of his fellow burgesses: success in his trade, good marriages, and conscientious performance in the lesser civic offices preceded election to the Corporation. He went on to become mayor in 1642. In spite of serious wartime losses he left an estate worth over £4,000. One of his daughters married a future Town Clerk, Richard Scovile; another became the wife of Samuel Bushrod, son of the former bailiff and MP.[33]

The reform leaders were a veritable cousinhood. How well they knew each other is apparent in their business dealings, and in the regularity with which they witnessed each other's wills, served as executors for each other, and acted as godparents for their children. They did similar favours for people below them in the social scale, provided they were among the godly. Richard Bushrod and Richard Savage, both prominent reformers, were witnesses when the pious tailor, James Yokeney, made his will in 1616; Yokeney also named them as his overseers, along with the Town Clerk, William Derby. It was a close-knit, intimate society.[34]

Such men dipped deeply into their pockets for the good of their neighbours. They lent money to buy grain for the poor during the 1631 famine; they contributed lavishly to all of John White's charitable projects. Some had special preoccupations. In 1636–7, his mayoral year, the ironmonger John Hill was particularly solicitous for the welfare of the sick and elderly, on at least one occasion entering orders for relief payments into the Corporation minutes in his own hand. When he made his will in 1657 he left one hundred pounds for one of White's pet schemes, an endowment to support a poor scholar from Dorchester at one of the universities. The elder Goulds and Richard Bushrod were all generous benefactors of the Hospital, the Free School, and the poor; Bushrod also left a lump sum of fifty pounds which was later used to reward godly tradespeople. John Parkins was another who responded liberally to White's appeals. He managed the fundraising campaign for the extension of Trinity church in 1612, made impressive contributions to the Hospital, and left five pounds a year to pay for a lecturer to assist Mr White.[35]

We should not idealise the reformers. They enthusiastically supported the campaign for godliness and sobriety, but they were human beings, and they had their occasional disputes and disagreements. James Gould the younger, son of old John Gould, seems to have been increasingly out of step with his colleagues. Elected to the Corporation in 1624, he went on to hold the usual list of offices: three times bailiff, and mayor in 1637. But his behaviour became more and more erratic. In 1629 he repeatedly refused to pay for a substitute watchman, and two years later, during the dearth, he would not contribute towards grain supplies for the poor. Later in the decade he was often in a minority of one at corporation meetings. When two new Capital Burgesses were elected in January 1641, Gould 'went away and would not set his hand'.[36]

Perhaps business worries affected Gould's behaviour. In 1633 a large consignment of his cloth was lost in a shipwreck off Portland (John Blachford also suffered in this incident), and at about the same time he was a defendant, along with Blachford, in an Exchequer suit about evasion of customs duties at Weymouth. Blachford was fined two thousand pounds, and although Gould was acquitted the affair led to serious divisions in the neighbourhood. The defendants claimed that they were acting on principle, standing up for the liberty of the subject, on the grounds that the House of Commons had condemned the levying of tonnage and poundage without consent of Parliament. Few believed that they were so altruistic, and John White sharply reproved them in his sermon at the 1633 Assizes. After his conviction John Blachford fled to France, though it was not until 1639 that he was expelled from the Corporation.[37]

The Blachfords were famous for their greed. A few years later a poor man named John Chimney began abusing one of John Blachford's sons when he came secretly back to Dorchester on business for his father. 'Thy father hath spoiled the town', he told the boy, 'and now he dares not to show his face but keeps in like a dog.' The boy's grandfather, old Richard Blachford, was another who had 'cozened men', Chimney went on, an 'old crippled knave', who like his son stayed indoors because he could not face his neighbours. Chimney was well informed about the affairs of his betters: Richard

Blachford had been absenting himself from Corporation meetings
for over a year, and he continued to do so until warned that he would
be expelled if he did not attend. He then resumed his place, but for
much of the 1630s the Blachfords, the only members of the 'Fifteen'
who were not enthusiastic reformers (unless we put the younger
James Gould into that category), were virtually without influence in
the Corporation.[38]

We may be certain that religion – in and out of the churches – was
at the heart of it, but beyond that it is difficult to reconstruct the
mental world of all but the most literate and articulate members of
society in an age so remote from our own. We can make certain
assumptions, for instance that Dorchester people were not likely to
be very different from men and women of similar rank and status in
other parts of the country, and can therefore apply to Dorchester
what we know about the general culture of the period, shared by
Puritans and non-Puritans alike. We can be more precise about the
culture of the educated minority, for we have a list of the books that
were available to them in the town library, housed in a room over
the Free School. Two prominent townsmen – Denis Bond and the
younger William Whiteway – left inventories of their private libraries, as well as some useful autobiographical material. Both kept
'chronologies', briefly listing what seemed to them the most important events in the history of their families and of the world around
them. Whiteway also kept a diary, and a commonplace book which
included among other things the notes he took on his impressively
wide reading.[39]

One further avenue into their mental world might at first sight
appear to be through the curriculum of the Free School, which
Whiteway and most of the others who had grown up in Dorchester
had attended. But although we can easily find out the general nature
of a grammar school curriculum during this period, we have very
little precise information on exactly what Robert Cheeke was teaching his Dorchester pupils. One of them could still remember some
of the old man's adages more than twenty years later – '*Res ipsa
loquitur*, out of his own mouth you may judge of him', for instance
– but for the most part we have to rely on guesswork.[40] Yet the

school is obviously relevant. It was well respected: many of the Dorset gentry sent their sons there, and it attracted pupils from further afield, some of whom boarded at Rector White's. It was rebuilt in 1618 at a cost of about £500, a considerable sum to raise at a time when there were other heavy demands on the charitable impulses of the townspeople. Most of the money came from the town, though Whiteway says that Cheeke received contributions from 'well disposed gentlemen of the county, and of many that had been his scholars'; even so, he had to dip into his own pockets. The school flourished, and when Robert Cheeke took over from his decrepit namesake William as parson at All Saints an Usher was hired to assist him. Cheeke died in 1627, and after a year's interval Gabriel Reeve, a Hampshire man, was appointed to replace him.[41]

The school must surely have helped to shape the outlook of Dorchester's seventeenth-century governors. They assumed, if they thought about it at all, that they lived in a world whose physical and political natures were both ordained by God, a world of interlocking hierarchies forming the system that modern historians have labelled 'the great chain of being'. All of nature, organic and inorganic, was arranged on a scale that ascended from immobile earth at the centre, upwards through the plants and the animal kingdom and humanity, to the stars in the heavens, and ultimately to God himself. There is no sign that Dorchester folk were interested in the works of ancient philosophy in which this intellectual system had originally been elaborated, but they could have found it in Augustine's *City of God* or in Aquinas's *Summa Theologica*, both of which were in the town library. It is more likely that they imbibed a watered-down version of it from the sermons, catechisms, and other religious works with which they were constantly bombarded; John White stressed 'the admirable and unchangeable order that God hath set in nature', without which everything 'must necessarily be in confusion'.[42] Knowledge of the Copernican heliocentric universe had as yet scarcely begun to undermine the older cosmology, though some people in Dorchester were certainly interested in both geography and the new astronomy: Whiteway owned works by Tycho Brahe and Kepler, and presented Mercator's *Tabulae Geographicae* to the public library, along with a couple of boxed globes.

Of more immediate concern, probably, to educated Dorchester people were the political aspects of the theory of cosmic order. Just as there were correspondences between the various hierarchies of the natural world, it was believed, so there were too within the system of political order which bound humankind together: between the family, the local community and the state. Authority in each sphere was assigned by divine command to those to whom it belonged 'by nature': to fathers and husbands; to lords, gentlemen and magistrates; to the King and his chosen ministers. White made the routine connection in his sermon at the 1633 Assizes. Obedience was ordained by God in the Fifth Commandment, 'in all duties between parents and children, magistrate and subject, husband and wife, master and servant'.[43] Disobedience by inferiors in one sphere encouraged disobedience in all others; disorder in one led inexorably to disorder throughout.

Rather surprisingly, the Dorchester library contained none of the popular prescriptive guides to the godly family, such as William Gouge's *Of Domesticall Duties*.[44] Still, its users could have found plenty of guidance in the works of luminaries like Perkins, Thomas Greenham and William Whately, all of which were on the shelves. Whiteway had his own copy of the latter two, while Bond owned the works of the ultimate authority, John Calvin, of which Whiteway's father had also given a set to the library. These were books that Puritans might be expected to read, but this part of their contents – the general theory of cosmic order and its application to the patriarchal family – would have been familiar to, and accepted by, virtually everyone. Whiteway was related, through his mother, to the author of one of the most popular of all works on the analogy between monarchy and the family, Richard Mocket's *God and the King*. James I had liked this book so much that he ordered it to be taught by every householder to his children and servants, as well as by all ministers and schoolmasters. Most people in Dorchester no doubt approved of Mocket's teachings on patriarchy, but by the 1620s some may have been less certain about their absolutist political implications. White, whose familial teaching was relentlessly patriarchal, was probably among them.[45]

What they would have accepted was that the well-governed family was at the heart of the social and political order. After some sporadic jottings on the early history of Christendom, Bond's chronology notes the arrival in Dorset in 1453 of an ancestor from Somerset – just before the fall of Constantinople to the Turks. Thereafter the family births, marriages and deaths follow thick and fast, and in the original version of the chronology a large proportion of the entries were of this kind.[46] Like most men of his position, Denis Bond was anxious to establish the antiquity of his family and be accepted as a gentleman. He jotted down genealogical notes on the Bonds and various related families, and when the heraldic Visitation of the county was held in 1623 he registered the family pedigree and paid the fee. He retained a healthy scepticism, however, adding 'I believe it not' when he acquired a fraudulent pedigree tracing the Bonds all the way back to the eleventh century. The mendacious source, he was quick to note, was a 'popish fellow'.[47]

Whiteway was interested in genealogy, too, though less so than Bond, perhaps because his family had weaker claims to gentility. Like all English diarists before Samuel Pepys, Whiteway is reticent about his personal feelings, both in his diary and in his commonplace book. He wrote some undistinguished youthful love-poetry, and later experimented with the pastoral mode. But he tells us nothing about his courtship of and marriage to Eleanor Parkins, apart from the inscription on the wedding ring – 'Conjugii firmi et casti sum pignus amoris'[48] – and the fact that they were married by Mr White in Trinity church, 'in the presence of the greatest part of the town'. It may have been an arranged marriage; there certainly were some careful financial provisions, as one might expect in an alliance of two of Dorchester's wealthiest families. Whiteway says little about the sadly early deaths – of six of the seven born between 1621 and 1633 – of his and Eleanor's children. 'God took her unto his mercy', he says of a daughter's death, and that conventional reflection is as far as he will go. Still, while emotional intensity is lacking, in his obsessive recording of the comings and goings of kinsfolk Whiteway shows that for him, as for Bond, his family was at the heart of his mental universe.[49]

Some of Whiteway's attitudes to personal and family matters can be deduced from the anecdotes which impressed him enough for him to write them down. They perhaps suggest a certain anxiety about sexuality. In one, a Somerton butcher is gored by an ox, which tears off one of his testicles: he pursues and kills the beast. In another, an Irishman with thirty-three children (by two different wives) gets his second wife's permission to sleep with the maid, to bring the number up to forty. From his reading in medieval Spanish history Whiteway noted the exploits of the promiscuous Margaret of Navarre, who had her lovers drowned in the river. Now we have no way of knowing how Whiteway reacted to these stories: whether with shock, amusement, or in some other way (he owned an edition of Rabelais, so his tastes were not necessarily puritanical in the conventional sense). They certainly imply a rather childish sense of humour. One of them is about a Dorchester attorney who gets drunk with some 'good fellows' on the way to Weymouth. His drinking companions empty the legal papers out of the box he is carrying and put in a swarm of bees, with predictable results when he opens it in the courtroom.

Some of Whiteway's anecdotes, however, may be more psychologically significant. There is surely a certain ambivalence about paternal authority in the story of the young wastrel at one of the Inns of Court who is saved from debtor's prison by the timely death of his father, and in Whiteway's version of the old tale of the father and son who quarrelled at the dinner table. The father boxed the young man's ears; patriarchal ideology made it unthinkable for the son to strike back, so he boxed the ears of his neighbour on the other side, asking him to pass it on: 'Box about, twill come to my father anon.' We might wish to know more about the relationship between the two William Whiteways. In spite of these ambiguities, the diarist had conventional views about the connection between morality and patriarchy. He notes the case of the impotent Enrique IV of Castile who in 1460 persuaded his Queen to let a courtier father her child, but to no avail because the people would not allow the bastard daughter to succeed. And he regarded the misdeeds of the infamous Earl of Castlehaven, executed in 1631 for a series of appalling sexual crimes against his wife and stepdaughter, as sufficiently noteworthy to merit mention in his diary. When he reports the number of people executed at each Assize he usually does so without comment, but if the crime involved members of the same family he was sometimes sufficiently shocked to record its nature, as when a man was hanged at Winchester in 1630 for murdering his own mother.[50]

Everyone accepted the importance of the family. But it was especially important for Puritans: the virtuous foundation of the godly society that Bond, Whiteway, and their friends were trying to create in Dorchester. Wives, children, apprentices and servants had to be provided for, educated in true religion, and if necessary disciplined and chastised. But the pious householder also had the duty, as one of God's elect, to promote order and godliness in the wider community of which he was a part. In that community each person had his or her role to play. John White reproved the sin of envy, condemning 'they that desire parity', and enlisting the Calvinist doctrine of the calling in the service of social order: 'Let it be our case to abide in the place, and exercise ourselves in the employments unto which God . . . hath assigned us.' 'Those that have not abilities for government', White consolingly continued, 'may be made use of for servants.'[51]

Fortunately there were those whose callings did make them fit for government. Bond and Whiteway both owned copies of Dalton's *Country Justice*, one of the most popular handbooks for JPs, and Bond also owned William Lambarde's famous *Eirenarcha*. They were proud of their town and dutifully recorded important events in its recent history: the foundation of the Free School, the 1610 charter, the 1613 fire. Leafing through Holinshed's *Chronicles*, Whiteway noted that Dorchester had in ancient times been the chief city of the West Saxons before their kings moved the capital to Winchester. Around 1625 he compiled a detailed account of Dorchester's charities. These things were important and ought to be recorded, particularly after a great fire in which so many records had been destroyed.[52]

Whiteway's annual listings of civic officeholders express his sense of being part of a community. So too with his recording of local births, marriages, and deaths, though here the socially selective nature of the entries indicates the privileged circles in which he moved. When he mentions the deaths of poorer townspeople it is normally only because some unusual kind of misfortune is involved, as when the blacksmith John Cobb collapses while bellringing, or John Gaylard's son freezes to death on the highway one December night. Still, these incidents give us some inkling of the sort of events that would have been topics of conversation in the Dorchester of his time. We naturally hear of the great public calamities: the 1623 fire, the 1630 dearth. But we also hear of the sensational crimes and accidents: the stabbing of the tapster in a brawl at the George; a poor woman's tragic murder of her baby; a man dying, 'bitten by a mad dog six weeks before'; a woman killed 'by mischance, by a sledge[hammer] that one was casting which beat out her brains'.[53]

The town of Dorchester was not the limit of the mental horizon of people like the Bonds and the Whiteways. Both families held lands elsewhere in Dorset. Denis Bond acquired a farm near Swanage and property in Weymouth on his marriage in 1610, and when his father died in 1633 he inherited the estate at Lutton. This brought him a country house (though its furnishings, which included a pair of virginals, were worth only a quarter the value of the contents of his town house in South Street, Dorchester), another good-sized farm, and a flock of sheep valued in 1636 at close to four hundred pounds. In 1641 he bought another two hundred acres at Chaldon Herring from the Earl of Suffolk, letting half of it to his Dorchester friend Edmund Dashwood. Bond might still be a small-town woollen draper, but he was moving up in the world. The elder Whiteway also had property in the county. In 1610 he bought land at Cary Mill, more at Woodsford in 1618, and in 1626 he took out a lease from the new Earl of Suffolk on six hundred acres at Winterbourne Ashton, with grazing for a large flock of sheep. Richard Bushrod, William Derby, and John Parkins also had substantial properties in various parts of Dorset.[54]

So Bond and Whiteway naturally took a keen interest in the affairs of their county. They record many of the movements of the leading gentry and their births, marriages, and deaths. Whiteway picks up gossip about local families, such as the story of Clement Walker stabbing his wife at the dinner table, which must have set Dorset tongues wagging. Both mention the county's afflictions almost as frequently as they do those of Dorchester: fires at Poole and Blandford, storms, epidemics (which led to the cancellation of the region's most important annual gathering, Woodbury Hill Fair, in three consecutive years), even a minor local earthquake. Sessions of the Assizes, big events in any county town, are regularly noted (Whiteway's father always entertained the judges on behalf of the town), as are ecclesiastical visitations by the Bishop of Bristol or the Archdeacon of Dorset. Whiteway also took a keen interest in the county militia, in which he was an officer.[55]

Concern for town and county was accompanied by similar curiosity about the world beyond their borders. Bond and Whiteway were clearly aware of the issues that were beginning to cause serious division in the kingdom. Both men were still loyal subjects who dutifully noted royal occasions like the death of Prince Henry and the marriage of Princess Elizabeth in 1612, and the birth of Prince Charles, the future Charles II, in 1630; Whiteway was impressed by reported observations of a new star on this occasion. They were patriotic Englishmen who conscientiously followed their country's military fortunes when Charles I got into wars with Spain and France, pathetically grasping at the rare successes and more often lamenting the occasions when expeditions 'shamefully' returned without having achieved anything. They were still conforming members of the Church of England, whose discipline, as Whiteway put it a few years later, was 'our discipline'.[56] There is nothing in his diary to suggest that, even as late as his death in 1635, he sensed the possibility that within a very few years Englishmen would be fighting each other in a civil war over the governance of church and state. Whiteway died before that recognition dawned. Bond did not, and he was to play a major role in the revolution that followed. But until the late 1630s there is no sign that he, any more than Whiteway, had any inkling of what was to come.

But both men knew that these were dangerous times. They were living, they believed, at one of the great turning-points, perhaps the greatest turning-point, of history: at the final stage of the eternal conflict between light and darkness, between good and evil, between Christ and Antichrist. Whiteway's diary begins in 1618, at the very outset of the Thirty Years War, which to many English Protestants seemed to be the final act of that great cosmic drama. After what was to become his regular annual listing of local officeholders, his first substantive entry records the appearance of the 'blazing star', the comet of 1618, which surely presaged great upheavals in the world. Like most of his contemporaries, Whiteway was interested in omens of this kind, though not excessively credulous about them. When he heard about a great battle in the sky over Ireland between huge flocks of starlings, he was torn between scepticism (he could not believe that twenty thousand birds had fallen dead) and the conventional reflection, 'malum omen avertat deus'.[57] He reports a solar eclipse without comment, and notes that a white circle round the sun is followed by a long spell of fine weather: the effect is meteorological, not supernatural. The appearance of the aurora borealis early in 1630 'much troubled the King and the Court', and a strange double tide on the Thames in 1632 was 'by divers curiously observed as a prognostic' – but these were other people's reactions, not necessarily those of the diarist. Bond may have found these events more meaningful. He gives no immediate explanation of the three suns that were seen all at one time at Rome in 1466, but a comet in 1577 appeared just before three kings were 'slain in Barbary'. Both he and Whiteway avidly noted instances of God's warnings and punishments being meted out to the Papists.[58]

Both of them, it will be recalled, grew up in families with personal experience of the bitter enmities generated by the European wars of religion, Bond's father narrowly escaping with his life at St Bartholomew, and Whiteway's being imprisoned by the Catholic League. When an uneasy peace returned early in the seventeenth century, the sons, like the fathers, found out what it was like to live under Catholic rule. The Bond family business sent Denis to St Malo for six weeks in 1603, and to Cádiz for two long years between 1605 and 1607. In 1616, at the age of seventeen, the younger Whiteway made what he describes as his 'first journey into France'.[59] Parental adventure stories, doubtless often retold, taught lessons repeated by teachers in their classrooms and ministers in their sermons, the lessons of sacred events in the protestant calendar: the 'fires of Smithfield' in Mary's reign, the miraculous defeat of the Armada in 1588, for example. From such sources Bond, Whiteway, and their contemporaries absorbed the ideology of protestant nationalism which had inspired their parents in the great Elizabethan days.

This outlook on the world was reinforced by the books they read. Bond's interests were heavily theological. He had copies, as we have noted, of the standard handbooks for JPs, a *Lex Mercatoria*, and one of Gervase Markham's books on equestrianism, perhaps the 1593 *Discourse on Horsemanship*. But most of his others were on religious matters: Calvin's *Institutes*; the works of Perkins, Greenham, and other puritan divines; 'a bible with Beza's notes'; Ursinus's 'Heidelberg Catechism'; and a book by 'Britman', presumably Thomas Brightman's *Revelation of the Apocalypse*, one of the most influential of English millenarian works. From Brightman, Bond and his friends would have gained a heightened sense that they were living in the 'last days' before the millennium, with the corresponding duty as members of the elect of preparing the way for God's kingdom.[60]

Whiteway's books duplicated many of Bond's, and both had access to the town library, which was stuffed with similar religious works. The list of donors is a roll-call of the leading Dorchester Puritans: Mr White, the Goulds, the elder Whiteway, John Parkins and many others. When an inventory was taken in 1632 only a book on 'the Conference at Hampton Court' in 1604 (possibly Bishop William Barlow's account) was missing: Whiteway had been using it and must have forgotten to return it.[61] He could also have found there the works of most of the great reformers: Calvin, Zwingli, Melanchthon, though, if the inventory is to be trusted, curiously not Luther. The library also possessed controversial works in abundance, most of them defending the protestant Church of England against Catholic attacks, or denouncing Rome as the agent of Satan: Thomas Beard's *Antichrist the Pope of Rome*, published in 1625, for example. Still, an assiduous reader at the library could have obtained a fairly balanced view of some of these exchanges, for among the holdings were Catholic works on the other side, including the answers to John Jewel's *Apology* written by John Rastell and Thomas Harding.

Whiteway's interests ranged far beyond religious controversy. It is curious that he did not go on to university after he left the Free School in 1615: Robert Cheeke had taken him to Oxford for a few days during the previous year, and he was obviously a compulsive reader.[62] As we have seen, he was well informed on astronomy and geography – besides the Mercator and the globes he gave to the library, he owned geographical works by Heylin and Ortelius, as well as travellers' accounts like *Purchas His Pilgrims*, and Captain John Smith on Virginia.[63] He also had books on logic, mathematics and medicine, and was interested in architecture (his commonplace book contains many architectural plans and drawings) and painting. When an itinerant French painter came to Dorchester in 1633, Whiteway was not content with passively sitting for his own portrait, but plied the artist with questions about mixing colours and other technicalities.[64]

But it was history that truly fascinated him. For its lessons he reached back into antiquity, taking copious notes on Herodotus, Livy and Procopius (he also owned copies of Josephus, and among later writers Froissart and Sir Walter Ralegh's *History of the World*). He owned George Buchanan's *History of Scotland*, and his books on English history included John Speed's *History of Great Britain* (he also had a collection of Speed's maps), Bacon's *History of King Henry VII*,

Camden's *Britannia*, and the chronicles of Stowe and Holinshed. His reading in continental history, especially of recent times, was equally extensive, ranging from Guicciardini's *History of Italy*, to modern histories of Venice, Spain, France, and the Netherlands. The *Histoire Universelle* by the French Huguenot Theodore D'Aubigné so impressed him that he laboriously translated it into English. This work, essentially a history of the French Wars of Religion between 1560 and 1601, had obvious relevance for one who, as Whiteway clearly did, worried about the threat of Catholic expansion on the continent and ultimately in England itself. He evidently contemplated writing a history of England in his own times, as he drew up a list of 'Materials for the History of the Reigns of K. J[ames] and K. C[harles]' that included many of the books, English and continental, noted above, as well as James I's published *Works*, and the book on the Hampton Court Conference that he had forgotten to return to the library.[65]

Whether Whiteway ever began such a work we do not know. It would have been a risky undertaking for someone of his political views in Charles I's England, and he must have been aware of the dangers. His commonplace book has had four leaves excised, presumably by the author, immediately following an entry commenting adversely on Arminianism, the dominant religion at Court at that time.[66] But his notes on his reading, and his choice of material for his diary, enable us to make a reasonable guess at the sort of line Whiteway might have taken. He would have started, surely, with the Reformation and the subsequent religious conflicts that convulsed Europe in the sixteenth century, culminating in the heroic English victory over the Armada. In more recent times he would have stressed the Catholic recovery that followed the deaths of Queen Elizabeth and King Henri IV of France, and traced the unfolding of events leading to the Thirty Years War. Whiteway shows much interest in the affairs of other countries, especially France, partly because of his family's trading interests there, but also because of his sympathy for the Huguenots. But the Spaniards and their Habsburg allies in Germany were the ultimate enemies of the Protestant cause. Englishmen might have serious maritime conflicts with the protestant Dutch, but, as some verses he recorded in October 1621 made clear, in the end only Spain stood to gain from them. Throughout the 1620s he watched helplessly as the Catholic tide swept over the

Palatinate and much of the rest of protestant Germany, obviously chafing at England's failure to do anything effective about it.

The dangers looming over protestant brethren in Europe seemed all the more serious in the light of developments in England, especially the change in the character of the national church that followed the accession of Charles I. James had never concealed his dislike of Puritans, but he was doctrinally orthodox, and throughout his reign the church was able to preserve the protestant consensus. In such a situation conformity was easy for moderate Puritans like John White, and although there might still be disputes over ceremonies they were not such as to drive people out of the church. But 'Puritan' had been a common term of abuse long before the 1620s, and after Charles's accession it became a wedge to split the church in two. The new king favoured churchmen like William Laud, who defined anyone who questioned his anti-Calvinist doctrine and rituals as a puritan rebel against authority. Laud's views, loosely described as Arminian' after the Dutch divine Arminius from whom they originated, challenged Calvinist orthodoxy at almost every point. Arminians rejected the doctrine of predestination, emphasised the sacraments above preaching, minimised the importance of strict sabbath observance, and wished to dilute the austere simplicity of protestant worship by the reintroduction of more elaborate rituals, in pursuit of what Laud called 'the beauty of holiness'.

Whiteway watched the Arminian advance with the same despair with which he followed the Catholics' continental victories. The two things were surely connected: Arminians must be crypto-Papists, at the very least fellow-travellers. Even in James's reign there were worries about Catholic influence. There had been the awful scheme to marry the heir to the throne, Prince Charles, to the daughter of the King of Spain. There had been the suspension of the penal laws against the Catholics; libels circulating at Court in 1621 had warned of a plot to 'bring in Popery'. Whiteway rejoiced at such manifestations of God's judgements as the collapse of Blackfriars Chapel in 1623, when at least a hundred Catholics were killed. Some of the stories he recorded were better founded in fiction than in fact, but they tell us what he wanted to believe; as when the dying James I sends for his son and charges him never to allow 'a toleration of popery'.[67]

Although Whiteway always worried about Popery, only in 1627

did he realise the seriousness of the Arminian menace. In that year
the moderate Archbishop Abbot was suspended and Laud, who was
to succeed him at Canterbury in 1633, became Charles's most influential ecclesiastical adviser. Soon the eminent Calvinist, John
Preston, lost his royal chaplaincy 'for preaching plainly against Idolatry' – Whiteway here uses the puritan codeword for Arminianism,
and he also speaks of it as 'the mother of Atheism'. Like many others,
Whiteway soon came to see a connection between Arminianism and
the authoritarian 'new counsels' now uppermost at Court. Abbot's
suspension, after all, was for refusing to license the publication of a
sermon about 'Catholic obedience' – unquestioning obedience to
royal authority, even royal authority to tax without parliamentary
consent. The imprisonment of the Arminian Roger Mainwaring by
Parliament in 1628 was provoked, Whiteway observed, by his
'seditious speeches against the liberty of the subject'.[68]

By this time Whiteway was becoming increasingly hostile to
bishops, as more and more of the hierarchy became Laudians. The
Basques, he was pleased to note during his readings in Spanish history, always refused to allow bishops to enter their country. When
Laud was elected Chancellor of Oxford in 1630 it was done,
Whiteway decided, by 'secret practices'. He savoured an anecdote
about one of Laud's predecessors, Richard Bancroft, who dreamt that
he had been made an archbishop and then cast into hell. Laudian
worship, with its devout ceremonial and elaborate music performed
by trained choirs rather than simple congregational psalm-singing,
was to Whiteway a hateful step on the road to Rome. From one of
White's former assistants he heard the story of a singing-man in
Exeter Cathedral observing a woman overcome by emotion during
the service. He asked her if she wept because of the beauty of the
music, and was told, no, it was because it reminded her of the noises
her old mare had made when it was dying.[69]

Laudian ceremonialism was now official policy, and although the
vigour with which it was enforced varied from diocese to diocese,
even in the least enthusiastic there was inevitably some effort to
enforce conformity. The destruction of Bristol's ecclesiastical court
records makes it impossible to tell how much formal pressure was
applied to Dorchester by the authorities there. Outwardly, relations
were always correct. When bishops came to conduct their Visitations
they were welcomed by pealing church bells, and were 'feasted by

the town'; in earlier days Robert Cheeke's pupils had acted Latin comedies in their honour. Archdeacons' Visitations were less elaborate, though still something of an occasion; Whiteway often records them, with the name of the visiting preacher.[70]

Whiteway had nothing against his own bishops, as the successive occupants of the see of Bristol in the 1630s – Robert Wright, George Coke, and Robert Skinner – were all moderate men, not Laudian persecutors. Still, bishops were royal servants, and soon after the turbulent parliamentary session of 1629 (in which upholders of Popery and Arminianism were voted 'enemies to the King and kingdom'), Bishop Wright had to order his clergy not to preach against either of these unpopular systems of belief. Whether White ignored the prohibition is unknown; if he did Wright must have turned a blind eye, as his successor did when White disregarded a royal proclamation in 1634. As the bishop well knew, to suspend White would be a foolish move, and would probably lead to his departure to New England with some of his leading parishioners. This sort of thing had happened in several East Anglian parishes, and by 1630 White was already encouraging lesser folk to leave and build God's kingdom in America. A few people in the town would have been glad to see him go. When Nathaniel Bernard was dismissed as Usher of the Free School he addressed an indignant petition to Laud, asking for protection against the Dorchester schismatics.[71]

Few if any of his fellow townsmen can have enjoyed anything like William Whiteway's sophisticated knowledge of recent history and international affairs. Still, a good number of them had a similar understanding of their world, and were convinced that they had a crucial role to play in the reformation of their community, their kingdom, and indeed the whole of Christendom. They were of course regularly reminded of this by John White and his clerical colleagues. The 'yoke of Antichrist', White later declared, had been removed at Queen Elizabeth's accession, but the 'perfecting of the work', the full reformation of the church, had been neglected or deferred for the current generation to complete.[72] It mattered, as it had not much mattered to Matthew Chubb, apparently, where England stood in the great world struggle of good against evil, of

Protestantism against Popery. And England, that 'elect nation' as the protestant advanced guard had always proclaimed it to be, could only play the role assigned by God if its rulers were sober, godly, and supportive of true (that is to say, Calvinist) religion. If the kingdom's rulers were backsliding, as by 1629 there were many regrettable signs that they were, it was all the more important that its component parts – towns like Dorchester and the households within it – should hold fast to the faith, should be reformed, godly, and industrious.

3

POVERTY AND DISORDER
IN DORCHESTER

YET AS John White well knew, Satan's grip was a tenacious one: far too many people in Dorchester were neither godly nor industrious. Long after White's arrival in the town idleness and immorality still reigned among a large segment of the population. Before we can understand how the Puritans tried to build their better world, the scale of the problems they confronted must first be appreciated. In this chapter we shall explore some of those problems; in the next the reformers' response to them.

How much work was needed before Satan's grip could be loosened will be apparent if we look at an incident in March 1634. It began hilariously, although if Whiteway is to be believed it did not end so. One Sunday evening a group of roisterers – Richard and Mary Veale, the shoemaker Anthony Penny, and a young fellow from Fordington named Roger Buck – called at the house of the carpenter John Wier, asking for food. Wier professed to have none to spare, but he and his wife, Joan, joined the party and they all went next door, where one of the butchering Haggards, Walter, was a lodger. There was more drinking and merriment, and Haggard offered Buck a halfpenny loaf if he would dance for them, which he promptly did, obviously far gone in drink. There are two versions of what happened next. According to one, after Buck had eaten Haggard asked him 'if he were well provided'. Buck did not miss the double entendre, and according to Haggard he immediately 'showed forth his privy members'. In the other version someone – either Haggard or Penny – offered Buck another loaf if he would expose himself. Both versions agree that Buck quickly did so. However, the women complained that the room was too dark, and Joan Wier held a lighted candle close to Buck so that everyone could see better. Alas, the jest went horribly wrong. Buck was burnt by the candle (none of those present admitted seeing it happen or hearing him cry out), and he died a few weeks later. It was never proved, apparently, that his death was caused by the burn: none of the perpetrators were charged with anything more serious than 'lewd carriage'. Mary Veale spent a month in the workhouse for it, and Whiteway says that she was 'well whipped' there; she and her husband also had to do penance after a sentence in the ecclesiastical court; presumably the others received similar punishment.[1]

So even after twenty years of reform this kind of merrymaking could occur in Dorchester. Matthew Chubb was dead, and so was Hunckes, the performing bear whose powers he had invoked, but in some circles their spirits lived on. Few parties got as completely out of hand as the one at Walter Haggard's, but less lurid anecdotes about others could easily be furnished. There were plenty of dissolute characters in the town who preferred drinking and fornicating to the sober routine of conscientious work and godliness that the Puritans were trying to inculcate. Some of them found that they could live better by stealing than by doing an honest day's work. Robert Sampson was by trade a shoemaker and John Chimney a glover. But between 1629 and 1637 they were also the champion petty thieves of Dorchester, cheerfully working together to help themselves to poultry, grain, clothing, fuel, and anything else they could lay their hands on. They often fell foul of the law in other ways. Sampson was charged with drunkenness or tippling ten times during this period, more than any other Dorchester offender, and also had half a dozen convictions for swearing. In 1632, egged on by Chimney, he abandoned his wife and ran away, but got only as far as Blandford before he lost his nerve or his money. A few months later he was charged with stealing clothes from his mother-in-law. Chimney was not much better, bound over in 1632 'for his idle course of life, refusing to work at his trade', though apart from his thieving he was less often in trouble than Sampson. It is remarkable that they were not hanged, and perhaps in the end they were, though Chimney at least was still in Dorchester after the civil war.[2]

Chimney, Sampson, and many like them were the victims of a social system in which property, access to education, and many other benefits were even more inequitably distributed than they are in our own times. They were, too, products of a culture which encouraged alcoholic evasion of responsibility rather than hard work and discipline. But their conduct suggests no conception of any alternative ordering of society. They would have been thieves and drunks, one feels, even if Matthew Chubb's vision of hospitality and good neighbourliness had prevailed. Like many other 'common drunkards' brought before the Dorchester JPs, they were the defeated flotsam of a seventeenth-century underclass. Yet they were also something more – for whether they realised it or not, they were adherents of an ancient tradition of popular sociability which stretched back, far beyond the Reformation, into medieval times. Plays, dancing, and communal feasting had been under sporadic attack in various parts of England long before John White came to Dorchester to give energy and direction to the local campaign against them. But the obstinate frivolity of many townspeople throughout the years of puritan reform shows how deeply rooted these traditions were. Much of the roistering in the alehouses was the work of visiting countrymen, but townsmen participated in it too. At virtually all the traditional holidays (which the Puritans were of course trying to suppress) there were outbreaks of alcoholic celebration. Fiddlers played and women danced at the Gaol on Easter morning in 1637, drunkenness and tippling regularly reached a peak around Whitsuntide, and Christmas was always kept up by the disorderly, whatever the town's governors thought about it. The irrepressible Sampson celebrated merrily in 1629. On Christmas Eve he was with John Merefield until long past midnight and had 'much drink'. He began Christmas Day with more drink in his own house, missing morning prayer, then slept it off and missed the afternoon service too. Seventeenth-century Christmas celebrations always continued at a hectic pace until Twelfth Night, or 'Twelfthtide'. There was a convivial gathering at the George – a 'tippling match' – on 27 December 1634, and two days later something that sounds like a festive dinner at Christopher Jenkins's house, with meat, drink, and tobacco.[3]

Even in Dorchester the old customs somehow survived: May Day was traditionally a time for music and dancing, so it is not surprising that when friends gathered at the house of the miller Thomas Norris on a Sunday evening early in May 1630 one of them should have brought a fiddle – though they insisted that 'there was no dancing at all'. Edward Hill, a blacksmith, was prosecuted for walking out in the middle of a Sunday service to go a-maying, while in the week before Whitsun 1635 one of a group of men drinking at Christopher Edmonds's alehouse brought a pole to make a 'malkin' – an effigy to be displayed at the maypole or in some festive procession. The old custom of midsummer bonfires on St John's Eve (23 June) was also still being observed. At about eleven o'clock on that night in 1634 Nicholas and Joan Jefferies, Thomas and Mary Hooper and some other revellers made a great fire at Glippath Bridge, 'between the dye house and the furze ricks'. Thomas Hooper later admitted carrying furzes to the bonfire, adding that 'divers of his neighbours did the like'. Eleanor Walbridge happened to be passing and quickly made her disapproval known. She professed to be worried about the danger to nearby houses, but it may also be that she was expressing moral disapproval, and that this is why she was so roundly abused: Hooper called her 'vrowdy faced carrion, jade, and toad's face'.[4]

Fiddling and dancing occurred at other times, when there was no such pretext as a traditional festival. The unfortunate Buck's dancing at Walter Haggard's party was entirely unpremeditated; so, apparently, was the merrymaking at John Brine's house in March 1637 when there was 'dancing all night long'. Some of the younger set, particularly in families where no good example was provided, were especially addicted. When Susannah Baily, daughter of a notoriously lawless alehousekeeper, was presented for tippling she also confessed to several dancing offences, both 'at home and abroad'. As we have seen, fiddlers were liable to turn up at drinking parties, even in the Gaol, and a group of them caused trouble at Fordington in September 1635, playing until three or four in the morning, 'to the great disturbance of the neighbours'. A Welsh vagrant ran into a fiddler of his acquaintance at one local sink of iniquity, Christopher Jenkins's house, in March 1630.[5]

Other traditional sports also survived. A gang of 'great boys' played at nineholes (a variant of marbles) in a field at Burton for a farthing a game one summer Sunday in 1632, and all missed divine service. Next spring they were at it again on Barrett's Hill and, even more audaciously, in Mr White's field at Frome Whitfield. Keeles (skittles) was also popular, and we find occasional references to cudgel-play and trapball. John Gape and his friends liked to play at fives in the prison courtyard; when told to stop they abused the Keeper and his daughter, 'in words and scoffs'. Fives was played by both men and boys. Some lads found playing against the walls of the Shire Hall in 1635 included many of the same ones prosecuted for nineholes a few years earlier; another group was caught playing in the churchyard at about the same time.[6]

High on the list of sports which seventeenth-century Puritans regarded with particular disfavour (because they so often led to drinking and violence) were bear-baiting and bull-baiting. There had been bear-baitings at other places in Dorset, if not in Dorchester, earlier in the century, and Matthew Chubb's reference to 'Hunckes the great bear' shows how familiar they were. But although they continued occasionally not far away, over the Somerset border, as late as the early 1620s, there is no sign of them in Dorset by then.[7] Bull-baiting was more common. It had some culinary justification in that it was supposed to make the meat tender, but it was also done for amusement, and it is not surprising to find Dorchester butchers engaging in it. A butcher's apprentice named John Hoskins met Edward Tewxbury and some other young men outside the town just after Christmas, 1634. There was a bull in the field, which they put into the pound and baited with a dog, the butchers all arriving at evening prayer gloriously late, after the sermon had begun. The younger Thomas Pouncey, a particularly violent member of the trade, also attended bull-baitings: in May 1637 it was reported that 'he did break the bullkeeper's head with his cudgel'.[8]

This kind of attachment to popular cultural traditions could be found among many of Dorchester's lower orders. Much of the play and feasting seems harmless enough to us, but to godly reformers it was deeply threatening. It was not only irresponsible young people who caused disorder, or were likely to sink into vice and ungodliness. Those present at the party at Walter Haggard's in 1634, it will be remembered, were all adults, and included two married couples. Satan made no distinctions of age when he sought adherents of his kingdom.

Misbehaviour among married people was especially serious, as it was likely to disrupt existing families, which were of course regarded as the essential foundations of any ordered, virtuous society. It is unlikely that Dorchester people were any more, or any less, loose in their sexual habits than their neighbours in other places. But stories of their misdeeds even in the years of puritan ascendancy are abundant. As we have seen, the town's population rose dramatically after 1600, and the housing shortage was intensified by the fire of 1613. Overcrowding was a serious problem, and many families took in lodgers. Some of them were Dorchester natives, like Walter Haggard, who, we may recall, was living at George Membry's when his friends came to call that memorable Sunday evening; more often the lodgers were new arrivals in the town. William and Christian Uphill had a room in Albion Bull's house; the cobbler William Way had another. Even married couples sometimes had to share houses. Inevitably there were suspicions of irregular sexual liaisons.[9]

Improper behaviour by married people was always a matter of public concern. The indiscretion of Ruth Browne, wife of a respectable bookseller, was particularly serious because it also involved a member of one of Dorchester's governing families. Young Richard Blachford, grandson of the Corporation member, met her at Matthew Miller's house and bought her a pint of wine. They then went upstairs and spent half an hour alone together; she naturally protested that she 'did no harm with him there'. The much less respectable Mary Veale, one of the women at Haggard's party, could scarcely have made this claim. Seeing the weaver George White go into her house early one morning, a neighbour's servant made an excuse to follow him. She found two neglected children and Veale lying in her smock, though White had managed to get out of the bed just in time. Another suspicious incident concerned Susan Lee, who had an affair with a Fordington miller named Francis Churchill. While Lee's husband was away at Woodbury Hill Fair a neighbour heard them in a nearby barn, where Churchill was murmuring endearments to his 'little sweet rogue'. The pair had innocently gone into the barn, they said, 'only to pass away the time'.[10]

Some of these relationships inevitably led to conflict. John Dowrage's wife, Mary, was certain that her husband had been unfaithful and that Rebecca Stillard, a carpenter's wife, was to blame: 'her husband did keep her and wash her guts.' She told her children that Rebecca 'must be their mother-in-law [i.e. stepmother]'. Passing

Stillard in the fields, Mary Dowrage turned and cursed her: 'all the devils in hell go with thee, would to God she were under ground.' Jealousies like this seriously undermined the neighbourly ideal of 'living in quiet'.[11]

A few accusations of sexual misconduct involved responsible townsfolk, people of 'good credit and reputation', and were taken particularly seriously, because people like this were supposed to set a good example. The clothier Joseph Parkins was a notorious delinquent. As a young man he had seemed destined for a substantial position in the town, but he then went completely off the rails. No relation, as far as is known, to the powerful and affluent John Parkins (the diarist Whiteway's father-in-law), Joseph first appears in the records in August 1610, when his friend Henry Edwards made his will, in which he left Parkins two pounds. Edwards died shortly afterwards, and by the time the will was proved in November Parkins had already married his widow, Julian.[12] For a time Parkins seemed to be doing well. He was a responsible member of Trinity parish, occupying the usual parochial offices held by men of his middling wealth and status – overseer of the poor in 1614, sidesman a year later. But after 1615 he held no more public offices, and it is not hard to see why. By 1617 he was frequenting Nicholas Hellier's extremely unsavoury alehouse in Fordington; worse, he was taking boys from the Free School to drink there too. His acquaintances by now included such undesirables as Anthony Barnes, a disorderly Fordington yeoman, and the surgeon Roger Haydon, a known Catholic sympathiser.[13]

An assault charge against Parkins in July 1629 was followed by a scattering of others for swearing, drinking, and absence from church. But it was his sexual promiscuity that really marked him out. In September 1629 he was alleged to be abusing his position as trustee for a neighbour imprisoned for debt, by sleeping with his wife. In May 1634 the constables found him in an upstairs room at Christopher Jenkins's notoriously disorderly house with an unmarried woman named Sarah Harris, and in the following August he was accused of having raped Mary Jefferies. Parkins was in a panic when he heard about the accusation, bolting the door against the constables, and giving extremely evasive answers to the JPs. The girl's mother swore that Parkins had offered to pay to have her spirited away to London, but the JPs must have felt that the family left it a bit late before making the complaint: the baby was born less than three weeks later. In January 1635 a more plausible charge of rape was made by Basil Cooke, daughter of a respectable alehousekeeper, William Cooke. Even then the girl's parents waited five days before going to the magistrates, during which time Parkins's friends the Hasselburys (in whose house the incident occurred) offered Basil's mother five pounds to hush it up.[14]

This time the JPs were sufficiently impressed to bind Parkins over to the Assizes. The outcome is unknown, but nothing very serious seems to have happened to him. He was again bound over on unspecified charges in 1635 and 1636, each time in the unusually large sum of eighty pounds, but he was still able to call on respectable people like the baker Joseph Purchase and the Hasselburys to give bail for him. By 1638 he may have been trying to reform himself, but perhaps that impression is simply the result of the absence of adequate judicial records after that date. At all events nothing more is heard of him until his death in May 1650. He had made no written will, but on his deathbed Parkins expressed his intentions to William Hasselbury and others present. He left everything to his wife Julian, he said, adding that 'all I now possess, and a great deal more, was her own before I married her, and therefore I will not give one penny from her.' He had spent her money and was confessing to a wasted life. Actually Julian had not been as totally ruined by her husband's excesses as this might imply. When she died seven years later she left a good deal of money to relatives and to various charities, including an impressive one hundred pounds for the poor of Dorchester.[15]

Nobody else of Parkins's status had as bad a reputation, but there were isolated accusations against a few others. Nicholas Stone, for more than twenty years an apparently virtuous pillar of Trinity parish, was denounced by the widow Elizabeth Hoskins, who had rooms in his house. Stone made repeated advances, and still kept after her when she moved out following the death of her husband, trying to get her to put her hand in his breeches and making other indecent suggestions. Eventually she lost patience and went to the mayor. The mercer Robert Cardrow was less prominent than Stone but he too came from a well-established and respectable family. A weaver named Thomas Croucher and his wife, Joan, lived in his house. When Thomas was away, Cardrow tried to invite himself into Joan's chamber, and repeatedly 'showed her his yard and bade her look what a dainty one he had'. She told him that she 'lived quietly' and did not want her husband to call her 'whore and common whore'. Cardrow dismissed her scruples: 'they were not whores that did a man a good turn.' She made the mistake of letting him kiss her ('to be rid of him'), and then belatedly told her husband the whole story. Cardrow was never punished, and Joan Croucher was well aware of the sexual double standard. When Cardrow told her 'how fondly he would use her', she could only think of the treatment given to other unfaithful wives: 'she should be used as Gasse's wife was, then, and whipped.'[16]

Joan Croucher and Elizabeth Hoskins were respectable women. But there were plenty who were not. The widow Margaret Pedwin, who already had one illegitimate child and was therefore thought to be fair game, was gathering fuel at Fordington when she met a man from Poole, who offered her a groat for sex. Pedwin indignantly replied that 'she would not go with him for a shilling'. He then raped her, though Pedwin admitted that he promised her 'some further recompense at his next meeting with her'. Several Dorchester houses appear to have been regular places of assignation. One, belonging to the joiner Christopher Jenkins, we have already encountered. His wife had briefly run off with a servant in 1617, spending several hours with the young man in a room at a Fordington alehouse. She must have returned to her husband, but their house was later much 'suspected of bawdry'. The blacksmith William Symes picked up a Fordington woman, Christian Tucker, in the market one Saturday in 1632. He was observed to nudge her with his shoulder, 'whereat the said Christian looked about', and they went by separate ways to the Jenkins's, where the constables found them later that afternoon. Two years later Sarah Harris and her sister Elizabeth came under suspicion. They lived at home with their widowed mother, taking on occasional household jobs for neighbours, but otherwise masterless. Sarah sometimes worked for Christopher Jenkins's wife; one evening she stayed to dinner after fetching water from the river at Glippath Bridge. When the constables arrived she was in an upstairs room with Joseph Parkins. She claimed that Jenkins was also in the room and that his wife had only just left, but the JPs were displeased, ordering her to get into service immediately and not 'go abroad a charring'.[17]

Among others who frequented the Jenkins's house were Mary Edwards, wife of a saddler, and William Barter, who was also married. The constables 'disliked' it, so they continued their meetings outside the town at Frome Whitfield. But Barter and his wife were also in trouble as a couple. They were bound over in 1630 when a Henstridge man and a local married woman were found suspiciously together in their house. Margaret Barter was several times fined for unlicensed aleselling and was told that 'if she keep not better order hereafter' she would be sent to the workhouse. Her husband's reputation was well known: when Bartholomew Hooper was abusing his daughter-in-law he called her 'bitch and whore and Barter's whore'. The millwright James Treamor and his wife Anne also had bad reputations. They were bound over in July 1629 for keeping a house 'suspected for bawdry', and some later incidents help us to see why. In September their servant, Elizabeth Masterson, was observed by neighbours (through the usual convenient chink in the wall), having sex with the shoemaker George Way. In December Anne Treamor was brought before the mayor for being alone with one of John Cooth's journeymen; he had been such a frequent visitor that her husband had given her a nasty beating because of it. And in the following spring the Treamors were entertaining company when Anne was called away by Joseph Parkins, 'to dress his supper'. James went with her, but knowing Parkins's reputation the JPs were understandably suspicious.[18]

The most shocking irregular liaisons were incestuous ones. Several incest cases surfaced in Dorchester in 1634 and 1635. The widow Margaret Pedwin, whom we have encountered already, had sex with her uncle in a barn at Burton; she claimed that he promised to marry her if she got pregnant. Katherine Maunders was the target of advances by her stepfather, the carpenter Thomas Hooper, who repeatedly got into bed with her, though she denied that he had actually tried 'to know her body'. There must have been suspicions about another household, the Merefields'; late one night the constables went to the house and found the grown son and daughter in bed together. Their mother claimed that a much younger child usually slept between them, but this had not happened on the night in question. Henry Pouncey, son of Thomas Pouncey the elder, admitted that he had asked his nine year-old sister Grace to let him 'have knowledge of her body'. The girl would have none of it, threatening that 'if he offered her any violence she would cry out to her father'. As with the Merefields, overcrowding was partly responsible; Henry and Grace Pouncey normally had a younger brother between them in the bed. Henry was promptly sent to the workhouse, it being noted that he was masterless and living in a 'lewd and uncivil manner'.[19]

Sexual misbehaviour was not the only thing that could disrupt a family. One of the worst things that could happen was desertion by a parent, usually the father. A threat to leave wife and children to be cared for by the parish was always a serious matter. Committed to the workhouse for swearing at the bailiffs, Robert Foote, a poor parchmentmaker, 'wished he might be hanged . . . if he did not leave his wife and children on the town or parish'. In another case it was the wife who was in the workhouse: Richard Veale threatened that unless she was released he too would abscond and leave his children behind. Some of these threats were not empty ones, as Robert Sampson showed when he abandoned his family and went off on his drinking spree through Puddletown and Blandford. William Croome, a Dorchester butcher, left his young son in London; the boy lived by begging before being caught, whipped, and sent home. Confronted with a husband's drinking or violence, a woman, too, might choose to run away. Margaret Pouncey, wife of a notoriously violent, abusive husband, left her children at the church porch; Christian Jacob left hers at the door of one of the overseers of St Peter's parish, the powerful William Joliffe.[20]

Then as now, domestic violence was probably under-reported, but there is still plenty of it in the records. It was often aggravated by drinking, and in the face of reproof many a drunken husband invoked his patriarchal rights. When the blacksmith Methuselah Notting's wife pleaded with him to stop drinking, he beat her up for questioning his authority. William Miller also insisted on his right to do as he pleased. After his wife had sent for the constables he said that 'in despite of their teeth he would go to the alehouse . . .

and have his cup and a pot of sack and a whore, and that his wife should stand by and see it, and that if she would dare to speak he would beat her to pieces.'[21]

During the five years ending at Michaelmas 1637, 1,386 cases are recorded in Dorchester's offenders' book. Of these, only about fifty – less than four per cent – have to do with sex or family problems. By far the biggest category of offences is the drink-related one: drunkenness, tippling, entertaining for unlawful drinking, and selling ale without a license, which together account for over thirty-five per cent of the cases. One obvious reason for its preponderance is that drink was so readily available. Dorchester being an Assize and market town, as well as on one of the main roads from the west towards London, the existence of a fair number of hostelries was only natural, and there is no sign that the reformers ever contemplated draconian measures to reduce their number. In 1629 there were thirteen licensed alesellers in the town, a number that grew to around twenty ten years later. Some of them kept large and impressive establishments like the George, the Antelope, the Crown and the Rose. The Ship, kept by William Wilson, was somewhat less respectable, to judge by the number of reports of disorders there, but such things were not unknown even at the George.[22]

Some of the alehousekeepers were respectable men like Robert Lawrence and Matthew Swaffield. There was only one complaint about the houses of either of them in the whole of the well-documented period between 1629 and 1637. At the other end of the scale were people like Jasper Brewer, who kept the Lion. Like many of the alehousekeepers, Brewer had another trade: he was a clothworker. He came to Dorchester as one of John Cooth's journeymen, and married a local woman, but was not allowed to follow his trade, so he ran the Lion instead. He was suppressed in 1631, possibly as a result of his servant's indiscretions (she had been too familiar with the customers, and got pregnant by one of them), licensed again two years later, and suppressed for good in 1635. Christopher Edmonds managed to keep his license throughout the 1630s, but it must have been touch and go several times. No great example to his patrons, around Whitsun 1635 he went on a pub-crawl with friends; they ended at the Rose, where Edmonds had to spend the night, too drunk to get home. One evening later that summer there was enough noise at Edmonds's to attract the vigilant Constable Righton. The maid detained him at the door long enough for the tapster to blow out the candle, but not long enough for a drunken patron to be able to escape by the back door. In 1636 the JPs began to crack down, distraining Edmonds's goods when he failed to pay a 10s. fine. Yet somehow he kept his license.[23]

Many alehousekeepers alternated between legality and illegality. Thomas Galton was suppressed and imprisoned in 1632, but got his license back when he came out. Several seem never to have been licensed at all, or at most for very brief periods. The most striking case is that of Clement Baily, nominally a shoemaker. He was constantly in trouble: charged with keeping a 'disorderly tippling house' in 1630, and suppressed in each of the next three years. But he was still at it in 1634, giving 'ill words' to the constable when told to close. Two years later the JPs lost patience and committed him to the Assizes. Baily gave bond not to sell ale any more, but he was soon being charged with keeping a 'house suspected of bawdry' after letting a room to a married woman from Alton Priors and her lover.[24]

Clement Baily was allowed to continue his aleselling because the JPs knew that if he did not he would be a burden on his parish. There were too many shoemakers in the town already, as the Freemen's Company explained when they refused to allow a new one to trade. Several other unlicensed sellers took it up because they could not support themselves at their regular trades. Sometimes they made a success of it, as the shoemaker William Symonds did at the Green Dragon. Others, including Brewer, did not last very long. Adam Smith, suppressed in 1633, was an unemployed weaver who had tried to get work as a paviour: the Freemen's Company ordered him to desist, 'not having been of that trade'.[25]

Women, particularly widows, often supplemented their meagre incomes by brewing or selling ale. Thomas Galton's wife ran the alehouse while her husband was in prison, and Rebecca Notting tried to carry on after she was widowed, though without much success. In other places magistrates tended to be tolerant of such people, but they were not in Dorchester. The widow Dorothy Bascombe used to sell ale at the trained-band musters, when the county militia drilled at Poundbury, always notoriously alcoholic occasions. After a muster in 1635 she tried to dispose of some of her unsold stock in the town, only to fall foul of the law.[26]

The results of excessive drinking could be seen every day. A sailor from London brought before the bailiff 'stank of drink'; Christopher Johnson and Philip Lockyer were both found 'reeling' in the street (Lockyer went home to sleep it off after 'pissing in his breeches'); Edmund Smith vomited in the parlour of the George. The number of people fined after being found drunk 'in view' of the mayor is legion. Offenders often made things worse by cursing the JPs. Matthias Mellege was 'very disordered' and abused the bailiffs, 'his hands playing with their faces'; his case was the more shocking because he was a minister, down from Oxford to visit his parents.[27]

Like sexual immorality, excessive drinking disrupted families, leaving a trail of neglected children and battered wives. Sometimes the punishment of drunkards was directly aimed at relieving their families: when Matthew North, a weaver, was fined five shillings his wife was awarded half of it. There were, of course, some incorrigible boozers: 'common alehousehaunters' like the carpenter Walter Wier, 'common drunkards' like the plumber Edmund Buckler and the glazier Elias Fry. Robert Sampson may have been the champion drinker between 1629 and 1637, but several others – the blacksmith Edward Hill, the butcher William Croome – were not far behind. The number of Dorchester people who drank to excess was probably no greater than in many other places: Richard Gough's memoir of his seventeenth-century Shropshire village is full of stories of marriages broken and lives ruined by drink. Dorchester was no different.[28]

Dorchester was like any other place, too, in that drink could lead to illicit sex. An unruly gardener named John Edwards turned up drunk at the house of Sarah Hancock; they had sex and he then collapsed in a stupor for a couple of hours. Anne Butler, the barber-surgeon's wife, got drunk in Fordington one evening and let Henry Reade come home with her. Reade got into her bed, but Butler collapsed on the stairs, making so much noise that it roused the neighbours. They told her to go to bed, but she retained sufficient presence of mind to reply: 'No, for there was a roguing knave in her bed already.'[29]

How much people actually consumed in their drinking-bouts is not always clear, though in the case of Nicholas Isack, one of James Gould's apprentices, it was enough to send him to bed 'without any stomach for his supper'. Usually the quantities are vaguely described: 'a sixpenny jug', a 'great pot of beer' found under the table. People rarely admitted drinking very much. Four men had only two 'hooped pots' between them at Keate's one Sunday evening in 1634, they said, and the younger Thomas Pouncey confessed to only two earthen pots' full in an all-night session a few months later. On the other hand, three young men got through a dozen beers one night at George Membry's. Ale was overwhelmingly the drink of choice, though a man got drunk on aqua vitae at the Ship in 1630, and at the same inn four years later seven roisterers got through seven pints of sack. On another occasion the linenweaver John Chapman went to sleep in the chimney corner after he and his wife had polished off a quart of claret.[30]

Next to sexual licence and drinking, the offences that most troubled Dorchester's reformers were absence from church and swearing. Under the Elizabethan statutes church attendance on Sundays was compulsory, with a shilling fine for each absence. Both town and parish officers – constables and churchwardens – routinely checked the houses of the negligent. The sidesmen also enforced attendance, although Robert Sampson declared that 'if the sidesman did beat down his doors' he still would not come to church. Attendance was compulsory not only on Sundays, but also for weekday Fast or Holy day observances, though the law appears to have been less regularly enforced in these latter cases.[31]

Absentees often had plausible excuses. Men tended to produce business-related ones, risking charges of sabbath-breaking. The barber-surgeon Gabriel Butler got away with one absence by pleading that he had been visiting a patient, but after going to Charminster on a similar errand he was fined for not attending church there instead. Other such excuses – gone to Charminster to fetch work, coming home from Blandford, at Fordington making a bargain – were also summarily rejected. Women were more likely to miss church, arrive late, or leave early, because of domestic chores: the needlemaker Thomas Lucas's wife and maid were getting dinner ready when Constable Bragge called during service time. Thomasine Hillgrove, wife of a currier, arrived at All Saints 'when the glass was half out in sermon'; she explained that she had 'many children to make ready'.[32]

There were other problems besides lax attendance. Elderly people often had to go out before the service was over because of physical infirmity, as well they might, given the length of the sermons: Henry White was one of many who left early 'upon extremity'. Elizabeth Bull may have sounded less than convincing when she gave this excuse: she had previously explained her repeated departures during the sermon by 'pretending she went to provide her dinner'. The clockmaker Thomas Walden left All Saints during evening prayer, 'taken with a fit of sickness'. Others who hung about outside the church door had no such excuse: Henry Hobbes and Hugh Haggard were both fined for talking in the street in service time, and Henry Merefield for loitering on the stairs outside St Peter's.[33]

Some people showed their contempt for the sabbath in other ways – by working illegally, for example. Such cases would normally have been dealt with by the ecclesiastical court at Blandford, but a few were heard in Dorchester. When a churchwarden asked Leonard Miller's servants what day it was, and 'whether it were a day fit to brew on?' the brewer contemptuously intervened: 'it was but ten groats . . . no more than drinking a quart of wine in an inn or alehouse.' John Facy admitted that he and his wife had been too busy baking to go to church; Mary Dowrage was 'proved by the churchwardens to hang out clothes' on a Sunday in 1631. A man who missed afternoon worship not unreasonably pleaded that his constitution could not stand three services in one day, but in spite of his poor health he had walked two miles to fetch a horse. Some people were incessant sabbath-breakers. In 1631 Thomas Southy was accused of conducting a regular Sunday business: 'he doth usually either send or carry abroad boots and shoes . . . to be sold,' an informer reported. Dorchester's reformers were successful in making most people come to church, but a great gulf still divided the godly from the unregenerate.[34]

Swearing, the next most common misdemeanour, was offensive to pious people both on religious grounds and because it violated that ideal of harmony and 'living in quiet' that was so important in the maintenance of civil order. The list of objectionable phrases uttered in Dorchester is endless: 'as God saved me', 'by God of heaven', 'in the name of Christ', 'God's wounds', 'God's blood', 'a pox of God', 'a plague of God', are only some of the most common. Bad language did not necessarily involve actually invoking the deity. The phrase 'a pox and a plague' was sometimes strengthened by adding 'of God' but might also be used without it. Two constables overheard a nice exchange between Robert Sampson and his wife. Sampson wished 'a pox and a plague of God' on her, to which she replied, 'a murrain on thee, husband'. That swearing occurred privately, within the family, did not make it any less offensive. 'A pox take thee,' said John Facy to his son; 'a pox on thee, hold thy peace,' the weaver Humphrey Perry told his wife: both were prosecuted.[35]

By punishing swearing the authorities were trying to control the vocabulary as well as the religious, sexual, and work habits of their neighbours. But swearing was so embedded in the language of the unreformed – of gentlemen as well as of the poorer sort – that it was an uphill task. The champion swearer in the offenders' book was the gentleman Henry Gollop, whom the watchmen claimed to have heard utter forty oaths. There were townsmen who could do nearly as well. The round figures often reported sound no better than approximations, though the counts made by JPs while cases were being heard are probably more accurate. A Rodden man was charged with swearing twenty oaths; while his case was being heard he added nine more and was fined for every one.[36]

Much of the invective was directed at authority-figures like the constables and magistrates. But even in ordinary discourse, the frequency with which terms like 'rogue', 'knave', and 'whore' were bandied about shows how difficult the task of building the godly community was going to be. Religious people were especially likely to be among the targets. We find the godly Matthew Swaffield denounced as 'hollow-hearted wretch', the pious Roger Turner as 'dissembling puritan knave'. George Brine was a turbulent and rebellious character, a carpenter by trade. He was constantly abusing people, calling his own brother 'slave' and 'toad', and an alehouse-keeper's wife 'witch and jade'. Young Robert Motier, a pipemaker, repeatedly denounced William Watts (who was in the same trade) and his wife as 'cuckold and whore'. Such terms were part of common speech. He would not 'allow a whore to call him a knave', Humphrey Perry told Elizabeth Hoskins.[37]

Women were just as inventive in their language. But when they did this sort of thing it was called scolding, and punished with a ducking. Mary Colliford called Elizabeth Lugge, the spinning teacher, 'gig, runagate, speakarse and baggage': bad enough, but what made it worse was that it was done in front of the Hospital children, so she was bound over to Sessions instead of being routinely ducked.[38] Ordinary street brawls between women were usually defined as scolding. The widow Katherine Gourd heard a noise one night in 1629; going outside she saw two quarrelling women emerge from a neighbour's house. One was Em Gawler, a terrifying apparition 'with her head clothes off, and her hair about her ears'. The other was the widow Anne Samways, who struck her with a 'wash kettle'. 'You old jade,' the widow Benfield screamed at Agnes Keate, 'you will be in Bridewell before me': Keate had called her 'common whore' and had noted that Benfield was about to have a second bastard. 'If she were upon calving, she should go home and calve,' Mary Dowrage advised her husband's mistress, Rebecca Stillard. Some of these shouting-matches went on for hours: evidence was given that in January 1633 Cicely Jenkins and three other women spent 'the most part of [two] days' in scolding. Women were ducked for much less.[39]

Scolds were women who rejected the submissive role conventionally assigned to them. So, even more dangerously, were witches: women whose satanic powers turned the natural hierarchies of gender, family, and class upside down, threatening to plunge their communities into a hellish maelstrom of chaos and disorder. Although Puritans firmly believed in the reality of witchcraft, serious accusations were rare in Dorchester during this period. But the word itself was much feared, even when used lightly as a term of abuse, for a frivolous accusation could cause almost as much division as a real one. The widow Margery Goodfellow was given a serious warning for disturbing the Women's Almshouse in 1634, for 'quarrelling and calling names, and in particular for calling Agnes Ashe a witch'. In several other cases, as when old William Lovelace called Rebecca Cornish 'whore and witch', the magistrates punished the accuser for abuse. Only two real accusations of witchcraft are recorded in the offenders' book, both in 1634, and again in both cases it was the accuser, not the alleged witch, who was brought before the JPs. Richard Shory, a labourer, was prosecuted for saying that the shoemaker John Merefield was a witch. He took wood from Merefield's house and threw it on the fire, saying, 'he would see if the witch would come' (the ritual was supposed to bring the witch into view), and went to the window to look for him. The other case was more serious, as it followed the sickness of a child. Old Margery Adyn had given a neighbour's daughter a cake, and according to the girl's mother, she was 'never well since'. Suspecting Adyn of having bewitched her, she got some thatch from her roof and burnt it, hoping that it would make Adyn appear and thus reveal her guilt. But the accusation seems to have gone no further, the JPs simply ordering the two women not to abuse each other any more.[40]

A large proportion of Dorchester's population thus stood in great need of reformation and discipline. One segment of them caused special concern: those of the younger generation. Noisy adolescents are always alarming to their respectable elders. And at this time there were so many of them: the products of that 'baby boom' generation born after 1600. Their families were sometimes too poor to support them, they often could not or would not enter covenanted service or apprenticeship, and they were always in danger of slipping outside the system of household discipline, the very foundation of the social order. They were part of the reservoir from which came that menacing figure, the masterless man or woman. But even if they were not masterless, even if they were apprenticed to respectable trades, they were always liable to be riotous and undisciplined.[41]

Their drinking was a particularly serious problem. The most dangerous kind of drinking involved young people, for in their case the authority of parents or masters was obviously at risk. The Recorder, Sir Francis Ashley, was particularly concerned about the lure of the alehouses in the poorly policed suburbs of Fordington and Colleton Row. In 1617 some Free School boys, boarders from good families, were caught drinking in a disreputable Fordington alehouse run by a man named Nicholas Hellier. Around Christmas 1618 Ashley unearthed two more unlicensed alehousekeepers in Colleton Row, both of whom had been 'entertaining townsmen and apprentices drinking'. But this could happen in the borough, too: Ashley also dealt with a man found in an alehouse who had been 'drawing other youths thither'. Three Dorchester alehousekeepers were in trouble some years later, in 1633, for serving mead and beer to boys from the Free School.[42]

The sons of Dorchester townspeople mixed freely with apprentices. Their social life may sound innocent enough to us, but to seventeenth-century moralists it could easily seem to undermine both filial obedience and good work habits. It was worst if it took place on the sabbath, as when an apprentice named Jonas Swarfridge spent a Sunday evening around Christmas 1629 drinking mead with the tailor William Parsons and a young unmarried woman named Mary Martin. After some of Simon Hasselbury's apprentices had wasted an evening at two unlicensed alehouses, they cheerfully staggered home, 'singing of songs'. A group of young fellows at the Antelope on Guy Fawkes night in 1632 included John Terrin and Matthew Bonger, both from respectable local families, and several apprentices; they got through four 'double jugs' of beer before the constables broke up the party. Robert Way, son of the eminently respectable Christopher Way, gave an interesting account of youthful sociability when questioned about his 'idleness and company keeping' in August 1631. His circle included Henry Whittle, Andrew Fooke the younger, and John Miller, all from fairly prominent families, as well as some less reputable apprentices. During Assize week they had taken tobacco, washed down with nine jugs of beer, at the house of the barber John Norton, and had also wasted time drinking at William Symes's place. On the following Saturday they were drinking again at John Hoskins's, in a group that included a woman from Fordington. They were late for church on Sunday morning because they were once more drinking at Symes's – William Martin's wife was there too, not in their company, she said, but the boys politely toasted her anyway – and on Monday, fair day, they were there again. What with breakfast on 'a neck of mutton and pottage' at Edmonds's none too reputable alehouse, Robert Way seems to have plunged into a veritable round of dissipation.[43]

To sober, God-fearing parents and employers it was all very worrying: their sons were getting into bad company and their servants were neglecting their work, possibly even trying to control their own lives by arranging their social calendar. Several apprentices questioned about their drinking denied that this was 'any meeting appointed by themselves' – they had just happened to take their 'morning draught' together. Another apprentice conceded that he had been lured to Richard Keate's alehouse by friends, but denied neglecting his master's business, though he admitted having some beer and a pipe of tobacco. Again this sounds little worse than a seventeenth-century equivalent of the coffee-break, but there were suspicions that the man was drunk, and the line of questioning is significant. Sometimes the culprits were not apprentices, but mature craftsmen who got drunk at the workplace, as Hugh Devenish did when doing some glazing at the Antelope.[44]

The young people were a constant worry. They were drinking too much, and this led them into many other kinds of trouble. Drunk or sober, they were all too likely to miss church on Sundays, or to misbehave when they got there. Many things besides Mr White's sermons beckoned them in the spring or summertime. Young Michael Colliford spent a Sunday afternoon picking nuts, 'till six of the clock'. Andrew Fooke and Robert Gillett went with their sweethearts to Bockington 'to eat milk and cream'; Fooke gallantly paid Katherine Goodfellow's fine for missing church. There were some incorrigible absentees. The servants Anne Chaldecote and Margaret Richardson were well known to be 'continual slack comers'; Thomas Tanner, a brewer's apprentice, missed five Sundays in a row in 1633.[45]

Trouble during church services was almost invariably the fault of noisy young people. The sidesmen were supposed to keep them in order – a 1634 case notes how they 'passed forth and came in to view such as were disorderly' – but their pomposity was likely to provoke youthful ridicule. John Hooper, a butcher's apprentice, sat 'with his hat on his head and laughed and flouted' at them as they paraded around the church. On some Sundays the sidesmen must have been busy. Giles Morey stuffed dirt down the neck of William Pouncey, and Richard Hoskins spat at one of the other boys; Henry Greene was charged with 'laughing and talking and walking up and down'. There was always a good deal of unseemly whispering and jostling, and it sometimes got out of hand. During one sermon in 1634, epithets like 'lousy rogue' and 'lousy bastard' were exchanged by boys from quite respectable families; young George Allambridge bit Lawrence Derby in the back. On a later Sunday John Hoskins was seen to 'pull Richard Butler out of his place and strike him a box in the ear'. The penalty for such juvenile hooliganism was usually a whipping, and when services were disturbed by young men no longer in their teens the authorities took an even more serious view of it. John King and Nicholas Symes, both previously charged with 'uncivil behaviour', were sent to prison after they were caught playing and laughing in All Saints church.[46]

This kind of loutishness was most likely to occur among adolescents who were not properly controlled by the system of household discipline. Young people no longer under the authority of their parents were supposed to have masters, and ensuring that they did so was one way of disciplining the disreputable. Ralph Perrin's son, who had been drinking and abusing the constables, had no master and would never adopt any 'honest calling'. For men as well as women masterlessness was often associated with other kinds of misbehaviour, such as drunkenness or absence from church. Henry Greene had no master and got into trouble playing fives at the Shire Hall.[47]

Masterlessness was particularly threatening when women were involved, and again it often accompanied other kinds of indiscipline. Sarah Hancock persistently refused to go into service; she was also several times ducked for scolding, and was accused of having casual sexual liaisons. Sarah Croome is another example: charged with scolding in May 1631, she too was found to be out of service. Mary Savage was stocked for drunkenness in 1630 and told to get into service; two years later she was again charged with being masterless, 'having lived of long time idly and disordered and out of service'. Sarah Coish was both 'a slack comer to church and a masterless person'. In 1634 she was accused of suspiciously keeping company with Nicholas Cox, and was given the choice of marrying him or finding a master within ten days.[48]

Apprentices being young people, their sexuality was a constant worry to their elders. While Rector White was catechising the young people one Sunday afternoon in 1636 there was much sniggering at the back of the church. A paper was being passed round which Henry Follett, a dyer's apprentice, described as 'a catechism for women that could not hold their legs together'. This corruption of youth naturally did not originate in Dorchester, Follett later said, but had been brought down from London by a son of the tailor John Russell. He may have been telling the truth, but it may also be that Follett, our only source of information about the paper's provenance, constructed his narrative to suit the prejudices of his inquisitors: London, everyone knew, was a sink of moral iniquity far beyond the imagination of pure-minded country folk. Be that as it may, the incident is further confirmation of the existence of a lively youth culture, a culture marked by much frivolous jesting, a good deal of drinking, and a keen adolescent interest in sex.[49]

But the sexuality of the young went far beyond sniggering. Employers' houses offered ample opportunities for pre-marital affairs. Young people of both sexes often shared the same rooms, and although this was quite customary even in respectable houses, sometimes suspicions were aroused: William Jacob, a weaver's apprentice, was called before the JPs for 'lying in one room with Mary Fry'. At the house of another weaver, Edward Chapman, female servants routinely slept in the same room as the male apprentices. Melchisadek Browne, who had left Chapman's service, came back to visit Honor Paine – he had long 'born her good will', he said – and they made love in her bed before the 'boys' came upstairs. Two other Chapman servants escaped from the overcrowded apprentices' chamber to have sex in the cellar; both said that they intended to marry if the girl got pregnant, which she soon did.[50]

Not all these romantic affairs had happy endings. Millicent Wier and John English were servants in the house of the baker John Facy. English professed love and promised marriage, so after she had moved on to work at the Ship Inn they went to bed on a day she describes as 'little wiven Sunday, as we call it, the Sunday before Palm Sunday'. She lent English 6s. to buy a hat, but the marriage did not take place and he was bound over to provide for Wier's bastard. Jane Harrison, servant to a saddler, gave in to the advances of his journeyman, and they regularly made love 'in a turf house upon the turves'; he promised to marry her, but when she got pregnant he fled and was not seen again. Charity Paine had known Christopher Wood, another of Facy's apprentices, less than a week before he 'made show of love' and promised to marry her. They were in the workshop of her master, John Rolle, a feltmaker, when Rolle's wife came home early from church and caught them. Women servants were notoriously vulnerable to their masters' advances, but accusations of such exploitation in Dorchester are extremely rare. This may or may not mean that Dorchester masters were more scrupulous than those in other places: perhaps they were more successful in covering up their sins.[51]

Pre-marital sex disrupted moral order. At worst it might lead to infanticide, as it did in the case of Elizabeth Lewes, servant to the Keeper of the Gaol, Thomas Sparrow. It was more likely to lead to the bastard's being a charge on the parish, another reason for people to worry about it. Ann Wythiman was a maid at one of the alehouses. 'Upon a fame given out by some' she was thought to be pregnant; she denied it, but examination by midwives confirmed that she was indeed 'far gone with child'. George Huntley, tapster at Christopher Edmonds's alehouse, could not remember how many times he had had sex with his fellow servant Urith Feaver, but the magistrates were convinced that it was pretty often. Two years after the issue of a paternity order Huntley absconded, and the Corporation had to sue his sureties to recover the money owing. Ralph Cake, a weaver's apprentice, already had an earlier paternity order against him, but had not learned his lesson. In 1630 he was drinking with Huntley and some other cronies at the Lion; the others left around midnight, but Cake stayed up with the maidservant until four in the morning, after which they had sex. The offspring of these and other liaisons were duly maintained by the parishes, but their prospects were scarcely alluring.[52]

Our response to the many stories of this kind found in Dorchester's offenders' book is very different from that of the people who observed them and wrote them down. Our reaction is likely to be that boys will be boys, and girls girls; that parents have always had problems with their offspring, yet somehow both generations have survived them. To seventeenth-century people, and particularly to the Puritans among them, the lessons were far more serious. Drinking, idleness and sabbath-breaking were violations of God's as well as of the kingdom's laws. The JPs' repeated warnings to young people to avoid 'idle company' were based on much sad experience: young Robert Way's 'idlesness and company keeping' got him into all sorts of bad habits. To the godly reformers, the frivolous behaviour of the young was one more symptom of Satan's power; one more set of evils to be stamped out.

Much of the disorder that plagued Dorchester was the result of the poverty that stalked it, as it did virtually all English towns. The realities of life for the majority of people in the seventeenth century should never be forgotten: the half-starved children, the women bringing up families in grinding, unending misery, the men demoralised and driven to drink or desertion by the hopelessness of it all. People without education and with few prospects in life inevitably took refuge in alcohol and irresponsibility. None of the other problems were likely to be solved until something was done about the poor. The able-bodied poor ought surely to be disciplined and punished for their idleness, and their children brought up in greater godliness and better work habits. But it was also the duty of every Christian to show compassion to the unfortunate and the afflicted. So the deserving poor – those who were poor through no fault of their own, but through age or physical affliction – also had to be cared for.

Like their counterparts everywhere in England, Dorchester's three parishes were responsible for the relief of their own poor: two overseers in each parish were required to assess their neighbours and collect a rate to supplement whatever funds were available from private charity. Seventeenth-century small towns were what modern historians like to call 'face to face' societies, in which everybody knew everybody else. So ratepayers not only knew in a broad impersonal way how their money was being spent: they knew as individuals the people to whom it was given. In All Saints parish in 1632, the shoemaker Matthew Butler, the butcher Michael Fooke, the hosier Christopher Way, and the chandler Richard Williams all knew that their rates had been set by their neighbours Edward Dashwood and Walter Hewett, overseers in that year. They also knew that their weekly fourpences were supporting the women like the widows Gourd and Robinson, and old men like Hugh Baker and Thomas Philpot. The deserving poor were overwhelmingly female or elderly.[53]

The system worked, more or less, to relieve the worst forms of poverty in normal years. But in the seventeenth century many years were far from normal, as the economy sank into depression after the Thirty Years War disrupted the market for cloth, England's main export, and as people struggled to cope with periods of high food prices whenever the harvest failed. The early years of the depression in the 1620s coincided with a couple of bad harvests, and caused some alarm in Dorchester, but did not require the introduction of emergency relief measures. However, a special watch was set in June 1622 in case, Whiteway informs us, 'any tumult should arise for want of trade', as had recently happened in Wiltshire and Gloucestershire. Some weavers tried to escape into other trades, because, as one explained, weaving was 'not sufficient to maintain himself and his family'. Others turned to part-time work. Henry Penny and Leonard Hoskins earned a few shillings shifting rubble from Trinity churchyard, cleaning gutters, and suchlike. But being further from the principal centres of the industry, Dorchester does not seem to have suffered from anything like the influx of unemployed clothworkers that beset some other towns – Salisbury, for example – in these years.[54]

There was a more serious crisis in 1630–1. In April 1630 wheat rose in Dorchester market from a moderate 4s. to as much as 6s.8d. a bushel, and although it fell slightly during the summer, by November it was up to 8s. Only when the next harvest reached the market – and there was always some delay before enough had been threshed to have much effect on prices – did the price begin to fall, reaching the more moderate level of 5s. a bushel in November 1631.[55]

The desperation of the poor during this bleak year is obvious from the sharp increase in the number of cases of theft of corn that were reported. Some of these suggest a certain touchiness about the ancient custom of gleaning: needing to maximise output to take advantage of high prices, farmers resented losing even small quantities to gleaners. There was a corresponding incentive for gleaners to expand the custom's boundaries as far as they could. In August 1630 two girls were spotted taking excessive amounts of barley from a field at Frome Whitfield, and at about the same time a local widow had to explain that the barley found in her house came only from gleaning – from 'her children scrabbling after the tithing cart'. The authorities certainly believed that gleaning rights were being abused, especially when the constables discovered quantities of 'swathe' barley – barley picked up from the swathes cut by the reaper's scythe, not from the scraps left after this had been gathered, which were fair game for gleaners – in six other Dorchester houses. Jane Dowrage was gleaning in Fordington field when her two stepsons brought her some swathe barley they claimed had been abandoned. In all these incidents

a reasonable case could be made that what had happened was gleaning, not outright theft. In others no such defence was possible, as
when two labourers took away whole sheaves of wheat from a field
at Walterston.[56]

Many of these cases involved women worried about the welfare
of their families. The widow Anne Samways more than once railed
at those responsible for the high prices. In June 1630 she tried to buy
wheat from a countryman in the market, only to be told that he had
none left. Samways exploded: such people ought to be 'served as
they were in France, to cut holes in their bags, for that they sold
all to the millers'. By October women were indeed doing this in
Dorchester; a crowd of women seized a sack of corn in the market
and egged each other on to slit it open. One had her knife at the
ready, but Dorothy Bascombe acted first, cut the sack, and poured
out the corn.[57]

Dorothy Bascombe was involved in another incident a year later,
when the values of the 'moral economy' (as distinct from the market
economy) were again invoked. Margaret Michell, one of the inmates
of the new Hospital, was working at her spinning when she heard a
cart rumbling along South Street. Thinking it was a corn cart, Goodwife Ashe 'held up her finger' to Michell – this sounds like a prearranged signal – and they went outside to follow it. They found it
at the town's end, surrounded by a group of angry women. Bascombe was making a great outcry about the selfishness of the town's
governors, and calling on the others to join her in seizing the corn.
By the time the beadle arrived to keep order another woman was
enlarging on Bascombe's complaints, instancing Mr John Blachford
who, she said, 'did send away the best fruits of the land, as butter,
cheese, wheat, etc, over the seas'. Margery Hayne called to the carter,
'She would have corn for her money.' The carter was sympathetic
– 'if it had been wheat and fit for them they should have had it' –
but, alas, it was only a brewery cart he was driving, loaded with
malt and a few hogsheads of beer. It ended in frustration, but the
episode has many features of the typical food riot: the prominent
role taken by women, the anger at the export of foodstuffs from an
area afflicted with shortage, the demand to purchase grain at a fair
price. If we add Anne Samways's earlier complaint about farmers
who sold wholesale to millers, the resemblance becomes complete.[58]

Poverty led inevitably to begging, and before the Reformation this

had been perfectly acceptable. But beggars were now seen as idle
and immoral. Many of them came from other places – vagrants
who had taken to the road because they had no land and no regular
employment. One of the many undesirable attributes of vagrants was
their propensity for begging. Recorder Ashley sent a Cornishman to
the workhouse in 1616: he was one of the all too familiar Low
Countries veterans, who had been found 'loitering and begging two
days together'. Most beggars were harmless, though there were
occasional criminals among them. A man from Frome caught 'begging for his victuals' in the town in 1637 was suspected, probably
correctly, of being one of a gang of horse thieves. There were local
beggars too. Prisoners from the Gaol and the local workhouse were
sometimes allowed 'to beg about the town'. Others drifted in from
Fordington: a poor, mentally retarded dumb boy, who, it was said,
'affrights and terrifies the children'; an old man named Robert
Hutton; a woman whipped and sent back across the parish boundary
in 1634.[59] During the 1631 dearth a certain George Jenkins was
whipped for begging, and warnings were given to several other
inhabitants. Six women, along with another from Fordington, were
ordered not to beg in 1636, and when trade again became bad
towards the end of the decade it was noted that begging was on the
increase again. The beadle was told to be vigilant about rounding up
beggars, and the parish officers were instructed to deduct a week's
poor relief for each offence by anyone in their parish.[60]

Poverty was endemic, and it contributed to many of the other evils
against which the godly were struggling. Some particular tragedies
dramatise its effects. Eleanor Galpin was literally driven out of her
wits when her husband, a poor clothworker, became ill just at the
time their child was born. She would 'come to misery and disgrace
by reason of poverty', she told her friends, on one occasion coming
downstairs in her smock crying 'she must go to work . . . she must
go to work'. The neighbours were worried and tried to help; one
'watched' with her for five nights, and then arrangements were made
for Nicholas Porter's children to stay with her. But it was to no
avail: her mind gave way and when the children were out of the
room she killed her ten-day old baby.[61]

The wheels of justice ground to their inexorable conclusion:
Eleanor Galpin was hanged on Gallows Hill. Her unutterable despair,
and the inability of the town's governors to respond to her act except

in the narrow terms of judicial culpability, may make us sceptical about their attitude to the poor and afflicted. But although nothing was done for Eleanor Galpin, serious efforts were made to relieve poverty and suffering in Dorchester. These efforts were at the very heart of the programme of godly reformation.

4

GODLY REFORMATION
1613–1642

TO THE godly the message of 6 August 1613 was clear. Fire from heaven: it was their mission, as members of God's appointed elect, to transform the disorderly, ill-governed town over which Matthew Chubb had presided – many of whose sinful manifestations, as we have just seen, continued to plague them long after Chubb had gone – into a reformed, disciplined, more truly godly community. The fire was the catalyst. Before that time, the younger William Whiteway lamented, 'little or no money was given to any charitable uses . . . men lay frozen in the dregs until it pleased God to awaken them by this fiery trial.' White quickly seized his opportunity. His sermons admonished the townsmen to set their hearts upon 'the true treasure that shall not perish', reminding them of 'the fading quality of all these earthly things'. The miseries of the homeless reinforced his appeals. 'Many men's bowels began to yearn in compassion,' says Whiteway. In meetings with their rector, some of the leading burgesses mapped out the first steps along the path that would, they hoped, turn their town into a haven of godliness, charity, and sobriety.[1]

Years later, White described the reformers' principal achievements: the new Hospital 'for the setting of poor children on work'; the vast increase in poor relief (the parish rates were doubled, he says); the enlargement of the churches to accommodate the increased population; and the policies which 'reduced the town into order by good government'.[2] But there were other features of the reformation: improved care for the sick and elderly, greater educational opportunities, a massive outpouring of private charity, and some ingenious funding mechanisms created to support it. A town, White reflected, was the ideal setting for such an experiment: 'bodies nearly compacted are more easily and better governed . . . than a people scattered and dispersed abroad.'[3] Good order would be enforced in family, workplace, town and parish; children educated in piety, obedience and industriousness; work provided for the able-bodied, support and relief for the aged and infirm; drunkenness, idleness and immorality punished and their perpetrators reformed; above all, God would be served by regular study of the scriptures and the sermons preached at the town's three churches. Dorchester would become a reformed Christian commonwealth in which God's purposes, already made clear to the elect, would be accomplished.

This vision is well expressed in the covenant, the 'ten vows', which White drew up at some time after 1630. Puritans often used covenants to confirm their fellowship with one another and reinforce their sense of mission, and this was certainly one purpose of the Dorchester one (it was also, as Archbishop Laud noted when he leafed through White's confiscated papers in 1635, a catechism to be used in preparation for communion). The preamble noted how God's indignation had been 'poured out upon the neighbour churches' (those of the French Huguenots and the defeated German Protestants), 'and threatened unto us by the preparations made against us' (by the Arminians perhaps), and asked 'how far we have been partakers in the causes of these fearful plagues?' Subscribers confessed that they had 'relapsed into lukewarmness' both towards God's truth and in their love for their neighbours, and had shown 'deadness of heart', pride, self-love, ambition, envy and contentiousness.[4]

But the backsliding sinners were repentant. They vowed to reform themselves through 'the true and pure worship of God . . . opposing ourselves to all ways of innovation' (another of the puritan code-words for Laudian, or as we might call them, high-church, cere-monies), and by 'reading, hearing and meditating God's word'. They would catechise and examine their families, and accept (and offer) suitable 'brotherly admonitions'. They repudiated 'all ways of gain which shall be adjudged scandalous by the godly wise', promising instead to devote 'persons and estates to the church's service': the puritan ethic of hard work did not justify the pursuit of wealth at the expense of the general welfare. They would respond to their 'afflicted brethren's distresses . . . in food, in clothing, and enlarging our hands to their necessities'. The vows require the pursuit of piety through religious exercises, education, and self-examination; but they also demand a spirit of fellowship and brotherhood, the elevation of the common good over individual self-interest.[5] There is the underlying assumption that these goals can only be achieved by rejecting both the old tolerance of sin displayed by Matthew Chubb and his like, and the doctrinal and liturgical 'innovations' of the Laudians.

Puritanism is often thought to have been an individualistic creed, a cover for the pursuit of material self-interest. It was not. When White, who was very active in promoting colonisation, heard that the settlers in Massachusetts were being exploited by entrepreneurs who took advantage of their shortages he immediately demanded regulation. 'I know it will be pretended that all manner of restraint is prejudicial to liberty,' he told the colony's governor, John Winthrop. But the only liberty that White approved of was the liberty to do good. 'I would fain know', he went on, 'what the general [public] shall gain by making half a dozen rich' at the expense of the rest. 'The applying of ourselves to further a common good is our greatest honour, profit, and safety,' White taught; we should seek 'not so much our good, as the good of the community', follow 'duty, and not gain to ourselves'.[6] This spirit inspired the entire edifice of charitable institutions that Dorchester created in the years after 1613.

Under questioning by High Commission in 1635, White described the vows as 'covenants to be observed by him and the other ministers of Dorchester . . . but never put in execution'. This was true in a literal sense, in that neither White nor his colleague at All Saints, William Benn, ever made subscription to the vows a necessary precondition of church membership. White, like other ministers of his time, did question notorious sinners before readmitting them to communion: one of that turbulent family, the Pounceys, was told to go to him 'to be examined before he came to the sacrament'.[7] And the spirit of the covenant was constantly disseminated in the rector's sermons and in his daily contacts with the townspeople.

White regularly visited his parishioners in their houses, to pray with and catechise them; he also lectured three times a week, and he conducted other services both on the sabbath and on weekdays. On Friday mornings throughout the year he expounded the scriptures, working his way inexorably through the Bible (it took him about six years) and then starting over again. He also conducted the special Fast Day services ordered by royal proclamation: one in April 1628 'for the good success of the Parliament'; others during various visitations by dearth and plague.[8]

Two dates stood out above all others in Dorchester's calendar: 6 August and 5 November. The town's deliverance from the great fire was celebrated every year until 1634, in a service at either Trinity or St Peter's at which money was collected for the poor, the Hospital, or some other worthy cause. Gunpowder Treason Day, 5 November, was of course the most powerfully evocative date in England's protestant calendar, the day on which God's mercies to his elect nation had been vividly confirmed by the frustration of the evil designs of Guy Fawkes and the Pope. In Dorchester it was celebrated not with the fireworks and bonfires common in other places, but by the ringing of church bells and other appropriate solemnities. There may have been some unofficial carousing by the unruly: in 1632 a group of apprentices got through four 'double jugs' of beer at the Antelope before the constables arrived. But the central feature of the day was the sermon in which White reminded his flock of the lessons of 1605, of the continuing Catholic menace, and of the importance of their regular bounty towards the poor. Like those of 6 August, the subsequent collections produced a steady income for Dorchester's charitable institutions.[9]

The effectiveness of these appeals depended on the esteem in which the preacher was held, and on the quality and intensity of his preaching. White was a powerful preacher – Thomas Fuller said that he could 'wind up' his congregation 'to what height he pleased' – and he was immensely respected both in and outside Dorchester. He was on close terms with Sir Walter Erle and other godly Dorset gentry, had a wide network of clerical acquaintances throughout the country and, after 1630, in America, and his fame was such that he attracted to Dorchester a stream of Protestants from the continent. Some came as students, some as refugees from the wars in Germany; one of them married White's niece, another, John Nicholas Rulizius, became his assistant at St Peter's. In 1634 the well-known Scottish apostle of ecumenicism, John Dury, came to discuss the prospects for Protestant unity. Within Dorchester White's stature was overwhelming. He was the essential mediator of disputes, public as well as private, did his best for the afflicted, and looked after his flock in the countless ways required of a conscientious parish minister, in spite of several bouts of ill-health.[10]

Eminent and respected, White was nevertheless seriously over-burdened. He was, it will be remembered, rector of both the upper parishes (though his income came almost entirely from Trinity). A succession of for the most part youthful curates, none of whom left much of a mark on Dorchester, enabled him to serve both parishes. The Palatinate refugee, Rulizius, is the most interesting; he assisted White for three years before leaving in 1631. In December 1633 the Corporation at last found one who would stay: an Oxford man named Hugh Thompson. The turnover is understandable, as until 1631 none of the assistants could be given a decent stipend. Thompson was offered sixty pounds a year, but he demanded – and got – a hundred.[11]

There were similar problems in poverty-stricken All Saints. William Cheeke, still much beloved by his flock, became so infirm that by 1617 the schoolmaster Robert Cheeke had to take over. Robert died in 1627; although Sir Francis Ashley commended his 'great pains and travail' in the parish, he does not appear to have been particularly energetic in his later years. Neither of his two immediate successors stayed very long, but a permanent incumbent was at last found in the person of William Benn. A north-countryman, he had held a living in Berkshire, and had then been chaplain to the puritanically-inclined Marchioness of Northampton. There may have been some opposition to the choice: Benn was elected 'with the approbation of the chiefest of the parishioners', but only by 'the major part of the Capital Burgesses'. Less popular than White or either of the Cheekes, he was, however, thoroughly in sympathy with the reformist path being followed in Dorchester.[12]

However confident he may have been of his and his colleagues' ministerial powers, John White had no illusions about human nature. Man's sinful desires made him 'impatient of government and subjection'; the 'petulancy of untamed spirits' required 'prisons and gallows, judgements and executions . . . to keep the world in quiet'.[13] If sin and poverty were to be overcome, the first requirement was to impose discipline on the undisciplined, to force the sinful to live orderly, virtuous lives. Magistrates everywhere strove to maintain household discipline, to punish drunkenness, fornication and vagrancy. Nowhere, however, was vice pursued as obsessively as in Dorchester.

So we must begin, as the reformers began, with the enforcement of the law. Like other towns, Dorchester employed a variety of officers to keep the peace and bring offenders to justice. They usually rotated annually, so most of the town's householders had some experience of such positions at one time or another. The parish offices all had some disciplinary functions. Sidesmen and churchwardens prosecuted absentees and people who misbehaved in church or profaned the sabbath. Non-communicants and other offenders were occasionally reported, as they should have been, to the Archdeacon's Court at Blandford, but Dorchester usually preferred to deal with its own offenders. A rebellious labourer named Stephen Pressley was presented at Blandford for not receiving the sacrament at Easter, but when two of the brewer Leonard Miller's servants were caught working on the sabbath, they were taken before the town JPs. People who slept or misbehaved in church were sometimes dealt with at Blandford, sometimes by the town. Officers of the ecclesiastical court, not a popular institution with Dorchester Puritans, had to be especially careful. When one of them rashly summoned a number of townspeople before the Blandford court he was promptly arrested and put in the stocks – 'in spleen', he complained – on a charge of drunkenness.[14]

Of the lay officials, the most important were the constables: two until 1619, three thereafter (usually, though not invariably, one from each parish). Before 1610 the office rotated among members of the Corporation, but after that date it was normally held by younger men, for whom it was a stepping-stone to higher things. Patrolling with their staffs of office, the constables personified the system of law and order – yet they were also neighbours, who would be encountered in a different role next year. Constables were always liable to be fetched out of bed by their indispensable assistants, the watchmen, if things got too far out of hand at one of the alehouses. The cutler Lawrence Righton, constable in 1634, gives us a picture of the law at work on a typical November night. 'Going about the town in search for suspicious persons', he reported, he could hear noisy company in the shoemaker Henry White's house. He sent the watch to ask what was going on, but they were denied entrance. Righton went himself, armed with a 'hue and cry' warrant, but he was told to go away, White's brother saying that they would obey no hue and cry. Eventually Righton told the watch to break down the door, and charged the White brothers with drunkenness.[15]

The constables were drawn from the upper and middling ranks of the town hierarchy. The watchmen were always their inferiors. In theory every householder was supposed to take his turn on the watch. In practice the wealthy usually paid for substitutes, though during times of danger these were allowed only with the mayor's permission. As they made their 'walks' – at least two each night – the watchmen were the first line of defence against violence and disorder. Human frailty being what it is, they sometimes slept on duty; if caught they might be given an extra turn at watch, or put in the stocks. Considering the opportunities available to poor men prowling about the streets in the middle of the night, it is remarkable that there were so few complaints of pilfering by watchmen: only one such case came before the JPs between 1629 and 1637. Drink was a more common temptation. The barber George Membry and his partner could not resist an offer of bread and beer when they came by the Ship Inn in October 1637, and a few weeks later some watchmen were totally demoralised by a group of countrymen from the Sherborne area. The watch had heard drunken singing coming from the Antelope, so two of them went to investigate. The Sherborne men hospitably offered them a jug of beer, and the news soon reached their colleagues, who promptly came to demand their share. Good fellowship prevailed; the watchmen promised not to fetch the constables, and agreed to guard the goods the visitors had left for the night at the town's end.[16]

Not all Dorchester watchmen were so easily corrupted. For all their occasional backslidings, their record during the years 1629–37 is impressive. They routinely arrested drunks, 'night walkers' (people abroad at suspiciously late hours), and swearers. They did not need to be watchmen to peer through windows or listen at doors – everyone did this in an age when private behaviour was thought to affect the functioning of the community – but as watchmen they had a particular responsibility for doing so. 'Looking in at the windows' as they were passing John Whittle's alehouse long after midnight, two watchmen saw Whittle and his wife drinking with a visitor, Henry Gollop. Gollop was far gone in drink, swearing incessantly, so they hastily sent for the constable. On another night in 1635 the watchmen heard a violent domestic row going on in the house of the barber-surgeon, Gabriel Butler. Butler was abusing his wife, threatening to 'slit her nose or cut her throat', and the attentive watchmen patiently counted thirty oaths before they intervened.[17]

Constables and watchmen were ordinary townsmen doing their public duty. But there were also some paid officers to assist them: the beadles and the serjeants at mace. The beadle was an assistant to the constables, paid a modest one pound a year (increased to two pounds by 1621), on duty during daylight hours when watchmen were not available. When John Pedwin was appointed in 1611 his duties included keeping vagrants out of the town, reporting the arrival of 'newcomers', and ensuring that beggars did not bother people at their own doors or at the inns; he was also to 'execute the whippings'. After Pedwin's time the job was sometimes combined with that of serjeant: in 1629 the offices were held jointly by the two puritan tailors, John Conduit and Benjamin Derby. Both were fairly vigorous officers, but even more active was their assistant, a shoemaker named Nathaniel Bower, who was eventually promoted to beadle. Bower brought in offenders with a zeal that soon made him one of the most unpopular men in Dorchester.[18]

The serjeants were less involved than the beadles in routine police work. They served warrants, collected fines, issued proclamations, and enforced market regulations; they had a room near the market where they weighed traders' goods to prevent them giving short weight. Conduit and Derby were in office together for almost ten years before Conduit's resignation in 1635; Derby stayed on until 'weakness and disability' led to his removal on the eve of the civil war, when the more energetic Patroclus Cooke replaced him. It was 'catching dealing', Cooke had once protested when Conduit and Derby came to collect a fine from him. Now it was his turn.[19]

Dorchester owned all the standard instruments of punishment: the pillory, stocks, and cucking-stool. The offenders' book contains no reference to anyone being actually sentenced to the pillory, but one was certainly in use: young Robert Way speaks of going from a drinking-party one August Saturday in 1631 to 'see the fellow stand in the pillory'. The stocks stood in the market-place, as we know

from George Brine's comment on seeing one of his friends being
stocked as he walked by the Bow. They were regularly occupied by
offenders too poor to pay their fines, most commonly for drunkenness. The JPs preferred to wait until drunks were 'fresh' before they
stocked them, both to ensure that they appreciated the shame of their
position, and for hygienic reasons. Women were less often stocked;
when they were it was also usually for drunkenness. Mary Lovelace
was put in the stocks for having missed church, but that was
uncommon: even the poorest husband would try to pay his wife's
fine rather than suffer the shame of seeing her stocked.[20] The
cucking-stool was used exclusively for women convicted of scolding. It presumably stood somewhere along the banks of the Frome,
but wherever it was it had plenty of work. The widow Mary
Tewxbury was treated leniently: in May 1631 she was sentenced to
be 'plounced' (the onomatopoeic local term for a ducking), but only
'when the weather is warmer'. No such favour was shown to Mary
Hooper, a repeat offender, who was ducked on 30 November.[21]

Prison sentences were less prominent in the penal repertoire of
seventeenth-century justice than they are today, but there were three
prisons in Dorchester: the County Gaol, the House of Correction,
and the Blindhouse. The Blindhouse, next to St Peter's churchyard,
was the town lockup, the place to put drunks for the night.[22] The
House of Correction, or Bridewell, was a cross between a workhouse
and a prison. It was where idle or immoral people were sent to be
disciplined and reformed: vagrants, runaway apprentices and other
masterless persons; unwed mothers and other sexual offenders. The
recipe for correction was hard work (beating hemp or making sackcloth) and a whipping. In a typical case, a suspicious couple from
Somerset, falsely claiming to be married, were committed there, 'to
be employed in labour and virtue'. Yet Bridewell discipline was not
always very strict; there were complaints of inmates being allowed
'to beg about the streets' on fair and market days. One of them was
only stopped from going into the town when he started cursing too
publicly, hoping that fire and brimstone would fall on Dorchester.
Another went on selling stolen goods while he was confined.[23]

The County Gaol had both economic and symbolic importance
for Dorchester, but it was not primarily a place where local people
were incarcerated – only debtors and those awaiting trial at the
county Sessions or the Assizes. It gave business to local traders

(Joseph Purchase had the baker's contract in 1632), and was also something of a social centre. The prisoners were locked up at night, but in the daytime they moved freely about the precincts. They entertained visitors (some prisoners had wives staying with them) and in spite of efforts to prevent it, young fellows from the town still came to play fives in the prison courtyard.[24]

Charming as all this may sound, the Gaol was still an awesome symbol of the power of the law. It housed a formidable collection of punitive implements. A 1660s inventory lists fifteen pairs of 'hand-bolts', a pair of 'cross bolt fetters', an instrument with the sinister name of 'the tailor's shears', and many other fetters, 'bazils', and chains. These were used on the 'better sort' as well as the poorer prisoners. When in 1628 the Dorset Grand Jury tried to clean up the prisoners' language, they ordered that poor prisoners who swore should lose their allowance of a penny a day and the wealthier ones be 'better laden with irons'. The Gaol was largely rebuilt in 1624, and Robert Cheeke obligingly composed an inscription to go above the gateway:

> Look in yourselves, this is the scope:
> Sin brings prison, prison the rope.

Religion was enlisted to make sure that prisoners did look in themselves. The Keeper or his deputy were supposed to read 'a chapter and prayers' to them twice a day, but they also had some clerical assistance. A minister named John Russell, in for debt in 1628, was paid ten pounds a year to preach to his fellow prisoners, and a few years later William Benn used to come over from All Saints to give occasional sermons. In the end, as Cheeke's inscription reminded them, the rope awaited the worst offenders. Public hangings, of which there were nearly always a few at each Assizes, theatrically portrayed the ultimate realities of power to attentive crowds. One condemned man committed suicide rather than be, as he put it, 'a spectacle for and gazing stock for the people'.[25]

Stocks and prisons were, however, a last resort. When order broke down in families – when members of a family were unable, in the common phrase, to 'live in quiet' – the Dorchester authorities, like those in other places, first tried to repair the damage through mediation. A couple named Oaten disturbed their neighbours by having a drunken row late one night. After receiving a lecture from the mayor, they promised to live 'in all quietness' in future. But when people persistently failed in their family responsibilities the magistrates had to intervene: the carpenter Thomas Hooper, for example, was told to pay a shilling a week to his aged father. Husbands were supposed to govern their wives, but if they abused or failed to exercise that power the JPs might take action. One persistent offender, the mentally unstable William Lovelace, was even ordered to be 'advised' by his wife and daughter, and to be sent to the House of Correction if he did not 'live quietly'.[26]

The Dorchester magistrates, like those elsewhere, also enforced the reciprocal obligations of wives to husbands. Backed by his neighbours, the shoemaker Albion Bull often complained of the 'ill carriage' of his wife Elizabeth. The JPs ordered her to stay at home and 'intend her husband, to dress his meat, etc, as a wife ought' on pain of being sent to Bridewell; a month later she was still 'unpeaceable' and was duly committed. And marital order was enforced by lawful authority, not by the raucous processes of popular justice. The west-country custom was that when wives too openly rebelled against their husbands the couple were subjected to the shaming ritual of the 'skimmington' – a disorderly procession in which surrogates for the offenders, preferably their next-door neighbours, rode backwards on a horse and acted out a semi-jocular version of the incident, accompanied by much blowing of horns and clanging of saucepans. Not so during the puritan years in Dorchester. When John Rideout and his wife had a quarrel which led to her beating him, two apprentices promptly went to find a horse 'for the next neighbour to ride'. They were preparing to organise a skimmington when they were summoned before the mayor.[27]

Moral standards were upheld by the formal actions of authorities, but also by the informal pressures of gossip and rumour. Often one led to the other. A Martinstown man was in the habit of visiting John Stibbs's wife when Stibbs was away, 'to the offence of the neighbours': he was ordered to stop it. There were some notorious town gossips. 'It had been as good half the town had known about it as she,' Joseph Parkins exclaimed on hearing that Margaret Barter had been told of one of his adventures. Occasionally we get a glimpse of the gossip network in action. Joyce Yeomans could hardly contain herself when she told her news to her friend Joan Maudit: 'O thou rogue, if thou hadst been where I was . . . thou shouldst have seen that would have made thine eyes dazzle.' Yeomans had been at the river washing clothes and had seen Margaret Richardson, Mrs Bury's maid, disappear into a chalk pit with John Edwards the gardener; when they resurfaced she saw Edwards 'pluck up his breeches with both hands'. Yeomans repeated the story several times in the rectory cellar, 'before the scholars and the other servants of the house', and it soon reached the responsible figure of Ralph Whitlock, who came to ask if it was true: 'he was one of the sidesmen and would make it good.' Word was soon passed on to the magistrates, who promptly investigated the incident.[28]

Household discipline was enforced by legal means, and parental authority was invariably upheld. Robert Fooke, a butcher's son, was bound over to the Sessions for sleeping out of his father's house. Young George Hillard, who had called his mother 'devil', was warned that he would go to the House of Correction if he abused her again. Children found guilty of minor offences were often ordered to be chastised by their parents, either at home or publicly in the Town Hall. When two brothers got into a fight in church their father agreed to 'whip them well'.[29]

Apprentices and servants being, in theory at least, as much part of the household as kinsfolk, their discipline was also of concern to magistrates. Masters were responsible for their servants, and were often required to punish them for public misdemeanours such as breaking windows or 'fighting with boys'. Few employers objected, though when John Colliford was sentenced to be flogged for repeatedly missing church, his master preferred to have it done by the beadle. The legitimate authority of masters and mistresses always received magisterial backing. Runaway apprentices were routinely returned to their employers, sometimes after a whipping and a spell in the House of Correction. Two runaways from Colyton, for example, were put in Bridewell before being sent home, though a 'blackamoor' servant seems to have suffered no worse fate than being returned to her master at Weymouth.[30]

But household discipline was to be exercised justly. As in other types of family conflict, the JPs usually tried to mediate disputes over terms of service. If that proved impossible the resulting court actions did not always end in the master's favour: in 1633, for example, the magistrates found that an apprentice named William Channon had been coerced into an illegal agreement and ordered him discharged. They always required that servants be provided with adequate clothing on release from service, and made sporadic efforts to protect them from abuse. Elizabeth Armstrong was released from the service of the clothier John Cooth after Cooth and his wife had misused her; the JPs again intervened when there were complaints of further violence by the Cooths against another servant. Such actions were, of course, no different from those of magistrates everywhere.[31]

The same can be said about other aspects of law and order in Dorchester. Every one of the forms of disorder and immorality described in the previous chapter was regarded with equal disfavour by the authorities of other English towns, puritan and non-puritan alike. Magistrates everywhere punished drunkards, brawlers, masterless people and vagrants. What was different in Dorchester was the intensity and energy with which the campaign against them was waged.[32]

The laws restricting access to the town by outsiders were enforced with particular severity. In a typical case, Richard Linnington was accused of unlawfully trading as a skinner; he was told to find a master or be sent to the House of Correction. Some illegal immigrants had families to support elsewhere. Thomas Gill had a wife and children at Wareham, but was treated as masterless because in Dorchester he worked 'sometimes with one, and then with another'. Recently arrived journeymen were often simply treated as masterless vagrants. The two categories sometimes overlapped, as in the case of Emmanuel Anstey, a new arrival who worked as a journeyman shoemaker; he was also accused of 'living disorderly' and as having been the father of a bastard child.[33]

The treatment of such newcomers reflects very traditional assumptions. The Freemen's Company, which regulated the town's economic life, clearly believed that this was still a small-scale economy of family enterprises. But they also had to take account of the needs of large employers like the clothiers John Cooth and Denis Bond, who could not always find the labour they needed locally, and who preferred more flexible conditions of employment than those of the old system of covenanted service. Bond was recruiting weavers from Somerset at least by 1630; the Company ordered them away, but then changed its mind and said they could stay, pending 'further conference with Mr Bond'. Even poor craftsmen sometimes took advantage of the free market for labour. In 1634 the parchmentmaker Robert Foote was employing a certain Robert Kiddle, 'for wages by the dozen'.[34]

The vagrant was easier to identify. Vagrancy was more prosaic than the colourful Elizabethan mythology of the criminal subculture, with its 'rufflers' and 'cony-catchers', portrayed it. Most vagrants were landless, unemployed people looking for work and subsistence – though this did not make them any less threatening to settled, propertied householders. Dorchester does not seem to have had a serious vagrancy problem. In the five years to November 1637 the JPs punished a total of thirty-five vagrants, an average of only seven a year, far fewer than the inundation that had been swamping places like Salisbury a few years earlier. Few in number, they nevertheless sometimes told highly picturesque stories. The more colourful and romantic, though, the less likely they were to be believed; more than one visitor to Dorchester with a good tale about having been enslaved by Turkish pirates spent a night in the Blindhouse before being whipped on his way. A few migrants claimed to be university students or even graduates, but they rarely had much luck in Dorchester. One twelve year-old said he was a scholar at Trinity College, Oxford, and that he had often been given relief by ministers in other places. When he told his story at the Free School and then at the rectory, however, he was promptly turned over to the magistrates. A man who claimed to be a Surrey vicar was also quickly unmasked, and the pass he was carrying found to be forged: Dorchester's JPs knew all about the business of bogus passes.[35]

The migrants most likely to run into trouble were couples trying to pass themselves off as man and wife. The JPs showed great persistence in interrogating such people, and often found them to be 'living incontinently'. In one such case the woman was sent back to Yorkshire after being branded with an 'R' (for 'rogue') on the left shoulder – the only time this penalty is recorded as having been inflicted during the eight years covered by the offenders' book. Most convicted vagrants were simply whipped and sent away with passes to their previous place of settlement, though a Taunton woman and her son were given six hours in the stocks for drunkenness first.[36]

In their war against disorder Dorchester's reformers had some successes, but also some failures. The most conspicuous failure was the campaign against excessive drinking. Nothing the magistrates could do seemed to make any difference to the deplorable habits of people like Robert Sampson. The JPs were unable even to reduce the number of alehouses. Unlicensed houses were constantly being suppressed, yet they nearly always managed to continue, or at least resume, operations. There were several particularly intensive purges. One was in October 1631, when high food prices were causing alarm and restrictions on brewing (to conserve barley) being considered. Four unlicensed alehouses were suppressed, and Christopher Edmonds, the least respectable licensee, was fined and given a sharp warning. In February 1631 Jasper Brewer was among a further half-dozen suppressed, the Dorchester JPs showing much more energy in response to urgings from Whitehall than their counterparts in the county, who by 12 March had suppressed only one alehouse in all the rest of the Dorchester division. There was another crack-down in May 1632, in which Brewer and several others were again told to close. Yet none of this activity permanently reduced the number of unlicensed alehouses. When Edward Streate, who had previously worked as a feltmaker, applied for a license in 1640 he was told that the Corporation would 'set up no more alehouses'. Streate ignored the prohibition and began selling anyway.[37]

With some other forms of disorder they were more successful. Although, as we have seen in the previous chapter, some features of the traditional festive culture survived the puritan onslaught, many did not, and some hitherto popular amusements were successfully suppressed. However dedicated they were, the reformers could never have succeeded in suppressing the old culture completely, particularly in a region as conservative as downland Dorset. Church ales and May games were still being held in villages only a few miles from Dorchester in the 1620s; fierce struggles raged over attempts to preserve festive customs even in towns with a significant puritan presence, like Weymouth and Lyme Regis. Ballad-sellers and showmen roamed the countryside, and must have been familiar sights to Dorchester folk at the neighbouring fairs, particularly the great annual gathering at Woodbury Hill.[38]

In Dorchester, however, such ungodly trades had been firmly put down. How long travelling theatrical companies continued their visits after the row over Lord Berkeley's men in 1607 is unknown, but by 1615 the battle had certainly been won. In July of that year another well-known company, the Prince's players, came to Dorchester, waving a patent from the Master of the Revels. The bailiff, John Gould, refused to look at it, and told their leader, Gilbert Reason, to take his company away forthwith. Reason promptly denounced him as 'little better than a traitor', showing that he well understood the political implications of the encounter (members of James I's government wished to protect, not suppress, the theatre), and abused Recorder Ashley in 'foul language'. There is no sign that anyone intervened in Reason's defence, and the offensive actor-manager spent two days in gaol before submitting.[39]

This was almost certainly the last attempt to perform a stage play in Dorchester before the civil war, apart from the edifying Latin comedies occasionally put on by Mr Cheeke's scholars to impress the Bishop. In 1630 a group of puppet-players who had caused trouble in other parts of Dorset (at Beaminster the inhabitants were unable to 'keep their children and servants in their houses' during their visit) were denied permission to perform; they were subsequently indicted at Dorset Sessions for illegally giving 'blasphemous shows and sights', but these had not been allowed in the town. An unfortunate Frenchwoman with no hands made a living entertaining people by doing tricks with her feet. She had a patent from the Revels Office, but, Whiteway tells us, it was 'not allowed here'; the diarist must have seen her perform somewhere, though, as he records that she could 'write, sew, wash, and do many other things with her feet'. Even the improving spectacle of a scale model of the city of Jerusalem, exhibited by a certain Will Gosling under a Revels patent, which had been allowed by some other puritan towns, was turned away by Dorchester, on the pretext that the crowds it attracted might increase the danger of infection.[40]

There were, as we have seen, a few prosecutions of people playing 'unlawful games' in Dorchester, but they were not very frequent, and in a town becoming so resolutely puritan this is unlikely to have been because such games were normally tolerated. The only real sign of tolerance by the JPs occurred in 1632, when two men were let off with a warning, their offence being 'but at quoits on Whitsun Monday'. They were treated leniently, but the fact remains that they had initially been prosecuted for playing. Bowls had certainly been tolerated at one time: the walk still known as the Bowling Alley existed under that name in the seventeenth century, but it was no longer used for bowling. In 1637 Fordington people were using it as a common 'trade way', driving their carts through it.[41]

One of the reformers' most striking successes was the enforcement of regular church attendance. That this improvement occurred cannot be simply attributed to the one shilling fine for absence imposed by the Elizabethan statutes. Such fines were regularly collected, and no doubt they helped, but the general pressure for conformity in a town with Dorchester's reputation must also have counted for something. How successful the campaign was can be deduced from the payments made by the churchwardens for bread and wine at communion services. Nothing is known about the frequency of communion services at the other churches, but at Holy Trinity in the year ending at Easter 1620 there were eleven communions. The churchwardens bought sixty-three quarts of wine (usually 'Malaga sack') for these eleven communions. This is about average for the decade ending in 1620, but then the quantity of wine bought increases sharply to an average of over a hundred quarts a year, reflecting the increase in the population of the parish. The churchwardens occasionally presented non-communicants to the Blandford court, but the quantity of wine consumed – enough, on average, for six hundred recipients at each communion – suggests that virtually the entire adult population of the parish regularly received the sacrament. The campaign for church attendance had been dramatically successful.[42]

So, it appears, was the campaign to clean up the townspeople's sexual habits. In Trinity parish, the only one in Dorchester for which reasonably complete records of births, marriages, and deaths have survived, we can chart changes in the frequency of illegitimate births (always carefully listed in the register); and can discover how many brides were pregnant before they got married, by noting the intervals between weddings and the baptisms of first children.

If the experience of Trinity parish is anything to go by, the Dorchester reformers were strikingly successful. After 1600 there was a sharp decline in the illegitimacy rate, and a less immediate but in the end equally striking decline in the proportion of first children born as a result of pre-marital intercourse.[43] In both respects Dorchester followed the national trend, but in a greatly exaggerated fashion. Over England as a whole bastardy rates had been climbing – arousing the concern of moralists, naturally – throughout Elizabeth's reign. They reached a peak around the end of the sixteenth century, and then began a steady decline. This is precisely what happened in Dorchester. The peak came in 1597–1601, when about 7 per cent of the births were illegitimate. The first decade of the new century was not much better, with a rate of about 5 per cent. But after 1611 the rate declined to 2 per cent or even less, reaching the remarkably low figure of less than 0.7 per cent in the ten years beginning in 1626, and rising to only 1.2 per cent in the later 1630s. Although Dorchester follows the national trend, it does so with remarkable abruptness. Before 1611 Trinity's illegitimacy rate was *higher* than the national average; in the decade 1611–20 it was less than half, and by the early 1630s less than a quarter, of that average. The transformation, it is hardly necessary to point out, occurred within a few years of John White's arrival in the parish.[44]

The decline in the frequency of bridal pregnancy is equally startling, and again Dorchester exaggerates the national trend. Before White's arrival about 13 per cent of the brides in Trinity parish were pregnant at the time of marriage. Between 1606 and 1620 there was only a slight decline, but in the 1620s the percentage fell to less than 8 and in the years 1631–42 to only 3.4 percent. White and his allies did not stamp out pre- and extra-marital sexual activity quite as completely as the Scottish reformer Andrew Melville is alleged to have done at St Andrews in the 1590s. But they still achieved a significant alteration of the sexual habits of the townspeople, particularly those in the middle ranks of society. Apart from delinquents like Joseph Parkins and Nicholas Stone, between 1606 and 1642 only one couple from this level in Trinity parish – Joseph Purchase and his wife – obviously deviated from the Puritans' strict sexual code. The decline of sexual laxity must surely reflect the reformers' ability to reach, and change the habits of, large numbers of people in the town.[45]

In their relentless pursuit of drunkards, fornicators, sabbath-breakers and masterless people, Dorchester's governors, like their counterparts in other English towns, were attempting to create a sober, godly, and disciplined population. Puritans enforced discipline with special conviction because they believed that as God's elect they had the singular duty of advancing His kingdom during these 'last days' before the millennium, when Satan's agents were so conspicuously aggressive. But the programme of godly reformation to which Puritans had dedicated themselves was not simply a negative and repressive one. Dorchester's reformers also showed a striking concern for relieving the deserving poor; for feeding, clothing, and educating their children; for providing shelter for the elderly and fuel for the indigent. These things were as much a part of godly reformation as the fining of drunkards, the stocking of swearers, or the flogging of the idle and vagrant. All stemmed from the vision inspired by the preaching of John White and his colleagues; the vision of a Dorchester that could become, even amid the spiritual wasteland of Laudian England, a reformed city on a hill, a veritable new Jerusalem.

Before these goals could be achieved, a better-endowed ministry was essential. Trinity's endowment was reasonably adequate, yielding an annual income of about sixty pounds, but St Peter's was pathetic, a mere fifteen pounds a year. When the town bought the advowson of All Saints from the crown in 1617, Sir Francis Ashley granted the minister the tithes of a chapel in the parish of Puddletown, but even with this addition Benn at first had no more than twenty-eight pounds a year. Both he and the assistants at St Peter's thus depended heavily on the 'benevolence and charity' of their parishioners. White recognised that he could expect no effective assistance until these financial problems were solved. He was not a member of the Feoffees for Impropriations, the puritan corporation in London that was trying to redistribute clerical income in favour of under-endowed parishes, but he had friends who were, and he subscribed to the fund they were raising. The example of the Feoffees suggested the possibility of buying the impropriation of an affluent parish, where the 'great tithes' had been siphoned off by a layman, and using them to relieve Dorchester's underpaid clergy. The minister of the parish whose tithes were being redirected would lose nothing, as he had only the 'small tithes' in the first place; indeed, if the example of the Feoffees was followed, he might be better off, as an augmented income could be provided for him too.[46]

By 1630 White was busy fundraising. Preaching at All Saints he persuaded the congregation to give 'very liberally', and the two more affluent parishes contributed proportionally. Even the miserly John Blachford gave one hundred pounds. Money was collected by White's clerical friends in London, and there were some timely bequests. John Gould must have been approached before he died, as he left thirty pounds to buy 'some impropriation or other lands' for the clergy, and there was a magnificent bequest of £300 from a Londoner named Henry Smith, with whom White was in touch through the Feoffees. In the end the impressive sum of £1,500 was collected, and at a meeting of about eighty contributors in St Peter's church it was agreed that it should be used to buy the parsonage of Seaton and Beer, just over the Devon border. The purchase produced an annual income of £100 to be shared among the Dorchester clergy. There were some anxious moments when the crown, alarmed by signs of puritan aggressiveness, took legal action against the London Feoffees: the Town Clerk was told to seek the advice of counsel 'for the assurance of Seaton Parsonage to the town'. But although Laud suppressed the Feoffees, no action was taken against Dorchester. In the mid 1630s the town seemed to have solved the problem of clerical poverty.[47]

By this time other parts of the programme of reformation were well under way. The teeming crowds of idle and irresponsible young people might be dangerous, but they also had souls to be saved and bodies to be corrected. It was too late, White reflected, to instil industry and 'family discipline' in unreformed adults; 'all the hope is in training up the youth in time.' So a central feature of the reform programme was an attempt to do something about the adolescent poor. The solution was the new Hospital. Dorchester, the Hospital's deed of foundation observed, contained 'great numbers of poor and needy people' who lived by 'begging and dishonest courses'. The magistrates wished to enhance the better order they had already achieved, by providing for 'the training up and instructing the children of the poor in honest labour'. At the Hospital fifty such children would be taught 'some lawful trade, mystery, or manual occupation', and thus learn to live godly and productive lives. Dorchester was not the only English town to attempt such a scheme, but few others were as successful. The Hospital was at the very heart of the programme of reformation.[48]

There had been careful planning, and the leading reformers contributed generously to the endowment. Of the approximately £450 originally subscribed, all but about twenty pounds was given by Dorchester townspeople, in amounts ranging from the elder Whiteway's seventy-five pounds to the tailor James Yokeney's modest one pound. Whiteway, John Gould, John Parkins, and Richard Bushrod also contributed annuities of between two and eight pounds in perpetuity. The money came principally from the town elite, but after 1617 countless humbler people must also have opened their purses at the great 6 August and 5 November commemorations.[49] Money continued to pour in for a few years, sometimes from surprising sources: from the officials conducting the national lottery for Virginia, for example. Besides many small bequests from townsmen, Margaret Chubb, Matthew's widow, gave £200, and there were legacies from Joan and John Gould, the elder Whiteway and Lady Browne of Frampton.[50]

A building was acquired in South Street, a 'discreet man', a fustian weaver named John Coke, appointed governor, and needy children were recruited. Coke was given full power to discipline the boys, but was not allowed to flog the girls, for whom a 'sober woman', presumably the 'teacher of the spinners' was to act as supervisor. By 1638 there was also an 'Overseer of the poor children', a man named John Torrington.[51] It is not clear exactly what craft skills the boys were taught in the early days, but for girls they were the typically female ones of spinning, carding, and bonelace-making: during the 1630s the Hospital was sometimes called 'the bonelace house'. Soon after Torrington's arrival a major reorganisation occurred. Denis Bond, who knew what was in the interests of large-scale clothiers like himself, proposed that bonelace be dropped and only spinning and burling (the process of removing lumps and knots from cloth) taught. The bonelace teacher was promptly dismissed, and the children who refused to do either spinning or burling told to leave. The children were to be taught craft skills, but only those approved of by the big local employers.[52]

Little else is known about the internal functioning of the Hospital. The Governor was required to keep a daily record of what each child produced, and they were paid every Saturday night for their week's work. The Corporation occasionally authorised special payments, to buy clothes for one or other 'hospital maid' (the cost was then deducted from the child's wages). Some of the children boarded at the Hospital: we hear of Mary Bankes arriving at four o'clock one May morning to wake them up and get them ready for work. Discipline was strict. There was a whipping post, and when Anne Smith displeased the bonelace teacher by being 'very negligent in following her work' he had her flogged. The girl's supervisor gave her only five 'stripes' with a birch rod, she said, but unfortunately the girl took sick and died a few weeks later.[53]

The Hospital was for children, which in seventeenth-century parlance included adolescents up to the age of twenty-one: this, after all, was the population that had to be disciplined. Mary Wood came home from five years' service in London but was refused admission because she was over age. But adults did sometimes work there, either voluntarily or as a more lenient alternative to the House of Correction. The weaver Nicholas Cox was sent there because he neglected his wife and children; his earnings were paid directly to his wife so that he could not drink them away. Most of the adults in the Hospital were women. In 1633 three young women who had been in trouble for masterlessness were sent to work at carding for a year. They soon quarrelled. Margaret Mitchell said that the Hospital boys 'could not sleep for fleas and lice', insinuating that this was the fault of Sarah Hancock, who 'used to pluck them out from under her sides and kill them'. Hancock replied in kind, Mitchell called her 'whore and jade', and punched one of Hancock's defenders in the face, all in front of an attentive juvenile audience. They were duly ducked in the cucking-stool, but the brawling soon resumed; after using more 'scurrilous terms in the hearing of the children' Hancock was expelled. In 1637 two more 'work women in the house' were flogged for scolding and fighting.[54]

Masterless young people were often put in the Hospital. Elizabeth

Merifield was told to find a master but 'in the meantime to work at the Hospital'. Children whose parents could not support them might also be sent there; in 1642 it sheltered two children of a refugee from the rebellion in Ireland. People sometimes petitioned for their children to be admitted, and there may have been more applicants than places. A spell at the Hospital gave the child of poor parents a better chance of being trained in a decent trade: in 1638 five Hospital boys were apprenticed, to a baker, a tailor, two shoemakers, and a clothier respectively. Help was provided for those going into service elsewhere, as when Nicholas Porter was given 10s. towards the cost of taking his daughter Joan, 'late of the Hospital', to London. It was also sometimes available for Hospital children years after they had left. When his apprenticeship to a blacksmith came to an end George Bartlett was given five pounds 'to begin the world'. He was still expected to 'demean himself well': Hospital boys were taught good conduct and morality as well as craftsmanship.[55]

For John White this moral and religious training was the Hospital's essential purpose. One way in which it was instilled was by regular catechising, the question–and–answer method of imparting the elements of doctrine which had become standard practice in the Church of England during the previous fifty years. It was also a necessary part of a protestant education: only 'popish prelates', White pointed out, wanted the laity to 'be kept in blindness and ignorance'. Catechising was done in many other places besides the Hospital: in church by the clergy; at home by parents and employers as part of the process of instilling household discipline; and, naturally, in the schools. But it was also central to the Hospital's system of instruction.[56] In 1641 Torrington was given precise instructions. Two or three times a week the children were to be taught 'the grounds of religion' using the printed Catechism by the moderate Puritan, John Ball. Each week they were to learn four of Ball's questions and answers. Ball imparted a simple protestant message: justification by faith; the primacy of scripture, which all were to 'read, hear, and understand'; the eternal, unchanging, and absolute power of God. The sabbath was to be strictly observed, 'set apart from all common uses', and not profaned by 'needless works, words, or thoughts about our calling or recreation'. And as usual the Fifth Commandment was interpreted to enjoin obedience to 'all superiors'

– to teachers, employers, and magistrates, in other words, as well as parents.[57]

So the Hospital's primary purpose was educational. But it was not the only place in Dorchester where the children of the poor could get a rudimentary education. One was yet another product of the campaign for godly reformation, the 'under school' established by the Corporation in Trinity parish in 1623, 'to train up boys and prepare them for the . . . Free School'. Boys, of course: the education of girls was not yet on anyone's agenda. The first master was the parish clerk, a former shoemaker named Aquila Purchase. Trinity School was a 'petty' or elementary school, teaching little beyond reading except religion and discipline. In 1628 Purchase was paid two pounds for teaching poor children; over half of them were from St Peter's parish, most of the others from Trinity, only a few from All Saints. The bulk of the financial assistance, in other words, went to boys from the wealthier parishes. Holy Trinity also regularly spent money of its own on 'the schooling of poor children'. There may have been other petty schools in the town. During a chicken-pox epidemic in 1638 the schools were ordered not to admit infected children, notice of this being given to the masters of the Free School, Trinity School, 'and the other teachers of the town'.[58]

Careful management of the funds collected for the Hospital and other charitable purposes was of crucial importance if the programme was to succeed. The town's leaders were practical businessmen who did not like to see money lying idle, yet in an age without banking facilities what else could they do with it in the interval between collection and expenditure? The traditional solution had been to lend unspent sums to wealthy townsmen – to themselves, in other words. This was done with some of John Whetstone's bequest when his Almshouse was built in 1621: Thomas Blachford and John Gould each had one hundred pounds of Whetstone's money in their custody for some years, paying interest at eight per cent.[59] At first the Hospital endowment was also held by individuals, and by 1622 there was some uneasiness about this. The town's governors were all no doubt men of the highest probity (though one might perhaps wonder about the Blachfords), but who knew what sudden disaster might befall them? An ingenious solution was found: to build a municipal brewery in which surplus funds would be invested, and which would also help to control the drink trade.

The Brewhouse was soon built, of 'good sound timber' faced with stone, in the Hospital grounds. It was finished by September 1622, and in the following January the tailor Benjamin Devenish was put in charge of it. He had a maltster working for him and at least one other assistant, a man named Jonas Palfrey. In 1639 a new maltster, Joseph Michell, was brought in from Salisbury, where there was a similar enterprise.[60] In spite of some set-backs – a fire in December 1623, problems with the furnace in 1639 – the Brewhouse soon became the biggest industrial operation in the town. In 1634 the 'Back Lane' had to be paved because of the constant brewery traffic, and a year later the Brewhouse had to pay for repaving South Street because of the damage done by its carts.[61]

The Dorchester Brewhouse was more successful, and encountered far less opposition from other local brewers, than its counterpart in Salisbury. This was partly because its competitors were tiny by comparison, partly because the brewers were no longer represented on the Corporation, as they still were (very strongly) at Salisbury. In spite of heavy damage during the civil war, the Dorchester brewery could still be let to tenants in 1649 for as much as £220 a year. So the house was a financial success.[62] But it had a more important function than brewing beer: the financing of Dorchester's charitable institutions. Surplus Hospital funds were invested in it from the start, and by 1625 the £200 still held by Gould and Blachford from Whetstone's gift had been put there too, along with other bequests. Proceeds of Fast Day collections were invested: one hundred pounds in 1625, for example. A few people even saw the possibility of using the Brewhouse as a bank. In December 1625 the Company of Freemen invested forty pounds, recoverable at a month's notice, and in 1648 a man received ten pounds interest on a deposit made there.[63]

The Brewhouse gave the Corporation much needed financial flexibility. From it came the money for maintaining the Hospital buildings, for paying the wages of employees, for 'the apparelling and teaching' and apprenticing of Hospital children. Interest on Whetstone's endowment paid for necessary repairs to his almshouse, and £150 of the capital was used for the purchase of lands at

Symondsbury when a good bargain became available in 1634.[64] Some of the schools' funds were also put there and used to pay for repairs and supplement the salary of the Usher. Brewhouse money paid for street repairs: not only to South Street, where the potholes could be blamed on its wagons, but also for other 'public places'. When in 1638 the town undertook some costly building operations at the Shire Hall, they turned to the Brewhouse to make up the deficit.[65]

But the Brewhouse's value went far beyond its ability to pay for urban improvements and to meet the cash-flow needs of the institutions whose money it held. Some of its profits were distributed to the poor at Christmas. In seven Decembers beginning in 1630, just over £212 was divided between the three parishes, and more than ninety pounds of this came from interest on the Brewhouse deposits. The Brewhouse made other occasional payments – in 1637, for example, the Corporation began using its funds to help lame and diseased persons – and altogether was a significant force in the relief of poverty in Dorchester.[66]

The Brewhouse smoothed the path of a multitude of financial transactions. It repaid the fifty pounds the town had borrowed from Margaret Cheeke, widow of Robert the schoolmaster. And in 1639 the Corporation borrowed one hundred pounds from it for legal expenses when they were sued in the Exchequer for arrears owing on the crown's Fee Farm Rents. Even more important were the Brewhouse's contributions to the maintenance of the local clergy. Before the purchase of Seaton Parsonage it paid supplements to the ministers' stipends. Without the Brewhouse it is hard to see how money could have been moved around quickly enough for the Seaton transaction to be completed. The Corporation's own contribution of one hundred pounds was borrowed from the Fast Day money deposited there, and the various debts incurred during the purchase were all paid off through the Brewhouse.[67]

The Brewhouse provided a valuable supplement to the support of the town's poor. But it was only part of an elaborate system of poor relief which the reformers tried to strengthen and make more efficient. One problem that confronted them was the extreme inequality in wealth between the three parishes. All Saints had the greatest number of poor people, but also the smallest resources from which to provide for them. So Dorchester did what other English towns had also attempted: it centralised poor relief through 'rates in aid'. The two richer parishes were required to subsidise All Saints, and during the ten years before the civil war about eighteen per cent of All Saints's revenues came from these subsidies.[68]

The policy began after the disastrous harvest of 1630. By 1633 the subsidy to All Saints amounted to seven shillings a week, with St Peter's paying two-thirds of it. In spite of their lighter burden, Trinity's parishioners always resented it. They paid for just four months under the original order, and gave only minimal compliance to later ones. At Easter 1640 the dispute came to a head. The Corporation refused to approve the overseers' accounts, and threatened to deprive the parish of its right to nominate a resident to one of the Almshouses. This did the trick: All Saints immediately got its 2s. a week. Yet many of Trinity's parishioners were still under-assessed, the Corporation thought, and they told the parish notables to put it right. This they did for a time, but as soon as new overseers took office in 1642 Trinity again defaulted. The Corporation had to raid funds collected for Irish refugees to make up the deficit.[69]

In the absence of complete overseers' accounts, there is no way of telling whether White exaggerated when he claimed that poor rates were doubled in the years after the fire. If he was right, Trinity's experience suggests that by 1640 some people resented it. Yet the system did work. There were roughly sixty ratepayers in All Saints parish, and although they paid their rates conscientiously they provided little more than half the money distributed to the parish's poor. Their rates, ranging from the shilling a week paid by Richard Blachford and the brewer Leonard Miller, down to the pennies and halfpennies assessed on humble people like George Oaten and Philip Lockyer, were paid with astonishing regularity. In the ten years before the civil war there is no record in All Saints of anyone falling into arrears, though in 1632 one ratepayer did in St Peter's parish; told to pay up, he called the overseer 'scurvy boy . . . knave and cozener'.[70] Relief payments ranged from the 2d. or 3d. a week paid to Alice Budden and Emma Gardner, who must have needed only small additions to whatever they received from their families, to as much as two shillings a week. Some of the poor had special needs which were met by the town. Until 1637 Joan Pedwin got the standard tenpence or a shilling a week, but she then became ill and the town gave her 2s.6d. a week out of the Brewhouse.[71] Both the yield of the poor rate and the size of the weekly payments gradually increased as the dearth conditions of the early 1630s receded. The average annual yield of the All Saints rate rose from less than thirty pounds between 1632 and 1637 to over thirty-five pounds during the next five years. At the same time the number of people on relief fell slightly, so that the average welfare recipient got £1.19s.0d. a year, compared with £1.8s.0d. during the earlier period.

Other forms of aid supplemented the weekly payments. The annual Christmas distributions of food and clothing were worth between ten and fifteen pounds a year to the All Saints poor; in December 1632 the overseers distributed twenty-eight woollen garments, as well as canvas shirts and smocks, and five bushels of wheat. At other times of the year they provided help for the sick, and in the more prosperous years after 1636 they occasionally made additional hand-outs: 6s.10d. for linen for Mary Haggard in 1641–2, for example. They looked after orphans, paying the costs of apprenticing them, and paid for paupers' funerals. The two richer parishes also gave money to the Fuel House that the town had established to help the poor with winter fuel.[72]

Some of the parish funds for the relief of poverty came from special collections like those on the 1625 Fast Days for plague relief. Dorchester was lucky and missed that year's epidemic, so two-thirds of the receipts were invested in the Brewhouse to support the poor. Another series of collections during the 1631 dearth produced £111, which was divided equally between the three parishes. There were other special collections: one during the arctic weather of February 1635, in which poor people suffered terribly; another in 1640. A more regular source of funds was the 'basin money' collected at communion services. The parishes used this for supplementary poor relief: small sums were given, for example, to 'divers poor people at sundry times'; to John Ryall, 'being in want'; to an unidentified poor woman. In 1619–20 a total of £14.16s.10d. was taken at communion services at Holy Trinity, and about half of this was given to the poor. In 1630 the parishioners drew up rules for disposing of the basin money: one third to the Fuel House, the remainder to those afflicted by sickness or misfortune. Churchwardens often raided the basin money for other purposes (in 1627 Trinity paid a carpenter's bill out of it); only in the more prosperous years of the later 1630s was it entirely devoted to the extraordinary needs of the poor.[73]

Such was the relief system in normal times. When a bad harvest brought high prices and the threat of famine, emergency measures had to be taken. There were several traditional remedies to which magistrates resorted at such times: regulating the markets, restraining food prices, distributing emergency stocks of grain. They were indeed statutorily required to do these things, and were often reminded of this by the Privy Council. When grain prices rose alarmingly in the summer of 1630 Dorchester's response was probably a bit more energetic than that of most other English towns, but it was not different in kind. The Corporation's first response was to survey stocks of barley and prohibit the making of malt; in August further restrictions were announced and the houses of maltsters searched for unlawful barley. Several maltsters were suppressed and one briefly imprisoned. But the restrictions were not always enforced, and two of the 'viewers of maltsters' who were supposed to keep watch on their brethren were themselves earlier offenders.[74]

By November 1630 it was clear that these measures were not working: not enough grain was reaching the market to keep the price within reach of the poor. The Privy Council was now ordering JPs to see that producers brought 'a certain quantity' to market and did not sell wholesale to dealers and middlemen. So Denis Bond was instructed to buy grain – one hundred bushels of wheat from Ralph Perrin, for example – which was then sold to the poor at 6s.8d. a bushel. This was a high price, but a good deal below the 8s. for which it was currently selling in Dorchester market. The viewers surveyed the maltsters' stocks and decided how much each ought to sell to the poor. Perrin, for example, was ordered to sell them two bushels a week, and a sack of barley every fortnight.[75]

Two developments early in 1631 were also related to the crisis. One was national: the Council's reissue of the Book of Orders, the official instructions for JPs which outlined, among other things, their responsibilities for poor relief and the regulation of markets. The other was local: the series of collections for the poor in the Dorchester churches which began on 13 February. None of the returns have survived which the Dorchester JPs, like those in other places, were now required to send to the Council, but their burst of activity in February 1631 was probably a response to the Book of Orders. Benjamin Devenish promised to supply ten quarters of barley from the Brewhouse, and Rector White sold twenty quarters to the Corporation for distribution at the controlled price of 4s. a bushel. The brewers and maltsters were persuaded to lend sums ranging from old John Adyn's two pounds to Perrin's fifteen pounds, interest free, from which further supplies were bought. The eighty pounds thus raised was divided between the three parishes. Substantial amounts of grain were acquired and distributed free: forty-five bushels in St Peter's, slightly less in each of the other two parishes.[76]

The 1631 harvest was better, and by November the Dorset JPs were assuring the Council that prices had fallen so much that it was now the countryman – the producer – rather than the urban consumer who was feeling the pinch. Only a return to free competition would solve the problem, they said; the previous year's high prices were the result of government interference, which had frightened people into hoarding grain unnecessarily.[77] The poor saw things rather differently: it was at this very time that the women of Dorchester were angrily demonstrating and demanding corn for their money. The town's magistrates were more compassionate than their rural brethren. Even when the immediate threat of dearth receded, they occasionally tried to enforce the old laws protecting the consumer. By the mid 1630s Whitehall, too, began encouraging 'common informers' to make sure that even archaic laws were enforced. Giles Foy gave information against five Dorchester men, as well as others from Fordington, for 'engrossing grain in the field contrary to statute'. Foy was probably in it for the money, but there were plenty of more genuine upholders of the 'moral economy'. In August 1632 Robert Foote was convinced that there were shady doings at the market, and raised his cudgel against a countryman he suspected of overcharging. A more prosperous townsman, Henry Bridges, intervened, and was himself promptly blamed for the high prices: 'Thou, Bridges, wilt thou forestall the market and buy up all the corn?'[78]

Unacceptable manipulation of the market was not always something done by the rich to the poor. Sometimes poor people were driven to regrating – buying in the market and then selling retail – which was frowned on because it drove up prices. Dorchester people seem to have been particularly inclined to regrate fruit, and almost every autumn a case or two of this came before the magistrates. In 1637 Dorothy Bascombe, one of the ringleaders in the attack on the brewery cart, was herself accused of it.[79]

Although conditions had certainly improved, the Dorset JPs were being over-optimistic when they assured the Council in 1633 that the days of food shortages were over. Whiteway reported high prices (though not as high as in 1631) throughout 1634, with wheat hovering at between six and seven shillings a bushel. But after 1633 there were no more emergency measures and the poor were left to their parishes. Even with some help from the town, they were in real 'extremity' during the frigid winter of 1634–5. A few years later there were renewed complaints of the 'deadness of trade', but grain prices remained reasonably stable. The brewers and maltsters were summoned to a special meeting in Christmas week, 1639, but no emergency measures were taken. When the JPs became alarmed by a subsequent epidemic of begging they simply used punitive measures to deal with it.[80]

Dorchester's reformers had no time for beggars, but they accepted that certain special needs of the poor could and should be met by the town. One of these was fuel for heating their houses. In 1618 the Corporation decided to supply cheap fuel for the poor. A public Fuel House was built in the Hospital garden, money obtained from the parishes, and by the end of January 1620 5,591 faggots had been distributed. The town governors were satisfied: they could now please the neighbouring gentry by prohibiting residents from going out of the town to scrounge wood or turves, 'they being well provided for fuel here'. Dorchester's poor would be looked after, but they would lose one more of their customary rights, and the town would protect the property of local landowners.[81]

The Fuel House languished during the 1620s, but it was eventually revived with the help of renewed grants from the two richer parishes. In the grim early 1630s the need was obviously pressing. Several cases before the magistrates show that the old tradition of use rights for the poor had not completely died out. It was only a few rotten roots and green furzes, one woman protested when caught stealing wood at Walterston; just some abandoned brushwood, another suspect declared. Some of the thefts involved habitual criminals like Robert Sampson and John Chimney, but others were the work of people driven to desperation by poverty. At such times there was also the temptation to profiteer: the shoemaker Martin Spring was several times ordered not to buy and sell fuel, and in 1630 he was one of several Dorchester people accused of forestalling wood and turves.[82]

The first 'purveyor of the fuel' was a certain Henry Hoskins, whose chief fault seems to have been what the Corporation regarded as excessive generosity; he was also illiterate and did not keep proper accounts. In 1638 'viewers for fuel' were appointed to inspect the operation and when they found irregularities Hoskins was dismissed. From the accounts kept by two of his successors (John Torrington, the Hospital overseer, and Joseph Michell of the Brewhouse) we can get some idea of how the Fuel House functioned. In Torrington's year just over fifty-eight pounds' worth of fuel was bought; it was sold to the poor for about fifty pounds. In Michell's year £47.10s.0d. worth of fuel was bought, and sold for £42.3s.0d. So the implied bargain under which the poor had given up their old right to pilfer fuel from nearby woods and fields was a fairly expensive one for them. In the two years for which we have good records, the amount of money the Fuel House received from the two contributing parishes was about double the subsidy that was being given to the poor: in 1641-2, for example, Michell received £13.11s.6d. from the two parishes, but the fuel was sold at only £5.7s.0d. below cost. This may have been good business, but it was not generous social policy.[83]

Besides helping the poor with fuel and extra relief, Dorchester's rulers also gave a helping hand to the sick and the elderly. The town was thought to be an agreeably healthy place because of its situation on the chalky soil above the damp Frome valley, and people sometimes moved there because of this. Dorchester had an unusual number of medical practitioners for a place of its size: half a dozen physicians, and about the same number of barber-surgeons. One of the latter, Matthew Barfoot, assisted at executions, regularly served as foreman of coroners' juries, and was an expert witness at inquests. There were also two families of apothecaries in the town: the Burys, who kept the Antelope, and the Colsons.[84]

The poor could ill afford apothecaries or surgeons, much less the far grander physicians. Such treatment as they got was usually provided by women, many of them with long experience and an accumulation of herbal lore. In the 1630s several Dorchester women nursed sick people, and were paid for it either by the parishes or the town. There were at least half a dozen midwives in Dorchester in these years, among them Joan Haggard, Agnes Hollard, and Katherine Keate, wives of a butcher, a feltmaker, and an alehousekeeper respectively. There is no evidence that Dorchester women acted as wet nurses, though some of them certainly earned money looking after sick children. When Sir Simonds D'Ewes was a baby he was taken ill during a journey and left in Dorchester in the care of 'a very honest woman', the wife of the glover Christopher Way.[85]

From all these sources – and, no doubt, from travelling quacks like the one sent to the House of Correction in 1629 for selling trusses without permission – Dorchester people got the medical attention they could afford. Many, of course, could afford very little, and for a few of these help was provided. Towns had always accepted some responsibility for public health, especially during epidemics. Most of the money collected for plague victims on the Fast Days in 1625 was either sent to infected Exeter or invested in the Brewhouse, but five pounds was spent on fitting out a makeshift isolation hospital. It was not needed in 1625, but a few people were placed there after outbreaks at Blandford, Bridport, and Salisbury in the two following years. An infected Dorchester couple, the Skinners, were given money, medicine ('Angellica water') and thirty shillings' worth of fruit and vegetables. Ten years later, when there was another serious epidemic in London, the town again took precautions: restrictions on carriers and a special watch to keep out travellers. Ralph Perrin's barn and another house were acquired to accommodate those infected, and they were soon sheltering three Dorchester men who had been to London.[86]

Such precautions would have been taken in any English town. But the Dorchester authorities went further than most in trying to alleviate the suffering caused by poverty and sickness. The parishes paid for nursing care and made direct payments to the sick. All Saints, where poverty was most acute, made substantial supplementary payments throughout the 1630s: a total of £4.18s.od. in 1633–4, for example. The town occasionally made similar payments, such as the one pound given to Thomas Churchill when he had to go to Bath for treatment. In such cases the Capital Burgesses expected results. The surgeon's bill for 'cutting of Giles Garrett's leg' was five pounds; he was to be paid half when he did the operation, the rest when Garrett was 'thoroughly cured'. The Corporation also helped the parishes deal with special cases, granting supplementary weekly relief to two badly afflicted All Saints parishioners, for example. Finally, in June 1637 they took the enlightened step of setting aside ten pounds a year out of the Brewhouse specifically for the relief of sick people. The regular use of town as well as parish revenues to help the sick strikingly demonstrates the Dorchester reformers' concern for their less fortunate neighbours.[87]

No such special diversion of public revenues was made for the elderly, who were in any case the main recipients of poor relief. But private benefactions had dramatic results in the years after the fire, and the Brewhouse was used for the management of the resulting funds. Before 1613 Dorchester's only almshouse was the 'Old' or Women's Almshouse near the Friary, of ancient foundation but now in decay. This received a major new endowment during the ten years after the fire, and at the same time two new almshouses, Whetstone's and Napper's, were established.[88]

The Women's Almshouse was later renamed Chubb's Almshouse, though, as we have seen, it was Margaret Chubb, not Matthew, whose benefaction this commemorated. In 1620 she covenanted to pay £400 to the town for charitable purposes, and when the first instalment was paid in the following year, £115 of it was assigned to 're-edifying' the Old Almshouse. When Margaret Chubb made her will a few years later she spoke of the Almshouse which she had 'newly built in Dorchester', making no mention of her husband. She was not the only benefactor: Joan Gould, the elder Whiteway, Sir Francis Ashley, Edmund Dashwood, John Parkins, and many others also remembered the Almshouse in their wills, though none as lavishly as Margaret Chubb.[89]

There were ten women in the Old Almshouse in 1625. The house could not afford to provide full maintenance, so additional support was required from either the inmate's parish or from relatives. There are signs of increasing budgetary stringency around 1640. Women newly admitted now received no weekly allowance during their first quarter of residence, the money saved being used for repairs to the building. Special supplementary payments were still sometimes made for particularly urgent cases, but it looks as if the almswomen were being meanly treated: eighty-five pounds left over from Margaret Chubb's gift was all the while lying unused in the Brewhouse.[90]

The other two almshouses were both founded soon after the fire. John Whetstone of Rodden, near Abbotsbury, had been a mercer in Dorchester during Elizabeth's reign, and bailiff in 1571. He left £500 to the town, for 'building of an almshouse for poor folk'. After his death in 1619 his executor, Thomas Blachford, had to be threatened with a lawsuit before he released the money, but a house was then bought in All Saints parish, and lands purchased to produce an annual income of ten pounds. The residue, in the Brewhouse, eventually generated another ten pounds a year. The new almshouse was in operation by March 1621, when the inmates' first allowances were paid. Whetstone's was for married couples, though survivors were allowed to remain after the death of a spouse. They received a weekly stipend large enough to make further relief payments by the parishes unnecessary. Careful management by the Brewhouse enabled running costs to be met, and new lands bought, with ease and promptness.[91]

The other new almshouse, Napper's, was founded not by a townsman, but by a Dorset landowner, Sir Robert Napper. In his will, made in 1615, Sir Robert noted that he had already begun building an almshouse in South Street, and this – the well-known 'Napper's Mite', built 'to the honour of God' – was completed the following year. Napper's housed ten poor men – four from the county, six from the town. There was one notable resident: old William Cheeke, the former rector of All Saints, who, blind and feeble and with no one to look after him, was sent there in 1636. He was obviously not someone who could be left to subsist on the inmates' usual modest fare, so he was given an extra shilling a week from the St Peter's 'basin money'. His gown, of higher quality than those bought for the other residents, reminded everybody that he was once a man of importance. The Dorchester haberdasher Robert Napper – presumably a distant relation of the founder's family – who became overseer of the Almshouse in 1636 obviously felt a special responsibility for him.[92]

Places at the almshouses were desirable options for elderly townsmen or women, and people occasionally petitioned for them. Little is known about the daily regime in the three houses, except that order was always enforced. Discipline at the Women's Almshouse was especially strict: the authorities were particularly sensitive to disorder when women were involved. Margery Goodfellow was threatened with expulsion in 1634 for 'disquieting of the whole house in quarrelling and calling names'. A few years later the widow Alice Allen was expelled. She was later readmitted, but was pathetically unable to look after herself: her daughter was told to 'keep her in better condition that she be not noisome and offensive to the house by vermin'.[93]

One of John White's greatest achievements was to unlock the philanthropic impulses of the townspeople; that he did so will be apparent from the numerous benefactions already mentioned. Other signs of success were the soaring receipts from charitable collections taken either during church services, or in great public fund drives. We know something about the procedures followed in the major campaigns from a Corporation order in February 1642. Before the next Fast Day the clergy were to announce the forthcoming collection (which in this case was to assist refugees fleeing the rebellion in Ireland), with suitable exhortations to their congregations. On the Fast Day the churchwardens and overseers were to go 'from house to house' as soon as evening prayer ended.[94]

Dorchester always responded to these appeals with remarkable generosity. Some figures to show the scale of ordinary church collections may help to put the special ones into perspective. We know that £14.16s.10d. was received at nine communion services at Holy Trinity in the year 1619–20, an average of £1.13s.0d. per Sunday. This is more or less in line with the collections for the poor during the 1631 dearth, at which an average of £1.8s.8d. was contributed. A total of £115.11s.6d. was collected in the town at the 1631 Fasts, of which just over half came from St Peter's, not quite a third from Trinity, and one fifth from All Saints. So we might expect ordinary Sundays to produce roughly five pounds, of which £2.10s.0d. would come from St Peter's, £1.10s.0d. from Trinity, and one pound from All Saints.[95]

When White and his clerical colleagues made special efforts the results were often spectacularly greater than this. Even more remarkably, they persuaded their flocks to contribute over and over again, and to do so on a scale surely unmatched by any other town in England. Between 1617 and 1623 collections at the great commemorative celebrations on 6 August, the anniversary of the great fire, and 5 November, Gunpowder Treason Day, were devoted to the new Hospital. After two years in each of which just over twenty-seven pounds was collected, annual receipts rose to between forty-three and fifty pounds in the years 1620–3. All told, over £267 was raised for the Hospital, and there were several other major appeals during these years. At least £150 was collected for the defence of the Palatinate (a great cause for Protestants) in November 1620, and over fifty-seven pounds at St Peter's on 1 February 1623 for victims of the second great fire.[96]

It is easy to understand the success of this last appeal. The victims were friends and neighbours, their sufferings immediately visible, and although there had been less damage, memories of 1613 were naturally awakened. However, when appeals involved a long series of collections over weeks or months even Dorchester's charitable stamina might be tested. Collections for the poor at the Wednesday Fasts in 1625 suggest initial enthusiasm, but a steadily dwindling response as the appeals were repeated. Over sixteen pounds was contributed on 20 July, but the yield gradually declined to an average of only eight pounds in October. Yet the results were still creditable enough. Dorchester raised well over a hundred pounds, duly invested in the Brewhouse, for its own poor, and sent on another £23.16s.7d. to plague victims at Exeter. Another series of collections a year later had similar results. At the first Fast Day over twenty-eight pounds was raised, but at no subsequent one did the take exceed ten pounds; on 12 November it fell to less than six, no doubt because the townspeople had made another major effort only a week earlier, on Gunpowder Treason Day. Still, over a hundred pounds was raised in 1626, and most of it went to Bridport, for plague relief there.[97]

Several other appeals had impressive results: twenty-three pounds for plague sufferers at Cambridge in 1630; forty pounds for victims of a fire at Bere Regis in 1634; over forty-five pounds for Shaftesbury during a plague epidemic two years later. In 1640 Dorchester was still pouring out its charity: over sixty pounds for plague-infected Taunton, with a further forty-four pounds being collected only a week later for people made homeless by a fire at Yeovil. The first of several collections for the Irish Protestants in 1642 realised over forty-five pounds. These are astonishing figures for a town of under 2,500 people – to obtain modern monetary equivalents we should have to multiply by several hundred – and when to them is added the regular charitable giving at the great annual services on 6 August and 5 November, and other special collections like those during the 1631 dearth and the 1636–7 plague epidemic, the scale of Dorchester's philanthropy appears even more striking. And local crises constantly demanded further aid for the needy. When a fire consumed four thatched cottages near the South gate in 1634, £22.9s.0d. was promptly raised for the victims. A collection to relieve the poor during the frigid weather of February 1635 gathered nearly nineteen pounds; one at yet another Fast Day before Christmas 1640 just under ten pounds.[98]

Not all the receipts of these early seventeenth-century collections have survived. But enough remain for us to recognise a remarkable outpouring of sympathy for human suffering. In one single week of 1640, in the two collections for Taunton and Yeovil, over one hundred pounds was collected, an average of almost four shillings for every household in Dorchester. We do not know what proportion of the inhabitants contributed, and obviously the rich must have given more than the poor. Yet we do know that at a 1643 Fast Day collection in nearby Bridport the contributions included many small sums from quite poor people, including inmates of the almshouse. If the poor in Bridport were being reached by these appeals, it is unlikely that they were deaf to them in Dorchester.[99]

Comparative statistics are hard to come by, so we have no *proof* that Dorchester was unique in its generosity. As we shall see, evidence from a few years later strongly suggests that it was indeed so;

that per capita Dorchester was the most philanthropically generous town in western England.[100] And some randomly collected figures support this impression. Other west-country towns' contributions to the relief fund after the 1623 fire were minuscule compared with Dorchester's efforts for other places. Sherborne, roughly the same size as Dorchester, gave a miserable two pounds to the 1623 fund, and although other Dorset towns did better, only Lyme Regis (about half the size of Dorchester, and also coming under puritan influence), produced as much as ten pounds. The only western town which made a really sizeable response was Exeter, where so many Dorchester people had friends and kinsfolk, and which had at least double Dorchester's population. Exeter contributed £23.8s.6d. in 1623, yet even this was considerably less than the forty pounds (more than half of it raised by public subscription) which Dorchester sent to Exeter during the plague epidemic two years later. On a Fast Day in July 1640 Dorchester's three churches collected £17.8s.11d. On the same Fast Day Bridport collected £2.3s.4d. Bridport was of course a smaller and poorer town, with only about sixty per cent of Dorchester's population, and less than half, possibly only a third, of its wealth.[101] On the most pessimistic estimate, though, if Bridport people had contributed as generously as their neighbours in Dorchester they would have given something like £5.16s.4d., whereas in fact they gave much less than half that amount. Contributions from other Dorset parishes to the 1623 relief fund confirm that Dorchester was far more philanthropically inclined than any other place in the county. White's message of compassion for the poor and afflicted had indeed struck home.

The generation who received the word of God from John White and William Benn effected a remarkable alteration in Dorchester. The permissive, loosely-governed town that Matthew Chubb had known became the reformed and disciplined community of the 1630s. Religion, education, the relief of poverty, and the care of the sick and elderly had all been transformed by a combination of public and private philanthropy. New institutions like the Hospital and Trinity school had been created; old ones like the Women's Almshouse made more efficient. Innovative financial strategies – notably through the establishment of the Brewhouse – had been devised to support them. The less discriminating hospitality of Chubb's time had been replaced by a policy which rewarded the virtuous but not the undeserving; which gave generous relief supplements to Joan Pedwin, the beadle's widow, when she became ill, but did nothing for the rebellious Dorothy Bascombe when her husband died.

There were, as we have seen, some obvious quid pro quos. In return for being better looked after, the poor lost some of their old perquisites – their right to scrounge fuel, for example, in return for firewood sold at slightly below the market price. For children as well as adults, the programme of reformation was twofold. At the Hospital children were taught useful trades. But they were the trades favoured by wealthy clothiers like Denis Bond, trades which did not encourage too much independence. One side of the coin was reform: the promotion of religion and education, the relief of the deserving. The other side was discipline: the enforcement of personal, familial, and communal order, and the punishment of the idle and the ungodly. The 'fire from heaven' that descended on Dorchester's reformers after the 1613 disaster inspired both. Not surprisingly, the campaign of reformation provoked both support and opposition in the neighbourhood.

5

REFORMATION'S FRIENDS
AND ENEMIES

THE WHITEWAYS and the other leaders of the campaign of reformation came almost without exception from the upper ranks of the town hierarchy. Those they were trying to reform seem to have been, typically, people from the bottom of the heap. But history is too complicated for broad generalisations of this kind to be anything more than approximately correct, and if we look more closely we shall discover that godly reformation had supporters and opponents at every social level. And both reformers and resisters had connections which linked them with people beyond the town's walls. Those outsiders, too, often had their own opinions about what was happening in Dorchester, opinions which in turn influenced events within the town.

When we go in search of the ordinary townspeople we at once encounter problems of evidence. Historians are the prisoners of their sources. We find only what is in our documents, and we may reasonably suspect that this will sometimes lead to distortion. Members of society's privileged upper ranks are not necessarily more law-abiding than those below them. True, having done pretty well out of the system, they have fewer temptations to operate outside laws that they and their kind have made, and are less likely to view the upholders of those laws as oppressive or hypocritical. Such people are likely to show up in the record when they do something positive: when they are appointed to public office, attend a meeting of some official body, give a donation, or make a will. If they break the law and get caught they will appear in court and we shall hear about it. Yet how often in Dorchester, we might wonder, did a constable pass quietly by the window of one of the town's governors while friends were being entertained, when he might have brought a charge of tippling against less affluent neighbours similarly engaged? People from those lower ranks are more likely to cross the historian's path in negative circumstances. They rarely hold office, and may be too poor to make a will; but they are far more frequently prosecuted for minor offences, particularly in the sort of moral climate that prevailed in seventeenth-century Dorchester. Drunkenness and irregular church-going are very visible in the sources: sobriety and godliness are not, yet they were probably much more common.

We do not know what the 'silent majority' in Dorchester – those who were neither conspicuously virtuous nor conspicuously sinful – thought about the programme of reformation. But there is sufficient evidence to show that its supporters included people of every social class, not just the members of the elite who presided over it. It may seem odd, but some of this evidence comes from the character of people who left the town: the Dorchester men and women who in the early 1630s, discouraged by the prospects before them in Laudian England, sailed away to build a puritan commonwealth in America. Their story is important and requires us to make a brief transatlantic digression.

The *Mary and John*, of four hundred tons, Thomas Squibb master, slipped out of Plymouth Sound one March day in 1630, and headed westward, bound for New England. On board were some 140 passengers, setting out to build their new Jerusalem in the American wilderness, and among them were at least a score of Dorchester people. John White, who had been a principal organiser of the expedition, was there to see them off and preach a farewell sermon – in a service held, appropriately, in Plymouth's 'New Hospital', modelled on the one at Dorchester. A few weeks later the first ships of the better-known 'Winthrop fleet' left the little ports of the Isle of Wight, also bound for America. It was the beginning of the great migration that was soon to establish flourishing colonies of the godly in New England. John White and his friends played an important part in this revolutionary development.

From the emigrants we can learn a good deal about the godly reformers, for those who stayed behind were not very different from those who left on the *Mary and John* and on other little ships during the next few years. Their outlook on the world was much the same, and so were their reasons for being interested in colonisation in the first place. As in other English towns, many people in Dorchester had shared in the growing excitement about transatlantic expansion during the early seventeenth century, and had seen its connection with the great struggle against Spain and Catholicism. In 1619 there was a lottery in Dorchester for the benefit of the Virginia Company. 'Men were cozened,' Denis Bond complained, but there were plenty of subscribers, and Thomas Blachford won a fine 'pyramided silver salt', appropriately, perhaps, as his family were active in the colonial trade.[1]

The Blachfords were not the only ones to look for profit across the Atlantic. Richard Bushrod had begun to invest in fishing and fur-trading ventures, and in 1623 he was one of a group who got a license to undertake preliminary exploration so that they could 'settle a plantation in New England'. By that time there may already have been Dorchester men at the little fishing base on Cape Ann, on the coast of what was soon to be known as Massachusetts, and others seem to have followed them there the next year. Some people in the town, among them Mr White, had more ambitious plans. The fishing and fur-trading outposts on the New England coast would be more secure if they were to become permanent, self-supporting colonies, rather than makeshift, temporary bases. They would provide a welcome outlet for England's surplus population, and they would advance the godly protestant cause by establishing an English barrier to further expansion by Catholic Spain. They would also enable Protestants to 'propagate the Gospel' among the native American population. John White was a member of a generation that was obsessed with the possibilities – both spiritual and material – of colonising projects, and he was in close touch with many other people who shared the same interests.

In 1624 his efforts led to the establishment of the Dorchester Company. Its governor was White's friend Sir Walter Erle, who presided over what Bond grandiosely calls the 'New England Plantation Parliament' at the Free School. Besides Erle, its members included Sir Richard Strode, John Browne of Frampton and others of the local puritan gentry, as well as a few neighbouring ministers and merchants from Weymouth and other ports. But fully a third of the investors were Dorchester townsmen: Bond, Bushrod, Hill, the two Whiteways, and other members of the Corporation, but also lesser people like Patroclus Cooke, Benjamin Devenish, the baker Matthew Bonger and a weaver named George Dyer.[2]

The Dorchester Company was never very successful. Several voyages sailed from Weymouth, none of them profitable as fishing ventures, though Bushrod and his friends did receive one good consignment of furs. The Cape Ann settlement was abandoned in 1626 and those of the survivors who had not returned to England moved a few miles down the coast to Salem. In 1629 they were reinforced by new settlers, of whom some may also have been from Dorchester. The *Lion's Whelp* left Gravesend at the end of April with, it was reported, 'about forty planters, especially from Dorchester and other places thereabouts', and another source says that six fishermen from the town were on board. It seems more likely that the fishermen were from Weymouth or some other coastal town, but that some people from Dorchester were among the passengers is likely enough. By now the Dorchester Company had been absorbed by the better-known Massachusetts Bay Company, and at the same time White's plans, like those of many other Puritans, were being transformed by the emerging menace of Arminianism. It was no longer enough to think of a few fishing outposts served by resident ministers. What was now urgently needed was a refuge for the godly – a refuge from the 'popish' innovations that were threatening the English church.[3]

So the pace of migration quickened dramatically in 1630. White was still active in the Massachusetts Bay Company, in close touch with John Winthrop and others who were planning the new settlements. Like Winthrop he wanted to create a safe haven for Puritans, and that this implied deep dissatisfaction with the King's government (which was openly promoting Arminian innovations) was widely recognised. A Lyme Regis man came to Dorchester and declared 'that all the projectors for [the] New England business are rebels', and that the emigrants were 'separatists'. The charge of separation always worried White. He was uneasy about what was happening at Salem, where the inhabitants had separated from the established church almost as completely as their 'Pilgrim' predecessors at

Plymouth, and he may have thought that some of Winthrop's friends had similar intentions. His solution was to establish a settlement that would be in full communion with the Church of England, and would allow open, rather than restricted church membership, just as White's own parishes did. This is why he had organised the *Mary and John* party, and he must have blessed them on their way with high hopes. Some of his parishioners were soon worrying that the rector might himself intend to desert them for New England. On 1 June a private fast was kept in Dorchester, Whiteway reports, 'for the turning away of the danger threatened, namely the removing of Mr White'. Later correspondence between White and Winthrop shows that these fears were well founded. In one letter White assured Winthrop of his long-standing wish 'to do that holy society with you service in mine own person'.[4]

Roger Clap, the young man from Devon whose memoirs provide the only surviving account of the *Mary and John* voyage, tells us little about the ten-week crossing, except that the two ministers on board preached and expounded scripture every day. But we can guess something of the feelings of the emigrants from the journal kept during his crossing five years later by the Lancashire clergyman Richard Mather, who was soon to minister to many of the Dorchester emigrants. There were the long days of impatient waiting at the point of embarkation – Bristol in the case of Mather's voyage – relieved by the 'friendship and courtesy of divers godly Christians'; there were the uplifting sermons and the sense of godly fellowship on board, alleviating the awful bouts of sea-sickness (many were 'ill at ease through much vomiting', Mather says). There were the amazing, unforgettable sea-creatures; the porpoises 'leaping and playing about our ship', the huge whales 'puffing and spewing up water as they went by'. Well might Mather intone his professional pieties as he beheld 'the works and wonders of the Almighty in the deep'. Clap and his fellow passengers landed at Nantasket, outside what is now Boston Harbour, on 30 May. A few days later they moved on to Mattapan, a few miles to the west, just south of what was soon to be the site of Boston, and they renamed it Dorchester.[5]

The new settlers were facing almost unimaginable dangers and uncertainties when they left the familiar fields and streets of old England for the untamed landscape of the new. Why did they do it?

Some, obviously, had earthily practical motives: to seek land, a better life, an escape from the deprivation and misery that was their likely fate in England. The material impulse undoubtedly explains the presence of so many unmarried young men, especially from the depressed clothing districts, among the early migrants. There were plenty of good reasons for wanting to escape from overcrowded Dorchester, beset as it was in the early 1630s by dearth and depression. Several of the emigrants were shoemakers – it was well known that there were too many shoemakers in the town.[6]

Some went because they had no choice, like young John Colliford, apprenticed to the weaver Thomas Croucher. We already know him as a 'disorderly and lewd boy' (he was publicly whipped for it), often absent from church. When Croucher died in 1635 his widow arranged for the young reprobate to be shipped to New England, paid part of the passage, and accompanied him for a few miles down the Weymouth road to make sure he got on board. New England was a good place to get rid of surplus, ill-disciplined young people. A runaway servant of Sir Richard Saltonstall was released from custody in March 1630 on condition that he rejoin his master, who was about to sail in Winthrop's fleet. True or false, a claim to be bound for New England was always a good story for vagrants to tell. That some people thought of the colonies as dumping-grounds for undesirables is evident in the surgeon Roger Haydon's drunken abuse of Constable John Bushrod: 'he would have him to go into Virginia shortly with the rest.'[7]

But unaccompanied young men might also be inspired by religion, as was the case with Roger Clap, and this was even more certainly true of the many substantial householders who went with their families. They went because they wished to build a godly community, and because that aspiration no longer seemed possible in an England polluted by Laudian idolatry and innovation. Clap gives us some idea of how the process worked. He and his friends were not deterred, he tells us, by the hardships they experienced during that bleak first winter in Massachusetts: 'our hearts were taken off from old England and set upon Heaven.' He wrote home to siblings in Devonshire urging them to come and join him, to such effect that several 'sold their means and came hither'.[8]

Something like this seems to have happened in at least one family in Dorchester. The *Mary and John* carried two daughters of the shoemaker Bernard Galpin,[9] one the wife of William Rockwell, the other of Nicholas Upsall. The Rockwells and two of their children (a third, Joseph, was too ill to travel – he was buried at Holy Trinity on 30 June), the newly married Upsalls, and a young man from Dorchester named William Hanham were all on the *Mary and John*. Like Clap, they must have found the new Dorchester to their liking, as within a few years they had been joined there by the old patriarch, Bernard, now well into his sixties, his son John, and two other daughters, one with her husband, Thomas Swift, the other still unmarried (she married William Hanham soon after her arrival). Bernard Galpin was at the centre of a remarkable family network of emigrants. It also included his brother-in-law Thomas Purchase and two other Purchase kinsmen: Oliver, who may have been Thomas's son, and Aquila, the master of Trinity School. The Purchases in turn were related to George Way, a prosperous glover who had held various civic offices and had been a member of the Dorchester Company. Way went briefly to New England during the 1630s, and after his return he retained a good deal of property there. Not all of Galpin's family crossed the seas with him. One son, Bernard the younger, carried on his father's trade of shoemaker in old Dorchester, and a daughter, Hannah, who had recently married Robert Gifford, also stayed. She was to make an important mark as one of the godly, living proof that the depth of religious commitment might be just as great in old Dorchester as it was in the new.[10]

When the years of Laudian idolatry ended in the 1640s some of the emigrants returned to Dorchester: William Horsford, for example, came back and fought for Parliament in the civil war. But most of them stayed in New England, though a good many left Massachusetts in the mid 1630s and moved west to establish a new community at Windsor, Connecticut. The Dorchester settlement was becoming overcrowded, and some may have objected to Richard Mather's restrictive ideas about church membership. But whether in Massachusetts or in Connecticut, the migrants from Dorchester played an important part in establishing the infant colonies. Among other cultural baggage, they brought with them expectations about how their communities ought to be governed, and those expectations invariably included a fairly wide popular participation. Whenever the Dorchester court met, it was agreed in 1633, 'upon the beating of the drum', the inhabitants would assemble at the meeting-house, to make 'such orders as may tend to the general good'. They realised, of course, that while general (male) participation might be desirable for consultative purposes, a smaller executive was also needed, so they provided for the choice of twelve 'select men' who were in effect a town council; legislation would require the consent of both the selectmen and a majority of the inhabitants.[11]

Among the early selectmen were several settlers from old Dorchester. George Dyer and Thomas Ford had both come over in the *Mary and John*. Nicholas Upsall was also a selectman, though in the end he was imprisoned and thrown out of Dorchester for speaking against persecution of the Quakers. The Dorchester men were also prominent in the church: William Rockwell was a deacon before he moved to Connecticut. The most active in both town and church, however, was John Galpin. He held every conceivable town office, including Recorder (or Town Clerk – 'keeping the books in good order', Dorchester's first historian, James Blake, commented admiringly) and deputy to the General Court of Massachusetts. He was also deacon of the church from 1658 until his death in 1692.[12]

So while John White and his allies strove to make their Dorchester a reformed community that would be a beacon to old England, others of the 'good people' of the town did the same on the other side of the Atlantic. They gave their children names like Experience, Deliverance, Takeheed, and Thankful, and they showed the same intense preoccupation with the state of their souls as their friends in England. They argued incessantly about what should be the qualifications for church membership: in the end public profession of conversion became the necessary requirement. But Roger Clap could recall, even in the early days, the 'many tears . . . shed in Dorchester meeting-house' as people 'declared God's work on their souls'. Their priorities were those of the puritan culture which had nurtured them. They looked after their poor (there were not many of them), contributed generously to good causes, and expelled people whose presence they saw as 'contrary to good order'. Within a few years of the settlement they established a school, for 'the training up of the children of the town in religion, learning and civility'. Unlike the Free School they had known, however, it really was free, open to all children, 'whether their parents be poor or rich'.[13]

We can learn a good deal from the emigrants about the supporters of the godly cause in Dorchester, not least the fact that they were drawn from a broad spectrum of the town's society. They were of course a handful of the elect, a 'small remnant', as people of their kind liked to call themselves. But they included people from the governing families like William Horsford as well as relatively humble shoemakers like Bernard Galpin. The middle level of the town hierarchy, from which many of them came, contained great variety of opinion. Yet the support of these people – the lesser clothiers, the better-off weavers, the shoemakers, tailors and suchlike tradesmen – was essential if the campaign was to succeed. These were the churchwardens and overseers of the poor, the constables, the holders of other important civic offices below the Capital Burgesses. We have often encountered them in these capacities, parading the streets to apprehend offenders, or to compel the laggard and unwilling to come to church, keeping order during the services, and upholding public morality in general.

Many people even of this type left few traces of their beliefs. It is often only the regularity with which they were called on to perform parochial or civic office that tells us anything about them. The joiner Ralph Whitlock is a good example. He served on juries, gave a respectable ten shillings towards rebuilding the Shire Hall in 1638, and was both sidesman and churchwarden of St Peter's parish. The tailor William Dry was three times churchwarden and three times overseer in All Saints between 1637 and 1658. In the same parish the hosier Christopher Way and the chandler Richard Williams also regularly served as churchwardens, and equally regularly held town office as constables; Way also became Steward of Whetstone's Almshouse. A similar example is the shoemaker Matthew Butler, an even more regular juryman than Whitlock. Constable in 1619 and 1629, he filled an impressive list of minor offices: warden of the Shoemakers' Company in 1632, twice churchwarden, twice overseer, and a trustee of both town and parish lands. His son William, also a shoemaker, followed in his footsteps – churchwarden twice and overseer once, all between 1638 and 1642.

These are people whom we must assume to have been among the godly primarily because they did their jobs without complaint – though we sometimes have other evidence, as when Williams was abused in language that suggests that he was known to be a Puritan. In some cases the evidence is even more circumstantial. Sons of Benjamin Devenish (who ran the Brewhouse), Robert Lawrence and Matthew Swaffield (both shoemakers turned alehousekeepers), John Churchill, and Gilbert Loder, were all to become ordained ministers of puritan persuasion. They must surely have been influenced by the town's religious climate during the 1630s, and it seems unlikely that their parents were immune to it. The Loders were part of the governing circle, but all the other families were in the middle rank of Dorchester society. Benjamin Devenish was a regular officeholder in his parish (Holy Trinity) – overseer in 1616 and churchwarden four times during the 1620s – and his appointment to the Brewhouse shows that he was well thought of. Churchill, a tailor, may have been a distant connection of the family at Colleton House, but if so he was very much a poor relation. Both he and Swaffield were men of good repute, regular recipients of 'Good Friday money' – the funds lent to respectable tradesmen from an old bequest of a former MP for the town, Dr Francis James. Swaffield married a daughter of the puritan tailor, Benjamin Derby, and there is a hint of his own outlook in the complaint that he was 'hollowhearted', a charge often levelled at puritans. All these were responsible men, and that their sons entered the ministry is not surprising.[14]

Of the fathers of these puritan divines, only Robert Lawrence seems to have been lacking in zeal. He had two spells as constable and was churchwarden and overseer in All Saints parish several times. He also kept an unusually orderly alehouse, his only indiscretion being in 1633 when he allowed boys from the Free School to drink there; unwittingly, of course, he said. Some thought Lawrence too much the genial host, a bit too partial to the bottle himself: he does not sound much of a reformer. Yet his son, Christopher, born and educated in Dorchester. certainly was. He went from the Free School to Oxford in 1631, and became a presbyterian minister of some note after the civil wars.[15]

There were of course a good many families whose attitudes to reform were ambiguous. Among the Galpins there was little difference between those who went to New England and those who stayed, but in the Purchase family the emigrants were certainly the more committed. Old Nicholas Purchase, who died in 1620, was a baker who was branching out into the brewing trade. Of his two sons, the younger, Aquila, was parish clerk and master of Trinity School, before emigrating to New England. The elder, Joseph, carried on the business and did well enough to leave his children a trust fund worth £280 when he died in 1638. He left small bequests to local charities, and held the usual parochial offices, but he was not active in borough affairs and may have been more interested in turning a good profit for himself than in godly reformation. In his younger days he had certainly not been a model of the purity that John White was preaching: his bride was six months pregnant when they were married in 1618.[16]

This lack of puritan zeal probably explains why Joseph Purchase did not rise higher in the town hierarchy. In the case of the grocer Joseph Underwood the reason was different: he went bankrupt. Born in 1586, Underwood seemed to be doing well until the early 1630s; he had been churchwarden and overseer in Trinity parish several times, was constable in 1624–6, and so forth. He was also a member of the Dorchester Company (he had relatives who went to New England), and was in the same tax bracket as Bond and several other members of the Corporation. But then he started to go downhill. He was arrested for debt in 1632, and although he managed to pay up, two years later he could not. He had been buying goods from London wholesalers who, he claimed, charged him for more than he had ordered. Summoned before the mayor, Underwood was indignant. He expected to be treated with courtesy in the old neighbourly way, he told the constable, not as a disgraced and broken debtor; 'if Mr Mayor had sent his boy he would go with him, but not with a constable without a warrant.' If the constable did bring a warrant he would come only if it was 'business for the King'. So his goods were distrained, and although his son came rushing home from the Shire Hall and secured some of the stock before the bailiffs arrived, the shop was soon being rifled both by the agents of the London dealers and by some distinctly unneighbourly neighbours. A crowd of over thirty people collected and took 'some fruit and other small things', while the Londoners helped themselves to nutmegs and drank some of Underwood's 'hot waters'. The grocer scurried off to London and eventually satisfied his creditors; he was back in business by the end of 1636. But his civic career was at an end.[17]

So even those who supported the campaign of godly discipline, as Underwood apparently did, might lose the confidence of the town's leaders. The mercer Thomas Hyatt was an officeholder in Trinity parish almost as regularly as Underwood, and was constable for two years – and a moderately active one. He might have gone further if he had been able to keep his temper. In 1631 he used 'contemptuous speeches' to the Governor of the Freemen's Company, and a year later he got into a fight with another respectable townsman, the haberdasher John Watts, when they met on the road coming back from Axminster Fair. Hyatt was a very active constable during his first year in that office, but in 1631-2 he was far overshadowed by his colleague John Bushrod. A customer at Robert Cuffe's barber's shop complained that Bushrod was as busy 'as a jackanapes was with his tail'; a veritable 'busy box', a Dorchester woman later declared.[18]

John Bushrod was no more committed to reformation than several other officeholders. Matthew Chubb's old enemy, the tailor John Conduit, also typifies the godly middling sort. Statements made in the 1607 Star Chamber case leave no room for doubt of his zeal for reformation. He w:s constable in 1616, unfortunately at a time when records are not very plentiful, and in 1629 he was sent to London to help Town Clerk Derby in the negotiations for the new charter. By this time, it will be recalled, he was both serjeant and beadle, offices of high visibility which brought him into regular and often noisy conflict with the unruly of the town. Conduit only did it for the fees, the younger Thomas Pouncey sneered: 'for 20d. he would undo any man.'[19]

By the 1630s a more vigorous brand of reformer was taking over. Among them were men like Conduit's successor as serjeant, Patroclus Cooke, the clothworker Henry Bridges, and the iron-monger Lawrence Righton. Cooke was a prickly character. He was constable in 1620 and was appointed beadle a year later. But at two pounds a year he felt underpaid and refused to continue in spite of being 'urged to it again and again'. In 1624 he was also dismissed from his other post, serjeant, for some indiscreet words at the Assizes. He neglected his widowed mother, and when ordered to pay a shilling a week towards her maintenance he still kept up the argument, and got a reduction to eightpence. Such indiscretions

delayed his further promotion, and for the next few years the only
office he held was that of sidesman in Trinity parish. By now he was
in his mid forties and must have been thought more responsible, so
in 1633 he was appointed overseer in his parish, and in 1636 was
constable again, and an extremely active one. In or out of office, he
was always a strong law and order man. One evening in February
1634 there was a disturbance at the George: a door was smashed by
a couple of Blackmore Vale butchers. Cooke went upstairs with the
constables to see 'all differences ended between them', and suggested
that those responsible should pay for the door. This, he says, was
'quietly taken', so he left – only to be assaulted in the street by the
butchers.[20]

An even more committed upholder of godly reformation, and a
far less turbulent character, was Lawrence Righton, who started out
as a cutler. Righton worked his way up from modest beginnings,
but he was never a rich man. In his early days he aroused the anger
of the saddlers by selling bridles and spurs, and there were complaints
that he intruded into other trades too. In 1630 he was allowed to
trade legally as an ironmonger, a sign that he was now fully accepted
in the town. We get occasional glimpses of the Righton family business: Lawrence chasing a thief who had stolen a knife from his stall
at Woodbury Hill Fair; his wife Amy tending the stall at the fair in
Dorchester market-place. He held parochial office for the first time
in 1631 and began an eventful term as constable three years later,
proving to be one of the most aggressively reformist of all the holders
of that office.[21]

Righton was a good townsman, always ready to do his civic duty.
His piety was well known. In 1635 he was cited to the ecclesiastical
court at Blandford for nonconformity; he greatly admired his rector,
William Benn; and he took the campaign against swearing and roistering very seriously. 'He should go to hell for it,' he warned Michael
Fooke after hearing the butcher utter some particularly lurid oaths.
Something about Righton's manner – a touch of officiousness, presumably – made people particularly inclined to resist or jeer at him.
To the town wags he was 'Constable Shit-on'; the 'sparrowbill constable' (a reference to items sold in his shop); a mere 'pedlar', a
drunken blacksmith declared. The innkeeper William Wilson resisted
violently when Righton seized his horse when executing a royal

warrant, wresting his staff of office away from him; the gardener John Edwards threatened to complain to the justices at the Assizes after Righton broke down his door. If the frequency of abuse is any indication of a constable's efficiency, then Lawrence Righton must have been one of the best. His service was appropriately rewarded when he eventually became a Capital Burgess after the civil war.[22]

Lawrence Righton spent a long lifetime in Dorchester. Henry Bridges, another active reformer, was in the town for only fourteen years. He was already an established clothworker, with his own apprentice, when he moved to Dorchester in 1629, possibly from Somerset (he had connections at Taunton and Yeovil). Bridges's integrity and technical knowledge were quickly welcomed. Denis Bond at once recognised a kindred spirit, his arrival important enough to be recorded in his chronology. Within a year Bridges had been appointed one of the 'searchers and sealers' – the officers who inspected cloth made within the borough, to maintain quality control – the other two being Richard Savage and Henry Maber, both members of the governing circle. Yet there was opposition when Bridges applied for admission as a freeman. He was given temporary permission to trade, but the clothiers objected, and in 1631 he was told to leave the town. Bond or one of the other notables must have arranged matters; the Freemen's Company soon reversed itself and admitted him. He became very active in municipal affairs, beginning a three-year stint as constable in 1636.[23]

Like Cooke, Bridges had a short temper, and like Righton he was somewhat officious. Perhaps he was right to intervene when he found Robert Foote in the market, cudgel raised against a visiting countryman, but he was inevitably dragged into the ensuing altercation. On another occasion, again with no office to protect him, he publicly reproved the saddler William Melmouth for swearing. A bystander, Henry Bishop, came to Melmouth's defence and gave Bridges 'lewd language'; Bridges called him 'saucy boy' (he was in fact just out of his apprenticeship), and there were further exchanges before he had them both hauled before the JPs. As constable, Bridges soon acquired a reputation for snooping – he 'hearkens at every door', it was said – and for being particularly tough on swearers. But although he encountered the usual abuse showered on constables who did their duty he did not provoke the kind of mockery so often directed at Righton. Churchwarden of All Saints in 1642, Bridges appeared destined for higher office, but the war came and led to his early death.[24]

All these were people from roughly the middle third of Dorchester society. The poorest third are harder to get at. Most of the visible opposition to reform came from this group: from the humbler shoe-makers, tailors, weavers, and other small craftsmen, the butchers, labourers, grooms, and tapsters. Some of them, like Robert Samp-son, make regular appearances in the records as drunkards, fornica-tors, or blasphemers. But only some of them – what of the others, probably the majority? We should not expect people like this to take many initiatives. They lived only a little above the minimum level of subsistence; they may have paid poor rates, but only at the lowest assessments of a penny a week or less; and when their working days were over they (and even more certainly their widows) were likely to go on relief, or if they were lucky, to end their days in one of the almshouses. Most of them were illiterate, which imposed a further barrier to active participation in the process of spiritual and moral awakening that John White was striving to inspire.

Granted all these difficulties, something can still be said about them. Stories in the offenders' book reveal a few of the successes of godly reformation. 'She would not buy repentance so dear, nor would she sell her child for money,' Elizabeth Cooke protested when Joseph Parkins's friends tried to bribe her into hushing up her daugh-ter's charge of rape. 'Never unkindness was done in secret but God knoweth it,' Joan Croucher told the persistent Robert Cardrow. So there were women in Dorchester who had internalised the official moral code and, at least in Joan Croucher's case, its religious founda-tion. But the same would have been true of women in many other less puritan towns, and we need not attribute their integrity entirely to the preaching of John White or William Benn, any more than we need suppose that Eleanor Galpin's agonized cry after stabbing her baby – 'the Devil did tempt her to do it' – expressed a religious outlook peculiar to Dorchester.[25]

Much of our knowledge of supporters of reformation is based on evidence about the enforcement of the law. The reformers relied heavily on the zeal of middling-level constables, but however vigilant they would have been powerless without the co-operation of their subordinates, the watchmen. The watch brought in malefactors partly out of fear: they would be punished if they neglected their duties too flagrantly. Yet watchmen often charged people with drinking or swearing even when there was no constable lurking nearby. They were 'hard fellows to interrupt honest men', a visiting gentleman complained when watchmen burst in on his carousing at John Whittle's alehouse.[26]

Two of the most active watchmen in the 1630s were the shoemakers William Chubb and Albion Bull. They arrested more offenders than anyone else, and we may reasonably conclude that they did it out of choice. Chubb, no relation to the great Matthew, turned in nine offenders in the eight years from 1629, and one of them was his sister, Em Gawler, whom he accused of slandering the minister, William Benn. Bull's record is even more impressive: sixteen accusations during the same period. This sort of energy naturally made him unpopular. A labourer named John Crimmell violently resisted when Bull tried to arrest him for drunkenness; the bystanders refused to help, so Bull had to let him go. After Bull had reported all this to the JPs, Crimmell found him working in Matthew Swaffield's shop – for another shoemaker of puritan views, it might be noted – and threatened to beat him up again. Bull's energy as a watchman may have provided some compensation for his marital difficulties, which culminated in his wife's being committed to the Assizes on a charge of theft. This was too much for Albion. In October 1636 he was caught tippling with Robert Sampson and John Chimney, and a year later he lost his unblemished record as a watchman by getting drunk on duty.[27]

Albion Bull reminds us that there was no absolute divide between the godly and the reprobate. He might strive to do his duty, but it was easy to fall into bad company. Still, those in authority knew pretty well who were the deserving poor and who were not. After the civil war part of Richard Bushrod's bequest was annually distributed to the godly poor, and the people who were chosen to receive it must have been approved by the reformers. One of them was the weaver Roger Turner: an active watchman in the 1630s, who stoutly assisted Constable Righton in an altercation with some very drunken country gentlemen in November 1634, and was later denounced by a fellow clothworker as a 'dissembling puritan knave'. Another was a shoemaker named Matthew Bennett; he served Parliament as a scout during the civil war and eventually succeeded Bower as beadle. A third recipient of Bushrod's charity was the Robert Gifford who married a daughter of the New England emigrant, Bernard Galpin; we shall encounter Hannah Gifford again as an ardent supporter of reform.[28] The shoemaker Thomas Grindham did not receive Bushrod money, but he was certainly one of the godly, giving security for John Martin, a weaver charged with seditiously denouncing the 'popish' ecclesiastical courts. He was also another of the active watchmen. One man he arrested threatened him with a rapier and denounced him as a 'bottle nosed rogue'. Later in the 1630s he injudiciously helped the constable, Gifford Bale, arrest a group of visiting fiddlers without having first got a warrant from the mayor.[29]

None of these people was as important to the cause of reform as Nathaniel Bower the beadle. Bower was a shoemaker, too poor to be assessed for the parish rate. But he was a responsible townsman, often called on to perform civic duties: as a 'viewer of maltsters', as a member of juries regulating the leather trade. He was clearly a Puritan, and in 1629 was prosecuted in the Archdeacon's Court at Blandford. When Conduit died and Benjamin Derby declined into inactivity Bower became the most visible and vigilant officer of the law in the borough, on the front line of moral reformation. Inevitably he was frequently ridiculed and reviled for it. He was a 'beggarly base knave', John Norrington shouted, adding that 'more beggarly knaves lived in Dorchester than in any town hereabout.' 'If Bower were not a knave,' a woman told the mayor, 'there was never a knave in England.' Solemnly patrolling the streets with his staff of office, conveying malefactors to the stocks or the Blindhouse, inflicting public whippings, collecting market tolls, reporting unauthorised traders, Bower could not help being unpopular. No wonder he made such a fuss about the fancy new uniform – the 'coat of black cotton, gathered and with two long skirts' – and the painted staff the Corporation provided for him in 1640. He had heard enough of the ungodly's mocking laughter already, though in the end he gave in and agreed to wear it.[30]

Godly reformation could not have succeeded without the enthusiastic support of people like Bower, and at least the acquiescence of a substantial proportion of Dorchester's lower orders. Both the enthusiasm and the acquiescence were for the most part forthcoming. Dorchester folk were inspired to journey forth into the unknown to establish new colonies of the godly in far-off New England. Those who stayed at home gave massively to charity, and a good many of them were active, sometimes very zealous, supporters of the reformers. Even those who were not found themselves coerced or persuaded into changing their sexual habits, so that there was a good deal less casual and pre-marital sex than in the old days.

But from the standpoint of the godly all was still not well. As the kingdom's divisions became increasingly pronounced in the later 1630s and early 1640s there were signs that even in Dorchester reformist zeal was on the wane. Holy Trinity's parishioners, always reluctant to subsidise their neighbours in All Saints, were now skimping on their obligations to their own poor.[31] Hints of apathy and disunity break through the normally bland corporation minutes. Sometimes there were good reasons why they could not find a quorum – in February 1640, for example, they wanted to avoid meeting because the Earl of Suffolk was trying to foist an unwanted MP on them. Sometimes it was because of the Assizes, or because it was a Fast Day, or because of 'the great muster in town'. But in June 1640 there was no other excuse than a general malaise: 'the meeting but slender and broke up in a kind of discontent, and nothing agreed on'.[32] These divisions among the godly were particularly ominous when we consider that beneath the veneer of conformity, there was always a substantial element of the Dorchester population which responded to godly reformation with indifference, anger, and mocking laughter.

The mocking laughter echoed around every street corner, haunted the godly from every tavern door. One August night in 1635 Nathaniel Bower was stopped in the street by the watch. It was late, past midnight; Bower had been helping with the harvest in Mr White's fields, and had supped at the rectory. The watchmen, two weavers named Philip Eliot and James Trayford, saw a glorious opportunity to deflate the officious beadle, so they pretended not to recognise him and took him to Constable Righton as a vagrant, abusing him as 'white livered knave' as they went. They had, of course, been

drinking, and were duly bound over to the Sessions, with what result
we do not know. Neither of these men were regular offenders, and
their obvious glee at making a fool of the beadle shows that hostility
to people like Bower was not confined to the most disorderly inhabitants of the town.[33]

We must be cautious about attributing such motives to individuals,
but it is clear that collectively episodes like this one were expressions
of that alternative, traditional, festive culture that the puritan
reformers were striving to eradicate. The vision of the reformed
new Jerusalem required the imposition of policies of economic and
cultural coercion that were deeply threatening to the way of life of
many of their poorer neighbours. To the reformers, indeed, those
old traditions were the very abominations of Satan. It is not surprising that they were resisted, often – as in the case of the watchmen
who apprehended Nathaniel Bower – in ways that made authority
look ridiculous.

The uses of ridicule were many and varied. Patroclus Cooke and
Henry Bridges, it will be recalled, were unusually active constables,
zealous for all forms of moral regulation. In 1637 they were assailed
in one of those satirical libels that occasionally cropped up in Dorchester. It was called 'The Song of the Constables', and we hear
snatches of it several times: in a quiet corner of the Shire Hall during
the Sessions, in the alley behind the Crown, and even in Hugh
Phillips's normally respectable grocer's shop. It was apparently a
joint composition of some of the young sparks of the town, of whom
one was Joseph Dare, often known as 'the blind boy', stepson of the
alehousekeeper Richard Keate; Dare knew it by heart and regularly
sang it to his admiring friends. The song took aim at each constable
in turn. Bridges, it complained 'goes about like a drudge, to hearken
to them that do swear' (or, in another version, 'he hearkens at every
door'). Cooke was equally disliked: ''tis in his book, he'll make you
pay for swearing.' The third constable, Thomas Clench, was more
affable, though: 'he will not us pinch, and will sit at home by the
fire, and won't wear out his shoes.' 'He'll never go about,' the other
version added, 'nor listen to the scout, nor hearken to them that do
swear.' It is true that Clench was less active than either Bridges or
Cooke, though the song may have made him bestir himself, as during the next few weeks he brought in a fair number of offenders.[34]

What the authors of the verses most objected to was the reformers' constant prying and snooping. The song reflects a spirit of genial good fellowship and neighbourliness reminiscent of Matthew Chubb. It pokes gentler fun at an earlier constable:

> Robert Lawrence is an honest man, pray let him be carried in the fore sedan;
> If thou art drunk and canst not stand, thou must go to Dorchester and be carried in the fore sedan.[35]

Dare and his friends may have been young hooligans, but they satirised their persecutors in language that echoed some of the themes constantly used by critics of the godly.

Opposition to puritan reform came from high-spirited, rebellious young people. But it also had other sources. Some of it certainly did come from people who resented the 'class' element in the reform campaign. The glazier Elias Fry, presented to Blandford court for 'sleeping and disorderly behaviour' during divine service, was incensed by the prosecution: 'It was a very small matter . . . the churchwardens could see him and such poor men to present them, but could not see the rich men.' After some routine invective against the churchwarden, Richard Williams, Fry gave his views on Dorchester's government: 'they choose such busy knaves into office that will present poor men and not rich, and they rule the town.' William Martin thought the clergy largely to blame for the fading of the old-fashioned neighbourliness. William Benn, for example, 'had gotten so much means that he was become so proud that he would not speak unto him, but cast up a great pair of eyes upon him'. It was all so much better in the old days: Martin fondly recalled 'the bounty of Mr Cheeke in giving at the collections', whereas Benn gave 'little or nothing'. Everywhere, Martin declared, ministers and lawyers 'had gotten all the riches of the land into their hands'.[36]

Not all the denunciations of greed and self-seeking were directed against allegedly hypocritical reformers: as we have seen, the Blachfords rightly came in for their share of them. But, however unfairly, some of the poorer people thought that White and his allies were interested only in lining their own pockets – by raiding the poor funds, the blacksmith John Bonger suspected. 'Every Monday morning after the sacrament' White and the mayor, John Hill, were said to send for 'the money given at the basin': 'what became of it [Bonger] knew not'. The widow Anne Samways blamed everything on the Rector: White 'did starve the country, and did join with the devil for money, and would be a merchant and farmer for his profit, and did send provision to New England in a colour to convey [them] to Spain'. The tirade continued, an onlooker reported, with 'many other unseemly words for a quarter of an hour space'.[37]

Another refractory member of Dorchester's lower orders, George Brine the carpenter, thought it was the offenders' money that the reformers were after: the whole purpose of fining poor men for trivial offences like drinking, he decided, 'was to get money to put into their own purses'. Brine was an inveterate rebel. Doing his turn as a watchman, he abused the constables and sneered that the town was run by 'a company of boys'. Brought before the JPs for tippling he denounced the constables as 'eavesdroppers', anticipating one of the points in his friend Joseph Dare's song. Brine had a strong sense of justice, and was in the habit of helping people escape from the stocks if he felt they had been unfairly convicted. 'It was not well done,' he assured Dare as he helped the blind boy get away after one spell in the stocks. The gunsmith Robert George was another rebel. 'He could cozen all the constables, the proudest of them all,' he boasted, adding that he had ways of conveying anyone away when the authorities came. Brine and George were unusually vocal; most people complained more quietly. 'These were hard laws,' John Gaylard mildly protested when he was fined for tippling – whereupon he was promptly bound over to the Sessions for contempt.[38]

'Class' insubordination could lead to retaliation, sometimes of a very savage nature. At the trained band muster at Poundbury in May 1635, William Paty, sergeant in a foot company, was infuriated beyond endurance by the insolence of one of his soldiers, the blacksmith Methuselah Notting. It was Whitsun week, always a time for boozy celebration, and Notting, as usual, had been drinking. Whenever Paty gave the order to turn right he would turn left, and vice versa, completely disrupting the drill, and provoking the sergeant into assaulting him with his cane. He died a few days later, ostensibly of a 'burning fever'.[39]

None of this amounted to an organised opposition within the town. Yet an explosion of factional conflict in 1631 is some indication that the memory of Matthew Chubb had not quite vanished. In 1621 the Company of Freemen had been established to regulate trading in the town, and to give its residents protection from outside competition; we have several times encountered it in action. When the new charter was obtained in 1629 the company received a somewhat more elaborate institutional structure. The freemen were given a Common Council of twenty-four, from whom the Governor of the Company and four 'Assistants' were to be elected. But this did not make the Company any more democratic, for the members of the Council were named in the charter, in other words chosen by the Capital Burgesses, who would also select replacements when councillors died or resigned. The Governor and his four Assistants would still be popularly elected, as they had been since 1621, but if they showed any signs of independence they could still be controlled by five other Assistants drawn from the Capital Burgesses, without whose approval the Governor could do nothing.[40]

The 1631 conflict involved a complicated mixture of issues. It began when some 'discontented persons', as Whiteway describes them, complained that the Corporation had 'wronged' them in the new charter by insisting on nominating members of the Common Council. A meeting was arranged between the Fifteen and the Company, at which John Coke and Joseph Paty spoke for the Freemen, Town Clerk Derby and Sir Francis Ashley for the Corporation. It turned into a blazing row. Derby argued that there had never been any intention of allowing the Freemen the right to elect their Council, so Paty and Coke then brought up other popular grievances, including the question of the Free School, which they claimed ought to be 'free for all'. No, Recorder Ashley replied, the deed of foundation stated that it was to be free only for 'poor men's children'. The Freemen thereupon walked out in what Whiteway describes as an 'insolent manner', chanting 'A Free School! A Free School!' A few days later the Corporation tried to pacify them by reducing the quarterly rate each freeman paid to the Company. To no avail: at the ensuing elections for the Governor and the four elected Assistants – the only opportunity the ordinary freemen had to express their opinions – the popular faction swept the board. Whiteway, needless to say, complains that they 'carried themselves tumultuously'.[41]

The row, inevitably, was mediated by Mr White. He got the antagonists to agree to a 'solemn pacification' which was accepted by everyone except Coke and a handful of others. To prepare the ground White had already initiated the first of a series of collections for the Free School at the 5 November commemoration. The idea was to build up the school's endowment until it could provide the schoolmaster with a salary of forty pounds a year, after which it would no longer be necessary to charge fees for the sons of 'men of ability'. This temporarily stilled the agitation, though much of the one hundred pounds raised in 1631 and at subsequent collections was frittered away on repairs to the school buildings, and the target of forty pounds a year for the master was never attained. Rumblings about the school continued. In 1639 the Commissioners for Charitable Uses investigated the matter, and two years later William Munden, a tailor who had been prominent in the 1631 campaign, and another freeman unsuccessfully demanded 'to be accounted poor men' and thus exempt from school fees for their sons. In Munden's case this was not very convincing, as he was a man of some substance, who had been churchwarden of his parish and had held other local offices. But there were no more organised challenges to the Corporation, and after 1632 the governing oligarchy managed to regain control of Freemen's Company elections.[42]

Was there anything more behind this dispute than the freemen's understandable resentment at the high-handed behaviour of the oligarchy? William Whiteway certainly thought there was, and although coloured by his usual discretion, his account hints at the presence of a real ideological division. Behind the vocal members of the Freemen's Company, he names some more influential people in the shadows: 'Mr William Savage their counsellor, Dr Bradish and Mr Ironside their divines', and 'old Mr Vawter the instigator of all'.

Nicholas Vawter we have encountered already: one of the old Chubb gang, expelled from the Corporation for non-attendance in 1625. Savage, a lawyer who moved to Dorchester from Sherborne in the mid 1620s, may have been related to the puritan Richard

Savage, a prominent member of the Corporation. He was, at all events, a man of strong opinions, one of the few in the county to resist the Forced Loan in 1627. Dr William Bradish was rector of Puddletown and had been a member of the Dorchester Company; he had also been educated at the most puritan of all Cambridge colleges, Emmanuel, which may or may not have moulded his opinions. But the other minister, Gilbert Ironside, the pluralist rector of Winterbourne Steepleton and Winterbourne Abbas, was clearly at odds with the reformers. As Bishop of Bristol after the Restoration he was to be reasonably lenient towards nonconformist clergy, but in the 1630s he was closer to the Laudians than to the Puritans, attacking the latters' sabbatarian views as a 'holy fraud'. In 1637 he sharply criticised White's 'Ten Vows', arguing that they would produce 'schism in the church and rebellion in the state', and were the fruit of attitudes that led to 'disaffection in the present government, turbulent commotions at home, needless fruitless plantations abroad'.[43]

That a parson so totally out of sympathy with White's brand of godly reformation was associated with the 'commons' faction suggests the presence of issues far deeper than the immediate, surface ones. The multiple connections between other members of the faction provide further clues to this. In the end, many of these links also connect them to Matthew Chubb. Vawter had been one of Chubb's protégés, and was the brother-in-law of the libellist Robert Adyn, from whose family he had acquired property. John Coke, the most obstinate of the freemen's leaders, married Vawter's sister, and the friends named as executors or witnesses to his will included several members of the faction, among them Ironside and the townsmen Edward Bragg and William Munden. Thomas Gollop, a gentleman from a distinctly anti-puritan Dorset family, and the cantankerous James Gould the younger (by now losing whatever enthusiasm for reform he had ever had) were also friends of Coke. Yet another of the leaders, Joseph Paty, was one of Vawter's overseers, managed property for the Adyn family, and had been a trustee in a great marriage settlement between the Chubbs' heir, the younger Matthew, and the daughter of their friend, the goldsmith Robert Coker. Margaret Chubb had also named Paty in her will as the recipient of a mourning ring, and Paty's son William (the trained band sergeant) married another of Robert Coker's daughters.[44]

Although some members of the faction may have been connected with Chubb, this does not necessarily mean that hostility to godly reformation was the link that united all of them. Several were in fact reformers at one stage or another of their careers. Patroclus Cooke, one of the most irreconcilable, never abandoned his reformist outlook, and although John Coke was removed from the governorship of the Hospital for his part in the affair, in earlier years he had been strongly for reform. Thomas Whittle, too, was one of the officeholding circle: three times churchwarden of All Saints between 1629 and 1642. Joseph Paty was less active in his parish after the dispute, but his son William continued to hold offices, first in Trinity parish and then in All Saints when he moved house in the mid 1630s; he was also constable in 1634 and Governor of the Freeman's Company five years later. Edward Bragg, overseer in St Peter's parish in 1632 and constable in that and the following year, was certainly no friend to the disorderly: on one occasion the younger Thomas Pouncey threatened to beat him up.[45]

But most people in the circle surrounding the Cokers and the Patys for one reason or another disliked the oligarchy now running the town. While serving as constable Edward Bragg continued to smoulder. In 1633 he grumbled about the partiality shown by the Mayor, Edmund Dashwood: if any of Dashwood's acquaintances were charged with anything, Bragg complained, the Mayor 'would bid them go home about their business'. A few of the faction managed to hang on to office in the Company, but even in that body the old customs of good fellowship were disappearing. In 1633 it was agreed that the annual dinner, at which the Common Councillors and Assistants were entertained by the retiring Governor, should no longer be held at the George, but at the Governor's own house, where the raucous behaviour acceptable at an inn would be less likely to occur.[46]

The commons faction brought together people who were discontented for a variety of reasons: men like William Munden who, for all we know, may not have wanted anything more than the abolition of tuition fees at the Free School, as well as others like Patroclus Cooke, who was staunchly for reform, but evidently wanted a real broadening of the governing oligarchy. Some, like John Coke and the Patys, may have initially been reformers, later becoming disenchanted as the campaign's puritan character became ever more rigorous; put off, perhaps, by White's 'Ten Vows' or Benn's uncompromising preaching. Under the guidance of such as Gilbert Ironside, they were taking the first steps on a path that was to land them on the opposite side from most of their fellow townsmen when the country divided in civil war in the following decade. They may have found it easier to do this because of their closeness to survivors of the old Chubb group, who had been hostile to godly reformation all along.

So there was resistance to godly reformation from within the town – from rebellious members of the lower orders, but also from more respectable members of Matthew Chubb's old circle. There were poor people who enthusiastically supported the reform programme; there were many more who acquiesced in it. But there was also a continuing struggle that ranged the unruly poor of Dorchester and their allies against those set in authority over them. Political and personal jealousies, class feeling, and resentment at interference with cherished recreations blended in a general hatred of the puritan oligarchy.

Hostility to over-zealous reformers also came from people at the other end of the social scale. Many of them were country gentlemen who resented being lectured or punished by plebeian townsmen: there was a geographical as well as a social dimension to the struggle. Examples are legion. A Chetnole gentleman scornfully addressed Constable Bridges as 'sirrah', and drunkenly proclaimed that he was 'a better man descended' than Mayor Hill. People did not have to be very far removed from their commercial origins to assert this kind of superiority. Lawrence Stafford, who left a large bequest for the Dorchester poor, had a son who in the 1630s was a clothier living at Fifehead Neville. When charged with swearing during a visit to Dorchester he accused the constable, John Bushrod, of lying, said he was 'a better man than he' and that his father 'had given more to the town than he [Bushrod] was worth'. Some years later the towns-men nabbed him again, this time for drunkenness.[47]

A succession of Dorset gentlemen flaunted their contempt for the upstart town magistrates, and invariably paid the penalty. In 1633 Richard Christmas of Sydling was brought, visibly drunk, before the JPs, where he continued to swear and insist that he was as good a man as the Mayor. Eventually he caved in: 'he would pay his

money and a fart for you all,' words which were naturally answered
by yet another summons to Sessions. Christmas was a notorious
enemy of the Puritans. Almost twenty years earlier he had set a cat
on a post in the street at Sydling, saying that it 'should make as good
a sermon as the best preacher in the country, and that there were
none but rogues and whores that would hear sermons'. When the
pious Lady Strode was returning to Parnham after hearing Mr White
preach in Dorchester, Christmas intercepted her coach, asked the
footman 'how many Puritans there were in that company?' and fired
a musket shot which terrified the party.[48]

The struggle between the two competing cultures – between puritan reformism and the old, permissive traditionalism with its ideals
of hospitality and good fellowship and its tolerance of festivals and
drinking – was particularly intense in the county of Dorset, where
the old ways were still strongly embedded, especially in the downlands and parts of Blackmore Vale.[49] Moral reformers were, of
course, to be found in all social classes, including the gentry, and
they looked to Dorchester for inspiration. Besides coming from
Parnham to hear Mr White's sermons, Sir Richard and Lady Strode
had several of their children baptised at Holy Trinity. John Browne
of Frampton, an active figure in county politics, lived in Dorchester
for a time. White was on familiar terms with Sir Walter Erle, and
Sir Thomas Trenchard was always a friendly presence; one of his
servants had a seat in the chancel at Trinity church.[50] But many of
the gentry were still untouched by, or resistant to, Calvinist notions
of godly reformation, and viewed Dorchester with suspicion. The
townsmen's self-assurance in suppressing ungodliness without
regard to rank or station affronted deeply-held beliefs about hierarchy, honour, and gentility. And the intolerance of revelling and
carousing by people of any class threatened that good old paternalist
order that the gentry, like Matthew Chubb, preferred above the
moral austerities of the reformed community.

There were many like Richard Christmas who came into Dorchester upon their lawful occasions and found themselves judged,
lectured, and fined by their social inferiors. What right had such
people to try them? Their cases crop up repeatedly: a certain Winter
Grant, Esquire, drunk at the Crown in 1629; a London gentleman,
Tobias Hooke, drunk and swearing repeatedly a year later; William
Hardy of nearby Bockhampton, drunk in 1634. A Wareham gentle-

man flatly refused to pay his fine for drunkenness in 1630, and in the same year Henry Gollop, one of a prominent Dorset family, caused the bailiffs a lot of trouble when he was hauled before them. 'He scorned what we can do to him,' the JPs recorded, scoffed at the constables, truculently warned that his connections would ensure swift retribution if the townsmen dared to put him in gaol, and repeated the familiar slur that the reform campaign was inspired by mercenary motives: if a stranger came with money in his pockets, 'we will pull it out.' In 1637 another genteel reveller was more explicit: the town 'should burn for it' if he had to pay his five-shilling fine for swearing. Wiser heads prevailed: somebody else, possibly a tradesman who valued his custom, paid it for him.[51] Gentlemen sometimes took advantage of accidental encounters to retaliate when Dorchester people were outside the town's protecting walls. In 1626 Stephen Ward of Knighton abused the bailiff, Edmund Dashwood, on the highway, while a few years later a group led by Ralph Arnold ambushed the mercer Henry Symes on his way home from Evershot Fair.[52]

The growing antagonism between town and country gentry is well illustrated by Dorchester's relations with the Williams family. The squires of Herringstone, it will be recalled, had long been prominent in Dorchester. Old Sir John Williams had been Matthew Chubb's friend, though also on good terms with William Kethe, the most prominent of Dorset's early puritan clergy. As long as Sir John was alive the family's influence survived, and they continued to cultivate it by subscribing to local charities.[53]

When Chubb and Sir John both died in 1617 the old harmony ended. The town was becoming increasingly independent – less willing to kowtow to the gentry – and increasingly puritan, which the younger members of the Williams family emphatically were not. In 1623 disaster struck. The new squire, John Williams, old Sir John's grandson, stabbed the tapster during a drunken brawl at the George and the man died of his wounds. The coroner's jury brought in a verdict of manslaughter, and at the Lent Assizes in 1624 Williams was convicted. Williams could not plead benefit of clergy under the archaic procedure which let off first offenders literate enough to read the biblical 'neck verse', because this procedure was statutorily denied to anyone convicted of manslaughter by stabbing. So he fled to France while his friends bestirred themselves. He was after all a gentleman, not the sort of person to be hanged for having had the bad luck to kill a mere tapster; a fit person for the King's mercy, the judge, Sir Richard Hutton, thought. Money changed hands (Whiteway heard that the pardon cost Williams £1,500), the Digbys, just beginning to establish themselves in the county at Sherborne Castle, used their influence, and at the summer Assizes the judges recommended the pardon, which was granted on 27 July. Dorchester people were outraged. Patroclus Cooke, never one to mince words, openly criticised Hutton's colleague on the bench, Chief Baron Tanfield, and had to be dismissed from his office of town serjeant. But Williams, returning to Herringstone after eight months in France, must have realised that his family's influence in the town was at an end. [54]

In 1629 he struck back. He had begun rebuilding his position in the county, courting the new Lord-Lieutenant, the second Earl of Suffolk, who got him a commission in the trained bands and appointment to one of those honorific posts so beloved of aspiring gentlemen, in this case Keeper of the King's Game in the Manor of Fordington. Dorchester residents had always been in the habit of poaching in the fields around the town, and it was not long before Williams was able to catch Henry Maber – a mere 'mechanic', Williams sneered, though he was in truth a highly respectable clothier – out there with his fowling piece. Williams confiscated the gun, but Maber continued his nefarious ways, now using a greyhound; 'as if he had no king to command him', Williams exploded to Suffolk, 'or himself had been exempted from the obedience of a subject, which is the damnable opinion of a Puritan'. He ordered Maber to hand over the greyhound, and sent his servant into Dorchester to collect it. By now, however, Maber was constable and in no mood to surrender. He refused to give up the dog, there was the inevitable scuffle, and the servant was locked up for assault. Williams asked Suffolk to report Maber's 'seditious' behaviour to the Council, and to urge them to curb 'the restless and turbulent daring spirit of these Dorcestrians, who factiously contemn all law and justice that is without their own precinct'. Maber was duly summoned to Whitehall, but no formal complaint was made so he was allowed to go home. A few months later the council directed five Dorset gentlemen to investigate the matter, but nothing came of it – not surprisingly in view of the inclusion of Recorder Ashley, John Browne, and Sir

Thomas Trenchard, all friends of the town, among them.[55]

John Williams died in 1632. He had long since given up paying his family's last paternalist tribute to the town, the annuity to the Women's Almshouse, and shortly before his death the Corporation was considering legal action over it. Whether it was ever paid again is not clear; his widow at least offered an olive branch in the shape of a gift of five pounds to Dorchester's poor. But it was not until the last decade of the century that members of the family were again buried in St Peter's church.[56]

John Williams of Herringstone was not the only member of his family to be at odds with the town. One evening in November 1634 Constables Righton and William Loder, with an accompanying watchman, were called to the alley behind the Antelope where three gentlemen were creating a disturbance. One of them was yet another John Williams, of Fryer Mayne, a cousin of the Herringstone family, and with him were Thomas Thornhurst, also of Mayne, and Robert Fitzjames of Bradford Peverel. Incensed at being questioned, the three gentlemen asked to see the 'hue and cry' warrant on which the constables claimed to be acting. Loder and Righton read it aloud, but refused to hand it over for them to examine. One of them thereupon blew out the constables' candle and knocked Loder down. Fitzjames threatened to beat out his brains, while Thornhurst called for a brace of pistols. More watchmen were summoned, and somehow the unruly trio were taken before the mayor, where there was more abuse before they agreed to pay their fines and Thornhurst and Fitzjames were bound over to keep the peace. Loder was conciliatory, however, presumably on the advice of people who did not want to embroil the town any further with influential county families, and a fortnight later withdrew the charges. The third member of the trio, Williams, wisely kept a low profile. He was fined only a shilling for swearing – Fitzjames and Thornhurst were each fined 17s. – and had sensibly stayed in the background during the scuffle behind the Antelope. But the incident was a classic confrontation between members of the landed gentry, accustomed to swaggering through the streets of county towns and doing more or less as they pleased, and Dorchester's determined reformers.[57]

The growing gulf between the townsmen and their gentry neighbours can be seen in other matters where their interests collided: the militia, for example. By 1629 Dorchester wanted its own militia company, free from the control of the gentry who ran the county trained bands. Having failed to get it in the new charter of that year, they petitioned the Council and the Lord-Lieutenant. Suffolk was not enthusiastic (he had been equally unhelpful during the charter negotiations), and referred the issue back to his Deputy Lieutenants in Dorset. Led by Sir Thomas Freke, the Deputies showed 'so much coldness and unwillingness', Whiteway tells us, that it came to nothing. Freke had originally not been unpopular in the town, but now he too was seen as an enemy: 'the county well rid of him', Denis Bond observed when he died in 1633. The town's suspicions of the Dorset gentry were fully reciprocated. During his travels around the county the topographer Thomas Gerard heard much about Dorchester's 'severe government', and the 'many censures' the gentry levelled at its magistrates because of it. One local squire, Angell Grey, was 'no friend to the Puritans', Anthony Ashley Cooper remarks, 'and by consequence not in love with his neighbours of Dorchester, who were totally devoted that way'.[58]

A case that occurred at some time between October 1638 and September 1639 again showed how easily Dorchester could become embroiled with powerful people in the county. A constable, Gifford Bale, assisted by the puritan shoemaker Thomas Grindham, had arrested some fiddlers and put them in prison. One of the Gollops (perhaps Henry again) tried to protect them – he may indeed have brought them to Dorchester in the first place – so Bale and Grindham imprisoned him too. Unfortunately they did all this without a proper warrant: Gollop brought suit at the Assizes for wrongful imprisonment, subjecting Bale and Grindham to heavy legal costs. Even more unfortunately, Gollop was protected by the powerful Digbys at Sherborne Castle; John White had to be enlisted to write to Lord Digby and compose the differences between Gollop and Bale. The whole affair illustrates once again how conflict in Dorchester so often ranged town against country, urban middling sort against country gentry.[59]

But it was not only the gentry who resented Dorchester's vigorous enforcement of godly reformation. It would be an exaggeration to portray the cultural conflict being waged in early seventeenth-

century England as one between reformist towns and a still unregenerate countryside – the distribution of godly and ungodly is too often
blurred in both directions – but this was certainly one element in the
situation in Dorset. As a thriving market as well as the Assize town,
Dorchester constantly attracted visitors from the surrounding rural
area, and those visitors often went looking for a good time when
their business was done. Many were the nights when the watch had
to be called to put down drunken carousing at the Ship, the George,
or one of the other hostelries, and discovered that the culprits were
countrymen – graziers from Blackmore Vale, husbandmen from one
of the downland villages. A Chaldon butcher went on a four-day
pub-crawl in the town in February 1637, and had to be put in prison
because he refused to leave. Such people often got into fights, like
the two Puddletown labourers who squared off outside Standish's
alehouse in 1632, or assaulted watchmen trying to keep the peace.
The innkeepers were totally unable to control them. When the constables told William Wilson to keep better order at the Ship after
finding a group of countrymen 'singing, tippling, and swearing', he
shrugged his shoulders and said he was powerless. Sometimes, as
we have seen, the watchmen were corrupted by offers of free beer.
The town authorities were struggling, they felt, to maintain an island
of godliness in a sea of depravity washing against, and over, their
walls.[60]

Confronted by the magistrates disorderly visitors were sometimes
appropriately contrite, like the Owermoigne man who was 'very
sorrowful': Mayor Joliffe remitted half his fine. More often, though,
the original offence was aggravated by additional abuse. A man from
Sydling, Richard Christmas's village, told the constables to be
hanged and said that Bailiff Savage could 'go shit'. A Maiden Newton man uttered dire threats against the mayor and boasted that he
'feared not the proudest in Dorchester'. Rural hostility to the austere
Dorchester magistrates was aggravated by the differing religious
complexions of town and region, and many people were conscious
of this. 'None but a Puritan would say so or tax him for it,' a Poxwell
man exclaimed when his friend was warned for swearing: 'it was a
puritan law which he spake.' Godly reformation, some Dorset folk
believed, had reduced the townsmen to an abject level of conformity.
'A plague of God on the slaves of Dorchester!' a Cerne Abbas man
shouted when arrested for drunkenness in April 1634. She would

'rather believe any drunkard in Chard than any Puritans of Dorchester', a woman who had recently moved to the town declared.[61]

So there was a rural component in the resistance to godly rule.
Restive townsfolk could take their cue from the gentry, for the ties
of patronage that had existed in Matthew Chubb's day had certainly
not withered away completely. Among the minor offices which the
gentry could staff with their dependants was that of sheriff's bailiff,
and it is striking how many of the bailiffs from Dorchester were at
odds with the town authorities. There were of course jurisdictional
as well as ideological reasons for this: the town was sensitive about
its privileges and quick to complain about the execution of warrants
without the mayor's permission. Not all the bailiffs were unruly
reprobates: a list of them in 1632 includes such virtuous borough
officers as Benjamin Derby and Nathaniel Bower. Still, the ones
who caused most trouble were on the other side: the two Roger
Pounceys (father and son), the shoemaker Robert Warman, the
weaver Sampson Harris, and a few others. They were often accused
of routine offences like drinking and swearing, and it must have
given the JPs especial pleasure to convict them, as they did when
Harris was late for church and they could reject his excuse that he
had been on official business for the under-sheriff, or when he was
caught tippling at Thomas Pouncey's.[62]

There was a typical affray at Dorchester Assizes in March 1631.
Two townsmen came to the Shire Hall to stand surety for a Purbeck
man. Roger Pouncey and Warman drove them out of the Hall, Pouncey shouting 'A pox of God on you! We have no greater enemies
than our townsmen.' 'For a company of such factious knaves [as]
Bower,' he went on, '. . . they could not be quiet.' Exactly why
Pouncey was so angry at Bower and the two sureties the sources do
not disclose, but that the quarrel ranged puritan townsmen against
the bailiffs and their gentry patrons is clear enough. Two months
later the younger Roger Pouncey was still complaining about the
town's obstructiveness. Bailiff Savage, he said, had 'cozened' the
High Sheriff in another case, and Pouncey also abused the constable,
Richard Williams (whom he attacked with a corn pike), and the
Keeper of the Gaol, Thomas Devenish. Williams, said Pouncey, was
a 'chandling knave and long nosed knave', thus combining sneers at
Williams's occupation and his puritan snooping.[63] The elder Pouncey had made himself useful to Matthew Chubb in earlier days: he

and his son were still serving the families of Chubb's gentry friends even as the town authorities became increasingly unsympathetic to their views.

It may help us to understand the division within the town if we take another look at the Pouncey family, which had always been at odds with the reformers. We often come across them in the offenders' book – in drunken brawls and punch-ups, sometimes stemming from their service to the country gentry as sheriff's bailiffs, and as authors of many a scathing comment about the constables and other agents of reformation, even about Mr White. Virtually all of them were butchers, and it may be that the nature of that occupation – the familiarity it engendered with blood, violence, and the physical – made its members particularly hostile to puritan discipline. Besides the Pounceys, several other families in the trade (the Haggards, Tewxburys, Hutchinses, and to a lesser extent the Fookes and Standishes) were notoriously on the same side.

The Pounceys had been in Dorchester at least since 1570, when a certain John Pouncey married Margaret Haggard. They raised a large family of children, including two sons, Thomas and Roger, who survived throughout our period. The first named – Thomas the elder – lived a fairly quiet life: one absence from church and a couple of drinking offences are the only charges recorded against him between 1629 and 1637, and he was sufficiently responsible to serve on juries occasionally. His son, Thomas the younger, on the other hand, was a hard-drinking, foul-mouthed thug, always in trouble. We encounter him on the Weymouth road, throwing his meat cleaver at Robert George and threatening to kill him; beating a Martinstown man on the highway; terrorising the maid at an alehouse; breaking the bullkeeper's head; and repeatedly abusing constables, serjeants, and anyone else who stood in his way. His family and neighbours were not spared. In 1633 he was bound over to keep the peace towards his stepmother, and in 1637, when he was charged with drunkenness and attempting to stab a female neighbour, it was noted that his wife had run away and left their children at the church door. She no doubt had a good deal to run away from.[64]

We can dismiss Thomas Pouncey as a brutal thug, but there is perhaps a bit more to be said about him. His moral code was very different from that of the town's governors, but he did have one. At its heart was a strong sense of personal identity and self-worth. If his rights were violated and he was the victim of what he thought was injustice Thomas was quick to protest, as we shall find him doing after he was conscripted for the Isle de Rhé expedition in 1627.[65] And he often did feel himself to be the victim of injustice, so his outbursts against mayors and other agents of authority were correspondingly frequent. His code is well illustrated by an incident in October 1637. He was drinking at Christopher Edmonds's alehouse in a group that included a young country fellow, Richard Paty. Words were exchanged, and Pouncey and Paty went out into the open space known as 'the Castle', where they had a fist fight. They then returned to the alehouse, 'all bloody with fighting', and resumed drinking together. It was a primitive code in which insults had to be avenged, but could then be forgotten after a fair fight.[66]

Thomas's cousin, the younger Roger Pouncey, was somewhat less violent, and most of his brushes with the law in Dorchester arose out of the performance of his duties as a sheriff's bailiff. Still, he had a colourful way with words – on one occasion he was alleged to have uttered twenty-four oaths at a sitting – and he too was more than willing to denounce the town authorities in violent terms, or even assault them, as he did Constable Williams.[67] Roger, however, was a far less significant figure than his father, Roger Pouncey senior.

This is the Roger Pouncey who, it will be recalled, was a member of Matthew Chubb's circle, the dependent to whom Chubb left a small legacy. He became by far the most prosperous member of his family, to judge by the number of occasions on which he gave bond for his kinsmen and neighbours, a service he performed more frequently than anyone else in Dorchester. When Anne and John Treamor are charged with 'keeping a house suspected of bawdry', it is to Roger Pouncey that they turn for help. When Joseph Dare is charged with escaping from prison, it is Roger Pouncey who gives bond for him. When the weaver Joseph Taylor is accused of drunkenly assaulting Constable Symonds, or the glover Peter Trask of 'riding at Constable Bridges's child', it is again Roger Pouncey who gives security. Mothers of bastards, keepers of unlicensed alehouses – whatever the offence, they all seem to go to Roger Pouncey for help. He was, in his way, a sort of godfather to the unruly and unregenerate of Dorchester.[68]

But Roger Pouncey was something more than a benign father figure to the disorderly. Like the rest of his family, he was deeply hostile to the reformist ruling group in the town. He may have had some attachment to the alternative belief system – which included beliefs in the efficacy of magical remedies against witchcraft and sorcery – that the Puritans were also trying to eradicate. In July 1634, in one of the few witchcraft cases that occurred in Dorchester during this period, thatch from the accused woman's roof was taken to his house and ceremonially burned in the fireplace, with the aim of luring the witch there. Like his son, old Roger had been a sheriff's bailiff; some of his anger against the Dorchester JPs may have arisen from this. But his earlier history, particularly the association with Chubb, suggests that the antagonism went deeper than the accident of his service to a rival authority.[69]

In 1637 all his hostility to the rule of the puritan reformers, and to their cultural repressiveness in particular, boiled over when Roger was involved in a lawsuit against his kinsman and fellow butcher, Matthew Haggard. The case began badly for him. 'He came to Mr Mayor for justice and could have none done,' Pouncey bellowed at Mayor Gould. He had already unwisely told Nathaniel Bower that the JPs had encouraged Haggard to 'take a false oath' against him, and had threatened to complain to Lord Chief Justice Finch at the next Assizes. According to Haggard, Pouncey had been using language like this for months, at least since the time of Gould's predecessor as mayor, John Hill. He would petition Finch, he said, to 'turn out Hill the mayor, Constable Blockhead and Constable Derrick' – Constables Cooke and Bridges, Haggard helpfully explained. 'Blockhead' needs no translation, but 'Derrick' calls for one: the word was an early seventeenth-century nickname for hangmen, which reveals a lot about Pouncey's feelings towards people like Bridges. But it is only one example of the old man's constant abuse of the authorities. If the constables came with a warrant, he declared on Whit Monday, he would 'kill them or knock them in head, though he were hanged tomorrow for it'. After a fire at a neighbour's house, Pouncey expressed the wish 'that all the town were on fire'. His most interesting idea, however, was to dream of getting 'a license from the King to bait a bear'; he would then 'bait the bear at Hill's nose . . . and Constable Blockhead and Constable Derrick's nose, in spite of their teeth'.[70]

Old Roger Pouncey was an angry and embittered man. But he had a good sense of symbolic action: next only to the maypole, bear-baiting was the most powerful available expression of the traditional culture that was now under attack from the reformers. He was obviously well aware that such symbols were greatly in favour with certain people at Court, and that bear-baiting would be as much of an affront to the Puritans in Dorchester as the Sunday theatrical performances that Matthew Chubb had once patronised. Had Roger himself attended that performance at the George Inn all those years before? He may well have done; he certainly remembered the performing bears that had been common in the neighbourhood in his youth, one of which his old patron had alluded to when he threatened to play 'Hunckes the great bear' and to break the Puritans' backs.

Better than anyone else in the Dorchester of the 1630s, the elder Pouncey personifies the constellation of forces ranged against the godly. He had served Matthew Chubb, and (as a bailiff) the county gentry who succeeded Chubb as the leading enemies of reform. He went to church, as he was required to do, but he also held some of the magical beliefs that the Puritans saw as survivals of pagan superstition. His allies were the idle and ungodly riff-raff who maintained, when they could, the ancient festive rituals on which the godly were waging relentless war. His enemies were the solemn reformers – Bridges the hanging constable, the officious Lawrence Righton, and their like. Roger Pouncey had counterparts in many parts of England. The day would come when the conflict between the Pounceys and their reforming enemies – a conflict about the entire moral nature of their communities – would move out of the courts and on to the battlefield.

6

DORCHESTER AND
THE KINGDOM
1600–1642

ENGLAND a battleground? The prospect was unthinkable, even in
1637. Yet for years there had been warnings of trouble ahead. One
day in February 1622 the quiet of Dorchester's streets had been inter-
rupted by an itinerant tailor named Spearing. He came running
through the town, shouting 'Woe, woe to Rome, that bloody city,'
adding, Whiteway tells us, 'many other woes to divers other persons,
but especially unto Papists and Jesuits.' Some said that he was mad
– 'distracted' – and so perhaps he was. Yet the timing of his demon-
stration, and the language used by the otherwise obscure Goodman
Spearing, suggest that if this was madness there was some method
in it.[1]

Six weeks earlier James I had dissolved Parliament. The 1621 session had opened in a mood of high optimism. Most of the members
looked forward to helping their king defend the territories of his
son-in-law, Frederick of the Palatinate, in other words to some effective intervention in the Thirty Years War on the protestant side. The
Commons voted two subsidies, were allowed to take proceedings
against corrupt officials, including Lord Chancellor Bacon, and
before they adjourned in the summer swore to sacrifice lives and
fortunes for the Palatinate. But the hopes of protestant firebrands
were disappointed. James I wished to restore his daughter and her
husband to their principality, but by diplomacy, not war: by enlisting
Spanish influence through the marriage of his son Charles to the
Infanta of Spain. When in November the Commons petitioned
against the 'Spanish Match' there was an angry response from James
– the adjournment and subsequent dissolution of Parliament.[2]

Spearing's appearance in Dorchester thus took place against a background of national uncertainty and fear – fear of the marriage of the heir to the throne to a Catholic princess. Who could forget the last time an English monarch had married a Habsburg, when Mary Tudor's union with Philip of Spain had led to the burning of the protestant martyrs at Smithfield? Already there were suspicions that James was too inclined to tolerate recusants, for he had recently rejected a petition for more forceful application of the laws against them.

Debate over two alternative foreign policies – between the protestant crusade and the Spanish match – dominated the early 1620s. The issue concerned many people in Dorchester, and is a constant subtext in Whiteway's diary. He, Bond, and their friends assumed, we may recall, that the ultimate conflict between good and evil, between the forces of Christ and of Antichrist, was imminent. That, rather than complicated dynastic intrigues, was for them what the Thirty Years War was about. Neutrality in such a struggle was inconceivable; James I's preference for diplomacy seemed pusillanimous and unmanly. The Spanish match would entangle England in an alliance with the wrong side, and lead to the toleration of English Catholics, perhaps eventually to their taking over the kingdom. Bond and Whiteway were loyal subjects, so such beliefs got them into difficulties. They were unwilling to question their lawful ruler, apt (like virtually all their contemporaries) to assume that when they protested it was only against his corrupt ministers. The inconsistencies which afflicted so many people because their political vocabulary precluded the notion of opposition to the crown were as evident in Dorchester as anywhere else. In the end some people were forced to resolve them in a civil war.

Dorchester was no rural backwater. Whiteway's writings are packed with information about both national and international affairs, information which he must have gleaned from newsletters, from gossip picked up through his family's trading contacts in London and abroad, and through its members' service in Parliament. His father-in-law, John Parkins, sat for Dorchester in 1621, his own father in 1624 and 1625, and he himself was elected to fill a vacancy during the 1626 Parliament, though there is no evidence that he actually attended. John White must have received plenty of news from the puritan clerical network, from friends among the Dorset gentry, and through his involvement in the colonial companies. Other sources of news must have included the Palatinate refugees who arrived later in the decade, bringing stories of Catholic oppression in their homeland. Rulizius, White's assistant at St Peter's, was an active fundraiser for the German Protestants, and when he left Dorchester it was to enter the service of James I's daughter Elizabeth of Bohemia, the 'Winter Queen' and protestant cult-figure.[3]

Dorchester people also had access to news at the many fairs and markets that were within easy reach; Woodbury Fair, the greatest of them, attracted traders from all over the country. A good many of the townspeople had visited London. When Whiteway was there on a sightseeing trip in 1631 he attended sessions of the Courts of Star Chamber and High Commission, each time when cases with strong political content were being heard. The town was also reminded of the business of the kingdom by royal proclamations and letters from the Council, and by the visits of the Justices of Assize, whose charges to grand juries regularly touched on public affairs. Occasionally there were more exalted visitors. During the 1625 war preparations the commander of the Cádiz expedition, Sir Edward Cecil, spent the night in Dorchester on his way to the fleet at Plymouth; the King himself was expected, though he did not come. After the fleet had sailed, the Earl of Holland and the great Duke of Buckingham passed through, incognito, during their journey back to London.[4]

So Dorchester folk knew what was happening in the world around them. We catch glimpses of them discussing the news of the day: in May 1635, for example, when some of the Brewhouse staff were chatting about a rumour that Spanish ships had anchored off the Isle of Wight. Members of the elite were naturally better informed, and as usual our best source for their outlook is William Whiteway. The diarist's upbringing, religion, and wide reading in continental history all predisposed him to a highly polarised view of the world. In his diary the 1618 comet is quickly followed by the beheading of Sir Walter Ralegh, and by the 'great stir' in Bohemia which precipitated the Thirty Years War. Whiteway must have seen the significance of Ralegh's execution – the symbolic sacrifice of the last great Elizabethan to James I's pro-Spanish policy – and he noted that it was 'much lamented by the Londoners'. It was also lamented in Dorset, where Sherborne Castle, which Ralegh had rebuilt, was soon to be handed over to James I's ambassador in Madrid, the future Earl of Bristol. In Dorchester verses were written in Ralegh's honour. Events in Germany were also closely watched by the townsmen. In November 1620 there was a nation-wide collection for the defence of the Palatinate (Dorchester contributed the impressive sum of £150), and Mr White held a 'solemn fast with long prayers' for the Bohemian Protestants. Alas, by the time a second such fast was held on 1 December news had already arrived of the protestant disaster at the Battle of the White Mountain.[5]

Even before the 1621 Parliament assembled James had tried to stifle criticism by issuing a proclamation that, as Whiteway read it, prohibited discussion of 'matters of state, either of this kingdom or of any other place'. In 1622, two days after the suspension of the Elizabethan penal laws against recusants, drastic restrictions on preaching were announced: only bishops and deans could discuss formerly uncontroversial doctrines like predestination, and all clergy were to avoid 'matters of state' and eschew 'bitter invectives' against the Catholics. But the tide of debate could not be stilled: the early 1620s were years of unprecedented political excitement.[6]

Whiteway, like most English Protestants outside the Court, followed the Spanish negotiations with gloomy resignation, particularly in 1623, when Prince Charles and Buckingham were in Madrid. In August of that year the fleet put in at Portland en route to Spain, Whiteway believed, to bring home 'the Prince and his lady'. Never one to miss a spectacle, he rode down to Portland to see it. While he was in London a few weeks later the situation changed dramatically. Rumours spread that Charles had become weary of the Spaniards' delays and evasions, even that he had come home and had landed at Portsmouth. This was what Englishmen wanted to hear, and, Whiteway reports, 'ballads were made of it'. The ballad-singers were promptly imprisoned, but they had been premature by less than a month, for on 5 October the Prince and Buckingham did arrive at Portsmouth, without the Infanta: the Spanish match was dead. Charles was mobbed by delirious crowds and there was jubilation throughout the kingdom, with bells and bonfires everywhere. There was greater sobriety in Dorchester, but the bells rang out joyfully, and Denis Bond, who had just become bailiff, had the town's 'great ordnance' dragged outside the walls to fire a salute.[7]

This was not the only time that the bells were rung on public occasions. Most of the ringing was uncontroversial, a conventional expression of loyalty. There was ringing at the proclamation of King Charles I, at the birth of his son, the future Charles II, on 29 May 1630, and annually on 27 March, the anniversary of the King's accession. Some of the other occasions for ringing had a more distinctly protestant flavour. There was always ringing on 5 November, a day that had special meaning for Puritans, whose hatred of Catholicism was even more profound than that of most of their compatriots. So had 17 November, Queen Elizabeth's accession day, when one could contrast what was remembered as her spiritedly anti-Catholic foreign policy with the feebleness of her successors'; nostalgia for Elizabeth was often a coded criticism of the Stuarts. Payments to ringers in Trinity parish are annually recorded on 5 November, but those on the 17th begin only in the 1630s, just when the good old protestant way established in the Queen's days was threatened by Arminian innovations. During that decade 'Queen Elizabeth's day' may have been celebrated with more enthusiasm than Charles I's accession day.[8]

One outburst of bellringing was even more explicitly political: the jubilant peals in October 1631 for the victory of King Gustavus Adolphus of Sweden at Breitenfeld. Whiteway had been recording the ruin of protestant hopes in Germany and the depressing outcome of Charles I's wars against France and Spain with his usual conscientiousness. The Swedish intervention gave him new hope, as it did Protestants everywhere. On 1 April there had been 'a solemn general private fast' in Dorchester to pray for Gustavus's success. 'How far must a man seek another man's good?' the preacher (undoubtedly White) asked, answering that any such decision to seek it must be followed by 'real performance'. Real performance: the Swedes, not the English, were providing it. Before May was out news arrived of further Swedish triumphs and the drums were beaten in Dorchester to raise volunteers for their armies. Breitenfeld confirmed that German Protestantism would after all be saved, and though Gustavus was slain at Lutzen a year later, Whiteway's admiration for Swedish valour remained undimmed. French intervention was to remove whatever religious motivation the Thirty Years War still possessed, but Whiteway died too soon to be disillusioned.[9]

Dorchester people had strong, no doubt oversimplified, views about the great events unfolding on the continent. When Whiteway first took note of conflict between the English and the Dutch in the East Indies he added some timely verses:

> While for their shares of Indian wares
> English and Dutch do brawl,
> The Spaniard watcheth, advantage catcheth
> To seize on them and all.

The lesson was never learned at Whitehall: in June 1634 he glumly observed how 'the whole Court leans much to the Spanish party'. People below Whiteway's social level shared his prejudices. When the Brewhouse employees heard that Spanish ships were off the Isle of Wight they convinced themselves that the servant from the Antelope looked suspicious; they questioned him and got him to say that if the Spaniards came he would 'fire the town and run away'. 'This is a Spanish rogue,' Jonas Palfrey decided. 'Let him be hanged out of the way,' somebody suggested, but Palfrey thought 'it were best to cut his throat first.' Ordinary folk in Dorchester had automatically anti-Spanish reflexes too.[10]

Worries about an apparently pro-Spanish foreign policy were accompanied by equivalent fears for the state of the English church. As the years passed, the concern of people like Bond and Whiteway about 'Popery and Arminianism' became increasingly evident. Whiteway commended the fortitude of puritan victims of Star Chamber: Alexander Leighton, whose ears were cut off, nose slit, and cheeks branded for writing against the bishops; William Prynne, sentenced to mutilation in 1634 for a book against stage plays that was held to reflect adversely on the Queen. Three years later Prynne was punished again, along with two other Puritans, Burton and Bastwick. 'They were wonderfully patient', Bond reported, so courageous 'that all the beholders, except some ruffians . . . shed many tears'. Whiteway was also interested in the case of Henry Sherfield,

Recorder of Salisbury, fined £600 in Star Chamber for smashing an 'idolatrous' stained-glass window in one of the town's churches. That Sherfield was a leader of a group of urban reformers similar to those in Dorchester would have been well known to Whiteway. While Puritans were being persecuted their enemies were flourishing. An Oxford divine had prayed for the dead, and one at Cambridge had upheld the Catholic doctrine of justification by works, 'and neither of them was questioned for it'.[11]

Equally disturbing was the toleration of sports and festivals which Laud was trying to force down the unwilling throats of the godly. The controversy boiled over in 1633 with the issue of Charles I's *Book of Sports*, enumerating the recreations which might be lawfully enjoyed after church on Sundays. Whiteway reports, not very accurately, the initial stages of the conflict over church ales in Somerset, and the reluctance of many of the clergy to read the 'morris book' (as it was often called, because of its toleration of the 'heathen' morris dances) from their pulpits, as they were ordered to do. John White, not surprisingly, would have nothing to do with it, and ignored all the pleadings of Bishop Coke and his Chancellor, neither of whom wanted to suspend him. There was much praying and self-examination, and White preached on 'The Morality of the Fourth Commandment', defining violating the sabbath by playing 'vain sports' as worse than violating it by working. Some of the local clergy debated questions 'concerning the Lord's Day' propounded by White's friend Richard Bernard. Whiteway seems not to have been entirely convinced that White ought to take the critical step of defying royal commands.[12]

The crisis came in July 1634. Sir Nathaniel Brent, Laud's Vicar-General, was to open the Metropolitan Visitation in Dorchester on the 15th. If White still refused to read the *Book of Sports* he would assuredly be suspended. Still he held out. On Friday the 11th, the day before Brent arrived as the guest of the Trenchards at nearby Wolveton, the churchwardens of St Peter's took matters into their own hands. They got hold of a visiting minister, a Mr Holliday, and persuaded him to read the Book in an empty church; empty, that is, except for the required presence of the parish clerk and the church-wardens. The Book had been publicly read, the proclamation obeyed, and they could certify as much to a grateful bishop. White was 'exceeding angry' when he heard about the subterfuge,

Whiteway tells us, but Brent was feasted by Mayor Joliffe 'at the charge of the town'. There were some uncomfortably anti-puritan sermons by preachers from rural Dorset, one of them denouncing magistrates who punished ministers for frequenting taverns. Fortunately it was Assize week, and the hostile sermons were counterbalanced by a more acceptable one preached by Thomas Fuller, later the author of *England's Worthies*, who was a great conciliator. Although Brent insisted on conformity in such matters as vestments and bowing at the name of Jesus, he assured the Dorset clergy that Laud 'would require no more than hath been required since the Reformation'. He seems not to have noticed that William Benn had also refused to read the *Book of Sports*.[13]

The immediate crisis was over, but Whiteway was still anxious. Ministers were being suspended in many places, and in October 1635 White was again believed to be in danger for refusing to read the Book. His troubles in fact had a different cause. Earlier in the autumn there had been a meeting at John Browne's house in Frampton, attended by White, Benn, and other local ministers. One purpose of the discussion was to dispose of money collected for godly ministers in either England or Massachusetts. Laudian suspicions were aroused – was a revival of the puritan Feoffees for Impropriations, with their nefarious schemes to augment the livings of sympathetic incumbents, in the wind? Browne, White, and their London contacts were summoned before High Commission, and White's study was searched. Documents seized there revealed the extent of his involvement in what was now seen as a seditious puritan network: correspondence with Sir Walter Erle about ministers in the west country, with John Winthrop in Massachusetts; and with someone at Batcombe (presumably Richard Bernard), who prayed that they might be delivered from 'absurd and unreasonable men'. Proceedings dragged on, requiring White's intermittent appearance in London, until they were apparently dropped in May 1636. Perhaps White benefited from the old boy network: the lawyer handling the case against him was another Wykehamist and New College man.[14]

By this time Holy Trinity, and no doubt the other parishes, had to face a different kind of danger. One of the central elements of the Laudian programme was the removal of the communion table from its unsanctified position in the nave, to the more exalted chancel, where it could be railed in and protected from the contaminating irreverence of the vulgar. It was one more insensitive attack on what was by now a well-rooted protestant tradition, threatening to turn the familiar communion table into a 'popish' altar: why else was it to be railed in if not for the celebration of the hated mass? Many English parishes complied, but many did not, and there were some famous acts of defiance, as when the churchwardens of Beckington in Somerset resisted their Laudian bishop. Fortunately for Dorchester Bishop Skinner was no Laudian. Preaching at the Visitation in September 1637 he assured the Dorset clergy that he would 'discountenance nothing but enormities'. Conformity to rites and ceremonies was necessary, of course, but the only ceremonies he mentioned were kneeling during prayers, use of the surplice and vestments by the clergy, and the sign of the cross in baptism – not a word about altar rails. Although Trinity's churchwardens had been cited to appear at Blandford 'about the communion table' there is no sign of their ever complying with any Laudian directives.[15]

Controversies in the church were accompanied by political ones in the state. For a long time the people of Dorchester, like their counterparts elsewhere, did not recognise the implications of their growing alienation from Court and government. And for a long time, partly because of the many institutional and symbolic links that connected them with the central state, they did not have to.

To begin with the obvious: Dorchester was the county town. Next to the churches, the Shire Hall was the most impressive building in the town, one of the major landmarks, a constant reminder of the connections between borough, county, and kingdom. Although the county Quarter Sessions were rarely held in Dorchester, the Assizes were, twice a year, so plenty of county business was transacted in the building. Public notices were exhibited there; in 1628, for example, new orders for the management of the Gaol and the House of Correction were placed on a table in the hall for public inspection. Special judicial commissions also used the Shire Hall. The burgesses did what they could to ensure that justice was dispensed in dignified surroundings. In 1628 they had the royal arms set up in the 'inner hall', and a few years later they provided a new chair for the High Sheriff; in 1638 the building was considerably enlarged at the town's expense.[16]

Twice a year, in March and July, the Assizes transformed the entire life of the town. Assize week was always a distinctive marker in the collective memory. It was during the Assize time, witnesses remembered, that Richard Cox abused his neighbours so scandalously; the Friday of Assize week that John Dowrage entertained his friends to a tippling party. During Assize week the JPs and the gentry, the litigants and the lawyers, all crowded into Dorchester's inns and taverns. That persistent offender against the licensing laws, Clement Baily, was given leave to stay open for a few more weeks in 1632, 'the Assize being near'. The tradespeople did good business: it was thought particularly reprehensible when an apprentice neglected his master's business 'in this busy time'. Even members of the Corporation were affected, and meetings of the Fifteen sometimes had to be cancelled while the Assizes were going on. For young sparks like Robert Way, Assize week was the occasion for a protracted round of merrymaking.[17]

At the Assizes, John White reflected, authority was 'represented as it were upon a stage', the behaviour of great men carefully observed and 'diversely censured' by the populace. The diarist Whiteway, whose father regularly entertained the judges on behalf of the town, kept careful record of who came on circuit, and which of the local clergy had the honour of preaching before them. Some of the preachers were eminent men: Gilbert Ironside in 1631, John White in 1633, Thomas Fuller a year later. Whiteway is usually reticent about the conduct of the judges, so he must have been shocked in 1635 when he noted Chief Justice Finch's bullying manner: Finch was 'exceeding high and quick with the [JPs], lawyers, and bailiffs and all others'.[18]

Occasionally Dorchester's own politics spilled over into the Assizes, as they did when Squire Williams was convicted and then pardoned. People like old Roger Pouncey who felt unjustly treated by the town authorities might bring a complaint at the Assizes, or threaten to do so. More often it was the politics of the region that surfaced, and Dorchester people were of course interested in them too. A case in 1626 had serious political implications. A parson from rural Dorset, Nicholas Day of Hooke, had preached a highly seditious sermon. The land, he said, 'was not governed by justice, but by bribery and extortion', and God's displeasure had been manifest in 'the late repulse' of English forces at Cádiz. Bound over to the Assizes, Day's sureties were Matthew Butler and Richard Williams, both Dorchester men of puritan opinions, who by giving bond for Day must surely have been expressing some support for his views. Another Assize case a few years later involved the inhabitants of Gillingham Forest, who had rioted after being swindled out of their grazing rights by Charles I's government. There was much sympathy for them in Dorchester and Joseph Paty went surety for one of their leaders charged with 'breaking up enclosures'.[19]

Dorchester was thus closely linked with the government of both county and kingdom. Normally there was little trouble; the system seemed part of the unchanging natural order of things. But in the early seventeenth century central government became more intrusive, particularly after Charles I's accession, and the impression grew that many of its priorities were not those of local people, in Dorchester or anywhere else. There had always been some friction over minor routine matters, like the requisitioning of horses for the King's service – as constables from Matthew Chubb to Lawrence Righton well knew. Occasional abuse from aggrieved neighbours was part of the price a constable paid for doing his public duty. But some things were new, like the additional burdens imposed on JPs by the revised regulations issued by the Council in 1631, the 'Book of Orders'. The Dorchester JPs probably did not mind having to publish a 1634 Star Chamber decree on the regulation of inns and alehouses, but they regarded it as a bit of a nuisance when they had to get a license for the Brewhouse. They decided to do so only if they could not 'with safety avoid it'.[20]

The belief that local liberties were being eroded became widespread during the 1620s. This was a war decade, and many of the tensions in and out of Parliament were the result of wartime pressures – generated by conscription, for example – on an inadequate bureaucratic system. This, at any rate, is how it appears to historians nowadays. To contemporaries it often seemed very different. Rightly or wrongly, many of them were convinced that the aggressiveness of central government in collecting taxes and in enforcing unpopular laws endangered ancient rights and liberties, and was the result of the Council's systematic policy of enlarging royal prerogatives. Among the irritants was Charles I's revival of outdated laws for revenue purposes. In 1629 one of the Heralds, Geoffrey Le Neve, arrived in Dorchester with a commission for the enforcement of an old statute requiring localities to provide facilities for archery. By now, too, common informers were becoming even busier than usual, bringing prosecutions against violators of under-enforced and archaic statutes. In this sort of climate the most fraudulent announcements of new government exactions were likely to be believed. A Wiltshire man turned up at the Rose Inn, claiming to have a commission to seize unmarked cattle. There was panic among the farmers and the price of pitch soared to record heights. The 'cheating companion' was unmasked and put in the pillory, but only after people's belief in the central government's inclination to fleece them had been strikingly confirmed. Impostors could be punished, but if the patent was genuine, as that of the man collecting saltpetre for gunpowder in 1635 presumably was, there was little that local magistrates could do to protect their neighbours.[21]

And in the 1620s the war itself had been divisive. The gentry in Parliament, and the populace in the streets, might celebrate the end of the Spanish Match and look forward to a renewal of the good old Elizabethan protestant crusade, but neither the elite (through their purses) nor the common folk (in their persons) seemed anxious to make the sacrifices necessary for that crusade to succeed. Part of the trouble was that when war did come, it was the wrong sort of war. In 1624 hawkish backbenchers thought they were voting for an old-fashioned naval war which would bring the Habsburgs to their knees and restore Frederick and Elizabeth to the Palatinate, simply through a well-timed interception of the Spanish treasure fleet. Instead, the taxpayers' money disappeared into the swamps of an ineffective land campaign under the German commander, Count Mansfeld, and a disastrous naval expedition to Cádiz. When Buckingham blundered into an equally mismanaged war with France, the alienation even of many of the Duke's erstwhile supporters was complete.

Whiteway and his friends were unhappy about misdirected strategy and incompetent tactics, and suspicious of both Buckingham's ability and his ultimate intentions, but they were not really against war with Spain. Among people of lower rank there was plenty of anti-Spanish, anti-Catholic feeling, but it is doubtful if there was much warlike enthusiasm. For the more substantial war meant increased taxation; for poor men it meant possible conscription, perhaps death on foreign soil. For everyone it meant the unwelcome presence of ill-paid, hungry, undisciplined soldiers in their neighbourhood.

Conscription – impressment, to use the seventeenth-century term – was a burden that fell almost entirely on poor, unmarried men. Between 1624 and 1628 Dorchester was subjected to at least seven bouts of impressment. Fourteen 'lusty fellows' were marched off to Dover in November 1624 to join Mansfeld; few of them came back. In 1625 ten were impressed for the fleet that was fitting out at Plymouth; eight more were subsequently called up but quickly demobilised, the fleet having already sailed for Cádiz. There were further demands in 1627 for Buckingham's ill-fated expedition to the Isle de Rhé: eighteen townsmen were sent to Portsmouth in the spring and a few more followed in the summer and autumn. In June the Dorset Deputy Lieutenants warned the Council that if more men were needed they would have to come from the normally exempt householders and trained band soldiers. In April 1628 they could find only seventy of the county's quota of one hundred, protesting that to get more they would have to take 'shepherds from their flocks, husbandmen from their ploughs, or poor labouring men from their wives and many children'.[22]

Almost without exception the Dorchester conscripts were the kind of poor, marginal riff-raff that constables always tried to unload on the army. Thirty-one of them can be identified, and they include some familiar names: Clement Baily, the often suppressed alehousekeeper; John Chimney, known to us for his 'idle course of life', the regular accomplice of Robert Sampson in many a nocturnal burglary; the disorderly parchmentmaker Robert Foote. Another, William Cox, deserted his wife and drifted from job to job; in 1632 he said he was 'breaking wool' for one of the clothiers but the JPs treated him as masterless and put him in Bridewell. Soon he was on poor relief and was sent to work at the Hospital. Equally, the journeyman

blacksmith Hugh Counter was regularly fined or stocked for drunkenness. Almost all the conscripts we know anything about were
people of this kind.[23]

Two of those impressed in 1627, however, were not. Thomas
Saunders later lived respectably as a journeyman shoemaker, conscientiously doing his duty as a watchman, and going on poor relief
only in the aftermath of the civil war, when many other people were
ruined, too. Another of the conscripts is better known to us: the
younger Thomas Pouncey. Violent and rebellious, he was also more
independent and self-reliant than any of the others. That he was also
among the very few from a level of society somewhat above the
bottom rung strongly suggests that he was deliberately singled out.
The constables who made the selection, Richard Bury and Richard
Williams, were both men of puritan sympathies, probably happy to
punish the Pounceys for the trouble they had so often caused the
godly.

Pouncey was so incensed by what happened to him that when he
got back to Dorchester he and one of his companions wrote, or more
likely dictated, a 'true relation' of their experiences. They told an
interesting story. After receiving the warrant from the Deputy Lieutenants, Sir John Browne and Henry Hastings, the constables went
round the town looking for suitable recruits. They came to the shop
of the weaver Robert Snook and found him at work with his four
men and a boy. The constables asked 'which of those he would
willingest spare to be a soldier?' Snook silently pointed to the boy,
even though the others were all 'very able men'. Things were no
better elsewhere in the county. Browne and Hastings released a
miller, 'an extraordinary stout man', and took instead another boy,
only fifteen years old. By the time Pouncey's company got to Portsmouth the 300 men who had left Dorset had dwindled to 160. Most
of the 'best and most able men' had bribed their way to freedom;
the price was either five or ten pounds, though it is not clear who
got the money. The remnant included men with various deformities,
including one with no toes. The unit must have resembled the one
an officer at Weymouth complained of a year later – 'more fitting
for an hospital than for the King's service'.[24]

Thomas Pouncey's relation tells us a lot about the quality of the
troops sent to the Isle de Rhé, as well as about early Stuart government and class relations. His willingness to speak out suggests that

even a butcher's son may have absorbed ideas about justice, good government, the rights of Englishmen. As sheriffs' bailiffs, the Pounceys were at the lower end of a patronage network controlled by the gentry. But this did not mean that they were obsequious boot-lickers. Anthony Ashley Cooper remembered Henry Hastings as the very epitome of the paternalist squire, genial and hospitable, a sort of rural Matthew Chubb. As with Chubb, there was another side to him, though, which offended Thomas Pouncey's standards of 'good rule'.[25]

A few dozen Dorchester men suffered from impressment during Buckingham's wars. Many more suffered from having disorderly soldiers billeted on them. Billeting troops on civilians was often unavoidable in the seventeenth century, and it always caused trouble. Householders were supposed to be compensated for it, but in practice they might not get the money for years. Dorchester's first serious encounter with billeting came in the autumn of 1626, when a thousand dispirited survivors of the Cádiz expedition were moved from Devon and Cornwall. They were quartered around Dorchester at a cost to the county of over ten thousand pounds; nobody ever received a penny for it, except to the extent that some of the money was later charged off against tax assessments. It is not clear how much of this force was billeted in Dorchester itself; Whiteway says only that it cost the townsmen two pounds a week for the lieutenant-colonel and 16s. a week for the other officers. In March 1627 the soldiers were ordered to march off to Winchester, but they refused to go until each man extracted 8s. from the householder on whom he had been billeted.[26]

The 'great ease' people received from their departure did not last long. In January 1628 some of the ragged remnants of the Isle de Rhé expedition marched into Dorset, and thirty-six men of Sir Thomas Fryer's regiment were billeted in the town. There were loud complaints – people had still not been paid for their losses during the previous year – and even the Deputy Lieutenants threatened to join in a protest petition. The 'richer sort', they announced, flatly refused to receive any more soldiers, and according to the officers the men were often forcibly 'turned out of their billets'. The country people told a different story. As Sir Walter Erle reported it to the House of Commons in April: the soldiers 'disturb markets and fairs, rob men on the highway, ravish women, breaking houses in the night and enforcing men to ransom themselves, killing men that have assisted constables'. During the previous year Ashley had got half a dozen of the Cádiz levies condemned to death for burglary. But the Council intervened – the men were 'able and experienced in the wars'. So they were pardoned and sent to the Isle de Rhé instead, which may not have been much of a reprieve.[27]

On 11 April 1628 Fryer's men marched away to join a force that was to assist the French Huguenots in La Rochelle. They never got there, and by the 23rd they were back again. The sporadic resistance of the previous winter flared up once more. Encouraged by the influential Richard Bushrod, several times bailiff and MP for the town, the wealthier householders refused to accept any soldiers at all. So they were quartered in the inns and taverns, and on 'divers poor men'; a year later only a third of the cost had been paid, and that out of Fryer's pocket. Sir Thomas complained to Buckingham, and got a special commission appointed to investigate Bushrod's conduct. Fortunately for Dorchester it included Sir Thomas Trenchard and two of the Brownes, always friends of the town, so nothing came of it. But the townspeople still wanted compensation. When John Conduit was in London about the charter in 1629 he was told to press for repayment, but he had no success, and in 1633 the Corporation again petitioned for the money. The Council blandly told them to get it from the proceeds of the 1627 Forced Loan, the balance of which was still in the collectors' hands. This was about as futile as the alternative of suing the Deputy Lieutenants for it, which was also discussed.[28]

The other great issue that embroiled the King's government with the localities was taxation. Compared with most European countries, England in the early seventeenth century was not heavily taxed. But this did not make its subjects any less indignant when they felt they were being taxed unfairly. Dorchester people had strong views about what was legal and what was not. The King's customary revenues and subsidies properly voted by Parliament were usually paid without dissent, even though during the 1620s the burden of parliamentary taxation was increasing. There were more subsidies, and more people were having to pay them: the twenty-nine Dorchester taxpayers of 1610 had increased to forty-five by 1628. Yet in the three subsidies voted in that year for which we have records there were only two defaulters. There were no serious complaints about taxes imposed 'in a parliamentary way'. Whiteway mentions the town's assessment in 1624, but does not bother with it on other occasions, and never records resistance to subsidies, in Dorchester or anywhere else.[29]

Other kinds of taxation might cause more trouble. Attitudes to it were coloured by people's views of its legality, and of the purpose for which it was intended. When James called for a 'voluntary' contribution for the Palatinate in 1620 Dorchester responded generously. The Palatinate was a popular cause; Charles I's wars were not. The 1625 Parliament refused to vote more than two subsidies, so the Council tried to raise the additional money it needed by other means. The first expedient was to ask for loans from selected individuals. Recorder Ashley was asked to 'lend' twenty pounds and eight other Dorchester people to produce ten pounds each, about three times as much as they would have paid under the two missing subsidies. The scheme had no more success in Dorchester than in other parts of the country. All but three of the local people were exempted on grounds of poverty – a not very convincing plea in the case of men like the elder Whiteway, John Parkins, and Richard Blachford. After the dissolution of the 1626 Parliament, which voted no subsidies at all, another attempt to collect a 'voluntary' loan was an equally abject failure, the 'free gift', or benevolence, being met with obstruction nearly everywhere. There is no sign of anyone subscribing in Dorchester; Whiteway says that in the whole county there was 'very little given, and that . . . by Papists and Popish persons'.[30]

The next such attempt, the Forced Loan of 1627, was more serious. It was carefully prepared, there was no pretence that it was anything but compulsory, and the Council wisely combined persuasion and coercion: a firm line with resisters, but a readiness to bargain with those who were unhappy but willing to pay. In the short run the Loan was a spectacular success, raising about £267,000 – about as much as the five subsidies the 1626 Parliament had failed to vote. There was serious resistance in other parts of the country, but in Dorset virtually everybody paid up. But the few local resisters included the lawyer William Savage, a recent arrival in Dorchester, and two powerful county magnates, Sir John Strangways and Sir

Walter Erle, both of whom were imprisoned. One reason for Dorchester's lack of resistance may have been the fact that the Council was holding out the carrot of charging off billeting claims against the Loan, as well as the stick of punishment for refusers. In fact, as we have seen, most of Dorchester's billeting costs were *not* paid out of the Loan, and the Corporation was still vainly petitioning for them years later.[31]

The Loan was a short-term success, but in the end it cost the Council much goodwill. People with unpaid billeting claims felt cheated; worse, the Loan raised fears of unrestrained prerogative taxation. Some who paid and said nothing in public revealed their true feelings in private. Whiteway surely did by his constant harping on the resistance in other places, as did Bond by stressing that the Loan really was 'forced' on the taxpayers.[32] The Loan was a constant undercurrent to the parliamentary debates of 1628, which produced the Petition of Right's famous clause outlawing it and similar exactions. But the Petition did not put an end to worries about unparliamentary taxation. Charles I still collected customs duties ('tonnage and poundage') even though Parliament's earlier grant of these duties had expired. If Whiteway's diary was our only source of information all that we should know about the matter was that there was a 'general refusal' to pay the duties, and that merchants who caved in under pressure were 'much hated', not that the levy was in fact generally paid. The first time Whiteway mentions another of the extra-parliamentary fiscal expedients, composition for knighthood (by which people paid not to have to incur the even greater expense of becoming knights), it is only to note that 'it raised little money, for most men made excuses'. This was true in 1630 when the knighthood commissioners first came to Dorchester, but in the two following years they were more successful, extracting fourteen pounds from John Parkins and ten from Edmund Dashwood. Several other Dorchester people, however, convinced them that their freehold lands were not worth the required forty pounds a year. Efforts to exploit other archaic sources of revenue show how anxious Charles I was not to have to go to Parliament again. In 1632, when the Council was trying to recover old debts due to the crown, the Corporation got a demand for the proceeds of the town's collection for the Palatinate more than ten years before.[33]

All these fiscal experiments paled into insignificance beside the most famous of Charles I's non-parliamentary revenues, Ship Money. Ostensibly raised to provide for coastal defence, and backed by good legal precedents, Ship Money was far more threatening than the earlier emergency levies. It was regular; it was more rationally assessed than the archaic parliamentary subsidies; and it was efficiently collected. The first writ, in November 1634, was directed only to the port towns. But the Weymouth merchants petitioned that Dorchester's trade was just as dependent on naval protection as their own, and one of them, Giles Greene, who had lands in the Isle of Purbeck, got up another petition to the Council asking that part of the Purbeck rate be transferred to Dorchester. The Attorney-General, Sir John Bankes, also lived in Purbeck, so the Council was easily persuaded, and the reluctant High Sheriff, Sir Thomas Trenchard, had to impose an assessment of £200 on the town. It was paid, Whiteway tells us, 'with much grudging'. When later writs extended Ship Money to inland towns and counties Dorchester came off rather better than might have been expected, never having to pay more than forty-five pounds; in 1638, when all assessments were lower, the bill was only eighteen pounds. Until 1638 Ship Money was highly successful. By April 1636 Trenchard had collected more than three quarters of Dorset's £5,000 assessment, and by October 1637 all but £1,200 of the £15,000 required from the county since 1634 had been received.[34]

From all this we might easily conclude that there was no significant opposition to Ship Money until war with the Scots precipitated the crisis of 1639–40. In fact the levy provoked resistance far beyond any previous form of taxation. Whiteway died in 1635, so he cannot be accused of hindsight; but his account emphasises the opposition to the tax – in London, Bristol, Exeter – rather than the fact that most people paid it. John Freke, High Sheriff of Dorset in 1636, had to distrain the goods of many defaulters, and noted that poor people paid it 'like drops of blood'. They 'sell their only cow, which should feed their children', he reflected, and in the end 'most come to the parish'. None of the Dorset towns would rate themselves, so he had to impose one on them. The next sheriff, Richard Rogers, took a tougher line, distraining the goods of influential resisters like John Browne and Sir Walter Erle, but he still had to report a long list of people with unpaid arrears, which included John Parkins, the elder Whiteway, and others from Dorchester.[35]

In 1638 the system began to fall apart as opposition mounted. The new sheriff was overwhelmed with rating appeals, constables refused to pay in money they had collected, and again there were some influential defaulters, including James Gould in his mayoral year. Many who had paid the first levies without serious complaint began to resist when it appeared that Ship Money was not after all a one-time, emergency levy, but an annual substitute for taxes voted 'in a parliamentary way'. By 1640 collapse was imminent. Dorchester would not agree to a rate, and when the sheriff imposed one the Corporation refused to apportion it among the inhabitants. The under-sheriff tried to collect in Dorchester, but could do nothing except by force. When he distrained horses belonging to the widowed Lady Ashley, he was threatened with violence by her servants. Her son-in-law, Denzil Holles, apologised to the Council on her behalf, but matters did not improve. By August neither Dorchester nor any of the other Dorset towns had paid in a penny. People of 'evil disposition', as the sheriff, William Churchill, described them, were obstructing collection all over the county, and some constables simply went into hiding. When cattle were distrained they were either forcibly recovered by their owners, or, if put up for sale, could find no buyers. Churchill did better than some other sheriffs, but still could collect only about half of his quota.[36]

There was a right and legal way of governing, and there was a wrong and oppressive way. In striking contrast to the fuss over Ship Money, when Parliament granted a new subsidy in 1641 the Dorchester Corporation immediately appointed assessors and the money was collected without any trouble.[37] They were loyal subjects; but loyalty to the King did not necessarily extend to confidence in his ministers, especially if they were suspected of lukewarmness, or worse, towards the protestant interest. Suspicion of 'evil councillors' was steadily growing. People like Bond and Whiteway, and others of the 'middling sort', were making up their own minds about the affairs of the kingdom.

They were making up their own minds, not being told what to do by their superiors. Some lesser folk in Dorchester, as we already know, were members of clientage networks controlled by the gentry. The town's governors had friends and allies among the county families – Erles, Brownes, Trenchards – from whom they could expect help if they needed it. But the gentry did not rule the town. There were some peers with local influence, but the Duke of Richmond was no more than a figurehead as High Steward, and of the two Earls of Suffolk, successively Lords Lieutenant of Dorset in this period, only Theophilus, the second Earl, had much to do with the region. Thomas, the first Earl, was more interested in a career at Whitehall; as Lord Treasurer his appetite for gain was too much even by the relaxed standards of the Jacobean Court and he was disgraced for corruption in 1618. His son, the second Earl, was more active in the lieutenancy and worked to build up an interest in the county. John Parkins and the elder Whiteway were among his tenants, and he occasionally made the symbolic gestures expected of the nobility, for example by sending the Corporation gifts of venison. But he was more concerned about his influence in gentry circles than among the plebeian townspeople. It was Suffolk who got John Williams the Keepership of the King's Game, and it was Suffolk who had Henry Maber summoned before the Council at Williams's request. When the Earl was asked to help the town get its own militia company he did nothing.[38]

Dorchester had by now almost completely escaped from the aristocratic and Court influences which had controlled its representation in Elizabethan parliaments. The nearest thing to a patron was the Recorder, Ashley, who was a man of influence both at Court and in legal circles, and always had some say in the election of one of the two members for the borough. He and a local gentleman, George Horsey, were returned for the town in 1614, and the courtier Sir Thomas Edmonds was elected when Ashley resigned his seat to him in 1621, the last time Dorchester was persuaded to accept a Court nominee. But Edmonds chose to sit for another constituency, so Ashley got the seat back. Sir Francis sat again in 1625, and a puritan newcomer, Michael Humphries, in the following year. The other MPs were mostly local men – Parkins, the Whiteways, Richard Bushrod, John Hill. In 1628 Hill was accompanied to Westminster by Ashley's son-in-law, Denzil Holles, younger son of the Earl of Clare, one of a family whose alienation from the Court was well known. At the last minute somebody remembered an old rule that MPs had to be freemen of the borough. The Freemen's Company was hastily assembled and Holles sworn in on the very morning of the election. It was the only business the Company did that day.[39]

These choices were not necessarily political ones. All the local men elected were sympathetic to godly reformation. But an equally important qualification was that they were *local*. The same localism is apparent in county elections, which were held just outside Dorchester – at Poundbury – and aroused keen interest among the townsmen, many of whom voted in the shire as freeholders. Whiteway mentions two particularly acrimonious elections, in 1624 and 1626. The 1624 one looks like a very traditional contest: a struggle for pre-eminence among county families, with no ideological content. Sir George Horsey assured Sir Nathaniel Napper that there would be no opposition to the latter's candidacy, but then swamped him when Napper's supporters did not bother to turn up on polling day. Foul play, certainly, but not the result of a conflict over principles.[40]

1626 was different. This was a distinctly more ideological election than the previous one, with a bloc of Dorchester voters supporting the puritan John Browne of Frampton, who had been living in the town, against Sir George Moreton. When the freeholders gathered at Poundbury they soon agreed on Sir Thomas Freke, not yet as unpopular in Dorchester as he was later to be, for one place. For the other, Whiteway tells us, 'the town cried "A Browne!" . . . and many of the country did the same.' But Sir John Strangways, the most powerful of the county magnates, had his own candidate, the comparative outsider Moreton – and the sheriff, Francis Chaldecote, was in his pocket. He required voters to take an oath that they had been present at the beginning of the election formalities, when the official writ was read out, and disqualified Browne supporters – but not Moreton ones – who could not swear to this. When the count was taken there were still not enough votes for Moreton, so Chaldecote moved the election down to the George Inn, shutting out most of the freeholders and continuing to take votes for Moreton until he had a majority. The Commons overturned the election, but Moreton won again at the second attempt – according to Whiteway because of Strangways's unscrupulous creation of new voters and manipulation of the count. Whatever may be the truth of this, it is striking how closely the alignment of forces corresponds with later ones in the county. On the one side stood Strangways and most of the gentry; on the other the Dorchester townsmen and a minority of gentry families like the Brownes. After Moreton's narrow victory his supporters carried him through the streets 'upon their shoulders in triumph'.[41]

During the 1620s some Dorchester people were beginning to think of politics in confrontational ways. There was no direct, signposted 'high road to civil war', and the divisions in the kingdom were slow to clarify. Still, even in 1624 Whiteway labelled one of the members for Lyme Regis a 'courtier', implying that he thought that such people had different interests from those of the 'country'. The Parliament of 1625 was dissolved, he also tells us, 'with great dislike of both sides' – a revealing remark, for according to the prevailing theory of consensus there could be no such thing as two sides in a seventeenth-century parliament. People *were* beginning to question the competence and integrity of Charles I's ministers; the 1626 Parliament, to which the diarist was elected, spent most of its time on impeachment proceedings against the Duke of Buckingham. The King saved him by a timely dissolution, but in the two following years Whiteway's conviction that the Duke was to blame for all the recent disasters became ever more clear. After the failure at the Isle de Rhé, he acidly comments, Buckingham was received at Court 'as if he had done excellent service', and he unsympathetically records several attacks on the Duke by mutinous sailors. He took the trouble to write down several of the anti-Buckingham verse libels that were being circulated in London, including the mock epitaph that begins, 'I, George Duke of Buckingham, I that my country did betray', and describes him as an 'agent for the Spanish state, the Papists' friend, the Gospel's foe'.[42]

But the issues confronting the kingdom went beyond the incompetence, or even malevolence, of a minister. Whiteway's impressions of the 1628 Parliament are relatively brief and general, but he was obviously aware that something profoundly important was happening. Other Dorchester people were no doubt reminded of it at the Fast Day service held on 21 April to pray for Parliament's success. Early in the session, Whiteway observes, the Commons 'began to vindicate their liberty', and he describes their great achievement, the Petition of Right, as being 'for the expressing of our liberties'. That indeed is how Englishmen everywhere saw it. The Petition summed up their most troubling grievances – the collection of taxes without consent of Parliament; imprisonment without due process of law;

compulsory billeting of soldiers; the use of martial law – and declared each one of them illegal. In many places there were bells and bonfires when Charles I gave his reluctant assent to the Petition. No such celebrations are recorded in Dorchester; perhaps the lack of an explicitly religious dimension to the Petition was the reason for this.[43]

Neither the Petition nor the subsequent assassination of Buckingham led to a return of harmony in the kingdom. During the Parliament's second session, in 1629, Whiteway noted the growing divisions. The Parliament ended in a scene of almost revolutionary passion and excitement. The Speaker, fearing the King's wrath, had tried to adjourn the House to prevent the passage of Sir John Eliot's inflammatory resolutions – against Popery and Arminianism and against the levying of tonnage and poundage – which Whiteway describes as the 'articles of liberty'. But he was forcibly held in the chair while the motions were carried by acclamation. Denzil Holles played a leading role in this violent scene, and after the dissolution he was duly sent to the Tower. All this was followed with close attention in Dorchester. John White and one of his former ministerial colleagues journeyed to London and tried to confer with their imprisoned MP, and in December 1629, while Holles was still in the Tower, the Corporation voted to present him with 'a standing cup of plate . . . for his service done the last Parliament'. It was an unprecedented gesture, and shows very clearly where Dorchester's governors stood in these disputes.[44]

Like Englishmen everywhere, by the end of the 1620s Dorchester people were beginning to feel alienated from the Court. Puritans as many of the leaders were, the increasing favour to Arminians in the church made them even more uncomfortable. Some, indeed, were willing to journey to New England to seek a purer air. Yet however deep the discontent, few thought of real resistance. In March 1633 John White preached before Lord Chief Justice Richardson and his colleague Baron Denham. An Assize sermon was always an impressive occasion, and the preacher was almost required to touch on public matters. White's sermon, like so many of the genre, was a meditation on the theme of 'godly magistracy'. But it also dealt, inevitably, with the two most pressing controversies of the day in Dorchester: the accusations of fraudulent evasion of customs duties by the Blachfords and other Dorset merchants, and the issue of church ales and Sunday recreations. For years the JPs of the western counties, backed by the justices of Assize, had issued repeated prohibitions of church ales and other such ungodly festivals. Chief Justice Richardson wished to continue the ban, but he had been ordered to command the JPs of each county on his circuit to revoke it. He complied with the order at this very session of the Assizes, though he did so 'gaily' (as a hostile witness reported), in a way that did not disguise his contempt for Laudian policies.[45]

White was flatly opposed to any toleration of ungodly pastimes, and was to make this plain in the following year by his obstinacy over the *Book of Sports*. Yet he believed in divinely appointed authority and could never have urged his parishioners to disobey it. He confronted agonizingly difficult issues, and this explains some of his ambiguities. At the heart of his sermon was the conventional argument from scripture that God had set kings on their thrones and magistrates in their offices, and that it was 'not in the power of men to pluck them down at their pleasure'. Nothing could justify the merchants' refusal to pay tonnage and poundage, even if they believed that its collection violated 'public liberty'. Indeed, White accused the Blachfords and their friends of hypocrisy in having joined with 'zealous and Godly patriots' only to advance their own private ends.

White had no time for people who used 'the liberty of the state' as a cover for their own self-interest, and his instincts always put him on the side of established authority. Nevertheless, he had some thinly-veiled criticisms of Charles I's more absolutist councillors – those who 'under colour of advancing authority, further their own ends' – and of swaggering, debauched courtiers. And there was always a higher power. The magistrate's commands, White argued, 'reach no further than the outward man; the spirit is God's peculiar'. Magistrates were required to enforce 'the sacred ordinances of God'. But if God's ordinances contradicted those of man, it was clear which must be obeyed: no one can have missed the reference to the issue of church ales and Sunday sports. The laws were 'a means of preserving purity', obedience was due to them only in so far as they were 'according to God's will'. Yet the apparent invitation to resist ungodly policies was hedged around with reservations. If the Christian decided that the law could not be obeyed, he must offer only a 'modest and respectful refusal'. He should accept the legitimacy of 'the power that commands' even while rejecting the particular command, and quietly submit to 'whatsoever authority lays on him'. White was not advocating resistance, but he was suggesting that the time might come when the subject had to submit to punishment rather than comply with ungodly commands. 'Blessed is the land where the ruler's godly zeal chaseth away wicked persons,' he concluded. But he did not say that this was *our* land.[46]

When White preached this sermon the kingdom, in spite of some disputes over tonnage and poundage, over Arminian ceremonies, and over church ales, was outwardly at peace with itself. Soon there came the trouble over Ship Money, and signs that Dorchester was becoming more self-consciously puritan than ever: it was 'Peter's church' now, not St Peter's. Hostility to Laudian rule was also more vocal. When a weaver named John Martin heard that the godly Constable Righton had been prosecuted for nonconformity, he burst out that 'the King maintains popish laws', through the oppressions of 'Blandford Court and other courts which were as that were'. The town JPs questioned him for his seditious talk, but soon dropped the matter. The real crisis began only in 1637 when the Scots were goaded into revolt by Archbishop Laud's attempt to inflict the Anglican liturgy on their Presbyterian kirk. In the 'Bishops' Wars' of 1639 and 1640 Charles I tried unsuccessfully to reduce them to obedience. In December 1639 writs went out for a new parliament which would, he hoped, enable him to fight an effective war and repair the kingdom's divisions. On 2 January, before the arrival of the writ, a majority of Dorchester's Corporation voted to elect Denzil Holles again, and to send Denis Bond with him to Westminster. But then the Earl of Suffolk intervened, nominating the courtier Sir Dudley Carleton. Not wishing to offend the Lord-Lieutenant, the mayor, Richard Savage, promised to pass on the message to the townsmen; but he also pointed out that by 'a constitution of this town' only freemen could be elected. That obstacle had been easily overcome for Holles in 1628, but nobody seems to have suggested a special meeting of the Freemen's Company for Carleton. Instead Savage took evasive action. Three Corporation meetings were cancelled for lack of a quorum before Holles and Bond were formally elected on 13 March. The town's electoral independence had been safely asserted. When another parliament, the famous Long Parliament, was summoned in the autumn nothing was heard from the Earl, and Holles and Bond were again returned for Dorchester.[47]

By the time of the Long Parliament election the second Bishops' War had been fought and lost; it was the presence of the Scots army in the northern counties that made Charles I swallow his distaste for parliaments, because he could only pay them off by getting a parliamentary grant. The 1639 campaign had passed Dorchester by, but a more serious military effort was made in 1640. The Dorset trained bands had to supply six hundred men for the campaign. They were mustered in April, but refused to march, arguing that as freeborn Englishmen they could not be forced to serve outside the country. Suffolk came scurrying down to Dorchester to deal with the mutiny and by 7 May claimed that the 'ill vapours' had been dissipated. On the surface the townsmen gave him what help he needed: tents for the muster at Poundbury, three townsmen for the Scottish service. But Suffolk wanted some symbolic recompense for his electoral rebuff, and reported Mayor Savage to the Council for not performing 'those respects due to his Lordship'. Savage was subjected to the inconvenience of a journey to Whitehall; but he made his excuses and was discharged on promising to be more careful in future.[48]

The town drum was repaired and the county's levies were reinforced by impressment: six more Dorchester men were taken by the constables towards the end of May. After some delays, in June they all left for the north. But the Dorset forces had no more stomach for the war than those from other counties, and some believed that they were the victims of a popish conspiracy to embroil them with their protestant brethren in Scotland. Marching through Berkshire they mutinied at Faringdon, murdering a Catholic officer.[49]

On the day the Long Parliament opened the Trenchards dined as usual in the great hall at Wolveton. Suddenly, according to a story recounted by John Aubrey, the sceptre held by the figure of the King carved on the hall screen came crashing to the floor. How many of the Trenchards' neighbours at Dorchester heard of this ill omen is unknown; most of them undoubtedly believed that they still lived in a kingdom whose problems could be solved in the familiar way, by the co-operation of King and Parliament. The bells of Holy Trinity pealed out on 20 February 1641, 'at the news of the happy success of the Parliament' (Charles I had given his assent to the Triennial Act, which guaranteed regular parliaments); and they rang as usual on 27 March, the King's accession day. In May rumours of Catholic plots prompted the Corporation to take a survey of the arms held by townsmen; any attempt by the ancient enemy would be met by the virtuous, armed, citizenry. But the Long Parliament completed its work of tearing down the bulwarks of Charles I's 'personal rule' – outlawing Ship Money, abolishing Star Chamber and the other prerogative courts, and having the King's hated chief minister, the Earl of Strafford, executed on Tower Hill. A great national reformation had apparently been achieved by a united parliament.[50]

The summer wore on, Charles I went off to Scotland, and the rumours of Catholic plots remained no more than rumours. For much of 1641 Dorchester's inhabitants seem to have been as concerned by the continued encroachment of Fordington people who had been sowing corn in the South Walls, and by fears of infection from plague outbreaks at Langport and Ilchester, as they were by the distant echoes of Westminster politics. Local opinion, it was reported in July, was firmly against the extremism of the 'pestilent sects and schismatics' in some of the London parishes, who were demanding the 'root and branch' reform of the church, including the total abolition of episcopacy. Dorchester people, the anonymous author claimed, had 'never kicked against the holy office of a bishop', and what they wanted was 'a pious reformation, not confusion in the church'.[51]

Whether this is an accurate assessment of Dorchester opinion is unknown; all we can say is that someone wanted to convey an impression of moderation. But whatever moderation existed was forgotten in November, when news came that Ireland was in revolt and that Protestants there were being massacred. All the old fears and hatreds boiled up, more virulently than ever. In the end, by raising the question of who should control the army sent against the rebels, the Irish rebellion precipitated civil war in England. But this did not happen for several more months, and in November 1641 the immediate reaction was one of panic. In Dorchester precautions were taken which must have heightened the prevailing anxiety. New shutters were made for the windows of the Shire Hall, an extra watch was set over the county magazine, and a 'discreet person' was stationed on the tower of St Peter's church, in case the Papists attacked during service time. Everyone was to have their arms ready 'for defence of the town'.[52]

As the winter dragged on, Dorchester people shared in the national mood of fear and anxiety. They took the loyalty-oath ordered by Parliament, the Protestation to uphold the 'true reformed Protestant religion . . . against all Popery and popish innovation'. They provided charity to refugees from Ireland, like the 'distressed Scotchman' who was given ten shillings in February 1642. But the refugees' lurid stories of massacre revived and intensified the anti-Catholic hysteria. From Bond and Holles in London the townspeople would have heard of the growing belief that the King was surrounded by a gang of crypto-Catholic evil councillors and irresponsible 'swordsmen', bent on using force to overturn the Long Parliament's reforms. They would have heard of the swelling street violence in London, of the mobs descending on Westminster to demand the exclusion of the bishops (now thought to be part of the Catholic plot against English liberties) from the House of Lords. They would have heard that their own MP, Denzil Holles, was one of the 'Five Members' whose arrest the King had unsuccessfully attempted when he led a party of soldiers into the House of Commons in January 1642. They would have observed the deepening impasse over the control of the army intended to suppress the Irish rebels, which Parliament dared not entrust to the King in case he should use it against themselves.[53]

All around them people were taking sides, pinning on their enemies those hostile labels – disloyal, morally repressive Roundhead or swaggering Cavalier – that were to become fixed in the historical memory. Many of their Dorset neighbours, particularly among the county gentry, were losing their earlier confidence in Parliament and rallying to the King's side, fearful that John Pym's supposed encouragement of the London mob against the bishops signalled impending anarchy and the destruction of the entire social system on which order and stability depended. In March 1642 came news that the King had gone to York, where he was raising forces. There were continuing propaganda exchanges, but the terrible prospect of civil war was no longer unimaginable. Before the March Assizes, worried about the 'many persons of several dispositions' pouring into the town, the Corporation again set a special watch over the arms and gunpowder in the Shire Hall. Assize week passed without incident, but no one could be certain that peace would last for long.[54]

The drift to war was accelerating. In May, responding to a letter from the Speaker, Dorchester raised £200 as a loan to Parliament; £170 of it came more or less voluntarily from the townspeople, and again there was none of the opposition provoked by Charles I's loans in the 1620s. By midsummer it was obvious that war was coming, and the town's leaders again agonized about the magazine in the Shire Hall. Nothing could legally be done about the county's arms – they were under the control of the gentry, of the Digbys, Strangways, Rogerses, and their friends, who could no longer be trusted. But the town could safeguard its own barrels of gunpowder. On 1 July they were removed from the Shire Hall and trundled down South Street to the greater security of the Brewhouse.[55]

7

DORCHESTER IN THE CIVIL
WAR AND REVOLUTION

BY THE middle of August Dorchester was an armed camp. Fighting
had already begun in other parts of England; not fifteen miles away,
Sherborne Castle was occupied by a band of Cavaliers. Yet somehow
the familiar rituals of the summer Assizes were performed in the
Shire Hall. The grand jury made its presentment, some routine
orders for an arbitration and the repair of a bridge were handed
down, and the usual crop of criminal cases disposed of. A Dorchester
woman was found guilty of stealing 12s. and some linen, while
another woman accused of taking a pair of shoes from Bernard Galpin's shop was acquitted. Politics, inevitably, intruded, and there
must have been passionate debate among the grand jurymen before
they reached the compromise position of petitioning the King to
withdraw his Commission of Array and the Parliament its Militia
Ordinance.[1]

Among the condemned prisoners were two Catholic priests.
They had disobeyed a proclamation requiring priests to leave the
country, and were thereupon convicted of treason. One of them
recanted, blaming his plight on the wicked machinations of the
Jesuits. The other, Hugh Green, did not, and on 18 August he
was taken to the place of execution at Gallows Hill. A Catholic
lady, Elizabeth Willoughby, bravely attended and left an account
of what followed.[2]

As usual at a seventeenth-century execution, a large crowd was
waiting; larger than usual, because today they would get something
more exciting than a couple of routine hangings. Prepared by generations of protestant preaching to see the Pope as Antichrist, and his

agents as satanically responsible for all the country's woes, their prejudices had been strengthened by the hysteria fostered by the Irish rebellion and by Parliament's continuing deluge of propaganda about Catholic plots. In his speech from the scaffold Green refused to play the condemned man's customary penitential role, and steadfastly insisted that he was no traitor. This inflamed the already excited crowd, and Sir Thomas Trenchard's chaplain screamed 'He blasphemeth! Stop the mouth of the blasphemer!' When the speech was finished the hideous cruelties of hanging, drawing and quartering were inflicted by the executioner and the local barber-surgeon, Matthew Barfoot, including the cutting out of the entrails of the still living victim – before the appreciative crowd. After Green, mercifully, had died, his heart was cut out, Elizabeth Willoughby recalls, 'put upon a spear, and showed to the people, and so thrown into the fire'. The mob was now thoroughly out of hand, and after Green had been dismembered and decapitated they appropriated the head and 'sported themselves' by playing football with it. Eventually they put sticks in the eyes, ears, nose and mouth, and buried the grisly object near the scaffold. According to Willoughby they would have liked to display it on one of the gates, but were deterred by the legend of God's punishment on the town after this was done with Father Cornelius's head in 1594.

The authorities were unable to keep order, and it is doubtful if they tried very hard, for to have done so might have led to the spilling of a lot more blood than that of the unfortunate priest. The High Sheriff, a Royalist, agreed to let some Catholic bystanders take away Green's dismembered corpse, but they were stopped by the mob. To have insisted would almost certainly have embroiled the sheriff in conflict with the 'blinded Dorcestrians', who had been arming and fortifying, in defiance of his orders, for more than a month. Civil war was obviously imminent, yet no one wanted to fire the first shot, and the horrifying scenes at the execution provided the wrong kind of pretext for what both sides knew was certainly going to happen before long.

Warlike preparations had been accelerating for months. In January the town had resurrected the old scheme to have its own militia company, and Bond had promoted it at Westminster. The parliamentary mills ground slowly, but on 19 July the ordinance authorising the Corporation to raise forces at last arrived. Volunteers were listed and training and drilling got under way. Work also began on fortifications: forty-two men and six boys were soon employed, and they were still busy at the time of the Assizes. The roundhead minority in the county was also preparing for battle, raising forces under Parliament's Militia Ordinance.[3]

As Assize week approached tensions rose still further. The Corporation warned the innkeepers not to overcharge, 'that there be no just cause given to the countrymen or strangers to except against the town'. The first week of August brought sensational news from Somerset: the royalist Marquis of Hertford had been driven out by a huge uprising of the country folk. He and his Cavaliers fled across the Dorset border to the Digbys' stronghold at Sherborne. Some of the local Royalists rallied to Hertford's support, while Parliament's friends prepared to eject him. At Dorchester the town gates were closed at eight o'clock every night, and a strong watch and ward set to prevent 'any insurrection or tumult'.[4]

The ugly scenes at Green's execution should now be easier to understand. For more than a week armed enemies had been ensconced a few miles away – Cavaliers, often equated with Catholics, and commonly labelled 'incendiaries'. Incendiaries: a dreaded word at Dorchester, with its memories of two great fires. When Judge Foster asked the magistrates by what right they were raising forces, they produced Parliament's ordinance, and told him they needed arms because they were in danger of being 'burnt up' by their enemies.[5] So although there were plenty of armed men in the town – indeed, precisely because there were so many armed men – there was no one willing to take the risks attendant on keeping order.

The royalist historian Clarendon thought Dorchester the most 'malignant' town in England, 'entirely disaffected to the King'. It was certainly the centre of Parliament's war effort in Dorset. Work continued on the fortifications after the Assizes, and the local artisans were busily employed; the carpenter John Haydon, for example, built gun carriages to be used against Sherborne. Henry Bridges and other messengers went galloping off with letters to parliamentarian leaders in Somerset. Upwards of forty men were soon under arms in Dorchester's new defence force, some recruited in the Dorset villages, two from as far away as Shepton Mallet.[6]

While preparations for the attack on Sherborne proceeded, Hertford sent emissaries to negotiate; they were told to submit to Parliament. At about this time a Dorchester merchant named George Leddoze, travelling through the countryside, was captured by Hertford's men and taken to Sherborne as a suspected spy. Asked if he was for King or Parliament, he stoutly replied, 'for both', indicating that he was for the latter: 'for King and Parliament' was the Roundheads' watchword. Leddoze warned his captors that the six 'great guns' at Dorchester would soon be used against them, and was treated to some choice invective in return before he was released.[7]

By the end of August troops under the Earl of Bedford had arrived from London, and on 2 September they marched away to begin the siege of Sherborne. The enlarged force contained many men from Dorchester – most of the able-bodied young men in the town, it was said. They were well supplied with arms and ammunition, the Roundheads having by now secured the Shire Hall magazine. Many of them soon lost their warlike enthusiasm however, running away, Bedford disgustedly reported, 'when they heard the bullets whistle about their ears'. John Whiteway claimed, though, that the Dorchester men played a useful part in the skirmish at Babylon Hill, near Yeovil, on 7 September. Bedford soon raised the siege, but he kept his headquarters at Dorchester, and guns and other supplies were still arriving there.[8]

On 19 September Hertford abandoned Sherborne and left the county. Life in Dorchester returned more or less to normal, though in the surrounding countryside Royalists were being imprisoned, and there was sporadic violence against suspected Catholics. But the town's leaders could resume discussion of such pressing matters as the repaving of the butchers' shambles and the leasing of market stalls. Yet the war was never far away. Preparations were made for possible street fighting: a chain was installed at the 'Bow' (at the junction of South and High East Streets), with only a narrow way through. Responsible men were put in charge of the gates, and the watch, warmed by a nightly issue of coal from the Brewhouse, was issued with pikes, halberds, and muskets.[9]

Three separate units were available for the defence of Dorchester: the militia company under Captain William Churchill, formerly part of the county trained bands; the town's own force, which was little more than an expanded and better equipped watch; and Sir Walter Erle's new troop of volunteers. Churchill's company spent eight days at the siege of Sherborne, but the part-time town force did not go there. In January 1643 the part-timers were divided into two companies of eighty men each, under the command of Joseph Paty and John Seward. Paty's enthusiasm for the parliamentary cause soon waned, so he was replaced by John Whiteway. The soldiers were on duty with the watch every third night, and mustered for training one afternoon a week. For this they received 2s. a week; if mobilised for 'constant service' they would get a shilling a day. The parish rate that was to pay for all this encountered opposition, however, and the system had to be changed. Except for the training sessions, service in the watch was again to be unpaid, though it required much more frequent attendance than in peacetime, as forty-five men were on duty every night. In February a third company of 'poor men' was recruited, with Richard Savage as its captain.[10]

Erle's volunteers were men of higher status. Of his troop's hundred-odd members more than a dozen came from Dorchester. Among them were Gilbert Whiffen, a future mayor, and several others – Edward Bragg, John Dashwood, William Horsford, Thomas Seward – from families within the governing circle. Bragg was later a commissioned officer for Parliament, as was another trooper from the town, Anthony Coombes. The troop also served for eight days before Sherborne, but it then disbanded, 'out of pay', and remustered only occasionally, presumably for training, during the winter. Some of the soldiers who came to join the troop were temporarily taken on by the town as guards and for work on the fortifications. In February yet another makeshift unit was formed, mainly out of men from west Dorset, though it also included a few with Dorchester connections. They were equipped by local house-holders – one received 'Mr Seward's arms', for example – in a way that reflects the improvisation common on both sides in the early months of the war.[11]

The lull that followed Hertford's departure lasted through the winter, and encouraged some of the local gentry to join those of other western counties in unsuccessful truce negotiations. But in April war returned to Dorset when a roundhead force from Somerset took Sherborne, which had again come under the control of the

Digbys in the Castle; some of the officers came to Dorchester and were entertained by the mayor, John Allambridge. Desultory work on the fortifications continued, and the blacksmiths were busy again, shoeing dragoons' horses and repairing muskets. Anticipating some sort of fighting during the summer, the authorities collected arms in private hands: Henry Woodcock spent six days 'receiving in of arms at the Shire Hall'.[12]

The crisis came in late May when Dorchester was suddenly threatened by two enemy armies. Sir Ralph Hopton's Cornishmen, fresh from victory at Stratton, were advancing eastward through Devon, and a second powerful force under Hertford and Prince Maurice was marching from Oxford to join them. The first sign of alarm came on the 27th, when the three companies of poor soldiers were mobilised. Extra labourers were recruited and urgently set to work on the defences. New earthworks were built and old ones improved; men worked all night on the fort near the East Gate. Bushes and hedges in the fields around the town were cut down to deny cover to attackers, and thatch stripped from roofs to reduce the danger of fire. Arms and ammunition were stockpiled, and scouts sent out to collect intelligence of enemy movements; Matthew Bennett was paid a shilling for 'scouting about the country'.[13]

During all this feverish activity Erle was at Dorchester with a force of five hundred men, sweeping the countryside to seize goods and money from people who had not previously contributed to Parliament. As the concentration of effort on the East Gate suggests, the immediate danger was from Hertford and Maurice. Attack seemed imminent when they advanced from Salisbury to Blandford; Hopton, meanwhile, was little more than a day's march away to the west. Erle regarded the new fortifications as 'slender works', but he was determined to defend the town, encouraged by the good spirit of the soldiers. The magistrates joined his officers in swearing 'to live and die together in defence of the place'. In the end Dorchester was spared. Hertford and Maurice marched by to the north, following a prearranged plan to link up with Hopton at Chard. They then turned north-east across the Somerset levels to confront Sir William Waller.[14]

The town's nerve had been tested, and people of all sorts and conditions had shown resolution and courage. Even Royalists were impressed by this example of the godly community in action, attributing it to the sermons of White, Benn, and Hugh Thompson. The ministers, an Oxford propagandist complained, brilliantly exploited the anti-Catholic prejudices of the townspeople, preaching that 'Mass was said openly at Oxford' and that 'none but Papists were about the King'. They had persuaded almost all their parishioners to take the Covenant – the latest of Parliament's loyalty-oaths – vowing that the clergy too would 'seal it with their blood'.[15]

With the contending armies far away, the tensions again relaxed. The midsummer fair was held as usual, though with understandable precautions 'for fear of incomers'. A constant watch was kept from St Peter's tower, the three companies of poor men remained in arms, and Erle's headquarters were still at Dorchester – though his forces were often away, dealing with royalist raiders in West Dorset, or besieging Corfe Castle. But in mid-July came news of Waller's disastrous defeat at Roundway. On the 24th Erle wrote anxiously to London for money, arms, and ammunition; the Dorset Cavaliers, emboldened by Waller's defeat, were again raising forces. Some 'honest men' from Dorchester and its environs hastily recruited another troop of horse, and both the Corporation and individual townsmen contributed large sums of money. It was not enough.[16]

'The curse of the Lord is in the house of the wicked,' an unknown scribe wrote, some time in 1643, in the account book of All Saints parish. Was he thinking of the Royalists, perhaps, or reflecting on Dorchester's own sins? For, confronted with a second crisis, the godly community collapsed humiliatingly. On 26 July Hopton's Cornishmen stormed Bristol's supposedly impregnable defences, and Parliament's most important stronghold in the west surrendered. A few days later a survivor of the fiasco, the Somerset officer William Strode, arrived in Dorchester telling 'strange stories' of the Cavaliers' achievements: they had thought nothing, he said, of 'running up walls twenty foot high'. Strode toured the town's cherished defences and was asked how long they would withstand the Royalists, replying 'about half an hour'. Morale, already low, disintegrated completely. The town's governors had sworn to live and die with Parliament, the clergy to seal the Covenant with their blood. They did nothing of the sort – they ran away. White and Benn fled to London, while the wealthier inhabitants feverishly tried to get their goods away to safety. The Royalists captured a ship leaving Weymouth laden with 'rich goods belonging to several persons well affected to the Parliament', and among those well affected persons were such leaders of the godly cause as John Whiteway and John Hill.[17]

By now the Earl of Caernarvon was marching from Bristol with two thousand men. Erle bitterly recounted the outcome. 'The distractions in the town were great,' he reported to Parliament. The soldiers were mutinous for lack of pay, and the 'poorer sort', disillusioned by their leaders' cowardice, would make no further sacrifices. Erle by now had six or seven hundred men, but he needed, he said, more than twice that number. So he marched off to Southampton and left Dorchester to its fate. Caernarvon appeared at the gates on 2 August, and agents were sent out to negotiate. The Royalists could afford to be generous, and terms were quickly agreed; in return for immediate surrender the townsmen would be spared both plundering and punishment.[18]

Clarendon thought that if Dorchester's inhabitants had had 'courage equal to their malice' the town might have been defended. Yet in 1643 Dorchester was not the only west-country town to belie a puritan reputation by ignominious surrender. Taunton did so too, though the Somerset town was to behave with greater resolution during two later sieges. For thirty years Dorchester's magistrates and clergy had proclaimed the cause of reformation. They now showed themselves unwilling to fight, or even risk their property, for that cause. But any chance the Royalists had of exploiting the townspeople's disillusionment was thrown away. Soon after the surrender Maurice arrived with fresh troops. They immediately began plundering and, according to Clarendon, Maurice made no effort to stop them. Caernarvon resigned his command in disgust.[19]

Dorchester had no reason to welcome the Cavaliers, but it had to live with them. The plundering by Maurice's troops was followed by other outrages. John White's study was pillaged (his papers were sold or given away), and contrary to the articles of surrender a collective fine was imposed on the inhabitants. There was even talk of burning the town as punishment for its puritan past. To avert worse disasters, Mayor Allambridge and his remaining Corporation colleagues persuaded William Churchill, one of the few leading townsmen who were not notorious Roundheads, to become Deputy Governor. Churchill had been in arms for Parliament at Sherborne, but by 1643 his royalist sympathies were clear. After 'much importunity' he agreed to take the job, and used his influence with the King's county commissioners (who often met at the George) to protect his neighbours from violence. Churchill was certainly in charge by December 1643, when he and Joseph Paty, who had also gone over to the King, were temporarily captured by a roundhead raiding party. Matthew Chubb's old friend, the goldsmith Robert Coker, was also alleged to be collaborating with the Royalists at this time. Somehow life went on. Edward Dashwood succeeded Allambridge as mayor, and it looks as if the great Thomas Fuller briefly officiated at the churches, though he refused the King's offer of the rectory because of his friendship with John White.[20]

Peace returned after the December raid, and the Royalists remained in control until midsummer 1644. At that time a great parliamentarian army under the Earl of Essex marched into Dorset, and Dorchester's parliamentarian loyalties resurfaced. During the next few months the townspeople several times fought valiantly when the King's forces tried to enter the town. In one incident women as well as men resisted the Cavaliers, 'pelting them with stones, and defending themselves with their spits'. In another, a force from Wareham (now in royalist hands) threatened to plunder and burn the place unless they were paid a thousand pounds; they were driven back into Fordington. After one unsuccessful raid on Poole, royalist cavalry were chased back to Dorchester. Major Sydenham, it was reported, 'charged them through and through', killing Major John Williams, another cousin of the Herringstone family. Williams was alleged to have killed Sydenham's mother in some earlier wartime atrocity. The soldiers of both sides were regular visitors. George Goring's Cavaliers, who arrived in February 1645, were no doubt the least welcome. Of all the civil war armies, Goring's was the worst: the crimes of 'Goring's crew' were to be legendary in the western counties. How much of the wartime damage done in Dorchester was their work and how much that of other armies is unknown; they were certainly blamed for smashing up the Brewhouse.[21]

The region's sufferings at last provoked the countrymen into action. In the spring of 1645 neutralist 'peace-keeping associations', commonly known as Clubmen, erupted all over Dorset. Although ostensibly neutral, most of the Clubmen were predisposed to royalism, so it is not surprising that Dorchester would have nothing to do with them. It is just possible that the townspeople may have been in touch with the more Parliament-inclined Somerset Clubmen, however, for messengers were sent into Somerset, one of them being imprisoned by the Cavaliers at Langport. Early in July, while Clubmen gathered in the downlands, Dorchester welcomed Fairfax's New Model Army, fresh from victory at Naseby, its soldiers already famous for their sobriety and godliness. By summer's end the war was virtually over in Dorset, though not the military presence. Fairfax's men marched through Dorchester early in October on their way to a mopping-up campaign in Devon and Cornwall, and again for one last time during their return in April 1646. The church bells rang joyously for their victories; it was peace at last.[22]

In spite of its leaders' unheroic behaviour in 1643, Dorchester had been overwhelmingly for the Parliament. Of the fifty-eight Dorchester men known to have been in arms, fifty fought for Parliament, only ten for the King. The two who supported both sides at different times – William Churchill and Joseph Paty – were from the town's upper crust, as were two other royalist sympathisers, the goldsmith Coker and the Keeper of the Gaol, Renaldo Knapton. All the other Royalists were from lower down the social scale: people like the butcher Matthew Haggard, the blacksmith Edward Hill, the tailor Robert Walbridge. The elder Roger Pouncey was too old to fight, but he was, inevitably, for the King, one of only four townsmen required to take the Negative Oath (administered to those 'aiding, assisting, or adhering unto the forces raised against the Parliament') when there were fears of royalist plots in 1647. Two of his sons were also open Royalists: William got a pension after the Restoration for his service in the King's army.[23]

On the other side stood virtually the entire town establishment, many of them (Bushrods, Dashwoods, Sewards, and others) with sons serving in the Parliament's forces. At least sixteen men held commissions, several after rising from the ranks – an indication that they were both efficient and highly motivated. Not all of them were unattached, ambitious young men with nothing to lose, of the type common in all armies. The younger Joseph Underwood was already married and a householder when he went off to war in September 1644; he rose to the rank of captain before he was demobilised. Most of the men who served were lucky and came home, though John Linnington received 'many dangerous wounds', and both Richard Pitt and James Stagge were 'maimed in the service'. Some never returned. Margaret Buckler lost both her husband and a son in the wars, and there were other widows. A few of the casualties were from prominent families. Joseph Cuffe, whose mother and stepfather kept the George Inn, died of an illness contracted in the service; Henry Bridges, Roger Pouncey's hanging constable, died, or was killed, in 1644; and the younger John Seward was killed in the summer of that year.[24]

What was life like for the majority who stayed home in wartime Dorchester? For some there were compensations: war contracts, employment on the fortifications or in the defence forces. The smiths and their fellow metalworkers did brisk business; when muskets arrived from London early in the war they were 'much out of order' and had to be repaired. Of those higher up the social scale, Richard Savage supplied cloth to the parliamentarians at Poole, but also to the Earl of Crawford's Royalists; John Hill sold provisions to the besiegers of Sherborne; and the grocer William White filled large orders for powder, match and bullets. Smaller contracts also went to people strongly identified with the parliamentarian cause. Patroclus Cooke provided ammunition when Irish troops attacked in July 1644. Lawrence Righton also supplied arms at various times; when he presented his bill it was noted that he was 'a very faithful servant to the state'.[25]

A few might find employment and even profit, but for most people the war brought misery and disaster. The sufferings inflicted by Buckingham's soldiers in the 1620s were as nothing compared with those from wartime armies. At first the town made no objection to billeting, paying 6s. a week to quarter three of Erle's men in February 1643, but as the armies moved in and out of the town the protests multiplied. Some of the innkeepers were still unpaid years later. In 1648 the Corporation itself reimbursed three wartime constables for their quartering expenses. Robert Cardrow, who had been forced to billet some of Crawford's Cavaliers, was still demanding payment in 1654. He was unusually persistent; most people had long since given up.[26]

In the first two years of the war there was still money about, in spite of the disruption of trade and the ravages of the armies. Wealthy townspeople dipped deep into their pockets to finance Parliament's war effort; they were in the best position to get to the head of the queue if ever there was a chance of getting loans repaid. Jane Trayte, widow of a prosperous clothier, lent £80 in September 1644 and was repaid less than a month later; Richard Savage and John Whiteway were both promptly repaid for money they had lent. Others were not so lucky. Even John Bushrod, whose family was certainly an influential one, claimed in 1654 that he had advanced 'a considerable part of his small estate' for Parliament's service, but had never got a penny of it back. Such self-interested statements have to be taken with a grain of salt, but there is no doubt that many people suffered from Parliament's dilatory accounting.[27]

The County Treasurer, Richard Bury, was one of the few who did well out of the war, but he had unusual opportunities. When he made his will in July 1644 John Seward complained that his estate was under enemy occupation and most of the debts owed him probably irrecoverable. Even some Capital Burgesses came close to ruin. Edmund Dashwood had the balance of John Churchill's charity in his hands, but most of it was 'lost by the wars'. His kinsman Edward, who succeeded Allambridge as mayor, got badly in arrears with his poor rate: he probably had spent a lot of his own money relieving the indigent. William Joliffe never recovered from the war and went bankrupt a few years later.[28]

The rich may have suffered, but as always the poor were far worse off. How bad things were can be seen in the mortality figures. Before the war there had been an average of about twenty-eight deaths annually in Trinity parish. In 1643 burials soared to sixty-six (three soldiers were also buried), an increase of over fifty per cent above even the worst prewar year. The heavy mortality appears to have been caused by the movement of troops – soldiers brought infections from distant places, to which local people had no immunity – and there may also have been an outbreak of plague in the autumn. After that terrible year mortality declined, though it was still well above the prewar average. Immediately after the war there was another plague epidemic: Dorchester was one of several Dorset towns affec-ted. Fifty-two people died in St Peter's parish, among them the parish clerk, so the names were never recorded. Trinity's register shows the tell-tale autumnal peak of deaths in 1645; four members of the Perrin family died, and several other families were almost as badly hit.[29]

With poor relief at the point of collapse, life was not enviable for the survivors. During the first year of the war there had been no sign of impending disaster, though some special measures had to be taken: in June 1643 the Corporation spent fifty pounds 'for the setting the poor a-work in the Hospital house'. But after the Royalists arrived funds for the poor were drastically curtailed. All Saints no longer received help from St Peter's, its Christmas distribution was cut in half, and the yield from its weekly rate was down by over a fifth. The parish struggled through, but only because fewer people received relief and the weekly allowances were cut.[30]

If the war years were bad, the years immediately afterwards were worse. In 1645–6 there were thirteen fewer ratepayers in All Saints than before the war, and their assessments had to be sharply reduced – Lawrence Righton was one of a number of middling-income parishioners whose weekly rates came down from fourpence to twopence. Receipts fell to less than half even the low figure of 1643–4, and with no subsidy from St Peter's and no Christmas distribution, the plight of the swelling numbers of the All Saints poor seemed desperate. Salvation came as usual from the Brewhouse. The 'New Brewhouse', as it was called after the wartime damage was repaired, had reopened by May 1645, when All Saints received a payment of ten shillings, and for the rest of the year it contributed 6s. 8d. a week, well over half the parish's total income. Payments were still drastically cut and sometimes not made at all, but the overseers managed to distribute over fifteen pounds by the weekly rate (less than half of the total even in the bad year of 1643–4) and to make other emergency payments, including a return to the traditional gift of clothing at Christmas. Many people who were not normally paupers now had to be given occasional relief. As always, most of them were widows, but a few unemployed men were also helped.[31]

In spite of it all the war had been won. How often, John White reflected as he looked back on the great struggle, had God 'stepped in between us and our utter ruin' – it was time to give thanks, to turn to His work again and once more 'lay up for ourselves treasures in heaven'.[32] The physical damage was quickly repaired and although economic recovery took longer, by the early 1650s most people were out of the wood. Townsmen who had fled in 1643 gradually drifted back, though some took their time about it: William Derby, for example, was still in London in September 1645. John Hill never came back, though he continued to sit on the County Committee. White, who had been serving a suburban London parish, announced in May 1646 that he wanted to return. He was getting old and feeble: preaching to the Lords a few months earlier he had spoken of being 'distracted by . . . pain and grief', and worried that his sermon might be dismissed as 'a sick man's dreams'. But by November 1646 he was home again in Dorchester.[33]

The old man no longer received quite the respect that he had once commanded. 'Factions and fond opinions crept in his flock,' his friend Thomas Fuller recalled. We can only speculate what those 'fond opinions' were, but all over England at this time there were those who said that there was no single universal church, but that like-minded Christians could separate and form their own churches, each with its own doctrines. Others believed that ministers had no more authority than laymen; some even said that there was no sin, and that to the godly all things were pure, even drunkenness, blasphemy, and fornication. Fuller may well have heard talk like this in Dorset during these turbulent postwar years. Such beliefs challenged the vision of the ordered, unified, godly community which the reformers had laboured so long to promote, threatening a hellish prospect of moral chaos and confusion. White put his foot down. In March 1647 he held a special Fast at St Peter's, 'to prevent heresies . . . the whole town attending'. He was, as he had always been, a bitter enemy of the radical sects. In 1645 he had denounced the 'dangerous heresies' of the Antinomians, Anabaptists, and others who had been uttering 'unheard-of blasphemies'. These doctrines were especially likely, he thought, to lead astray 'silly women, laden with sin'. If there were no laws against such heresies Parliament should immediately pass some.[34]

One of those who no longer regarded White with the old reverence was William Paty. He had never openly gone over to the King, as his father had done, but his sympathies clearly lay in that direction. Somehow he got hold of White's 1633 Assize sermon, and had it published to show how far the rector's behaviour during the civil war had contradicted his former professions of loyalty. The Corporation, of course, remained firm in their admiration, and were seriously concerned when they heard that Lord Saye was trying to lure White back to Oxford as Warden of New College. His problems in Dorchester, as always, were partly financial: Trinity and St Peter's parishes had been too impoverished by the war to pay the supplements to his stipend that they had promised. Temporary augmentations of fifty pounds each for both White and Benn were obtained from Parliament's Committee for Plundered Ministers, as well as another fifty pounds to support a lecturer who would 'ease Mr White in his weakness'. Some further inducement was needed, so the Corporation bought the impropriated rectory of Fordington from the Trustees for the Sale of Dean and Chapter Lands. The purchase gave them control over a parish whose disorders so often spilled over into Dorchester. They would now nominate the incumbent (always consulting the 'honest people' of the parish) and ensure that he was sympathetic to Dorchester's brand of godly reformation. The income from Fordington would allow them to pay thirty-five or forty pounds a year to the minister there, eighty pounds a year to an assistant at St Peter's, an additional sixty pounds a year to Benn at All Saints, and twenty a year to the master of the Free School. To pay for Fordington, Seaton Parsonage was sold back to Walter Yonge.[35]

It was easier to solve the financial problems than to get an assistant for Mr White, and on 21 July 1648, before one was found, the Rector died. A solemn 'day of humiliation' was held to seek God's help in the choice of a successor, and for more than a month the church porch was draped in black. Benn and a succession of stopgap preachers filled in until a new rector was appointed. The new man was another conservative Presbyterian: Stanley Gower, born in Glasgow and educated at Trinity College, Dublin. In the autumn of 1648 Gower was in the Isle of Wight with several of his ministerial colleagues, trying to persuade the captive Charles I to save his throne by agreeing to the establishment of Presbyterianism. William Benn went there with a delegation of townsmen to investigate Gower's fitness for the post, and he was instituted to the rectory of Holy Trinity on 24 January 1649.[36]

John White had led Dorchester through its transformation from the sleepy backwater presided over by Matthew Chubb to the reformed, godly community of the 1630s. The limits of reformation had become all too clear in the abject surrender of 1643, and in the signs of division that greeted White on his return after the war. Yet something of the old spirit lived on, even in a community battered by war and economic depression. As he made his will the patriarch acknowledged 'the infinite goodness and mercy of God' in enabling his preaching to produce 'such effects as I have cause to look upon with much comfort'. He warned his flock not to be 'carried up and down with every wind of doctrine', every plausible novelty. But he could still give thanks for 'the favours and honours' he had received from his people during forty-three arduous years.[37]

White died at a time of great tension and anxiety throughout the kingdom. Resentment at high taxes and an expensive, radical army boiled over all across southern England during the summer of 1648. Dorset did not experience actual fighting in this 'second civil war', but it was a near thing. In March a cavalier newsbook sneered that the 'holy brethren of Dorchester' were much alarmed by the resurgence of royalism in the locality. A county petition claiming ten thousand signatures listed familiar complaints: about centralisation and military rule, violations of ancient laws and liberties, and the promotion of men of 'broken condition' to positions of power. These were the grievances of rural Dorset, and they aroused few echoes in Dorchester; the town's leaders included some of those 'men of ruinous fortunes and despicable estates' whose authority in the county the petitioners so disliked. The Committee met several times at the George to 'preserve the peace of the county', and a new volunteer force was raised. John Whiteway and Richard Bury were among the officers who marched with it towards Shaftesbury on 15 July. This and other precautions prevented any royalist rebellion, but the military presence was as unpopular as ever.[38]

Men like Whiteway and Bury were still enthusiastic Parliamentarians in the summer of 1648. It is not clear whether they remained so as the country drifted further into revolution during the autumn and winter – as the House of Commons was purged by Colonel

Pride's soldiers (Denzil Holles was one victim), and as the King was tried and executed. They retained their local offices, doing their jobs as magistrates and committeemen. But so did many other Englishmen who had no love for the republic – the Commonwealth that replaced the monarchy. Most people in Dorchester certainly viewed the revolution with grave misgivings. They kept quiet about it, of course: it was dangerous to speak out. But Dorchester was a presbyterian town, and Presbyterians, though they had fought against Charles I, had no wish to destroy him or his whole system of government. Monarchy was part of the divinely-ordained natural order which Presbyterians believed in just as much as their former enemies did. White's successor Stanley Gower, who arrived in Dorchester within a few days of the King's death, loathed the radicals who had thrown his world into chaos.

Dorchester people kept their heads down during these upheavals, but there are some clues to their opinions in, of all things, their contributions to church collections. They had always responded generously to charitable appeals, and they still did so even in the years of poverty and privation that followed the civil war. At a series of monthly public Fasts in 1646 and 1647 collections were taken for the poor, which produced an average yield of £4.15s.3d. Further economic adversity, and also perhaps White's failing preaching powers, led to a decline to an average of only £2.14s.0d. in 1648, before recovery began in the following year. Routine collections of this kind were probably not much affected by the political climate, but it was a different matter when Parliament appointed Days of Thanksgiving to celebrate the victories of its armies. Before 1649 Dorchester people still gave thanks for the New Model Army's successes: celebrations in 1648 for victories in Wales and over the Scots at Preston each produced around £5.10s.0d. – more than double the average takings at the monthly Fasts, more even than at the Day of Humiliation after White's death. During the Commonwealth Dorchester's charity could still be awakened – the townsfolk subscribed over seven pounds for fire victims at Broadway in 1649, fifteen pounds for another fire at Stratton in 1651 – but not on public Days of Thanksgiving. In October 1650 they gave only three pounds when asked to celebrate Cromwell's victory at Dunbar, and even less than that at the Thanksgiving for Worcester a year later. These sums were smaller than those gathered on the regular Fast Days. The decline surely reflects the townsmen's ambivalence towards the Commonwealth.[39]

The defeated enemies were Scots, to be sure; but they were also Presbyterians, as the Scots routed by Cromwell at Preston had not been. The Dunbar collection was entered in the records with the note that it was for the 'success of our army in Scotland'; someone crossed out the word 'success'. On 22 August 1651 there was a great storm in Dorchester, so bad that the clerk thought it worth describing it in the parish register – torrents of rain, gigantic hailstones, 'great thunder and lightning, such as had not been known by any living in this age'. On that same day, he added, two godly presbyterian ministers had been executed in London for conspiring against the Commonwealth: God's anger at their martyrdom had been tempestuously proclaimed.[40]

The Commonwealth had to be obeyed, but many Dorchester people were unhappy about it. When Josiah Terry was installed as mayor in October 1649 the oath of office had to be revised, as there was now no king to swear allegiance to. Terry swore that he would 'do equal right to the poor and to the rich', as mayors had always done, and he promised to perform the office according to 'the laws of the land'. But nothing was said about allegiance to the Parliament or Commonwealth. By this time the Rump Parliament had decreed that all holders of municipal office should take a new loyalty oath: the 'Engagement' to be 'true and faithful to the Commonwealth of England, as it is now established, without a King or House of Lords'. Presbyterians in many town corporations refused to subscribe, and there were massive purges. In Dorchester no one was dismissed for refusing the oath, even though several burgesses took it with reservations that made it virtually meaningless. Richard Bury and John Bushrod subscribed 'in this sense only, that I will live peaceably under this present power and obey them in lawful things'; William Benn used the same formula. Some members of the Corporation apparently avoided taking the Engagement altogether; George Cole managed to put it off until October 1652. There was little enthusiasm for the republic in Dorchester.[41]

In spite of being so clearly out of sympathy with the government at Westminster, Dorchester came through the Commonwealth unscathed. There were occasional disputes over Corporation elections, but these were rarely political matters. The prewar generation was passing: William Derby and old Richard Blachford both died in the early 1650s, and several of the others were generally absent. Like John Hill, James Gould rarely attended Corporation meetings (he was expelled in 1653 for refusing to serve as mayor), and Denis Bond was totally preoccupied with parliamentary affairs. Before Pride's Purge the town had paid him lavishly – two hundred pounds for the years 1645–7, for example – but after he threw in his lot with the illegal republic his pay was cut off. The Corporation discussed what further sum to allow him, but in the end all they did was present him with six sugar loaves.[42]

In April 1653 Oliver Cromwell threw out the Rump, and in December he was installed as Lord Protector of the realm. The Protectorate was at first a relatively moderate regime – Cromwell's watchword was 'healing and settling' – but it led to much greater meddling in local affairs by Whitehall. The Corporation was apparently under pressure to get rid of possible dissidents as early as 1654. A replacement for Gould was belatedly found in the person of the puritan Philip Stansby (a grocer who had been Richard Bury's apprentice) and another member, William Paty, was forced to resign. Given the known royalist sympathies of his family, it is remarkable that Paty had been elected to the Fifteen at all. He now resigned, he said, 'in discharge of my conscience and according to my duty'.[43]

What was left of 'healing and settling' vanished after the royalist rising of 1655. The rebellion was mainly a Wiltshire affair, but it had some support in downland Dorset, and a few prisoners were lodged in Dorchester Gaol to await trial at the Assizes. Angered by the interminable plotting, Cromwell turned to repression. After the rising many of the local gentry who had played no part in it were rounded up and brought to Dorchester; the Dorset magnate Sir John Strangways passed the time in gaol by writing a poem 'Upon a private and retired life'.[44] The country was now divided into military districts, each under a Major-General (Dorset's was that hard-bitten Puritan, John Disbrowe), and Commissioners 'for securing the peace of the Commonwealth' were appointed to raise a new militia and impose a discriminatory tax on Cavaliers to pay for it.

The Dorset commissioners met at Dorchester in December 1655, and Major-General Disbrowe was there to instruct then. In February he was back again, and it is no coincidence that within a few days George Cole, one of the least puritan of the Corporation, resigned. He was readmitted a year later, but only after Disbrowe's approval had been obtained. The Corporation wisely cultivated their new overlord. During the 1656 summer Assizes he was entertained by Philip Stansby, and was presented with the sort of gifts – of wine, sugar, and mutton – normally reserved for the judges. The town obediently provided the names of local Royalists, which were kept on file at a central security office in London. Among the eleven suspects listed from Dorchester were Matthew Haggard and, inevitably, one of the Pounceys. The Major-Generals were supposed to suppress the idle and immoral as well as the politically deviant; to the godly the two categories were virtually identical. Dorchester needed little encouragement when it came to moral reformation, but the Corporation could always invoke Disbrowe's backing if it suited them. A former soldier who asked for permission to open an alehouse was told that no more licenses would be granted without approval from the Major-General.[45]

Cromwell abandoned the unpopular new officials in 1657, and normal government was resumed. But there were still divisions in the Corporation: another protracted dispute arose over the election of new members, eventually resolved by the admission of the physician Frederick Losse and the pious cutler, Lawrence Righton. The choice of Righton, a man of only modest wealth, shows that the revolution had opened some doors to people from outside the usual governing circle.[46] But the Corporation was still liable to fall into conflict, even over religious exercises. When Cromwell died in September 1658, Mayor Stansby proposed that the clergy be asked to preach, with the aim of 'stirring our cold hearts, the more to be quickened in the ways of piety'. This innocuous resolution was opposed by two of the burgesses, who thought that the ministers ought to be consulted first. Stansby was right about the cold hearts: the collection on the Fast Day to mark Oliver's death produced only £2.10s.0d. in the two richer parishes, the two pounds from All Saints being an unusually high proportion of the town's total. It looks as if the Protector's passing inspired quite different levels of urgency on the part of the preachers. Gower had no love for Cromwell's memory, whereas

Benn at All Saints had always been the most radical of the ministers.[47]

Cromwell's death was followed by other unsettling signs. In January 1659 there were elections for a new Parliament. In earlier Protectorate Parliaments Dorchester had had only one MP, but that member had been elected fairly democratically. Traditionally the franchise had been restricted to freemen, but when John Whiteway was chosen in 1654 the election was held as usual at the Town Hall, and was 'by the voices and consent of all that were present'. But the 1659 Parliament, summoned by Cromwell's amiable but ineffective son, Richard, was elected on the old system. Dorchester again had two members, and although the evidence is not absolutely certain, it looks as if the conservatives got their way on the voting qualifications, too, and that the restricted franchise was also restored. The Corporation stalwart, John Bushrod, was elected, but so was the refractory James Gould, which suggests that the ordinary freemen were again tiring of the reformers' oligarchic rule. When the Protectorate collapsed in the spring and the Rump gerontocracy resurrected itself, the Corporation must have felt more vulnerable than ever. Many of them, too, were getting old – Bury and Savage were well into their seventies and several others were not much younger – and there were now three vacancies, as Bond, Joliffe, and Cole had all recently died. In July 1659 there was a debate about choosing new members, but nothing came of it.[48]

Stansby's concern about his neighbours' cold hearts reflected a common anxiety about the state of religion in Dorchester. The old problem – only two ministers serving three parishes – was as intractable as ever. Benn normally doubled as assistant in the upper parishes, as well as serving his own parish of All Saints. In 1653 the Corporation decided to search for an assistant, but not until 1656 did they seriously start looking, and only in 1658 was their eventual choice – Richard Russell – installed at St Peter's. The delay was largely Gower's fault. He insisted that his title as rector of both Trinity and St Peter's be formally confirmed, and also caused trouble over the distribution of the income from Fordington parsonage.[49]

The coming of the republic had other, more dramatic, effects, particularly in All Saints parish. William Benn had always been more radical than White or any of the other ministers, and after the war he was free to go his own way. That way was the ultra-Calvinist way of restricting communion to the elect, which meant that the sacrament was never officially administered at All Saints throughout the 1650s: no purchases of bread or wine are recorded during the entire decade. Benn may have formed a 'gathered church' of the elect which received communion privately: when a Fordington widow named Alice Limbury made her will in 1655 she left money to 'the church whereof I am a member in Dorchester' (she did not say 'parish', or give the church a name), and she asked Benn and the Fordington minister John Loder, who was certainly a Congregationalist, to be her overseers.[50]

The familiar liturgy had gone. Instead of Common Prayer, both Gower and Benn used the presbyterian service-book, the Directory. Baptisms and burials continued, but church weddings became much less common after 1653, when the so-called Barebones Parliament instituted civil marriage, conducted by JPs. Some people still wanted to be married in church, even if they had to go outside their own parishes; many couples with no apparent connection to Dorchester were married in the town churches in 1656 and 1657. There was also an unsuccessful attempt to put an end to bellringing. An All Saints parish meeting in March 1649 ordered 'that the churchwardens pay the ringers no more money', but knells were still rung for the deceased before burials, and money continued to be spent on repairing bells and bellropes.[51]

One thing the revolution had not changed was the involvement of parishioners in matters affecting their church. At a 'full meeting' of All Saints parish in 1657 it was agreed that the steeple was so badly decayed that it should be taken down and replaced by a clock tower. St Peter's had a clock: why not All Saints? A special church rate was authorised and the tower quickly completed. The other major problem at All Saints was that old bone of contention, church seating. The war had led to a massive turnover of population and made the old seating arrangements obsolete, so in 1656–7 the churchwardens made 'a new map for the church'. A second parish meeting had to be called, however, to authorise the ejection of people who had been moved into new seats but refused to pay the rents set out in 'the old church book'.[52]

White had worried about the spread of unorthodox opinions, and so did the Corporation, who in 1653 felt that it was urgently necessary to obtain a third minister, 'for prevention of disorder'. There is no sign that any congregations of radical separatists formed in Dorchester during the 1650s, though such things were happening in many other places. The town's governors were distinctly unfriendly to the sects. Delegates from west-country Baptist congregations met in Dorchester in May 1658, but the town was chosen for its location, not its religious climate. Mayor Stansby refused to let the Baptists meet in any of the churches, so they had to use the George instead, where their discussions were observed by a government spy. Nor were the Quakers, the Baptists' chief sectarian rivals, any more welcome. Several were imprisoned in Dorchester Gaol by the county magistrates in 1656, and when he was mayor John Whiteway was particularly hostile, often having Quakers whipped as vagrants.[53]

Dorchester's presbyterian orthodoxy seems to have been unaffected by the example being set in Fordington, where two successive ministers, both of Dorchester stock, were Congregationalists. John Loder, son of the prominent attorney Gilbert Loder, was appointed to the living in 1649, even though he had not been ordained and was apparently under age. His views caused no trouble at Fordington, but they did when he moved to St Bartholomew Exchange in London: he provoked violent controversy by forming a gathered church and excluding most parishioners from communion. Loder was succeeded at Fordington by another Dorchester native, Joshua Churchill, also a Congregationalist.[54]

In the dark days at the end of the war, John White's vision of a reformed, God-fearing Dorchester seemed to have come to a dead end. The Brewhouse was in ruins, the schools empty, the charities crippled, the town oppressed with misery and disease. Yet in a remarkably short time recovery was under way. Old programmes were revived, and important new initiatives begun. Indeed the post-war period was the climax of the puritan attack on poverty and ignorance.

The Brewhouse was the key; without it, none of the expensive welfare schemes started before the war could succeed. Its worst problems were the damage done by Goring's soldiers, and the long list of bad debts. The physical damage was quickly repaired, but the debts, totalling over a thousand pounds, were more difficult. In 1648 Richard Savage paid one hundred pounds for the right to collect them, with what success is unknown. Benjamin Devenish died during the war, and the house clerk was now his former assistant, Jonas Palfrey, whose son James was head brewer; John Bushrod exercised general supervision as steward. The Brewhouse quickly resumed its old role in the management of Dorchester's charitable funds.[55]

The first priority was to rebuild the Brewhouse's wasted capital. One hundred pounds was invested after the sale of Seaton Parsonage, and other money – from Fast Day collections and the rents of Free School lands – also found its way there. Although the Brewhouse was perfectly well managed, the Corporation decided in 1649 to privatise it, and it was let for £220 a year to a syndicate, the 'farmers of the Brewhouse', which included Bushrod, Savage, and the clerk, Jonas Palfrey. Farmed or not farmed, the Brewhouse's outlays were of a familiar kind: financing repairs to school buildings, paying for clothing for the poor at Christmas, supporting the Fuel House, and making special payments to the afflicted. Brewhouse money was also used to help deserving shoemakers get started in their trade, to relieve the families of soldiers sent to Jersey, and to buy a new parsonage house. It was used when the town needed extra cash to 'double' on earlier loans to Parliament. Whatever the need, the Brewhouse seemed able to supply it.[56]

The recovery of the town's charitable institutions followed automatically. The Hospital had been 'dissolved' during the war, and even in 1647 poor children were still roaming the streets. John Bushrod headed a committee to get the house reopened, and see that the children were 'supplied with labour'. Thomas Clench was appointed Master, and a man named Clement Brine became the resident supervisor. There was also a woman supervisor for the girls, a spinning teacher, and in 1659 a Wimborne woman was brought in to teach children 'to knit worsted and silk'. But spinning had regained its old pre-eminence: the children received $3\frac{1}{2}d$. a pound for the yarn they produced. The house was again sometimes used as a workhouse for adults as well as children: in 1658 stocks of hemp were bought for them. Clench was not a satisfactory master – when Brine moved out in 1655 he showed no great enthusiasm at having to 'teach and correct' the children himself, or to 'see that they neglect not the sabbath'. But as in earlier days, the Hospital enabled many Dorchester children to get a start in life. Young Thomas Saunders was there for at least five years before he was apprenticed. Hannah Corbin was given clothing and linen when she left to move to Ireland with her parents. Examples like this could easily be multiplied.[57]

The almshouses had come through the war with less interruption, in spite of occasional raids on their funds. The Corporation had borrowed the unspent balance of Margaret Chubb's bequest to the Women's Almshouse, and in 1648 this had still not been repaid. Some of the rents on which Napper's Almshouse depended could not be collected in 1644, yet the almsmen were still paid their full allowance of 1s. 9d. a week throughout the war. With the return of peace there were special treats like the Christmas dinner arranged in 1653. Whetstone's and the Women's Almshouses also survived without much harm, though in 1653 the former was still in debt; when one couple were admitted their parish had to go on paying their weekly relief.[58]

Some charities were more seriously affected by the war than others. John Churchill's gift (for loans to poor artisans) had been almost totally at the disposal of the treasurer, Edmund Dashwood. He died in 1643, in reduced financial circumstances, and it was not until 1659 that new loans could be made. But Dr James's similar gift – the 'Good Friday money' – was back in operation by 1648, when the Corporation raided it to pay the beadle's wages. Some of those assisted with Good Friday money were people clearly in the puritan camp – John Bushrod's brother Henry and the millwright William Haydon, for example – but the fund was not restricted to the politically correct, as Robert Pouncey was lent five pounds from it in 1658.[59]

All this was little more than the revival of earlier philanthropy. But the postwar years saw two developments in social policy that went far beyond the programmes of the 1630s: the care of the sick, and the education of poor children. In the former case the new policies reflected the Corporation's more interventionist attitude towards poor relief. The parishes, of course, retained the primary responsibility for their own poor. Yet even after the appalling penury of the immediate postwar years had lifted, parish relief never returned to its prewar level. In the more prosperous 1650s the relief budget of All Saints, for example, was only about three-quarters of what it had been before the war. Receipts from the parish rate settled down to average about thirty pounds a year, slightly below the prewar figure, and neither St Peter's nor Trinity could afford to resume the old subsidies. If the parish rate had been all they had to rely on, the poor of Dorchester's poorest parish would have been much worse off after the civil war than they had been before it.[60]

Fortunately this was not all they had to rely on. Dwindling parish relief was offset by the many special hand-outs made by the town, out of receipts from Fast Day collections and from Brewhouse funds. These did not go only to the virtuous and the deserving: old Thomas Pouncey frequently received the town's charity. But he was ill and decrepit; at the same time the usual efforts were made to force the allegedly idle, able-bodied poor to work. In 1650 the Corporation considered a scheme for 'setting the poor on work in spinning of worsted and knitting of stockings, and . . . making sackcloth', though apparently nothing came of it. When another bout of unemployment struck in 1658 it was decided to make such people work at the Hospital, beating hemp for sixpence a day. Experience had shown that unemployed adults did not always set the seemliest of examples for the Hospital children, so the operation was soon moved to the 'gaol room' at the Shire Hall. This took care of those unsympathetically described by the authorities as 'such loitering persons of the town as pretend want of work'. A few payments were made from the Brewhouse to people working on the hemp, but the operation was soon abandoned.[61]

Some of the 'extraordinary payments to the poor' were made by the parish overseers, who were reimbursed from the Brewhouse. But others were made directly by the Corporation, and these payments became extremely common in the 1650s. Some applicants made nuisances of themselves; one was given a final shilling, 'upon promise to come no more'. Money was sometimes given, sometimes lent, but in either case it was part of a systematic attempt to meet the special needs of the poor. The Fuel House was revived, with Brewhouse money, in 1649, and Stephen Bedford, a former ensign in the Parliament's forces, was put in charge. Fuel was still sold below market prices, but only to approved customers. In 1658 William Levitt, Bedford's successor, was given 'a new list of the poor to whom he shall deliver turves and faggots'.[62]

While the poor always needed help, those who were ill were especially deserving. Before the war the Corporation had begun using Brewhouse money to relieve the sick, and after 1645 this practice was greatly expanded. Sometimes the town made special payments to parishes whose resources had been strained during epidemics. At other times money was paid to named individuals, usually widows, the elderly, or the particularly deserving – such people as Alexander Biles, parish clerk at All Saints, who was given ten shillings in 1651 to help him through the illness of his wife and children. Those who could afford it were expected to bear part of their medical expenses. When the widow Devenish was sent to Weymouth for an expensive course of treatment she had to pay a third of the cost, the town paid another third, and the rest was raised 'out of honest people's purses'. Even family members were sometimes paid for looking after sick relatives: Henry Chappell got ten shillings for curing his wife's lameness, William Savage's wife the same sum for 'attending her mother in her sickness'.[63]

For a brief moment in history Dorchester had something very like a municipal health service. Between 1646 and 1650 the physician, Dr Losse, received a stipend of eight pounds a year for treating poor patients. Other local doctors were employed in individual cases; in 1659 one at Crewkerne was paid three pounds for performing cataract operations on an elderly Dorchester couple. Regular payments were also made to the apothecaries. Jasper Colson began providing 'physic for the poor people' in 1648; three years later he handed in an itemised bill for almost three pounds' worth of medicine supplied to twelve persons 'not able to pay for it', and in 1655 he received a total of eleven pounds for such services. Richard Bury and a new apothecary, Richard Atkins, also provided medicines on a less regular basis.[64]

Physicians, surgeons and apothecaries were what in our day we should regard as medical professionals. But in an age when people without formal qualifications (usually women) were under attack from those formally certified by such bodies as the Royal College of Physicians (men, of course), it is interesting to find the Dorchester authorities still employing healers of the traditional type. In the early

1650s Anne Butler, widow of the abusive barber-surgeon Gabriel Butler, was the most regularly used. In 1650 the Corporation commended her 'great pains in dressing the widow Hopkins's son, who had very bad legs'. Other healing women were also paid from public funds; later in the decade Cassandra Haggard was the most active of them. Not all the healers were women, though: the men included Robert Griffen and 'young Mr Wilson', perhaps the son of the innkeeper William Wilson, who was paid for 'several cures done on poor people'.[65] John White had urged the townspeople to hear the cries of the poor and the afflicted. In the decade after his death his teachings were still being heeded.

Dorchester's leaders were still much interested in education. They responded to one of White's earlier appeals, voting in 1650 to contribute twenty-five pounds to poor scholars at the universities currently maintained by 'ministers or others of this county'. They did their best to revive the Free School, whose master, Gabriel Reeve, had fled in 1643 and was still absent in November 1646. When he at last returned he seems to have been more concerned about drawing the interest on what was left of the prewar Fast Money than about teaching his pupils. In 1650 the Corporation noted the 'low condition' of the school and concluded that Reeve had 'lost his esteem both in the town and country'. When he refused to resign, the trustees ('upon the earnest solicitation of the townsmen') kicked him out. With him went the Usher, Edward Archbold, dismissed for 'offensive carriage'. Reeve was replaced by the sub-master of St Paul's School, Samuel Cromelholme, who served until he was lured back to St Paul's as master in 1657. The Free School's reputation must have fully recovered, for Cromelholme's successor, Anthony Wither, was soon being talked of as the next master of Winchester, though in the end he stayed in Dorchester.[66]

But it was the education of poor children that most concerned the Dorchester reformers. Trinity School, which they founded before the war, was for boys whose parents, while not rich, could afford to keep them out of the labour force for a few years, perhaps as a prelude to going to the Free School. Some public money had been spent on the education of really poor children, and this continued after the war, when Christopher Gould, the Trinity schoolmaster, was occasionally paid for teaching them to read. Some townswomen were also paid for teaching either by the town or the parishes. Hester Saunders, wife of the godly Thomas Saunders, received eight shillings for teaching two children for a whole year. It is unclear how much teaching these women did; some were probably simply childminders.[67] One of them, however, was a real teacher, and became an important figure in the life of the town.

In October 1651 the Corporation decided that poor children should be 'taught to read at the charge of the Hospital'. So a school was established in an upstairs room there, and Hannah Gifford was chosen as the teacher, at a stipend of ten pounds a year if there were fewer than thirty children, twelve pounds if there were more. Hannah Gifford was a determined and deeply religious woman. She was the daughter of old Bernard Galpin, who had gone to New England years before with so many of his family; she had married Robert Gifford in 1629 and had stayed behind in Dorchester, where she brought up several children of her own. At the new school she taught reading and later the catechism, being commended by the Corporation for her 'extraordinary pains' in this.

The school was immediately popular and the numbers had to be limited to sixty. On 5 November the children solemnly processed to St Peter's church for the Gunpowder Treason service, neatly dressed in the new clothes provided for them by the town; they had to make a good impression, as a collection was going to be taken for the school. Alas, some children had been sent only to get the free clothing. In May 1653 Gifford drew up a list of the delinquents. Several children had not been seen since Christmas; Edward Allen's three had come for only a week, the widow Counter's had been absent for a month, one of John Brine's boys was a confirmed absentee, the other 'seldom there'. The Corporation stopped paying for clothing after this disillusioning experience, though they still did it in special cases: three in 1658 were given clothes, to be 'fit to go unto the school at the Hospital'.[68]

Some children did come regularly. The town paid for the books, from money collected at the Gunpowder Treason services. In December 1658 John Long the bookseller sent in his bill for £3.5s.7d. for bibles, testaments, primers, and 'other small books' delivered to Goodwife Gifford. The spiritual as well as the educational needs of the children were naturally kept in mind. Bibles had sometimes been given to deserving children even before the school was established, and this continued. John Counter got one when he was apprenticed in 1659 – he must have learned to read after all, in spite of his poor attendance. Girls may have attended the Hospital school as well as boys, though the evidence is uncertain. The 1653 list describes some of the absentees as boys, others as 'children'. The Counter family can be reconstructed from the Trinity parish register. Only two of them were young enough to have been at the school; the boy John, and his sister, Alice. Matthew Butler's daughter must have been able to read too, as the churchwardens of All Saints presented her with a New Testament, but the Butlers were better off than the kind of people whose children went to the Hospital school. Whether restricted to boys or open to girls, Hannah Gifford's school was one of the most striking achievements of puritan Dorchester.[69]

No offenders' book has survived from the postwar period, so we know much less about the other side of the programme of reformation – the campaign for discipline and morality – than we do before 1640. The reformers now had the backing of the government at Westminster, and of a bench of county JPs who shared their preoccupations, so it is unlikely that there was any slackening of their efforts. Scattered entries in the Corporation minutes show that people were still being fined for swearing, drunkenness, unlicensed aleselling, and absence from church, which is no more than we should expect. The town still tried to keep out unwelcome outsiders. In 1650 a Charminster labourer agreed to leave, 'whether he marrieth the maid with whom he is in league or no'. The prewar decline in bastardy continued, if the parish registers can be trusted – we must be cautious, for there may have been under-reporting during these chaotic years. In the best recorded parish, Holy Trinity, two bastards were baptised during the war, and only two more between 1646 and 1660. Baptismal records for the other two parishes begin only in 1653, and in neither are any bastards recorded before the Restoration.[70]

The Interregnum JPs were just as hostile as their predecessors to ungodly amusements. Local fairs continued, but it was their economic, not their festive function that kept them alive. In September 1648 the Corporation actually postponed an official Day of Thanksgiving because it fell just before Woodbury Hill Fair, when 'most of the town will be from home'. The great fair still loomed large in the local calendar; two Dorchester people promised to see that lodgers in their houses left by 'the Monday after Woodbury day'. In 1654 a visiting showman turned up with a one-animal menagerie, a camel, 'pretending the Lord Protector's license'; he was told to take the beast away. Although in other parts of the west country old festive customs were being defiantly revived in the 1650s, there is no sign of this in Dorchester. But popular traditions were remarkably resilient, and we can be sure that the mocking laughter was still heard occasionally in the dark back streets and in Colleton Row.[71]

The sarcastic laughter was never quite extinguished, yet John White's vision lived on. After the civil war Dorchester people were still mindful of the needs of their less fortunate neighbours. Wills made in the immediate aftermath of the war not surprisingly contained smaller charitable bequests than many of those in earlier days: there was a lot less money about. But within a few years the old generosity was again in evidence. Some testators spread their charity around, as the wealthy lawyer Matthew Derby did: he left small bequests to the poor of Dorchester and several nearby villages, to the Hospital children, the almspeople, and destitute prisoners in the Gaol. Others, like Julian Parkins, widow of the reprobate Joseph, made fewer, but larger bequests – twenty pounds to the poor of Merriott, Somerset (her birthplace), and a splendid one hundred pounds, which generated six pounds a year from the Brewhouse, for the poor of Dorchester. John Hill was no longer active in Dorchester, but he implemented one of White's cherished projects by setting up an exhibition for a boy from the Free School to go to one of the universities.[72]

Few could afford such generosity. Even known adherents of the godly cause like the schoolmaster Christopher Gould and the combative Patroclus Cooke left little or nothing to charity (we do not know, of course, what they had done during their lifetimes). Yet some less affluent people expressed strong religious commitment, as

Alice Limbury did, for example. Several testators wanted their charity to benefit only the godly poor: Gilbert Loder and the brewer Jonas Palfrey, among others. As Richard Bushrod's bequest was at last producing income for them, the godly poor were being well looked   after.[73]

Dorchester people were also responding to charitable appeals from the pulpit, though not quite as freely as before the war. During the depressed years of 1646 and 1647 Fast Day collections in the churches produced less than half the prewar yield, and recovery began only after 1650. When Gunpowder Treason collections were resumed they too were devoted to the poor, and the yield was usually about the same as on Fast Days. With the establishment of Hannah Gifford's school, however, a new purpose was found which stimulated enough interest for the response to be substantially higher than on Fast Days.[74]

The townspeople also contributed generously to appeals for the relief of suffering elsewhere in Britain, and for the Protestant cause abroad. Appeals for victims of fire or plague were invariably well supported, and even in the impoverished postwar years impressive sums were collected: twenty pounds for plague victims at Honiton in 1646; not much less after an epidemic at Totnes in the following year. Memories of the 1613 fire could still induce Dorchester folk to dip into their pockets for people who suffered similar disasters. Over twenty-eight pounds was collected for Andover in 1647, more than thirty-two pounds for Milton Abbas in 1658, while the huge fire at Marlborough in 1653, the worst of the decade, produced a collection of sixty-five pounds. Special efforts were made in these cases. At the morning services the clergy whipped up their congregations, and the churchwardens took the collection in the afternoon at the church door. Much depended on local knowledge of the places affected, but the intensity of the preaching was also important: Gower extracted over twenty pounds for an appeal from his birthplace, Glasgow.[75]

But it was the old cause of religion that was most likely to arouse the townspeople. As we have seen, they were not much inclined to celebrate victories over their Scots brethren; they contributed three or four times as much to appeals for the rebuilding of churches at Salisbury and the Somerset village of West Camel. Protestant Europe was a different matter. When Protector Cromwell ordered a national appeal on behalf of Protestants driven out of Poland and Bohemia

Dorchester gave almost eighty pounds. Even this pales before the £147.1s.10d. contributed in 1655 for the Vaudois Protestants – the survivors of Milton's 'late massacre in Piedmont'. In this case comparisons with other places can be made, which strikingly confirm the vitality of Dorchester's Protestantism. The collection yielded a pathetic £10.7s.10d. at Sherborne, a place of about the same size as Dorchester, but probably the least puritan town in the entire west country. Other royalist towns – Blandford, Shaftesbury – did little better. On the other hand Lyme Regis, like Dorchester a puritan bastion, contributed just over sixty-three pounds, somewhat less per capita than Dorchester, but far better than the royalist towns. When we look further afield Dorchester's achievement appears even more remarkable. Taunton, which like Lyme sustained an heroic siege during the civil war and had an equally puritan reputation, gave over seventy-five pounds to the Vaudois fund, but from a considerably larger population than Dorchester's. Salisbury was three times the size of Dorchester, yet its contribution was less than a hundred pounds, only two-thirds that of Dorchester. Bristol, the greatest city in the west, five or six times as big, gave £270 – an impressive sum, but again a much smaller one per capita. The Vaudois appeal confirms that Dorchester was more devoted to the protestant cause than any other town in the west of England.[76]

Dorchester had kept the faith. Yet times were changing, and like other puritan towns it had to contend with one more great transformation: the restoration of monarchy in 1660. After the downfall of the ineffective Richard Cromwell, the revived Rump had failed either to govern or prevent the disintegration of the once mighty New Model Army. In April 1660 elections were held for a 'Convention' Parliament that would end the threat of anarchy. In Dorchester old James Gould, still not forgiven by the Corporation, was again a candidate, and there was the inevitable dispute over the franchise. Could all male inhabitants vote, or only freeholders and freemen? Some 'ancient men' were trotted out to swear that the restricted franchise had been 'the custom of the borough time out of mind'; the Protectorate's experiment in wider electoral participation would not be revived. It made little difference, as Gould was narrowly beaten under both franchises, the victors being John Whiteway, the man of the 1650s, and Denzil Holles, back from exile to assist in the restoration of order in church and state. They went off to Westminster and on 1 May Parliament voted that 'according to the ancient and fundamental laws of this kingdom, the government is, and ought to be, by King, Lords and Commons'. The revolution was over.[77]

8

THE END OF GODLY
REFORMATION

ON 10 MAY 1660 King Charles II was proclaimed at Dorchester. Salutes were fired, drums beaten, the bells rang out, and a solemn procession with colours flying followed the Mayor and Corporation to the town centre. The Company of Freemen distributed two pounds among the poor, though there was none of the free beer or the fountains running with wine that we hear of in other places. But if the Dorchester celebrations were not as alcoholic or extravagant as the ones we usually associate with the Restoration, they were none the less sincere. Good Presbyterians that they were, Dorchester people had recoiled in horror from the republican and sectarian excesses of the past decade – the abolition of monarchy and House of Lords, the eruption of dangerous ideas of religious pluralism and toleration – almost as much as Royalists had done. So the Mayor, John Daniell, made a short speech – 'much savouring of loyalty', an observer commented – and then it was the turn of the Town Clerk, Joseph Derby. He looked back over the 'world of confusions' from which they had just escaped, the 'strange and . . . unheard of governments' that had 'wasted our treasure and much precious blood in the nation'. He then proclaimed Charles II, adding a prayer that his throne might be 'established in righteousness'. There were loud cheers, and the gathering dispersed.[1]

A few days later there was a second celebration in the town when the county also proclaimed the King. Again there were banners and noisy acclamations, and the ceremony ended with a sermon by John White's old antagonist, Gilbert Ironside, who had been adviser to the Freemen's Company during the 1631 dispute. His text was from the eighty-fifth Psalm: 'He will speak peace to his people and to his Saints; but let them not turn again to folly'. Ironside denounced the sectarians who had destroyed 'brotherly union', but he also warned the Cavaliers not to think that just because they could now 'insult over others' and drink the King's health until they vomited they were necessarily his most faithful subjects. The cautious moderation of Derby's speech and Ironside's sermon was just as typical of the Restoration as the wild rejoicings at places like Sherborne.[2]

The revolution was over, but godly reformation survived for a few more years; indeed, its last echoes died away only towards the end of the century. Dorchester's governors had never regarded their objectives as being incompatible with monarchy. Charles II was to prove a sad disappointment to those who had so gladly welcomed him as a Christian prince, but in 1660 the outlook seemed promising. Most people expected an accommodation between the royalist Anglicans and the moderate Presbyterians who had been the main architects of the Restoration, and many of the presbyterian clergy managed to conform to the restored Church of England. Some even became bishops. In the end, moderation was to founder on the obstinacy of some Presbyterians, and the opposition of high churchmen and vengeful Cavaliers determined to exact retribution for their sufferings during the previous twenty years. But this became clear only gradually during the months after Charles II's return.

So while the Dorset gentry busied themselves with a loyal address to Charles, Dorchester's reformers went quietly on with their lives. Somebody had had the foresight to hide the royal arms when they were taken down from All Saints church in 1649; they were now put up again, and the churchwardens spent three pounds on 'new gilting of them'. There was a renewed bout of celebration in 1661 when Charles II was crowned at Westminster. On 23 April, Coronation Day, the Company of Freemen gave another hand-out to the poor; once again there are no signs of convivial festivity. But royal occasions were still dutifully commemorated. The bells were rung on 29 May, which was both the King's birthday and the anniversary of his triumphant entry into London. This day, 'Oak Apple Day', as it was later called because of Charles's refuge in the oak tree after

Worcester, was to be one of the most evocative dates in the royalist calendar.[3]

For two years after the Restoration Dorchester was still governed by the men who had steered the town through the treacherous waters of the Interregnum. Richard Savage was elected mayor in October 1660, Josiah Terry a year later. The other Capital Burgesses shuffled the lesser offices around among themselves, as they had always done. But there was trouble about filling vacancies – Bond, Cole and Joliffe had still not been replaced – and the divisions seriously obstructed town business. In February 1661 the Corporation managed to elect Joseph Seward, the mercer William Twisse, and old James Gould, who was restored to his position as 'eldest Alderman'. But Gould once again attended only when it suited him, and Seward refused the oath of office, saying 'Mr Mayor knew his mind; he would not come'. In the course of 1661 Richard Bury died and Frederick Losse resigned, and when replacements were elected they too refused the oath.[4]

People were uneasy about accepting office in so uncertain a political climate, particularly in a town with a notoriously parliamentarian past. The Corporation realised that they needed protectors, so in November 1660 they invested the Lord-Lieutenant of the county, the Duke of Richmond, with the largely decorative title of High Steward. He was not very active, and a far more useful patron was the town's MP, Denzil Holles, named to the Privy Council in June 1660 for his services at the Restoration, and soon raised to the peerage as Baron Holles of Ifield. He was consulted about the choice of a new rector when Gower died, and about the replacement of the Recorder, William Hussey. When he came home to the Friary in October 1661 he was given a lavish welcome of the kind normally reserved for the judges. But he was rarely in Dorchester, and the Corporation normally dealt with him through his steward, John Damer.[5]

Holles could help to divert reprisals for the town's unfashionably puritan past. By the end of 1661 there were ominous rumblings, including the threat of *quo warranto* proceedings – which would require the Corporation to show by what warrant the town's privileges were held, in courts that were likely to be distinctly unfriendly. Recorder Hussey was too politically suspect to be of much help, so in December he was asked to resign. Hussey was furious. Ever since he knew 'what belongs to order and government', he stormed, he had 'honoured Dorchester as a place scarce admitting a second', and it was a shock to be abruptly laid aside. But he bowed to the inevitable, and was replaced by William Constantine, a lawyer who had been MP for Poole in 1640 and had steered a moderate course in the civil war, ending on the King's side. He was an ideal choice: a former Royalist who nevertheless sympathised with the course of reformation being followed in Dorchester. He was retained for 'preventing and stopping the *quo warranto*' even before being sworn in as Recorder.[6]

This was a danger from afar. Within the town, apart from the general unwillingness to serve on the now beleaguered Corporation, the years of revolution had left few obvious scars, though there may have been feuds which have left no traces in the records. In a rare instance of political invective, Joseph Guy told a fellow watchman that they had 'an excise constable, and a runaway constable, and a penny constable'. No doubt he had been drinking (it was midsummer night), and we can only guess what lay behind his outburst. More serious signs of division occurred during the election to the new Parliament in March 1661, when there was the inevitable argument over the franchise. The Corporation had announced that the vote was restricted to freeholders or men paying local rates and taxes, and Mayor Savage rigidly enforced this rule. Holles and old James Gould were elected, and when the former became a peer shortly afterwards his place was taken by John Churchill of Colleton House. The town was edging towards royalism, either by choice or out of self-interest.[7]

So although political life went on much as it had done under the republic, there were hints of changes to come. The same was true in matters of religion. Gilbert Ironside, who became the new bishop, was reasonably accommodating, but there were others who were not. Some of the local Cavaliers tried to unseat William Benn: he and Joshua Churchill were among a number of Dorset ministers presented at the Assizes in September 1660 for not using the Anglican liturgy. But although he suffered a spell of imprisonment, Benn remained at All Saints for another two years. The ecclesiastical courts were restored, but the All Saints churchwardens' accounts suggest that they made little impact until after Easter 1662. Even some Royalists were being conciliatory. Renaldo Knapton had been reappointed

Keeper of the County Gaol, and in March 1662 the churchwardens reduced the rent for his pew because of his 'civility and courtesy' to Mr Benn.[8]

There were some difficulties in the upper parishes, but they too were not very serious. Gower died a few weeks after the Restoration, and the assistant, Russell, left to become Holles's chaplain. The Corporation's first choice to succeed Gower was the minister at Sherborne, Francis Bampfield, a curious character who was always unlucky in his timing – deprived as a Royalist during the civil war, and repeatedly imprisoned as a nonconformist in the 1660s. Some of the town's leaders rode over to Sherborne in July to talk to him; perhaps fortunately for Dorchester he was not interested. Instead a far more orthodox Presbyterian, George Hammond, was persuaded to move from his Devonshire parish. Even this nomination was not unanimous – scattered votes were cast for two other candidates – but he took over in February 1661.[9]

When Hammond arrived the prospect of finding adequate maintenance for the town clergy was more remote than ever. Fordington Parsonage, bought in the postwar sale of confiscated church property, now reverted to its legal owner, the Deanery of Salisbury. The town's gamble that the ecclesiastical revolution would be permanent had failed. A dejected local scribe lamented the consequences of having sold Seaton to buy Fordington: 'all is gone from the ministers, and not one farthing benefit accrues to them'. By the spring of 1662 the stipends of both Benn and the schoolmaster were badly in arrears. Even after John Bushrod had obligingly come forward with a loan there was a shortfall of £6.10s.0d. which had to be raised from 'particular persons'.[10]

The welfare programme which had shaped so much of the character of prewar Dorchester at first continued without much change. There were differences, of course. One of the first medical payments made after the Restoration went to a woman going to London to be touched for the King's Evil: the belief in the monarch's miraculous healing touch had not been extinguished by years of republican rule. Other people going on the same errand were helped, and there were also the familiar payments to local healers like Cassandra Haggard. The Hospital still functioned, though there were complaints that the children 'frequently go abroad a-begging at doors', and dire warnings were issued to those who did this. A new scheme to teach cardmaking was introduced; it was housed in a loft above the 'breaking shop', and nearly fifteen pounds was spent on equipment. Children were still being apprenticed when they left the Hospital: one was sent to Newfoundland to serve a mariner for seven years. William Levitt was still in charge of the Fuel House until his death in 1661, after which his widow and son took over. And Hannah Gifford still ran the reading school, regularly supplied with books by Long the bookseller, as usual paid for out of the Gunpowder Treason collections. Dorchester remained true to its mission of relieving its poor and afflicted, and the townspeople still responded generously to appeals for victims of misfortune in other places: in 1661, for example, a collection for those made homeless by a fire at Ilminster realised over thirty-six pounds.[11]

The Brewhouse was, as always, the key. It provided money for specially deserving welfare cases: for William Arnold's children when he absconded and left them on the parish; for Lazarus Moore, because he was such a 'laborious, painful man'; for Joseph Gray when he migrated to Ireland. It reimbursed overseers of the poor if they had to overspend, and paid off an old debt for Whetstone's Almshouse. But the additional payments now needed for the clergy were a serious drain on its finances, and things got worse when the brewer, Jonas Palfrey, died. He had invested two hundred pounds of his own money in the house, and his widow insisted on repayment at the worst possible time. Frantic efforts to collect outstanding debts had little success, and when barley had to be provided for the poor during a period of scarcity early in 1662 it was paid for by a loan from one of the town serjeants, instead of by the Brewhouse, as would have been the case in the old days. When they wanted to give extra money to the almswomen, the Corporation had to raid funds belonging to the Fuel House.[12]

The reformers knew that their days were numbered, especially after the passage of the Corporation Act in 1661. The measure fulfilled the Cavalier Parliament's aim of purging their enemies from borough governments: commissioners were appointed to remove all members of corporations who refused the oaths of supremacy and allegiance, would not receive the sacrament according to the rites of the Church of England, repudiate Parliament's 1643 oath of loyalty, the Solemn League and Covenant, and swear that it was unlawful 'upon any pretext whatsoever to take arms against the King'. The commissioners, who included the town's new MP, John Churchill, took their time, but they arrived in Dorchester at last in September 1662.[13]

Before the purge the Corporation had a nominal membership of only eleven (three others had been elected, it will be recalled, but had refused to serve). Only three of the eleven survived: the inactive James Gould, Edward Dashwood, and – more surprisingly – Josiah Terry, who was John White's nephew. The other eight refused to betray their pasts by repudiating the Covenant. So out went the ageing survivors of the prewar Corporation: Savage, Bushrod, and John Whiteway. Out went the men of the 1650s: Daniell, Stansby, and Righton. Out went the newly elected William Twisse. Their replacements, elected not by the Corporation but by the commissioners, included the three who had previously refused the oath along with five others. Among them were some familiar names: Robert Napper, yet another of the Gould clan, Richard Churchill of Colleton. Dashwood succeeded Terry as mayor, and as an olive branch to those expelled it was resolved that if any of them changed their minds and returned to the Corporation they would get their old seniority back.[14]

While the Corporation was being transformed, so too were the parishes. Under the new Act of Uniformity ministers were required to declare their loyalty to the re-established Church of England by 24 August 1662, and take the same oath and declaration as in the Corporation Act. When Ironside conducted his visitation in September neither Benn nor Hammond had done so, but both managed to hang on for a few months longer. There may have been hopes that Hammond would change his mind, and no action was taken against him until March 1663. Benn, on the other hand, was clearly going to be obstinate. His living was sequestered, and on 10 September Ironside issued the 'intimation' removing him from All Saints. But the Town Clerk somehow intercepted it, and it was not delivered to the Apparitor, the appropriate officer of the ecclesiastical court, until 12 January 1663. Some of Benn's flock regarded him as their minister whatever his status in the parish. When William Dry made his will in December he left ten shillings to Benn, and the same sum to 'the poor of the church under his ministry of which I am a member', language which suggests that he was one of the gathered church that Benn had formed at All Saints. The new rector, Richard Wine, arrived in February 1663, and was treated generously, getting half the parish's Easter gift, even though he had been there for only about six weeks. Hammond stayed even longer at Trinity. The intimation removing him was dated only 4 March 1663 and was 'affixed' on the 16th. A week later the Corporation was still hoping to persuade him to stay, and asked the trustees of the living to present him to it again, without success. His successor, John Knightsbridge, was installed in July. In 1664 the Corporation offered Hammond the mastership of the Free School, but the Bishop objected, and the High Steward, Richmond, also had some 'prejudice' against him.[15]

That Benn and Hammond lasted so long after August 1662 shows that there were plenty of people more moderate than the Cavalier Ultras in Parliament who were enacting the intolerant Clarendon Code against the dissenters. At the March Assizes in 1663 the preacher was Henry Glover, a client of Denzil Holles's whom the Corporation had once tried to lure to Dorchester as Gower's assistant. Glover's message was one of reconciliation. He found his text in Romans 12: 18 – 'if it be possible . . . live peaceably with all men' – and he prayed that God would 'pour down a spirit of peace and love amongst us'. He uttered the ritual condemnation of ministers who encouraged disobedience and rebellion, but he also denounced those who called 'for fire from heaven against all dissenters'. The war that 'begins in the pulpit', he reminded them, 'must be ended in the field'.[16]

Many people in Dorchester were happy with preaching of this kind, but there were others in the county who were not, and who saw in the Corporation's very moderation signs of disaffection. One such was Renaldo Knapton, the Keeper of the Gaol. Knapton's initial friendliness to Benn and other old enemies quickly evaporated when his job was threatened. In 1664 a group of Dorset gentry led by Elias Bond (who was an Admiralty Judge even though his father, Denis, had been so notorious a republican) tried to replace Knapton with John Wilson, a former parliamentarian soldier who was the son of the innkeeper at the Ship. According to Knapton the purpose was to obtain more lenient treatment for the many nonconformist clergy now in the Gaol. To the fury of the 'fanatic party', Knapton had managed to stop their sermons, but he had been unable to prevent the clerical prisoners being brought food and drink by factious townspeople, or stop them conducting baptisms and churchings. Knapton's letters and petitions depict a town whose puritan character had been little affected by the Restoration.[17]

Dorchester, Knapton declared, was still 'as factious as any place in England'. He was the only person in the town, he claimed with a little exaggeration, who had suffered sequestration or imprisonment, or who had 'served his majesty in the late wars'. The purge of 1662 had left Dorchester in the hands of people only slightly less disaffected than the ones who had been thrown out. The town was a haven for dissenters, protected by magistrates who had no interest in enforcing the punitive Clarendon Code, as Cavalier justices in the county were doing. The town's JPs deliberately avoided disturbing the nonconformist conventicles that met both in and outside the Gaol.

Knapton was exaggerating, for Dorchester was no longer as rabidly puritan as it once had been. The men of the new Corporation were less marked by their parliamentarian past than their predecessors, and they knew that they had to live in a monarchist, Anglican world. So they took care to stay on the right side of powerful people. Edward Dashwood entertained Richmond when the Duke came to Dorchester in 1664, and a few years later the Corporation spent fifteen pounds on feasting Ironside's successor as bishop, Guy Carleton. They could still rely on Holles, who was again lavishly welcomed when he came to the town in 1668. When Recorder Constantine died in 1670 they reluctantly accepted Holles's recommendation to appoint Daubeny Williams, a member of a family too well known in Dorchester for anyone to be comfortable with him. The Corporation protested and argued vehemently that somebody – anybody – else should be offered the job, but to no avail; Williams became Recorder.[18]

The town's leaders had shown pragmatic good sense in adapting to the new climate of the Restoration. But Knapton was partly right: many of the Capital Burgesses had roundhead pasts even if they were willing to disavow them for the sake of staying in office. Several of the new recruits to the Corporation after 1662 were ex-parliamentarians or nonconformists, or came from families which were. Gilbert Whiffen, elected in 1664, had fought for Parliament under Sir Walter Erle; it took him a year to overcome his scruples and take the necessary oaths. Hugh Baker, another 1664 recruit, delayed even longer, while a third person elected in that year, Thomas Hall, was certainly a nonconformist a few years later. Other new Capital Burgesses in the 1660s included Samuel Bond, one more of Denis's sons, and Andrew Loder, a kinsman of the puritan lawyer, Gilbert Loder. Four more known nonconformists had joined, or rejoined, the Corporation by 1676.[19]

One day in September 1665 the King came to Dorchester. He was greeted with loyal enthusiasm: the bells were rung and the Corporation spent freely for his entertainment. The Court was at Salisbury, having been driven out of London by the great plague, and Charles took the opportunity to make a leisurely tour through Dorset, which he had not seen since his escape after Worcester. But his visit to Dorchester had a more politically symbolic purpose. While in the town the King ceremonially gave the royal assent to an act recently passed by Parliament. The measure had been carefully chosen as one conveying an important message for Dorchester. It is known to history as the 'Five Mile Act' because it prohibited nonconformist ministers who would not swear the oath of non-resistance from living within five miles of any corporate town, or any place where they had previously held a living. The act was to prove something of a paper tiger, but in the short run it led to a swift clerical exodus from Dorchester and many other places. Dorchester was the biggest nest of ejected ministers in the western counties, and few towns had so large and influential a dissenting community. The symbolic significance of the King's visit cannot have been lost on his loyal subjects in Dorchester.[20]

Sporadic persecution of nonconformists had begun in Dorset soon after the Restoration, but it became serious only towards the end of 1663, following the discovery of a nonconformist plot in Yorkshire. Benn and other ejected ministers were rounded up and imprisoned, though most of them gave bonds for good behaviour and were released. But as Knapton reported, several stayed in the town and preached to illegal conventicles. Benn was not the only one with close ties to Dorchester. Christopher Lawrence and Joshua Churchill (recently ejected from Fordington) had grown up there and had attended the Free School. John Thompson had married Benn's daughter, and his father had been White's assistant at St Peter's before the war. Benjamin Way, born at Bridport of a family with many relatives in Dorchester, had married a sister of another curate, Richard Russell. And there were other dissenting ministers still in the town – George Hammond, for example – who had not been imprisoned.[21]

Hammond, Way, and a few of the others took the oath prescribed in the Five Mile Act and stayed in Dorchester. The rest dispersed – Benn to Maiden Newton, Churchill to Compton Valence, Lawrence to Frampton – though Bishop Ironside was certain that they were still meeting secretly, 'about what, no man knows'. Benn and Churchill soon drifted back, and by 1669 were preaching to a congregation at Fordington. In 1672 Charles II issued his Declaration of Indulgence allowing nonconformists to worship publicly. Four dissenting congregations were quickly licensed in Dorchester: Hammond served the local Presbyterians, and Benn, Churchill and Way the Congregationalists. The doctrinal differences between them were probably not very great, though it is true that Benn and Churchill had always been more radical than the other local ministers, and lay Presbyterians were likely to be closer to the established church, especially in places as accommodating as Dorchester.[22]

The conventicles included some of the most powerful people in the town. Hammond's congregation met in the houses of William Twisse, Jasper Samways, and John West. Samways was a member of the Corporation, as Twisse had been in 1662 and was to be again; West was Stanley Gower's stepson. The congregation contained two other current or future Capital Burgesses, two men soon afterwards elected to the Common Council, and two recent churchwardens of St Peter's parish. Apart from Stansby, in whose house Benn's conventicle met, the Congregationalists were less prominent – but they were even more numerous. For much of Charles II's reign the dissenters shared power in Dorchester with the conformists on equal terms. Between 1671 and 1682 seven mayors were nonconformists or occasional conformists. Nonconformists attended parish meetings, signed churchwardens' accounts – if they were not churchwardens or overseers themselves, as they often were – and as a matter of course had members of their families baptised or buried in the parish churches. The various confessional groups were linked by innumerable ties of birth, marriage, and friendship. The Terrys are a good example. Josiah Terry had conformed in 1662, but his wife, Margaret, was a sister of the presbyterian William Twisse, and was also related to the Rightons; she left money in her will to Hammond and to another prominent dissenter, Abraham Templeman. The grocer John Symonds balked at the oath and declaration required by the Corporation Act when he was chosen as a Capital Burgess, but he served as churchwarden in Trinity parish just the same. Even hardliners like Stansby and Whiteway, who would not stoop to occasional conformity, continued to be trustees of Trinity parish, and signed the letter inviting Samuel Reyner to succeed Knightsbridge as rector in 1670.[23]

Before 1681 only the Baptists and Quakers suffered anything more than intermittent persecution. A Baptist conventicle at Fordington, some of whose members were Dorchester people, was broken up by soldiers in March 1665. Four years later there were said to be two hundred dissenters in Fordington, that number presumably including members of Benn's and Churchill's congregation as well as Baptists. Governed as it was by Anglican county magistrates, Fordington was a more dangerous place for nonconformists than Dorchester: in 1670 the JP Robert Williams levied fines totalling over sixteen pounds from people caught at a conventicle there. But juries were more inclined to be sympathetic. When Williams brought another charge against members of the Fordington conventicle they were acquitted at Bridport Sessions.[24]

In the town even more than in the county harassment of dissenters was sporadic, varying according to the amount of pressure from above, the nature of the dissent (Quakers being the most and Presbyterians the least likely to suffer), and the inclinations of those temporarily in authority. Even in Dorchester it did not pay to speak out too robustly against the established church. John Lilly told the All Saints churchwardens that he would come to church only once a month – he could not bear such 'babbling' – and when taken before the JPs, abused them in 'gross language' and said that he would not go to church at all. He also refused to contribute to the minister's maintenance – he would give nothing, he said, 'to maintain Wine's wife in a black bag' – and protested bitterly when his poor rate was increased, accusing the overseer, Walter Hewett, of being 'a turncoat indeed'. After the withdrawal of the Declaration of Indulgence dissenters were more often punished for being absent from their parish churches: Stansby, West, and John Bushrod were all fined for this in 1673. Quakers were always fair game, and in the following spring two of them, William Biles and Thomas Strong, were presented at the Assizes. Four leaders of more mainstream dissent – Stansby, the younger Righton, Clement Brine and Abraham Templeman – were also bound over at the Assizes in 1676.[25]

The handful of prosecuted cases probably represents only a small fraction of Dorchester nonconformity. Wills made by townspeople during this period often show their admiration for the dissenting clergy. In 1671 the widow Joan Bartlett left two pounds apiece to a long list of them: Hammond, Benn, Joshua Churchill, Benjamin Way, Joseph Swaffield (son of Matthew, the shoemaker) and others. When James Palfrey, whose father had kept the Brewhouse, died in 1673, his executor and overseer were Stansby and another uncompromising dissenter, William Haydon; the will left sums ranging from two to five pounds to the same group of ministers, only Hammond being omitted. Besides the usual bequests to the poor of the three parishes, Palfrey left five pounds to be disposed of by Stansby, Haydon, and several other dissenters, presumably for the benefit of the congregation of which they were all members. Elizabeth Bedford was more explicit about her intentions: besides two pounds to Joshua Churchill, she left money for 'the poor of the society I belong to in Dorchester'. Thomas Poole left money to the poor of the three parishes, and a further five pounds to be distributed to 'several poor persons' by his executor, the nonconformist John Yeate; he also left ten pounds to Benn and one hundred to Joshua Churchill's wife. Some dissenters made their views plain in their burial instructions: the most extreme was William Haydon, who asked to be buried 'by my dear wife in my garden'. Another strikingly nonconformist will was Philip Stansby's. Besides the usual bequests to the poor of Dorchester and of Lyme Regis (his birthplace), he left five pounds to Joshua Churchill (the most frequent beneficiary of bequests to the clergy), and two pounds to the poor of the congregation 'with whom I have walked in the fellowship of the Gospel'.[26]

However numerous they may have been, the dissenters did not comprise the entire population of Dorchester. After the arrival of Wine and Knightsbridge, services in the churches must have sufficiently resembled those prescribed in the Prayer Book to satisfy the Bishop and Archdeacon. The All Saints churchwardens got into trouble at Blandford for not having provided Wine with a surplice, but after Easter 1664 they quickly remedied this. Puritan symbols, linguistic as well as liturgical, were slowly disappearing; by the end of 1664 the town records revert to the old usage, 'St Peter's', instead of the puritan 'Peter's', for the church and parish. Another sign of the times was the resumption of regular communions at All Saints, where they had been abandoned during the Interregnum. In the year ending at Easter 1666 there were five communions, for each of which 3s. 2d. was spent on bread and wine. This suggests that about eighty people must have received the sacrament at each communion, a far smaller percentage of the population than at Holy Trinity in 1618–20. The churches were still central to the life of the town, but not quite as central as they had been in John White's day.[27]

In one respect at least the clergy were very much worse off. The loss of Fordington Parsonage deprived them of the considerable augmentations to their stipends that first Seaton and then Fordington had provided. In 1663 the Corporation tried to recover something for them by claiming that the sale of Seaton back to Walter Yonge in 1647 had been an illegal transaction. It was a mistake, involving the town in expensive litigation, which they eventually had to settle out of court. The Corporation tried to keep Wine's head above water, and in 1668 agreed to pay him twenty pounds a year. But neither Wine nor the other ministers ever had anything like the income that their predecessors had enjoyed before the Restoration.[28]

After 1662 the vision of a reformed, godly community which had inspired Dorchester's leaders ever since the fire of 1613 gradually faded. The reason in part was generational: great causes are always likely to lose their vitality as the original leaders are supplanted by others who have grown up in a different moral climate. The new men of 1662 may have been sympathetic to nonconformity, but most of them lacked the zeal of those who had fought the good fight against Laudian innovation and the Popish Antichrist in the prewar years. Ageing Puritans like John Whiteway and Richard Savage were losing some of their enthusiasm, but they had spent a lifetime in the service of godly reformation and could never turn their backs on it.

Philip Stansby was an idealistic reformer of the old type, but after 1662 he too was out of office. The men who took over were the realists, the pragmatists, the opportunists, the occasional conformists. Most were financially honest, though one of them, Jasper Samways, helped himself to the Good Friday money during his year of office as mayor.[29] His colleagues were suitably shocked and expelled him, but they too were men of the Restoration, less concerned than their predecessors with improving the morals of their neighbours.

A more practical reason for the decline of the programmes of social betterment was financial. After the loss of Fordington and other property acquired during the revolution the town was chronically short of money, constantly in debt. In November 1662 the Corporation borrowed two hundred pounds from a certain John Henley, and two years later they had to go cap in hand to the Company of Freemen for a loan of twenty pounds. The Brewhouse, the financial engine of the whole programme, never recovered its earlier prosperity. It had originated in the idealism of the 1620s, and when that disappeared after the Restoration the Brewhouse was correspondingly neglected. It seems to have gone back under the Corporation's direct management in 1660, but it was so short of capital that the Steward, William Pitt, had to come to the rescue with a loan of one hundred pounds. A few years later the clerk was sacked for inefficiency, and the Corporation had to raid one of the charities – Churchill's gift – to enable the Brewhouse to pay the new excise. Politics may have led to the loss of one major contract. When Renaldo Knapton was pressed for payment in 1663 he said he would pay, but would then transfer the Gaol's custom to Miller's brewery. Things improved in the later 1660s, when a syndicate headed by John Cole took over at the old rent of £240 a year, but before many years had passed it became impossible to find tenants at this rate. The brewing equipment deteriorated, and in 1672, when Benjamin Spearing got a lease at the much reduced rent of £150, the Corporation had to grant him a rebate because of the 'imperfections'; two years later the malting cistern was repaired at the town's expense. A succession of tenants tried and failed to make a go of it, and the rent asked by the Corporation steadily declined. In 1682 the magistrates ordered St Peter's parish to halve the Brewhouse's poor rate assessment, a sure sign of trouble.[30]

The Brewhouse still made its traditional payments to the poor and the sick throughout the 1660s, but on a much reduced scale compared with the previous decade, and it was becoming less and less central to the system of philanthropy it had previously supported. Weekly relief supplements to deserving individuals were paid until 1674: 1s.6d. a week to old Thomas Walbridge and his wife, 'they being very weak', for example. Responsibility for special medical payments was also sometimes accepted, as when apothecaries' bills were paid for Nathaniel Grindham and Josiah Panchard. The Brewhouse still supplied what was in effect a public discretionary fund, enabling the Corporation to help a poor woman named Honor Bradford with a loan of ten shillings when her husband was at sea during the second Dutch war. But as the Brewhouse declined, the 'weekly payments to several poor persons' had to be abandoned. They were stopped in the upper parishes early in 1674, and in All Saints soon afterwards.[31]

The Brewhouse's difficulties had other disastrous results. There was no distribution of clothing to the poor at Christmas 1662, and although a year later the Steward was told to divide the usual twenty pounds between the three parishes, he was unable to provide it. By 1665 the cupboard was completely bare. The parishes were told to find the money elsewhere (the Brewhouse would reimburse them at midsummer) and the next year the whole distribution was put off until Lady Day. Some years were better than others, but the parishes by now appear to have been losing interest. In 1670 Trinity's overseers did not bother to spend even the little money that was available, and there were 'daily complaints' from the poor that they had not received their clothing. The Christmas distribution continued at an ever declining rate; by 1674 each parish was getting only five pounds a year, and by the end of the decade even this had come to an end. While it lasted, the Brewhouse made the required annual payments from charitable funds invested there – in 1682 All Saints was still getting its two pounds a year from Julian Parkins's gift – but its days as a source of extra money for charity were over.[32]

The Brewhouse had originally been established to finance the Hospital. That institution, too, declined during the Restoration years. By 1660 its character was changing and it was becoming increasingly a workhouse for poor adults as well as children. When Thomas Clench was confirmed as Master in December 1662 his job was to 'keep the poor people a-work'. A subsequent agreement was more specific: Clench was to keep twenty spinning 'turns', and 'set all the poor people and children a-work'. In 1665 Benjamin Spearing took over, agreeing to provide 'spinning work' for fifteen poor people and to pay them at the 'usual rates'; this arrangement continued under Spearing's successor, John Daw. After an investigation in 1673, however, the Corporation noted that the founders' intentions of maintaining fifty poor children had not been implemented 'for many years past'. The Brewhouse's weekly payments to selected poor people were among the first casualties of the subsequent reforms: the endowment was to be again used only to support poor children. What then happened is not clear, because after 1676 the Hospital virtually disappears from the records.[33]

The Hospital school had already vanished by this time. Hannah Gifford was still the teacher until 1668, and the 5 November collections still paid for the books. In 1666 she received eight New Testaments, eleven Psalters, thirteen primers and a dozen hornbooks, and more were bought from the bookseller William Churchill. The Gunpowder Treason collections were still designated for books as late as 1676, but by this time there is no evidence that they were used at the school, or indeed that it functioned at all. In 1670 the book fund was used to make a loan to a certain Peter Wills, and for several years nothing was done with a gradually accumulating balance. The greater toleration allowed to dissent in 1672 may have helped to revive the old activism; the money really was spent on books for a few years after that date. Yet the collections were pathetically small compared with those of prewar years. On 5 November 1661 £3.7s.10d. was collected, but after 1662 receipts fell abruptly. The average for the years 1665–76 was less than £1.5s.0d. – a far cry from the Cromwellian decade, when four pounds would have been thought a poor collection.[34]

As the Hospital and its school declined, Dorchester became more and more like any other small town. In the 1660s the Brewhouse still made occasional payments to young people going to be apprenticed elsewhere: Will Pouncey's son was given a suit of clothes in 1668, 'being to go an apprentice in London'. The merchants John Cole and Maximilian Gollop got the town to pay for the apprenticing of young people sent to work on their lands in New England, and older emigrants were also sometimes subsidised: the town paid Cole three pounds 'for the transportation of John Barber and his family to New England'. Apprentices were far more often bound, with either town or parish help, to local masters, but the Corporation still worried over the number of masterless young people. In 1668 the overseers were told to go from house to house and take the names of 'all such poor children as are fit to be bound out apprentices and go to service', and there was discussion of 'raising a stock for placing poor children apprentice'. The notion that the town might educate them and teach them to read had been abandoned.[35]

How vigorously the regulation of the townspeople's morals continued after the Restoration is hard to say, because only a few fragmentary bits of evidence survive. The JPs still dealt with some old problems: scolding women, for example, as when one of Jane Haggard's neighbours called her 'jaybird, whore, drunken whore and murderous whore'. They still regulated alehouses and suppressed unlicensed ones just as their counterparts did in other towns. In 1674 Benjamin Spearing was promised that a special effort would be made to eliminate the Brewhouse's illegal competitors. This was not easy to do, as in his later years Town Clerk Derby was in the habit of selling alehouse licenses. After his dismissal for this and other offences regulation had more success; four illegal alesellers were fined at the April 1681 Sessions. Apart from this there seems to have been little interest in the reformation of manners. In 1673–4 the constables collected a good many fines from nonconformists who had been absent from church, but only two for drunkenness and three for swearing, two of the culprits being 'strangers'. Borough Sessions records, available from 1676 onwards, disclose a handful of prosecutions for drunkenness, swearing, masterlessness, and illicit sex, but do not suggest anything like the level of regulation that had been the rule fifty years earlier.[36]

In most places in England the popular sports and festivals that the Puritans had struggled to suppress promptly resumed after the Restoration, often with official encouragement. Maypoles reappeared in profusion, and many a boisterous church ale or revel feast was held in villages where they had not been known for years. But not in Dorchester. Itinerant puppeteers who came to the town were routinely turned away; 'we have no waste money for such idle things,' one of them was told. The county JPs were more permissive than their early Stuart predecessors, but they too still suppressed popular amusements in times of crisis. In October 1666, with plague still threatening, the Dorset JPs prohibited 'all sports and pastimes, as bear-baiting, bull-baiting, interludes, common plays, cock-fightings' and so on, because the crowds they attracted made it easier for infection to spread. The Dorchester magistrates made a distinction between legitimate commerce and entertainment. When a man turned up with a license from the King to sell 'remedies and balsoms, and erecting a stage for that purpose', the Corporation gave permission, but not if he used 'any plays, music' etc. As late as 1684 a woman was fined for 'keeping an alley to play kittlepins'. The division between the respectable and the ungodly was as sharp as ever, as the contrasting behaviour of members of two by now familiar families during the Dutch Wars reminds us. On one side we find young Matthew Swaffield, serving faithfully and severely wounded 'in the late engagement against the Dutch' and duly rewarded with a pension. On the other, as usual, we find the Pounceys, still in trouble with the law. Two of them were arrested in 1676, 'affronted' the court, and escaped. In 1672 a Dutch sloop had done a lot of damage to English shipping near Portland. The sloop's crew, an observer reported, included 'one Pouncey, our countryman, who was born at Dorchester . . . and as I am informed served a butcher in [Weymouth]'. He had two wives, it was noted: one in London, the other in Holland.[37]

Yet Dorchester was changing. When an All Saints parish meeting in 1674 decided that they would no longer pay the bellringers, custom was too strong for them. The ringers were not paid that year, but in 1675 they rang on 29 May and 5 November and received their customary shilling each time. Four years later, however, after memories of the 'Good Old Cause' had been reawakened by the great crisis of the Popish Plot, the bells were rung on 5 November, but not on the King's birthday. Trinity was distinctly more patriotic and monarchist than All Saints, by the 1680s at any rate. The parish always rang its bells on St George's Day, and in 1685 they also celebrated James II's accession and birthday, the Day of Thanksgiving for the defeat of Monmouth's rebels, and the feast of Epiphany, or Twelfth Night. Even after Charles II's death, 29 May was generally celebrated with ringing, as the anniversary of the Restoration. Dorchester was becoming a distinctly livelier place by the end of Charles II's reign. There were even two of the now fashionable coffee-houses in the town, one licensed to the widow Margery Gould in 1671, the other to a man named Morris Gauntlett eight years later.[38]

The way Dorchester was changing after the Restoration is also reflected in the slackening of the townspeople's philanthropic generosity. There were no more major bequests of the sort made by the Goulds, Margaret Chubb, and old William Whiteway earlier in the century. Edward Dashwood, one of the last survivors of the prewar oligarchy, showed some of the old spirit when he made his will in 1667: he left fifty pounds from which the interest was to be distributed annually to the poor. John Whiteway and William Twisse, by contrast, left nothing to Dorchester charities. James Gould left money for the poor and the almspeople, and £1.2s.0d. each for eighteen needy craftsmen who were 'of best report for their good conversation'. It sounds a lot, but Gould was much richer than many earlier benefactors who had given more. He was not the only prosperous townsman whose will included only minimal bequests to charity. In 1667 the merchant William Wade left only four pounds to the poor, and although his son John, who died a few years later, did rather better (twenty-five pounds to the poor, five pounds to the Free School), his gift to the Hospital was a paper one, involving the writing-off of a debt owed his father by the Corporation. Margaret Terry, Josiah's widow, left only four pounds to Dorchester's poor, but added an interesting provision that Holy Trinity's share of this should go principally to 'the widows of that parish'. Of the postwar newcomers, the lawyer Henry Bestland did most for the poor – thirty pounds for six parishes, including the three Dorchester ones – but, like Gould, he was immensely rich, capable of leaving five hundred pounds to a son and a thousand each to four daughters. Some of the lesser folk gave more, proportionally, to charity, and as we have seen, a good many of those who did were nonconformists.[39]

Dorchester people still responded well to charitable appeals when they were suitably inspired. Most of the 'briefs' authorising collections for victims of misfortune produced only trivial sums, but when proper preparations were made the results were often impressive.

Before an appeal for plague victims at Southampton in 1665 the ministers were asked to 'stir up the inhabitants . . . to an ample and cheerful contribution'; after evening prayer the collectors would go from house to house. The result was an excellent collection amounting to fifty pounds. In the following year several substantial sums were gathered: twenty pounds for plague victims at Salisbury, just over fifty-five for people made homeless by the great fire of London, and – most impressively because it came only a few days after the collection for London – over twenty-one pounds for plague victims at Winchester.[40]

As always, Dorchester people were more inclined to respond to local appeals than to more distant ones: the £3.13s.0d. given in All Saints parish in 1667 for people made homeless by a fire at Fordington was much bigger than any of the other collections on briefs in that year. They were also still easily touched by the sufferings of sailors taken captive by Barbary pirates. In 1674 nearly four pounds was collected in St Peter's parish to redeem a local man imprisoned in Turkey, and later there were equally successful collections for captives in Algiers. But the town had less control over the disposition of the money collected than it had had before the war. Receipts at Fast Days in 1666 were to be spent only 'as the Lord Bishop . . . shall order'. This may help to account for the declining yield of the 5 November collections, though there were other reasons besides episcopal interference. Many of the leading townspeople were now nonconformists, who might or might not contribute, and people of all social levels were less driven by the high religious zeal that had animated them before the war. When James II authorised a national collection for the persecuted French Huguenots in 1687, Trinity parish contributed a modest seven pounds, far short of the massive sums that had been poured out for the Vaudois and Polish Protestants in the 1650s, or for the Palatinate in James I's reign.[41]

So godly reformation steadily dwindled in Restoration Dorchester. The ideals which had inspired John White and his allies survived, at least for a time, rather better in the new Dorchester than in the old, but there too they slowly faded. Whether or not they had joined the exodus to Windsor, Connecticut, or other places, the emigrants of the 1630s shared in the trials and tribulations in which the New England way was tested. They had watched intently the distant struggles in an England torn by civil war. 'Pray for England, that is now in the battle,' Richard Mather exhorted his Massachusetts congregation in 1644, pray that 'God's people' may be saved from 'the bloody hands of the Papists'. Yet Mather reminded them that England's troubles were the just results of God's righteous wrath: 'there hath been much idolatry.' In 1659 the Dorchester settlers were still holding regular Days of Humiliation on behalf of the brethren they had left behind, praying for God's help as the puritan cause disintegrated and they heard of 'commotions and troubles breaking forth in country and Parliament'.[42]

For Massachusetts colonists as for those they had left behind them in old Dorchester, the goal was the harmonious, unified community. It was easier to proclaim as an ideal than to achieve in practice. In 1645, it was noted, there were 'intemperate clashings in our town meetings', and the selectmen were directed to draw up stricter rules of debate. Naturally there were similar conflicts in the church, for no more in New England than in old England could spiritual matters be disentangled from secular ones. In the 1640s the same disputes erupted over church government – over the people's right to control their elders and ministers – as were raging in England. In one such debate a speaker denounced 'opinions that make a people to be supreme, which have done so much harm in this country', and wished to 'confute that exorbitant Independency that some would establish . . . , and to pluck it up root and branch'. Denzil Holles would have nodded in agreement.[43]

By the time the emigrant Roger Clap wrote his memoirs in the 1680s the ideal of the religious community that had inspired the first settlers had long since begun to wane. Clap looked back with nostalgia to the early days, when people had shown 'great love one to another; very ready to help each other; not seeking their own, but every one another's wealth' in the spirit that John White had taught. But by now New England was becoming too much like the England Clap had tried to get away from, with sin, not grace, openly abounding: 'drunkenness, adultery, fornication, oppression, and abominable pride'.[44] Old men forget, and no doubt Clap heightened the contrast between the glorious past and the sinful present in order to drive home the lesson to his descendants. He was right, though: by the end of the seventeenth century puritan idealism was certainly on the wane in New as well as old England. Yet the new Dorchester and the settlements it had spawned inherited much of the political culture of their English forebears. In the eighteenth century, while old Dorchester was becoming increasingly controlled by the aristocracy and gentry, its American counterpart retained its independence, its town meeting, and a somewhat wider distribution of political power. These alternative political values, driven underground in England, never completely disappeared in New England, and were easily revived during the struggle for independence in the 1770s.

Protestant enthusiasm could still be reawakened in the old Dorchester, however, as it was during the later years of Charles II's reign, when anxiety grew over the prospective succession of his Catholic brother, James. An earlier episode shows that local anti-Catholic feeling was as strong as ever. In 1667 a new arrival in the town took over the Red Lion and foolishly decided to change the inn's 'ancient sign', setting up the Pope as its replacement. As a letter from Weymouth reported, there was, not surprisingly, 'much murmuring both in town and country'. On the next fair day a 'lusty fellow' ordered a jug of beer and then told the host that he 'was sworn against the Pope and popish innovations and he would be faithful to his oath' – he obviously remembered the language of the 1642 Protestation. 'The Pope', he announced, 'should come down this day.' Climbing up on a butcher's stall, he produced a hammer and smashed the sign to the ground. Some bystanders unexpectedly objected – there was 'a great tumult, some taking part of one side and some the other' – and the innkeeper had the sign-breaker put in the lockup. But the mayor, William Wade, soon released him and sent him home.[45]

The choice of the Pope's head as an inn sign, stupid in 1667, would have been unthinkable ten years later, when fears of Catholic conspiracy on behalf of the hated James were beginning to ignite. Who were the real enemies of the state, the Catholics or the protestant dissenters? Few had any doubts in Dorchester, where nonconformists were so comfortably entrenched in the government of the town. The nation became increasingly politicised during the 1670s,

as fears of that menacing combination, 'popery and arbitrary government', became ever more widespread. Anthony Ashley Cooper,
now Earl of Shaftesbury, was busily exploiting these 'country' fears
and trying to turn them against the Court. The 'Cavalier' Parliament,
elected long ago in 1661, had not been dissolved, but its character had
changed dramatically. In a Dorset by-election in 1675 Shaftesbury's
candidate was heavily beaten, but, as a government agent noted, he
had the support of the 'nonconformist party'. Anti-Court feeling
was always strong in Dorchester. When James Gould died in 1676
he was replaced at Westminster by his son, another James, never
very active in the House of Commons, but sufficiently acceptable to
Shaftesbury for the Earl to characterise him as 'worthy'. Even John
Churchill, the other 1661 MP, had moved far enough from his earlier
royalism for Shaftesbury to give him the same label. The Churchills
must by now have been confident of their standing with the ordinary
freemen, as they protested loudly when the mayor certified that the
younger Gould had been elected by the 'burgesses'. The Corporation
was asserting a right to elect MPs by itself, the Churchills complained, excluding 'us and the generality of the said town, who are
above six times more in number'.[46]

In 1678 came the great explosion of the Popish Plot, triggered by
Titus Oates's sensational allegations about a Catholic scheme to burn
London, kill Charles II, and install James as king. Shaftesbury
responded with the proposal to exclude James from the throne,
making the revolutionary claim that Parliament could alter the succession. Amid mounting excitement Dorchester returned members
who soon became supporters of James's exclusion – 'Whigs', as
Shaftesbury's friends were coming to be called – to the two short-
lived Parliaments elected in 1679. The same men were returned to
both: Sir Francis Holles – Denzil's son – and Nicholas Gould, a
cousin of the Dorchester Goulds who had made his money in London
but still had property in the neighbourhood. As usual, the townsmen
were also involved in the county elections, most of them supporting
the Whig, Thomas Freke of Shroton, who was Denzil Holles's stepson. On the day of the election Freke made a substantial gift to
the poor of Dorchester, and the town's close relationship with him
continued until at least 1685.[47]

But by 1681, when Charles II dissolved the third 'exclusion' Parliament, the tide was turning against the Whigs. People of moderate

opinions felt that Shaftesbury had led the country perilously close to civil war by his constitutional extremism and his dangerous appeal to the London mob. In January 1680 only fifteen jurors could be empanelled at Dorchester's Borough Sessions (the normal minimum was twenty-one); grand juries were being pushed into making highly partisan presentments, and many people were uneasy about it. By the time of the August 1681 Sessions it was clear that serious dangers threatened a town so well known for its puritan, dissenting, Whiggish, past. It was time to make known the town's loyalty to its King.[48]

Ever since the dissolution of the recent Parliament (to which Dorchester had once again elected Whig MPs), town corporations had been hastening to express their respect for the legitimate succession and their hatred of Whig extremism. Dorchester's governors now did the same – belatedly, they admitted – and a grand jury of thirty-five, headed by Richard Churchill, produced an appropriately Tory Loyal Address. It contained language, however, that enabled moderate men – even some of those who a few months earlier had been cheering for the Whigs – to subscribe without too much embarrassment. The Address began by recalling the miseries of the Interregnum, blaming them on 'the insinuations and subtle designs of Jesuits, popish priests, and other pretending zealots', and arguing that the recent 'false suggestions of arbitrary government' had been spread by the same sort of people, 'to the same anarchical end'. The signatories thanked Charles for his promise to govern 'by the known laws' (which, of course, only 'ill men' had ever doubted), and promised to hazard lives and fortunes for Charles, his heirs and 'lawful successors' and 'the true Protestant religion'. What might happen if one of those heirs and successors tried to undermine that religion was not specified. An impressive list of 317 inhabitants signed the document, including William Haydon and a few other nonconformists, though most of them followed Philip Stansby's example and had nothing to do with it.[49]

Harassment of dissenters, relaxed in the later 1670s when they could justly claim to be loyal defenders of the state against the Catholic menace, was intensifying. The younger Lawrence Righton was bound over at the April 1681 Sessions, and two years later William Haydon's wife was fined for repeated absences from church. Stansby, the town's most eminent nonconformist, was also prosecuted in 1684 for having been absent for three months. Angered by the treatment he was receiving, the old man told the JPs that he was 'as good a subject as any man that sits in court, or any of you'. He might have reminded Gilbert Whiffen, now sitting in judgement on him as a JP, that forty years earlier he too had fought against his king. Even some who were not dissenters were occasionally stirred to protest at the vindictiveness of the persecution. In 1683 Richard Wine preached at All Saints against the county magistrates' excessive zeal. His sermon, the Bishop of Bristol noted, contained 'passages that tended to the encouragement of the Fanatics, and discouragement of loyal men'. Wine had to make a humiliating public recantation, acknowledging that he had been wrong to criticise JPs for enforcing the laws against 'seditious and schismatical sectaries and other criminals'. In future, he said, he would try to 'reform all such sectaries as shall be within my charge and ministry'.[50]

Somehow Dorchester escaped the worst of the Tory reaction of the early 1680s. In some well-known centres of dissent – Taunton, for example – meeting-houses were reduced to heaps of rubble, and in many others borough charters had to be surrendered and remodelled after *quo warranto* proceedings had required the corporations to show by what warrant they were held. Such proceedings had been threatened against Dorchester in 1661, and they were again pending when Charles II died in February 1685. But the stonewalling tactics of the Town Clerk, Andrew Loder, succeeded, and no action was taken against the town. Loder's family had once been stout Puritans, and he inherited their deep hostility to Catholics: 'a man inveterate against liberty' and 'tenacious for the Test and Penal laws', one of James II's agents reported. The town was wise enough to elect two Tory loyalists (one of them was William Churchill, brother of the 1661 MP) to the new Parliament that met, full of enthusiasm for James, in April 1685.[51]

In February the bells had pealed for James's accession, but there were many who thought that the protestant Duke of Monmouth, Charles II's illegitimate son, was the rightful heir. In Dorchester, William Dowle said that Monmouth ought to be king, 'for he was right heir to the crown because the late king was married to his mother'; John Greybard held similar opinions. When two months later Monmouth landed at Lyme Regis to begin his ill-fated rebellion Dorchester remained remarkably quiet. The town was no more than twenty miles from the route taken by the rebels; but the roads were watched, the militia (with little enthusiasm for James II) on foot, units of the regular army moving into the neighbourhood. Yet it is still surprising that only three men from so notorious a nonconformist stronghold are known to have taken part in the rebellion. Matthew Bragg, a lawyer whose father had been a member of the Corporation in the 1650s, was hanged as a rebel, and two other townsmen were accused of being in arms, though neither seems to have been captured or tried; perhaps they were killed at Sedgemoor.[52]

Dorchester experienced the horrors of the rebellion principally through being the site of the most bloody session of the 'Bloody Assizes'. The County Gaol was soon packed with prisoners – twenty to a cell in some cases – and All Saints church had to be commandeered as overflow accommodation. On 4 September Lord Chief Justice Jeffreys arrived from Salisbury and was lodged in the Bestlands' fine house on High West Street. The next day the Assizes opened in the Shire Hall, and by the time they ended on the 10th Jeffreys had freely displayed the brutal contempt for both law and common humanity that made him justly hated throughout the west country. Well over three hundred prisoners were tried, of whom seventy-four were condemned to death by hanging, drawing, and quartering, after trials that were farcical even by seventeenth-century standards. Another 175 were sentenced to transportation – a good racket much exploited by favoured courtiers. The nonconformist minister John Pinney, father of one transported rebel, expressed heartfelt relief when he heard the news of his son's reprieve from a death sentence. Andrew Loder was Clerk of Assize as well as Town Clerk, and Pinney feared that his son could expect no help from him, indeed that Loder would have 'hastened his death'; yet in the end Loder befriended him. Thirteen of those condemned were executed at Dorchester, the others at various places around the county, and their dismembered remains were for several years a grim reminder of the fate that awaited rebels.[53]

The Gaol was still crowded after the executions, and during the winter gaol-fever took the lives of at least fourteen prisoners; another outbreak a year later, in February 1687, killed off four more, at least one of whom had been a rebel. Conditions, bad at the best of times, must have been appalling. Both the Gaol and All Saints church had to be thoroughly fumigated with burning pitch; the churchwardens claimed that the interior of the church had been virtually 'demolished' by the prisoners. Windows had been smashed, seats broken, and the mayor's seat had to be given a special scrubbing (the rest of the church was only mopped). The 'people of God' from other western towns and villages had participated far more massively in the rebellion than those from Dorchester, but the subsequent reign of terror was long remembered there.[54]

Within a few short years, the bells of Dorchester were clanging again, in 1688, for the acquittal of the 'seven bishops' – put on trial for having petitioned James against having his Declaration of Indulgence read in churches. Before the year was out the town was celebrating the flight of the Catholic king, and the arrival of the protestant saviour, William of Orange.[55] The danger of a return to Catholicism, that nagging fear, which had beset generations of Englishmen for over a century, had been averted. The Glorious Revolution ensured that Dorchester would remain a protestant community in a protestant country, with a constitution which (so men of property believed) guaranteed traditional English liberties under the law, and in the end made the crown's ministers accountable to Parliament. To that extent the long struggle whose course we have traced for almost a hundred years had ended in victory for the reformers.

Yet in Dorchester there can have been little sense of triumph. The high ideals of John White's time had long since been compromised by Restoration pragmatists, by occasional conformists unable or unwilling to continue the programmes that had made Dorchester a more godly, more disciplined, but at the same time more compassionate community. By now all the old reformers had passed from the scene. In 1681 William Benn had been buried at All Saints, the church to which he had come as a young firebrand fifty-two years before, and from which he had been ejected in 1662. In November 1686 another of the reform generation, Philip Stansby, was buried at Holy Trinity. Earlier in that year a general meeting of the Trinity parishioners had agreed, by majority vote, 'that the church should be forthwith vaulted, and the Communion Table railed in, according to the command of the . . . Lord Bishop of this Diocese'.

The church was expensively redecorated, with gilt applied to the pillars and 'the pedestals about the communion table and the font'. By a final irony, the new altar rails were installed by Dorchester's most skilled carpenter, the nonconformist William Haydon. It had taken the bishops almost fifty years, but in the end they had done it. Dorchester had submitted.[56]

EPILOGUE

ON TO CASTERBRIDGE

T W O   L O N G centuries separate the Dorchester we have been exploring from Thomas Hardy's Casterbridge. Early Victorian Dorchester/ Casterbridge was a very different place from the disciplined, godly community that John White and his allies had tried to create after the great fire. Gone was the passionate soul-searching, the high idealism – the fire from heaven – that gave the town its distinctive character in the seventeenth century. Casterbridge had been a '*hoary place o' wickedness*', one of the regulars at the Three Mariners reflected: ''*Tis recorded in history that we rebelled against the King one or two hundred years ago, in the time of the Romans, and that lots of us was hanged on Gallows Hill, and quartered, and our different jints sent about the country like butcher's meat.*''[1] Buzzford gets no marks for his history, though Hardy may well have heard something like this from the local folk memory. The old stories of violence and heroism seemed strange in nineteenth-century Casterbridge, none of whose inhabitants would have been likely to hazard their lives for a cause larger than themselves.

But although Dorchester had been very different in John White's days, by the time of the Glorious Revolution the main outlines of Casterbridge were already in place. Holy Trinity had given up the fight against Laudian ceremonialism, had caved in to Bishop Trelawney over the communion table and the altar rails. Adornment and beautification were now in fashion: gilding the pillars, planting yews and sycamores to shade the churchyard, as All Saints had been doing in the 1680s. Public celebrations were noisier, the bells rung more often, beer was freely available for the ringers. On George I's Coronation Day in 1714 there were bells and bonfires, an ox to be roasted, and enough ale for a crowd of two thousand. The day ended with the burning of an effigy of the Pretender; some local Jacobites riotously tried to rescue it, and moved on to attack one of the nonconformist meeting-houses. They had come a long way from the sober, restrained celebrations of 1660. The nonconformist presence in the town was still strong, and the establishment's close ties with the leading dissenters help to explain the general harmony of the eighteenth century, for the 1714 riot was exceptional. When Daniel Defoe came there he thought Dorchester 'less divided into factions and parties, than in other places'. He was delighted to find the dissenting preacher taking tea with the Anglican clergy, 'conversing with civility and good neighbourhood, like . . . men of a catholic and extensive charity'.[2]

Toleration and civility were one side of the coin; the other was the loss of reformist energy and altruism. By 1693 the Brewhouse was 'void and untenanted'. It still existed in 1706, when iron bars were stolen from the premises, but it was no longer generating funds for charity. Without the Brewhouse to finance it, it was only a matter of time before the Hospital also collapsed. In 1725 it was noted that the 'charity school and workhouse', as the Hospital was by now remembered, had been 'for many years . . . disused, and are now very much out of repair'. It was rebuilt as an ordinary workhouse, with none of the educational intentions of the original foundation, although those intentions were not entirely absent from the Corporation's mind when they first considered repairing it.[3]

There may have been slightly less poverty in Restoration Dorchester as the population stabilised, but the impetus to reform had sunk gently between the waves of conformity and inertia. A changing attitude to worldly pomp is surely reflected in the monument erected in St Peter's church to Denzil Holles after his death in 1680. He was of course an aristocrat, a son of the Earl of Clare, no ordinary member of the reform generation. Yet it still comes as something of a shock, even today, to confront this pompous Augustan figure, so far removed from the puritan simplicities of the people with whom he had thrown in his lot in 1628.

Dorchester's late seventeenth-century records are less than perfect, but they do give some impression of the daily life of the town. Some things had not changed. In 1699 the constables complained about eight unlicensed alehouses, and about certain people who had been absent from church on 8 January, among them – can we be surprised? – three of the Pouncey family. A year later they were concerned about a disorderly house where vagrants had been entertained, but in 1707 their return simply stated, 'All things are well.' The grand inquests at the Borough Sessions showed some interest in practical matters like repairing the streets and removing rubbish, in illegal trading and the unauthorised digging of chalk, but their main concern seems to have been to keep women in their place: several were presented for masterlessness in 1699 and 1700, and another for scolding in 1707.[4]

A new offenders' book reveals the same lack of disciplinary vigour. In the ten years beginning with 1697, the busiest year (1705) saw only twenty-six cases recorded, a tenth of the number in any normal year in the 1630s. The early eighteenth-century cases were, to be sure, mostly of the old, familiar type – the usual list of bastardy, swearing, tippling and assault cases. In several of the bastardy cases soldiers were named as the alleged fathers. Dorchester's new status as a garrison town is also apparent in some other episodes, including one in which Mary, wife of Lawrence Pouncey, was denounced as 'Captain Wallis's whore'. Once again the Pounceys make regular appearances. Young Thomas is charged with stealing wood; Robert and his son are had up for tippling; Lawrence is fined for missing church one Sunday in 1704, and in the same year three of Robert's family are charged with tippling during service time. The town still had other disorderly families, though they were not policed with the same energy as their ancestors two generations before.[5]

The boisterous characters of seventeenth-century Dorchester, bursting into the record with the panache of people like the Pounceys, had less colourful successors. By the time we reach Casterbridge they have dwindled into the pathetic and mean-spirited Christopher Coney, Solomon Longways, and their like. Even the Pounceys became respectable: in 1748 one of them was appointed Master of Trinity School.[6] Dorchester shared in the 'urban renaissance' that improved so many English country towns in the eighteenth century; it had its coffee-houses, its polite balls and assemblies, eventually a playhouse, and was always the social as well as the administrative centre of the county. But the fire from heaven no longer inspired either its preachers or their congregations. And the town lost its political distinctiveness, its franchise invaded by absentee gentry voters, its MPs no longer independent townsmen but clients of the Duke of Newcastle or Lord Milton. For twenty years after 1727 there was a cosy election agreement: one Whig, one Tory. We are in Walpole's England.[7]

Worldliness, ambition, conformity, and sheer inertia in the end defeated reformist idealism, the urge to build a better society that had inspired John White, Hannah Gifford, Philip Stansby and their like. But so did the obstinate tenacity of popular cultural traditions. By 1640 the reformers had apparently eradicated many of the festive customs, the heathenish maypoles and morris-dances, the disorderly bonfires and Christmas games on which they had waged incessant war. Yet the old customs were never forgotten, always lurking not far beneath the surface of popular consciousness. There were important differences between Hardy's Casterbridge and seventeenth-century Dorchester, but in some ways they were surprisingly alike. Mixen Lane in Durnover, *'the Adullam of all the surrounding villages'*, where *'vice ran freely in and out certain of the doors of the neighbourhood'*, had its ancient counterparts in the ill-governed suburbs of Colleton Row and parts of Fordington – Durnover itself. Nicholas Hellier's unsavoury alehouse in Fordington often attracted the attention of Sir Francis Ashley; it was a base for poaching (even of swans and herons) and for many other kinds of iniquity. Joseph Parkins used to take the schoolboys drinking there; Christopher Jenkins's wife used it for a tryst with her husband's servant.[8]

One day in February 1707 Mary Smith was working in Joseph Cave's house in Dorchester when she was alarmed by the discordant noise of a great crowd of people coming up the street, 'with a drum and staves'.[9]

Which way be they going now? 'I can't be sure for a moment . . . because of the malter's chimbley. O yes – I can see 'em . . . They are coming up Corn Street after all.'

Joseph Ford, a servant, admitted that he was 'forced upon a ladder to be carried about the street (by George Cline of this borough)'.

What – two of 'em – are there two figures? 'Yes. Two images on a donkey, back to back, their elbows tied to one another's! She's facing the head, and he's facing the tail.'

They 'came to the said Joseph Cave's house, and some of them said they would go and ride skimmington for Mr Cave'.

Elizabeth-Jane attempted to close the window, but Lucetta held her by main force. ''Tis me!' she said, with a face pale as death. 'A procession – a scandal – an effigy of me, and him!'

They broke doors and windows, 'and affrighted with their threatening the said Joseph Cave's wife, being great with child, so that she is at present in great danger of her life'.

She stood motionless for one second – then fell heavily to the floor. Almost at the instant of her fall the rude music of the skimmington ceased. The roars of sarcastic laughter went off in ripples, and the trampling died out like the rustle of a spent wind.

And so, unwittingly, Thomas Hardy wrote the epitaph of the great seventeenth-century experiment. Whether in the 'real' Dorchester or the fictional Casterbridge, if we look at history through the eyes of the patrons of the Mixen Lane establishments nothing had ever changed. Puritan efforts to reform them had always foundered in a chorus of mocking laughter.

NOTE ON SOURCES

COMPARED with those of many other towns Dorchester's seventeenth-century records are extraordinarily rich, particularly for the first half of the century; a valuable selection from them was published by C.H. Mayo in 1908 in his *Municipal Records of the Borough of Dorchester*. But for all its excellence – Mayo was an extremely careful, reliable editor – his volume is only a selection, and this book is based on many other documents from the Corporation archives (now in the Dorset Record Office) which he did not print. The most revealing for the day-to-day life of the townspeople is the offenders' book (B2/8/1), but much other information has been obtained from the Corporation's minutes (B2/16/1–5), and many other miscellaneous town documents. Besides the Corporation archives, the Dorset Record Office also contains the surviving records of the town's three parishes, William Whiteway's account of town charities (D1/10,448), and two versions of Denis Bond's chronology (D 413/22/1 and D1/JC8).

Apart from the holdings of the Dorset Record Office, the sources that have been most widely used in this book include two recently published by the Dorset Record Society: *The Casebook of Sir Francis Ashley* (a useful supplement to the town's offenders' book); and *William Whiteway of Dorchester: His Diary 1618 to 1635*, which gives us a window into the mental world of one of the leading townsmen, as does Whiteway's Commonplace Book in the Cambridge University Library. For the civil war period two sources are of particular value: *The Minute Books of the Dorset Standing Committee* (another of C.H. Mayo's fine editions); and the accounts of the Treasurer of that committee, Richard Bury, in the Bodleian Library.

I have used the pamphlets, newspapers, and governmental records in the British Library and the Public Record Office that are standard fare for any historian working in the period, always wishing that I had more. But the historian's life is never easy, and some of the limitations of the sources should be mentioned. There is, as one might expect, very little material from before the fire of 1613. The offenders' book exists only for the years 1629 to 1637; another one has survived from the end of the century, but in between there are only a few sporadic constables' accounts and sessions records. The most obvious gap in the sources is the almost complete absence of ecclesiastical court records from the Diocese of Bristol or its Arch-deacon's Court at Blandford, which perished in eighteenth-century fires. But this is not as serious as it might seem, as the town's JPs dealt with many of the offences that at first sight one would expect to have been heard at Blandford. The records of the three parishes become reasonably plentiful after 1653 (except for St Peter's), but before that we have only a register and churchwardens' accounts from Holy Trinity, and overseers' accounts from All Saints.

The sources are not perfect, but I hope that this book has shown that it is possible to reconstruct some of the life of a seventeenth-century community even in less than ideal circumstances. The reader who wishes for more detailed references to the sources and to the secondary works used should consult the Reference Notes.

ABBREVIATIONS

APC: Acts of the Privy Council

Ashley: J.H. Bettey (ed.), *The Casebook of Sir Francis Ashley JP Recorder of Dorchester 1614–1635* (Dorset Record Soc., 7, 1981)

BL: British Library

Bury's accounts: Accounts of Richard Bury, Treasurer to Dorset County Committee (Bodleian, MS Gough Dorset, 14)

CJ: Journals of the House of Commons

Commonplace Book: Commonplace Book of William Whiteway (Cambridge University Library, MS Dd. xi. 73)

CSPD: Calendar of State Papers, Domestic

DNB: Dictionary of National Biography

Dorset Proc.: Proceedings of the Dorset Natural History and Antiquarian Field Club (under various titles)

DRO: Dorset Record Office

DSC: C.H. Mayo (ed.), *Minute Books of the Dorset Standing Committee, 23rd Sept., 1646, to 8th May, 1650* (Exeter, 1902)

HMC: Historical Manuscripts Commission

Hutchins: John Hutchins, *The History and Antiquities of the County of Dorset* (3rd edn., ed. W. Shipp and J.W. Hodson, 1861–73)

LJ: Journals of the House of Lords

MRBD: C.H. Mayo (ed.), *The Municipal Records of the Borough of Dorchester, Dorset* (Exeter, 1908)

PRO: Public Record Office

QS: Quarter Sessions

SDNQ: Somerset and Dorset Notes and Queries

TT: Thomason Tracts

Whiteway: William Whiteway of Dorchester: His Diary 1618 to 1635 (Dorset Record Society, 12, 1991)

NOTES

PROLOGUE
THE GREAT FIRE

1. Thomas Fuller, *History of the Worthies of England*, ed. P.A. Nuttall (1840), I, 451. Although the weather in August seems to have been good, the 1613 harvest was not in the end a particularly bountiful one: see Joan Thirsk (ed.), *Agrarian History of England and Wales*, Vol. IV: *1500–1640* (Cambridge, 1967), Table I, p. 820.

2. 'The lamentable and fearfull Burning . . .', in *Fire From Heaven* (1613); my description of the fire in this Prologue comes mainly from this source. It is reprinted in *Dorset Proc.*, 13 (1892), 77–81. See also Hutchins, II, 340.

3. *Fire From Heaven* says that the barrels were in a merchant's house, but the Shire Hall is more likely. See 1639 inventory in *MRBD*, pp. 678–9. There is some dispute about which side of the street the fire started: PRO, C5 (Bridges)/53/8: Bestland v Haviland, 1668.

4. PRO, C2 (Chancery Proc., James I)/L 13/38: Lawrence v Clarke, 1623.

5. The losses give a rough impression of the distribution of wealth between the three Dorchester parishes: 33 houses, valued at just over £18,000, destroyed in St Peter's parish; 59, worth £13,495, in Trinity parish; 78, worth only £7,599, in All Saints.

6. Hutchins, II, 340. *CSPD, 1611–18*, p. 244. PRO, REQ 2/299/12: Fry v Owen, 1621. See also PRO, C22 (Chancery Depositions)/604/24: Blachford v Short, 1631.

7. *Fire From Heaven*. Hutchins, II, 340. Estimates of the number of houses in Dorchester over the centuries are remarkably stable: 349 in 1529, 368 in 1594; just over 350 in 1749; about 350 in 1763: A.L. Clegg, *A History of Dorchester* (1972), p. 134; *MRBD*, pp. 690–5; Hutchins, II, 337.

8. DRO, PE/DO (HT) CW 1, 1613–14 and 1615–16 accounts, also fols. 73v–74v. PRO, C2 James I/L 13/38: Lawrence v Clarke. William Jones, *The Mysterie of Christes Nativitie: A Sermon Preached in the Parish Church of All-Saints in Dorchester the 25 Day of December, 1613* (1614). I know of no evidence to support the statement by D.W. Lloyd ('Dorchester Buildings', *Dorset Proc.*, 89 (1967), 191), that Trinity was destroyed and St Peter's escaped.

9. *Fire From Heaven*. PRO, PROB 11/125: 19 Rudd (Greene); 11/139: 94 Dale (Barker). PRO, C22/604/24: Blachford v Short.

10. DRO, D 413/22/1: Bond, 'Chronology', p. 41. Hutchins, II, 340. Frances Rose-Troup, *John White* (New York, 1930), p. 30.

11. D 413/22/1, pp. 11, 41. Bond's household goods were worth £220 in 1636: ib. p. 15.

12. PRO, C22/604/24: Blachford v Short. PRO, REQ 2/412/113: Skinner v Gould,

1617. PRO, C5 (Bridges)/53/8: Bestland v Haviland.

13. PRO, PROB 11/350: 1676/50.

14. DRO, D1/10,448: 'William Whiteway's Book'.

CHAPTER ONE
DORCHESTER BEFORE THE FIRE

1. *MRBD*, p. 33. Clegg, *Dorchester*, p. 146. Lucy Toulmin Smith (ed.), *The Itinerary of John Leland* (1906–8), I, 249–50.

2. *MRBD*, pp. xxviii – xxix, xxxi, 1–41, 107.

3. *MRBD*, pp. 35–7.

4. *MRBD*, pp. lii – liii, 102–3, 120, 296. DRO, B2/26/1. The standings noted above are nos. 15 and 34.

5. *Fire From Heaven.*

6. Hutchins, II, 382–3, 522–7. *MRBD*, pp. 306, 325, 340, 343, 347, 355, 358, 360. DRO, B2/26/1, burgages nos. 28, 35. PRO, C22/604/24: Blachford v Short. PRO, PROB 11/127: 44 Cope (Yokeney).

7. Hutchins, II, 415–16. *MRBD*, p. 336. Bodleian, MS Willis 48, fol. 227.

8. P.W. Hasler, *The House of Commons 1558–1603* (1981), I, 151–2. Russell property in Dorchester is mentioned in *MRBD*, p. 359; and PRO, C5/53/8: Bestland v Haviland.

9. *MRBD*, pp. 42, 302, 320, 326, 346, 349, 355, 359, 379, 443, 480–1. V.L. Oliver, 'An Additional Calendar of Dorset Deeds', *Dorset Proc.*, 53 (1931), 72. Clegg, *Dorchester*, p. 57. PRO, PROB 11/129: 11 Weldon. Hasler, *House of Commons*, III, 526–7.

10. Peter Clark and Paul Slack, *English Towns in Transition 1500–1700* (1976), pp. 13, 82–4, 101–2. C.S.L. Davies, *Peace, Print and Protestantism 1450–1558* (1977), p. 246; but cf. E.A. Wrigley and R.S. Schofield, *The Population History of England 1541–1871* (Cambridge, 1989), p. 531.

11. These estimates are derived from the Holy Trinity parish register, DRO, PE/DO (HT) RE 1, and are based on the assumption that the parish contained the same proportion of the

total population of the town as it did after 1653, when registers for the other two parishes become available. My estimates of the population of Trinity parish are obtained by using the crude birth rate figures in Wrigley and Schofield, *Population History*, Table A3.3, pp. 531–2.

12. See Keith Wrightson, *English Society 1580–1680* (1982); and, for witchcraft, Keith Thomas, *Religion and the Decline of Magic* (1971).

13. See W.K. Jordan, *Philanthropy in England 1485–1660* (1959).

14. *MRBD*, pp. 552–5. DRO, D1/10,448, p. 10. W.K. Jordan, *The Forming of the Charitable Institutions of the West of England* (Philadelphia, 1960), p. 59.

15. *MRBD*, p. 480. See also below, n. 34.

16. W.M. Barnes, 'Church Goods, Dorset, 1552', *Dorset Proc.*, 25 (1904), 221–2.

17. See Prologue, n. 5.

18. E.T. Long, 'The Religious Houses of Dorset', *Dorset Proc.*, 53 (1932), 44. Clegg, *Dorchester*, pp. 65–6. Hutchins, II, 365. *MRBD*, pp. xlviii – xlix, 308, 314, 322, 337, 345, 355. Fry, 'Dorset Chantries', II, *Dorset Proc.*, 28 (1907), 15.

19. J.J. Scarisbrick, *The Reformation and the English People* (Oxford, 1984), pp. 19–20. I have followed Scarisbrick for the ensuing discussion of fraternities and chantries.

20. Hutchins, II, 387–9. Clegg, *Dorchester*, pp. 58–60. E.A. Fry, 'Dorset Chantries', 1, *Dorset Proc.*, 27 (1906), 216–17. *MRBD*, pp. xlv–xlvii, 116, 244, 315–18, 322, 586–7: the index shows the overwhelming predominance of the Fraternity of the Blessed Virgin Mary.

21. Clegg, *Dorchester*, p. 66. *MRBD*, pp. 323, 479.

22. Clegg, *Dorchester*, p. 60. *MRBD*, pp. 342–3, 589–93. Fry, 'Dorset Chantries', II, *Dorset Proc.*, 28 (1907), 15; and III, Ibid., 29 (1908), 35–40,. Bodleian, MS Willis 48, fol. 227.

23. *MRBD*, p. 479 (and cf. p. 364). PRO, STAC 8/94/17, deposition of Thomas Foy. DRO, B2/8/1, fol. 190v.

24. Hutchins, II, 393. *MRBD*, p. 346. PE/DO (HT) RE 1, baptisms and burials 1560–1600. G.D. Squibb, 'Dorset Incumbents 1542 – 1731', II, *Dorset Proc.*, 71 (1950), 127.

25. A.G. Dickens, *The English Reformation* (1964), p. 227. David Underdown, *Revel, Riot and Rebellion* (Oxford, 1985), p. 47.

26. HMC, *Salisbury*, V, 225–6.

27. *CSPD, 1581–90*, p. 361; *1591–4*, p. 488. *APC, 1590–1*, p. 358. HMC, *Salisbury*, XII, 366–7, 536; XVII, 591. Hutchins, II, 340. Joseph Gillow, *Literary and Biographical History . . . of the English Catholics* (1885–1902), I, 274. W.M. Barnes, 'A Contribution to the History of Dorchester', *Dorset Proc.*, 20 (1899), 128–36.

28. On the growth of Protestantism in Elizabeth's reign, see Patrick Collinson, *The Birthpangs of Protestant England* (1988).

29. See Roy Strong, *The Cult of Elizabeth* (1977), chap. 4; and David Cressy, *Bonfires and Bells: National Memory and the Protestant Calendar in Elizabethan and Stuart England* (1989).

30. *MRBD*, pp. 478, 480–1. *APC, 1588*, pp. 133, 301, 354. HMC, *Salisbury*, IX, 337.

31. Hutchins, II, 367–8. *MRBD*, pp. 563–4. M.B. Weinstock, *Old Dorset* (Newton Abbot, 1967), p. 142. DRO, D1/10,448, p. 26; B2/27/2 (notes of school accounts, 1597). *SDNQ*, 8 (1902–4), 178.

32. The best guides to all this are Patrick Collinson and Peter Lake. See Collinson, *The Elizabethan Puritan Movement* (Berkeley, Cal., 1967), and *The Religion of Protestants* (Oxford, 1982); and Lake, *Moderate Puritans and the Elizabethan Church* (Cambridge, 1982).

33. John Greene and Oliver Hayne, for example: PRO, PROB 11/125: 19 Rudd (Greene); 11/141: 13 Swann (Hayne). Hutchins, II, 398.

34. In 1606 they still owed the poor fund over £30: see DRO, B2/21/2, 1601–6 accounts.

35. PRO, E 178/4117: Inquisition into goods of William Anthony, 9 James I.

36. PRO, PROB 11/115: 47 Wingfield (Palmer); 11/124: 115 Lawe (Eyres); 11/138: 94 Dale (Barker); 11/174: 61 Goare (Vawter).

37. *MRBD*, pp. 43–56.

38. PRO, PROB 11/129: 74 Weldon; 11/155: 45 Barrington (Margaret and Matthew Chubb wills). *MRBD*, pp. 39, 346–9, 364–5, 378–9, 478–9, 705. *CSPD, 1581–90*, p. 594. PRO, E 179/105/198 (1610 subsidy). Interrogatories in PRO, STAC 8/94/17 confirm that Chubb taught school; the schoolhouse is mentioned in *MRBD*, p. 563. See also L.J. Chubb, 'Matthew and Margaret Chubb', *SDNQ*, 28 (1961–7), 213–18, 230–5.

39. *MRBD*, p. 479. Hasler, *House of Commons 1558–1603*, I, 607. Bodleian, MS Willis 48, fol. 229.

40. Rose-Troup, *White*, pp. 4–19.

41. Rose-Troup, *White*, p. 19. For Cambridge's reputation, see especially William Haller, *The Rise of Puritanism* (New York, 1938), chap. 2. I am grateful to Richard Ollard for information about New College.

42. *DNB*: Burges, Twisse. Collinson, *Religion of Protestants*, pp. 85–9. Paul Seaver, *The Puritan Lectureships* (Stanford, 1970), p. 112. Rose-Troup, *White*, chap. 3.

CHAPTER TWO
DORCHESTER'S GOVERNORS

1. This account of events in Dorchester between 1606 and 1608 is based mainly on the Star Chamber suit, PRO, STAC 8/94/17: Conduit v Chubb.

2. There had also been a fourth libel, 'The Puritan's Profession', not recited in the lawsuit.

3. *MRBD*, pp. 308–64 passim, 449–50, 594–5. *CJ*, II, 432.

4. Other evidence shows that Gould was in fact literate. Perhaps he found Adyn's handwriting difficult; Chubb would have been more familiar with it from his business dealings with him.

5. Jones, *The Mysterie of Christes Nativitie* (1614).

6. John T. Murray, *English Dramatic Companies 1558–1642* (Boston & New York, 1910), II, 26–8. Murray does not record any performances in Dorchester, but we know from Chubb's statements that they had often occurred.

7. The ideal is described by Felicity Heal, 'The Idea of Hospitality in Early Modern England', *Past and Present*, no. 102 (1984), 66–93.

8. PRO, PROB 11/155: 45 Barrington.

9. PRO, PROB 11/101: 26 Bolein. DRO, B2/21/2, 18 March 1597/8; D 413/22/1, p. 42. There were also allegations that Chubb was part of a conspiracy to cheat Robert Corbin's daughter out of her inheritance: PRO, C2 James I/ C11/15: Cage v Corbin, 1603.

10. Chubb's heir was his nephew, son of another Matthew; he also had a brother John. There were other Chubbs in Dorchester, so the genealogy is confusing. See also *MRBD*, pp. 346–7; Hutchins, II, 378; and above, p. 23.

11. *CJ*, II, 435–6. PRO, PROB 11/129: 74 Weldon; 11/155: 45 Barrington (Chubb wills). Clegg, *Dorchester*, p. 97. L.J. Chubb, 'Matthew and Margaret Chubb', *SDNQ*, 28 (1961–7), 213–18, 230–5.

12. PRO, STAC 8/104/10: Chubb v Conduit.

13. *APC, 1613–14*, p. 264. HMC, *Tenth Report*, IV (Capt. Stewart's MSS), p. 62. PRO, PROB 11/138 fol. 245 (R.Barker will). DRO, B2/16/1, 1 Feb. 1619/20 (acquittance to John Barker); D1/10,448. Hutchins, II, 340.

14. *CSPD, 1611–18*, p. 206. T.L. Moir, *The Addled Parliament* (Oxford, 1958).

15. PRO, C2 James I/L 13/38: Lawrence v.

Clarke. There is the counterpart of a three-year lease of the George to Chubb, dated 6 Aug. 1616 in DRO, B2/21/2 (steward's accounts).

16. *Whiteway*, p. 50. See also Hutchins, II, 340–1.

17. All this from *MRBD*, pp. 538–9, with further details from B2/16/6. See also Wyndham A. Bewes, *Church Briefs* (1896), p. 97.

18. *Whiteway*, p. 87. *MRBD*, p. 597.

19. The seating plan is in PE/DO (HT) CW I, fols. 70v–2v (at reverse end of volume). See also 1616–41 accounts, passim.

20. PE/DO (HT) CW I, fols. 24v, 69v. B2/8/1, fol. 35. There may well have been other cases in the now missing diocesan court records.

21. PE/DO (HT) CW I, 1616–40 accounts.

22. PE/DO (HT) CW I, passim. *MRBD*, p. 617. See also Rose-Troup, *White*, p. 395.

23. Rose-Troup, *White*, chap. 22, esp. p. 283. Bodleian, Rawlinson MS B 158, pp. 176–7. For the 1633 sermon, see below, pp. 190–2.

24. *MRBD*, pp. 594–5, 597, 617. PE/DO (HT) CW I, 1617–18, 1634 – 5, and 1635–6 accounts. B2/8/1 fols. 110v, 243.

25. PE/DO (AS) OV I, fol. 7v (between 1634 and 1635 accounts).

26. *Whiteway*, pp. 144, 147, 149. D 413/22/ I, p. 52.

27. See Rose-Troup, *White*, pp. 49–51 (which, however, conflates Edmund and Edward Dashwood); PE/DO (HT) RE I, fols. 27v, 29; D 413/22/1, pp. 32–41.

28. *MRBD*, pp. 165–279 passim. B2/21/1 (1597 accs). PRO, E 179/105/298; REQ 2/412/113: Skinner v Gould, 1617; PROB 11/158: 109 and 92 Scrope.

29. For the elder Whiteway, see his son's Commonplace Book (Cambridge University Library, MS Dd. xi. 73) pp. 43–4, and *Whiteway*, p. 184. For the St Bartholomew incident, see D 413/ 22/1, p. 34.

30. Their wills reveal many of these

connections. See PRO, PROB 11/155: 5 Ridley (Bushrod); 11/183: 60 Coventry (Whiteway, Sr.); 11/158: 92 and 109 Scrope (John and Joan Gould); 11/169: 94 Sadler (Whiteway, Jr.), printed in *Whiteway*, pp. 166–7.

31. *Whiteway*, pp. 56, 68. Changes in membership of the Corporation are established by the signatures in DRO, B2/16/1.

32. Information from subsidy assessments in PRO, E 179/105/298, 313, 320, 322.

33. PRO, PROB 11/148: 88 Rivers. C6/194/33: Cooth v Allambridge et al., 1669.

34. PRO, PROB 11/127: 44 Cope.

35. DRO, B2/16/3, fol. 31. *MRBD*, p. 578. PRO, PROB 11/155: 5 Ridley (Bushrod); 11/301: 225 Nabbs (Parkins). Parkins's will was less generous than Bushrod's, but he had a lot of children to provide for, and may have felt that he had done enough for charity during his lifetime.

36. DRO, B2/8/1, fol. 18v. B2/16/6E, fol. 24. B2/16/4, p. 15. B2/16/3, fol. 33v.

37. Rose-Troup, *White*, pp. 279–85. *Whiteway*, pp. 128, 136, 142, 148, 153. PRO, C22 (Chancery Depositions)/358/40: Gardner v Blachford, 1636. *CSPD, 1625–49, Addenda*, p. 604. *MRBD*, pp. 466, 716. Not that the reformers were entirely blameless: John Hill was accused of being hand in glove with the Blachfords: *CSPD, 1648–9*, p. 379.

38. DRO, B2/8/1, fols. 101, 287. Corporation attendances from B2/16/2–4, passim.

39. *MRBD*, pp. 581–3. D 413/22/1; there is a transcript of a later version of Bond's chronology in D 53/1. Whiteway's chronology is printed in *Dorset Proc.*, 16 (1895), 64–74. His books are inventoried in BL, Egerton MS. 784, fols. 114v–18.

40. Rose-Troup, *White*, p. 290. For the grammar school curriculum, see Kenneth Charlton, *Education in Renaissance England* (1965), chap. 4.

41. DRO B2/8/1, fol. 227v. D 413/22/1, p. 44. D1/10,448, p. 26 (also in Hutchins, II, 368). *Whiteway*, pp. 94,

97. *MRBD*, pp. 564–5. See also Clegg, *Dorchester*, p. 100.

42. White, *A Commentary Upon Genesis* (1656), I, 49, 58–9.

43. John White, *A Sermon preached at Dorchester in the County of Dorset, at the General Assizes held the 7 of March, 1632* [– 33] (1648), pp. 9, 22.

44. One of the first things the Londoner Nehemiah Wallington did after his marriage was to go out and buy a copy of Gouge: Paul Seaver, *Wallington's World* (Stanford, 1985), p. 79.

45. For Mocket, see Gordon J. Schochet, *Patriarchalism in Political Thought* (New York, 1975), pp. 88–90; and Susan D. Amussen, *An Ordered Society: Gender and Class in Early Modern England* (Oxford, 1988), pp. 55–6. For White's views, see his *Sermon preached at Dorchester*, pp. 7, 9, 21–2; and *Commentary Upon Genesis*, II, 85–101; III, 207–8.

46. Bond later added many entries dealing with civil wars and revolutions.

47. DRO, D 413/22/1, pp. 58–81; also D 413/22, Notebook 2. J.P. Rylands (ed.), *Visitation of the County of Dorset taken in the Year 1623* (Harleian Soc., 20, 1885), p. 16.

48. I am the pledge of a strong marriage and a pure love.

49. *Whiteway*, passim. Pastoral poems in Commonplace Book, fol. 159. John Parkins paid the dowry of over £600, including interest, by the time of final settlement in December 1623.

50. Commonplace Book, fols. 152–60v, for these stories. See also *Whiteway*, pp. 109, 116. On the ear-boxing, see John Aubrey's account of Sir Walter Raleigh: O.L. Dick (ed.), *Aubrey's Brief Lives* (1949), p. 256.

51. *Commentary Upon Genesis*, I, 59, 71–2; II, 55–8.

52. Whiteway, Commonplace Book, fol. 175. DRO, D1/10,448.

53. *Whiteway*, pp. 55, 77, 89, 126, 141, 155. For the tapster, see below, p. 157; for the murder of the baby, below, p. 88.

54. D 413/22/1, pp. 7–18, 52. PRO, PROB 11/183: 60 Coventry.

55. DRO, D 413/22/1, passim; *Whiteway*, passim. *MRBD*, p. 644. PRO, SP 16/

147, fol. 71. Whiteway was listed as a defaulter at the 29 July 1629 muster, for not fulfilling his obligations in East Dorset, where his family had lands at Woodford: ib. fol. 90.

56. *Whiteway*, p. 141.

57. May God avert an ill omen.

58. *Whiteway*, passim. DRO, D 413/22/1, pp. 32, 34.

59. D 413/22/1, pp. 39–40. Whiteway, Commonplace Book, fol. 45.

60. Inventory of Bond's library in D 413/22/1, p. 17. We cannot be certain of the full extent of Bond's library because, besides the titles listed, the inventory mentions four unidentified Spanish books and thirty-three 'small books' (pamphlets or almanacs) worth a total of £2.15s.6d.

61. *MRBD*, p. 583. Whiteway, Commonplace Book, fol. 2. Collinson, *Religion of Protestants*, pp. 28–9.

62. His health may have had something to do with it. He had an attack of pleurisy in 1616, though it did not stop him from going to France during that year.

63. Whether Smith's *True Relation* or *General History* is not clear: cf. Commonplace Book, fol. 2. There was another copy of Purchas in the town library.

64. *Whiteway*, p. 134. Commonplace Book, fols. 23–8, 32–4.

65. Commonplace Book, fols. 2, 8–11, 12v–17v, 29–30, 39–40, 42, 154v–6, 175–83v. *Whiteway*, p. 119.

66. Between fols. 183 and 184.

67. *Whiteway*, pp. 41, 43–4, 55, 59, 70.

68. *Whiteway*, pp. 91, 93; Commonplace Book, fol. 138.

69. Whiteway, Commonplace Book, fols. 147, 155, 158v; *Whiteway*, pp. 110, 133.

70. PE/DO (HT) CW 1, 1621–41 accounts, passim. D 413/22/1, p. 48. *Whiteway*, pp. 55, 88, 117, 122, 132, 134, 152. Bodleian, Add. MS B97, fol. 63. *MRBD*, p. 645.

71. BL, Add. MS 35,331 (Walter Yonge's Diary, 1627–42), fol. 29v. Rose-Troup, *White*, p. 294. Laud's minute on Bernard's petition describes it as being directed against White: PRO, SP 16/219, fol. 20.

72. John White, *The Troubles of Jerusalems Restauration* (1645), p. 3.

CHAPTER THREE
POVERTY AND DISORDER IN DORCHESTER

1. DRO, B2/8/1, fols. 210–10v, 213–13v. *Whiteway*, p. 145.

2. B2/8/1, fols. 127v, 134v, 146v, 193, 203v, 218v–19, 246, 270v, 288, 293v–5v, 307, 311v, 315v, 341v. B2/16/4, p. 194.

3. *MRBD*, p. 668. B2/8/1, fols. 21, 63v, 250v, 251v–2.

4. *MRBD*, pp. 658, 665. B2/8/1, fols. 40, 220v–1, 274.

5. B2/8/1, fols. 33, 331v, 343. Wiltshire Record Office, Dean's Peculiar, Presentments, 1635, no. 57.

6. *MRBD*, pp. 651, 661, 663. B2/8/1, fols. 84, 127, 133v, 141, 148, 167v, 169v, 275v, 283.

7. Underdown, *Revel, Riot and Rebellion*, pp. 98–9.

8. *MRBD*, p. 668. B2/8/1, fol. 252v.

9. B2/8/1, fols. 9, 42, 155v, 200, 290.

10. B2/8/1, fols. 290, 334v, 361. Susan Lee had previously been convicted in the ecclesiastical court and excommunicated.

11. B2/8/1, fol. 231. Dowrage was already suspicious two years earlier: fol. 134.

12. PRO, PROB 11/116: 105 Wingfield. Edwards was buried on 17 August 1610, and his widow married Parkins on 7 November: DRO, PE/DO (HT) RE 1, fol. 59v; W.P.W. Phillimore and E.R. Nevill (eds.), *Dorset Parish Registers, Marriages*, VII (1914), 7.

13. PE/DO (HT) CW 1, 1614–17 accounts; CW 2 (1685–1732), copy of 1612 accounts at end of volume. *Ashley*, pp. 16, 36, 41.

14. B2/8/1, fols. 8–9, 216, 231v–3, 254–8. PE/DO (HT) RE 1, fol. 39.

15. B2/8/1, fols. 306v, 308v. B2/16/3, fol.

115. PRO, PROB 11/212: 99 Pembroke (Joseph Parkins); 11/273: 85 Wootton (Julian Parkins).

16. DRO, B2/8/1, fols. 246v–7, 318v.

17. *Ashley*, p. 45. B2/8/1, fols. 120v, 156v, 162, 224. When Elizabeth Harris, Sarah's sister, was bound over for similarly suspicious conduct, Christopher Jenkins was one of her sureties (fol. 216). Dorchester's magistrates were not the only ones to be suspicious of 'charmaids': Underdown, *Revel, Riot and Rebellion*, pp. 36–7.

18. B2/8/1, fols. 2, 9, 20v, 31v, 34v, 138–9, 175v, 182v.

19. B2/8/1, fols. 10v, 203v, 219v–21, 278v.

20. B2/8/1, fols. 8, 22, 74v, 127v, 152v, 213v, 326v. B2/16/4, p. 37.

21. B2/8/1, fols. 235, 350.

22. For the licensees, see annual recognizances in B2/8/1, also fols. 188, 228v. For the George, see Buckler v Combe, 1632, in F.J. Pope, 'Dorset Depositions' (MS at Dorset County Museum), VII, 4–5; and DRO, B2/16/2, 28 Sept. 1632.

23. B2/8/1, fols. 36, 56, 70v, 101v, 119v, 133, 274, 288v, 298v–9, 306v, 318v. Lawrence and Swaffield both had sons who entered the ministry: A.G. Matthews, *Calamy Revised* (Oxford, 1934), pp. 317, 470.

24. *MRBD*, p. 658. B2/8/1, fols. 10v, 43–4, 57v, 65v, 70v, 113v, 134v, 148v, 169v, 174v, 180v, 215v, 248, 281, 301, 309, 315–16.

25. B2/13/1, 16 April and 30 June 1625. B2/8/1, fols. 175–6, 177v, 179, 180v, 185v, 237, 240, 283, 338v.

26. B2/8/1, fols. 143, 185v, 278, 345. See also Peter Clark, *The English Alehouse: A Social History 1200–1830* (1983), pp. 73, 79–80.

27. B2/8/1, fols. 53, 91, 188v, 322, 334. *MRBD*, p. 658.

28. B2/8/1, fols. 57v, 145, 237, 313v, and many other entries. Richard Gough, *The History of Myddle* (ed. David Hey, Harmondsworth, 1981), passim. For a good general survey, see Clark, *English Alehouse*, chaps. 3–8; and note his analysis of customers at Dorchester

alehouses, p. 126.

29. B2/8/1, fols. 290, 310.

30. B2/8/1, fols. 48, 127, 162, 211, 223, 239, 241, 265, 348v, 351.

31. B2/8/1, fols. 37v, 61v, 65, 104, 323v–4v.

32. *MRBD*, p. 654. B2/8/1, fols. 20v, 49v, 90, 146v, 147v, 183v, 186v, 192v, 230v, 243.

33. *MRBD*, p. 660. B2/8/1, fols. 108, 110v, 140, 161, 181, 192v.

34. *MRBD*, pp. 651, 658. B2/8/1, fols. 16v, 105, 323v, 350.

35. B2/8/1, fols. 142, 152v, 298v.

36. B2/8/1, fols. 37v, 50v, 177, 268, 318v, 345.

37. *MRBD*, pp. 650, 661. B2/8/1, fols. 3v, 100, 156v–7, 216v, 220v.

38. Gig: a flighty girl. Runagate: a vagrant (*OED*). The other two terms require no explanation.

39. *MRBD*, pp. 654, 660, 663–4. B2/8/1, fols. 16v, 31, 100v, 122, 134, 160v, 227.

40. *MRBD*, pp. 664–5. B2/8/1, fol. 265v. For witchcraft accusations, see Thomas, *Religion and the Decline of Magic*, esp. p. 544 (for the burning ritual).

41. See A.L. Beier, *Masterless Men* (1985), esp. pp. 9–12.

42. *Ashley*, pp. 36, 55–6. B2/8/1, fol. 169v.

43. B2/8/1, fols. 21, 87–8, 151, 313.

44. B2/8/1, fols. 168, 183, 292v.

45. *MRBD*, pp. 655, 658–9, 661. B2/8/1, fols. 21, 82, 90, 106, 117, 144v, 174v, 196, 227, 230, 237–8, 242. Andrew Fooke and Katherine Goodfellow later got married.

46. *MRBD*, pp. 656, 669. B2/8/1, fols. 4v, 39, 52, 89, 90, 110v–11, 261v, 317v.

47. B2/8/1, fols. 42, 57–8v, 65v, 72, 84v, 105, 128v, 221, 282v, 339v.

48. B2/8/1, fols. 41v, 81v, 152, 161, 218, 237v.

49. B2/8/1, fols. 314–15. Not all Follett's friends were juveniles: Leonard Gaylard was bound apprentice in 1631, and must therefore have been 18 or 19.

50. B2/13/1, 9 April 1632. B2/8/1, fols. 44, 216, 270v, 279, 293v, 322.

51. B2/8/1, fols. 92, 169, 172–3, 183. For

masters and servants, see also Amussen, *Ordered Society*, pp. 159, 167.

52. *Ashley*, pp. 18–20. B2/8/1, fols. 56, 170v, 298v. B2/16/1, 18 Feb. 1618/19. B2/16/4, p. 9.

53. For this and the following paragraphs, see PE/DO (AS) OV 1, 1632–42 accounts.

54. DRO, QSOB, 1625–38, fol. 34. *Whiteway*, pp. 39, 46. PE/DO (HT) CW 1, 1618–21 accounts. B2/13/1, 10 April 1623. *MRBD*, p. 393. For Salisbury during this depression, see Paul Slack, 'Poverty and Politics in Salisbury', in Peter Clark and Paul Slack (eds.), *Crisis and Order in English Towns 1500–1700* (1972), pp. 164–203; and Paul Slack (ed.), *Poverty in Early-Stuart Salisbury* (Wilts. Record Soc., 31, 1975).

55. *Whiteway*, pp. 110, 113. *CSPD, 1629–31*, p. 547; *1631–3*, pp. 185–6. For index of cereal prices during these years, see Thirsk (ed.), *Agrarian History of England*

and Wales, IV, Table I, p. 821.

56. B2/8/1, fols. 50–3, 63, 68v.

57. *MRBD*, pp. 594, 655–6. B2/8/1, fol. 59. For another Samways outburst, see below, p. 150.

58. B2/8/1, fol. 100v–101. For food riots in general, see John Walter and Keith Wrightson, 'Dearth and the Social Order in Early Modern England', in Paul Slack (ed.), *Rebellion, Popular Protest and the Social Order in Early Modern England* (Cambridge, 1984), pp. 108–28.

59. *Ashley*, p. 22. B2/8/1, fols. 212, 214v, 356. *APC, 1629–30*, p. 262. DRO, QSOB, 1625–37, fols. 51, 130v.

60. B2/8/1, fols. 72, 75, 90, 107v, 308v. *MRBD*, p. 669. B2/16/4, p. 20.

61. B2/8/1, fols. 208–9. Seventeenth-century justice did not customarily entertain an insanity plea as a defence. However, the JPs' line of questioning suggests that they wished to establish that Galpin was of sound mind at the time of the murder.

CHAPTER FOUR
GODLY REFORMATION, 1613–1642

1. DRO, D1/10,448. Hutchins, II, 341.

2. Rose-Troup, *White*, p. 30, citing White's *Tree Of Life* (1647).

3. *Troubles of Jerusalems Restauration*, p. 49.

4. Two versions of the covenant are printed in Rose-Troup, *White*, pp. 418–22. See also Collinson, *Religion of Protestants*, pp. 269–70.

5. As Collinson observes, White's vows expressed 'a civic ethic of the common good which would not have been out of place in a south German city in the first age of the Reformation': *Religion of Protestants*, p. 272.

6. *Winthrop Papers* (Boston, 1929–47), III, 322. White, *Commentary Upon Genesis*, I, 44; II, 58.

7. PRO, SP 16/301, fol. 6 (*CSPD, 1635*, p. 459). See also SP 16/535, fol. 306 (*CSPD, 1625–49, Addenda*, p. 62). *MRBD*, p. 596. But cf. Bodleian, Rawlinson MS B 158, p. 177, which says that White did make subscription

a condition for being admitted to communion.

8. Bodleian, Rawl. MS B 158, p. 177. *Whiteway*, pp. 76, 87, 96, 100, 156. White's *Commentary Upon Genesis* was presumably a product of these scriptural exercises.

9. *Whiteway*, p. 149. DRO, B2/8/1, fol. 151. For 5 November, see Cressy, *Bonfires and Bells*, esp. chap. 9.

10. Fuller, *Worthies* (ed. Nuttall), II, 25. Rose-Troup, *White*, esp. pp. 43–8, 264–5. *CSPD, 1635*, p. 500. B2/16/6E, fol. 24. *MRBD*, p. 597.

11. Rose-Troup, *White*, pp. 241, 256, 258–60, 453. *MRBD*, pp. 596–601. *Whiteway*, pp. 123, 127, 132, 136.

12. *MRBD*, pp. 613–17. Rose-Troup, *White*, pp. 244–5, 256–7. *DNB*: Benn.

13. 1633 *Sermon*, pp. 7, 21.

14. *MRBD*, pp. 651, 654. B2/8/1, fols. 2v, 123v, 261v, 314–15.

15. *Whiteway*, p. 27. B2/8/1, fols. 97, 100,

153, 179, 245v, 282, 289. For an excellent survey of constables and their duties, see Joan Kent, *The English Village Constable 1580–1642* (Oxford, 1986).

16. B2/8/1, fols. 20, 39, 124, 197, 227, 235, 277v, 320, 348v, 358v–60. *MRBD*, pp. 532–3, 535, 652.

17. B2/8/1, fols. 25, 50v, 268, and passim.

18. *Whiteway*, p. 86. B2/13/1, 4 Nov. 1622. B2/16/3, fol. 72.

19. *MRBD*, pp. 467, 502, 658. B2/8/1, fols. 108, 214v, 228, 266, 294. B2/16/3, fol. 25. B2/16/4, pp. 16, 61–2.

20. B2/8/1, fols. 41v, 83–4, 87v, 117, 136v, 274. There was another set of stocks outside the County Gaol: *APC, 1629–30*, p. 262.

21. *MRBD*, p. 658. B2/8/1, fol. 103, among many other possible examples.

22. For examples, B2/8/1, fols. 34, 177v, 269, 281, 315v, 354. Perhaps the 'cage house' built in 1565–6: *MRBD*, pp. 479, 708. See also B2/16/3, fol. 23; and B2/16/4, p. 57.

23. B2/8/1, fols. 10v, 134v, 140, 265v, 328. *Whiteway*, p. 145. *APC, 1629–30*, pp. 261–2. DRO, QSOB, 1625–37, fol. 488.

24. *MRBD*, pp. 594–6, 651, 668. *Ashley*, pp. 18–20. B2/8/1, fols. 6v, 28v, 214, 354v–7. *Whiteway*, p. 143. DRO, QSOB, 1625 – 37, fol. 381v.

25. DRO, QSOB, 1625–37, fol. 150v; 1663–74, p. 42. *APC, 1629 – 30*, pp. 260–2. *Whiteway*, p. 63; Commonplace Book, fol. 151v. D 413/22/1, p. 45. B2/8/1, fols. 258v, 280v.

26. B2/8/1, fols. 3, 13v, 18v, 109v, 149, 156v, 248, 265v.

27. *MRBD*, pp. 655, 665. B2/8/1, fols. 48v, 244v. See below, pp. 264–5, for a later skimmington in Dorchester, resembling the one in Thomas Hardy's *The Mayor of Casterbridge*.

28. B2/8/1, fols. 146v, 227v–8, 253.

29. B2/8/1, fols. 60, 84v, 111, 320, 322.

30. *MRBD*, p. 656. B2/8/1, fols. 18v, 30, 77, 81v, 90, 110, 113v, 164v, 174v, 181v, 242, 261v, 269, 295, 321v–2, 345.

31. B2/8/1, fols. 2, 10, 25v, 29–31, 44v, 173, 199, 291v. DRO, QSOB, 1625–37, fol. 346.

32. For the seventeenth-century campaign to suppress disorder, see Anthony Fletcher, *Reform in the Provinces: The Government of Stuart England* (New Haven, 1986), chap. 8.

33. B2/13/1, 30 June 1625. B2/8/1, fols. 38, 161, 174v, 181, 189v. For the whole subject of masterlessness and vagrancy, see Beier, *Masterless Men*.

34. B2/13/1, 30 Jan. 1622, 3 March 1631. B2/8/1, fols. 41v–2, 49v, 186, 215.

35. *MRBD*, pp. 652, 654, 658, 663–4, 666. B2/8/1, fols. 12, 14, 279, 299, 340–1. See also Paul Slack, 'Vagrants and Vagrancy in England, 1598–1664', *Economic History Review*, 2nd ser., 27 (1974), 360–1, 369–70, 375.

36. *MRBD*, pp. 654–5. B2/8/1, fols. 14v–15v, 25, 29, 106v–7, 222v–3, 229–30, 307.

37. B2/8/1, fols. 56v–8v, 70v, 129, 131v–3v. PRO, SP 16/187, fol. 32. DRO, B2/16/4, pp. 23, 30.

38. See Underdown, *Revel, Riot and Rebellion*, pp. 56–8, 93. For ballad-sellers at Dorset fairs see also B2/8/1, fol. 95v.

39. *Ashley*, p. 10 (the transcription misprints John as Henry Gould). For Reason, see G.E. Bentley, *The Jacobean and Caroline Stage* (Oxford, 1941–68), II, 541–3. For the Prince's company, see *Ibid.*, I, chap. 5. For the political implications of cultural conflict, see also Leah S. Marcus, *The Politics of Mirth* (Chicago, 1986).

40. *Whiteway*, pp. 55, 111, 154. DRO, QSOB, 1625–37, fol. 272v. Murray, *Dramatic Companies*, II, 206. *MRBD*, p. 667. The prologue to one of Cheeke's Latin plays is in Bodleian, Add. MS 97, fol. 63.

41. DRO, B2/8/1, fol. 146v (wrongly printed as 'but at Corfe', instead of 'but at Coits', in *Dorset Proc.*, 10, 76). B2/16/3, fol. 30v. See also *Ashley*, p. 44; and B2/16/4, p. 11.

42. For presentments of non-communicants, see, for example, PE/DO (HT) CW 1, 1619–20 accounts.

43. Before 1597 the Trinity register is often imperfect or illegible. However, averages for several four- or five-year

periods can be obtained, and after 1601 the quality of the register makes it possible to obtain five-year averages without difficulty.

44. Comparative figures from Wrigley and Schofield, *Population History*; and Peter Laslett, *Family Life and Illicit Love in Earlier Generations* (Cambridge, 1977), pp. 116–17.

45. The decline in pre-marital pregnancy, from an average of over 16 per cent of brides before 1600, to just over 11 per cent in the years 1600–42, can be seen in the sample parishes used in P.E.M. Hair, 'Bridal Pregnancy in England Further Examined', *Population Studies*, 24 (1970), 60. For St Andrews, see Geoffrey Parker, 'The "Kirk by law established" and the origins of the taming of Scotland: St Andrews 1559–1600', in Leah Leneman (ed.), *Perspectives in Scottish Social History: Essays in Honour of Rosalind Mitchison* (Aberdeen, 1988).

46. *MRBD*, pp. 620–1. *CSPD, 1611–18*, p. 506. DRO, D1/10,448, p. 27. Rose-Troup, *White*, chap. 19, esp. pp. 254–5, 257. For the Feoffees, see Seaver, *The Puritan Lectureships*.

47. *MRBD*, pp. 596–7, 601, 622–5, 712–13. Rose-Troup, *White*, pp. 260–3. B2/16/3, fols. 11, 16Av. *Whiteway*, p. 123.

48. *Winthrop Papers*, III, 336. Hutchins, II, 397. Rose-Troup, *White*, pp. 34–5. For a similar programme in Salisbury, see Slack (ed.), *Poverty in Early-Stuart Salisbury*.

49. Hutchins, II, 397–8. The proceeds of these collections rose from just over £27 at the two services in 1617 to over £49 in 1621, before falling back slightly during the next two years.

50. D 413/22/1, p. 43. Hutchins, II, 398. *MRBD*, pp. 514–15, 559, 562. D1/10,448, p. 10.

51. Hutchins, II, 397, 399. *MRBD*, pp. 514–17. B2/8/1, fols. 100v, 237, 338. B2/16/1, 16 July 1619. B2/16/3, fols. 50, 70, 92v.

52. *MRBD*, pp. 515–16. Hutchins, II, 399. B2/16/3, fol. 14. B2/8/1, fols. 170v, 239v, 308. B2/16/4, p. 52. See also Eric

Kerridge, *Textile Manufactures in Early Modern England* (Manchester, 1985), pp. 138–9, 198–9; I am grateful to Paul Slack for this reference.

53. Hutchins, II, 399. B2/16/4, pp. 41, 45. B2/8/1, fols. 218, 337v–8. A 'Hospital Book' recorded these transactions in more detail, but has unfortunately not survived.

54. B2/8/1, fols. 170v, 185, 218, 237, 281v, 337v. *MRBD*, p. 667.

55. B2/8/1, fols. 84, 292v. B2/16/3, fols. 14, 24v, 92v. B2/16/4, pp. 7, 46, 48, 52, 54. Payments for apprenticeship out of the Hospital stock were presumably also for Hospital children even if this is not specified. See e.g. B2/16/3, fol. 25; B2/16/4, pp. 7, 9.

56. White, *Commentary Upon Genesis*, III, 66. *MRBD*, pp. 515–16, 564. B2/16/3, fols. 4v, 8v. B2/8/1, fols. 100v, 314. B2/16/4, pp. 8, 40. See also Ian Green, "For Children in Yeeres and Children in Understanding": The Emergence of the English Catechism under Elizabeth and the Early Stuarts', *Journal of Ecclesiastical History*, 37 (1986), 408–9, 419–20.

57. Rose-Troup, *White*, pp. 32–3. Hutchins, II, 399. Ball published four different catechisms; this presumably was the most popular of them, the *Short Catechism*, reprinted over thirty times by 1645: Green, 'For Children in Yeeres', pp. 400, 419.

58. Rose-Troup, *White*, p. 37. D 413/22/1, p. 44. D1/10,448, p. 27. PE/DO (HT) CW 1, fol. 5v, and 1636–40 accounts. *MRBD*, p. 534. On petty schools in general, see David Cressy, *Literacy and the Social Order: Reading and Writing in Tudor and Stuart England* (Cambridge, 1980), pp. 35–8.

59. Reduced in 1623 to six per cent. For the management of Whetstone's money, see B2/16/6, fols. 1–4 (Whetstone's accounts); B2/16/1, 8 April 1619; *MRBD*, p. 560.

60. *MRBD*, p. 525. B2/16/1, 18 March and 8 April 1622. B2/16/3, fol. 131v. B2/16/4, p. 11. *Whiteway*, p. 47. For the Salisbury brewhouse, see Slack, 'Poverty and Politics in Salisbury', esp.

pp. 183–4, 190–1; and Slack (ed.),
Poverty in Early-Stuart Salisbury,
pp. 10–12.

61. B2/16/1, 24 April 1622. B2/16/3, fols.
19v, 23, 92v. B2/16/4, pp. 19, 22, 29.
Whiteway, p. 56.

62. Its operations can be followed in
MRBD, pp. 525–8; B2/16/3, fol. 72;
B2/16/4, pp. 17, 37–8; B2/8/1, fols.
180v, 190; and B2/13/1, 16 April 1635.

63. Hutchins, II, 398. D1/10,448, pp. 3,
10, 25, 27. B2/16/6 (Whetstone's
accounts), fol. 4. B2/16/3, fols. 12–
13v. *MRBD*, p. 494. B2/13/1, 9 Nov.
and 8 Dec. 1625. B2/16/4, p. 81.

64. Hutchins, II, 398. B2/16/3, fols. 14, 16,
17v, 20, 22v, 24 – 5. B2/16/4, p. 5.
B2/16/6, fol. 5. *MRBD*, p. 560.

65. *MRBD*, pp. 507, 564–5, 713–14. B2/
16/3, fol. 22v. B2/16/4, pp. 8, 17.

66. *MRBD*, pp. 657, 659, 668. B2/8/1,
fols. 155, 194, 250, 297. B2/16/3, fols.
19v, 25. B2/16/4, p. 6. For the relief
of the sick and lame, see below,
p. 122–3.

67. D1/10,448, pp. 25, 27. *MRBD*,
pp. 86–7, 597, 601, 615–16, 625. B2/16/
3, fols. 5v, 13, 92.

68. PE/DO (AS) OV 1. Summary of All
Saints poor relief receipts, 1632–42:
parish rate £323 (54 per cent); subsidies
from other parishes £110 (18 per cent);
Christmas distribution (including
Brewhouse) £122 (20 per cent);
miscellaneous (gifts etc) £42 (7 per
cent). Total £597. Bristol was among the
towns imposing 'rates in aid': Paul
Slack, *Poverty and Policy in Tudor and
Stuart England* (1988), p. 191.

69. PE/DO (AS) OV 1, 1630–42 accounts.
B2/8/1, fols. 67v, 347v, 350. B2/16/
3, fols. 16Av, 25. B2/16/4, pp. 7, 12,
23, 31, 41–5, 56, 60.

70. B2/8/1, fol. 107v.

71. B2/16/3, fol. 31. She may have been
the widow of John Pedwin, beadle in
1611.

72. Salisbury was in some ways even more
systematic, setting up a storehouse to
provide cheap food for the poor: Slack
(ed.), *Poverty in Early-Stuart Salisbury*,
pp. 11–14.

73. D1/10,448, pp. 25, 27. *Whiteway*,

p. 76. B2/16/6E, fols. 20–1, 24v–6v.
PE/DO (AS) OV 1, 1632–42 accounts.
PE/DO (HT) CW 1, 1619–40 accounts.

74. *MRBD*, pp. 655, 657. B2/8/1, fols. 36,
43v, 46, 54v, 59v–60. *Whiteway*,
p. 112. For a good survey of the
subject, see Fletcher, *Reform in the
Provinces*, chap. 7.

75. *Whiteway*, p. 113. *MRBD*, p. 657. B2/
8/1, fol. 62–2v. For similar regulations
in Norfolk in the 1590s, see Amussen,
An Ordered Society, pp. 26–7.

76. *APC, 1630–1*, pp. 214–15. B2/16/6E,
fols. 22–4. In St Peter's parish the grain
was stored in the elder Whiteway's loft.

77. *CSPD, 1631–3*, pp. 185–6.

78. *Ashley*, p. 115 (and for other informers,
see pp. 113, 118). B2/8/1, fol. 142v.

79. *MRBD*, p. 660. B2/8/1, fols. 113v,
147, 148, 186, 313v, 347v–8.

80. *Whiteway*, pp. 142, 154. B2/8/1, fol.
190. B2/16/3, fols. 22, 92v. *MRBD*,
p. 669. B2/16/4, pp. 14, 20.

81. B2/16/1, 2 June 1618, 8 Nov. 1619, 25
Jan. 1619/20. *MRBD*, p. 529. PE/DO
(HT) CW 1, fol. 20.

82. B2/8/1, fols. 29, 31v, 68v, 123–4,
160v, 185v, 193, 204. B2/13/1, 30
Sept. 1630.

83. B2/16/2, 29 March 1633. B2/16/4,
pp. 8, 11–12, 22–4. *MRBD*,
pp. 529–31.

84. B2/8/1 and other town records contain
frequent references to the medical
practitioners. See also *Whiteway*,
pp. 127, 133, 150, 157; and
Rose-Troup, *White*, pp. 383–4, 399,
413.

85. B2/8/1, fols. 23v, 208v, 242. *Ashley*,
p. 20. J.O. Halliwell (ed.),
Autobiography of Sir Simonds D'Ewes
(1845), I, 25. PE/DO (AS) OV 1, 1640–
1 accounts. PE/DO (HT) CW 1, 1630–
1 accounts. B2/16/3, fol. 92.

86. *Whiteway*, pp. 84, 86, 89. DRO,
QSOB, 1625–37, fol. 52v. D1/10,448,
p. 25. *MRBD*, pp. 532–4. B2/8/1, fol.
314. B2/18/4, p. 3. For the general
subject of plague precautions, see Paul
Slack, *The Impact of Plague in Tudor
and Stuart England* (1985), pp. 44–7,
and chap. 8.

87. PE/DO (HT) CW 1, 1617–18 and

1630-1 accounts. PE/DO (AS) OV 1, 1632-4 accounts. *MRBD*, pp. 515-17. B2/16/3, fols. 31, 91v-2. B2/16/4, pp. 37, 40, 58.

88. For the Women's Almshouse's earlier benefactions, see D1/10,448, p. 1; and Hutchins, II, 368.

89. *MRBD*, p. 562. D1/10,448, pp. 1, 10-11. PRO, PROB 11/155 45 Barrington; 11/158: 109 Scrope.

90. *MRBD*, p. 562. DRO, D1/10,448, p. 2. B2/16/3, fols. 2v, 24, 29, 31-3. B2/16/4, pp. 17-18, 41, 44-5.

91. *MRBD*, pp. 355-65, 450, 560. B2/16/1, 8 April and 9 Nov. 1619. B2/16/6, fols. 1-4. D1/10,448, p. 4. B2/16/3, fols. 2v, 22, 32. B2/16/4, p. 63.

92. *MRBD*, pp. 561, 613-14. Clegg, *Dorchester*, pp. 98-9. D1/10,448, pp. 5-6. B2/16/4, p. 41. PE/DO (AS) OV 1, 1632-40 accounts. D1/MJ 51 (Napper's Almshouse accounts, 1636-53).

93. *MRBD*, p. 664. B2/8/1, fols. 79v, 199v. B2/16/3, fol. 93. B2/16/4, pp. 18, 22.

94. B2/16/4, pp. 52-3. *MRBD*, p. 544.

95. PE/DO (HT) CW 1, 1619-20 accounts. B2/16/6E, fols. 20-6v. The 1619-20 average is depressed by the fact that only 2s. 11d. was collected at the Palm Sunday communion – perhaps Mr White was preaching at St Peter's that morning. The parishes responded to charitable appeals roughly in proportion to the distribution of wealth between them: see, for example, D1/10,448, p. 25.

96. Hutchins, II, 398. *Whiteway*, p. 31. *MRBD*, pp. 538, 677.

97. D1/10,448, p. 25. *Whiteway*, p. 76.

98. *Whiteway*, pp. 112, 146, 150, 157. *MRBD*, pp. 534-5, 544, 667. B2/16/4, pp. 39, 53. D1/10,448, p. 28. PE/DO (AS) OV 1, 1634-5 accounts.

99. For the Bridport contributions, see Thomas Wainwright, *Bridport Records and Ancient Manuscripts* (Bridport, n.d.), p. 42.

100. See below, p. 229.

101. B2/16/6E, fols. 2v-3. *Whiteway*, p. 76. *MRBD*, pp. 543 – 4. Wainwright, *Bridport*, p. 52. The Council's Ship Money assessments rated Bridport at 30 per cent of Dorchester; sheriffs' assessments usually at 40 per cent: *MRBD*, p. 707; *CSPD, 1635*, p. 331; PRO, SP 16/302, fol. 151; 333, fol. 171; 351, fol. 182; 401, fols. 84v, 87v.

CHAPTER FIVE
REFORMATION'S FRIENDS AND ENEMIES

1. *Whiteway*, p. 26. DRO, D 413/22/1, p. 43. PRO, C22/604/24: Blachford v Short, 1630. *MRBD*, p. 543.

2. *Whiteway*, pp. 56, 61. DRO, D 413/22/1, p. 44. Rose-Troup, *White*, pp. 49-63, 448-60. Charles M. Andrews, *The Colonial Period of American History* (New Haven, 1934-8), I, 344-7.

3. Rose-Troup, *White*, chaps. 9-11. Andrews, *Colonial Period*, I, 349-52, 360. Charles E. Banks, *Planters of the Commonwealth* (Boston, Mass., 1930), p. 61. Frank Thistlethwaite, *Dorset Pilgrims* (1988), pp. 38-43.

4. Rose-Troup, *White*, pp. 197-203. *MRBD*, p. 657. *Whiteway*, p. 111. *Winthrop Papers*, III, 87, 321.

5. *Memoirs of Roger Clap* (Boston, Mass., 1844), esp. pp. 19, 39 – 40. *Journal of Richard Mather* (Boston, Mass., 1850), esp. pp. 1 – 14, 15, 17, 21, 23, 33. See also David Cressy, *Coming Over: Migration and Communication between England and New England in the Seventeenth Century* (Cambridge, 1987), chap. 6.

6. DRO, B2/13/1, 30 June 1625. For migration in general, see Anthony Salerno, 'The Social Background of Seventeenth-Century Emigration to America', *Journal of British Studies*, 19 (1979), 31-52; David Souden, "Rogues, Whores, and Vagabonds": Indentured Servant Emigrants to North America', *Social History*, 3 (1978), 23-41; and Cressy, *Coming Over*, chaps. 2, 3.

7. B2/8/1, fols. 30, 43, 161v, 242, 274.

MRBD, pp. 666–7.

8. *Memoirs of Roger Clap*, pp. 20–1. For a general analysis of the *Mary and John* company, see Thistlethwaite, *Dorset Pilgrims*, pp. 45–56.

9. In the New England sources Galpin is usually spelt Capen or Cawpen. I use the English spelling to avoid confusion, because of the Galpins left behind in old Dorchester.

10. This paragraph is based mainly on *Dorchester Town Records* (Fourth Report of the Record Commissioners of the City of Boston, 2nd edn., 1883); and *Records of the First Church at Dorchester in New England* (Boston, 1891). See also *Whiteway*, p. 129. For Way, see PRO, PROB 11/187: 155 Evelyn; *Dorchester Town Records*, pp. 2, 27; *Winthrop Papers*, III, 337; and Thistlethwaite, *Dorset Pilgrims*, p. 88. For Hannah Gifford, see below, pp. 225–6.

11. *Dorchester Town Records*, pp. 3–4. *Records of the First Church at Dorchester*, p. xiv. Clarence A. Torrey, *New England Marriages prior to 1700* (Baltimore, 1985), p. 389. B.R. Burg, *Richard Mather of Dorchester* (Lexington, Kentucky, 1976), pp. 27 – 9. Thistlethwaite, *Dorset Pilgrims*, pp. 95–7, 107–11, and chap. 7.

12. *Dorchester Town Records*, pp. 1–16. *Records of the First Church at Dorchester*, pp. 1–9. [Ebenezer Clapp], *History of the Town of Dorchester, Massachusetts* (Boston, 1859), pp. 42–5. James Blake, *Annals of the Town of Dorchester* (Boston, 1846), pp. 16–33.

13. *Dorchester Births, Marriages and Deaths* (Boston, 1890), pp. 1–7. *Memoirs of Roger Clap*, p. 21. Patricia Caldwell, *The Puritan Conversion Narrative* (Cambridge, 1983), pp. 69–71. Stephen Foster, *Their Solitary Way: The Puritan Social Ethic in the First Century of Settlement in New England* (New Haven, 1971), pp. 137, 141. *Dorchester Town Records*, pp. 54–7.

14. Matthews, *Calamy Revised*, pp. 116, 326, 470. *MRBD*, pp. 555–6, 650. For Good Friday money, see Hutchins, II, 404; DRO, D1/10,448, p. 10; B2/8/1,

fol. 3 and passim. It resembled 'Churchill's gift', for which see above, p. 13.

15. B2/8/1, fols. 169v, 340. Matthews, *Calamy Revised*, pp. 317 – 18.

16. PRO, PROB 11/133: 41 Swann (N. Purchase); 11/178: 167 Lee (J. Purchase). DRO, PE/DO (HT) CW 1, 1624–8 accounts. B2/16/1, 7 May 1621. *Whiteway*, p. 129. *MRBD*, p. 584. DRO, QSOB, 1625–37, fol. 381v.

17. Rose-Troup, *White*, p. 448. *MRBD*, p. 661. PRO, E 179/105/313. DRO, B2/8/1, fols. 209v, 249, 314v. *Whiteway*, p. 153. PRO, E 134 (Exchequer Depositions)/ 11 Charles I, Mich. 10: Underwood v Parker, 1635. DRO, B2/16/3, fol. 115. 'Hot waters' means aniseed water.

18. B2/13/1, 3 March 1630/31, and 'Thursday' [? Jan. 1634/5]. B2/8/1, fols. 96, 143v–4.

19. *MRBD*, pp. 370, 664. B2/8/1, fol. 38v. B2/16/3, fol. 25.

20. B2/13/1, 4 Nov. 1622. *Whiteway*, p. 65. B2/8/1, fols. 3, 13v, 199v–200, 339.

21. *MRBD*, pp. 393–4. B2/13/1, 19 Oct. 1626; 30 Sept. 1630. *Ashley*, p. 101. B2/8/1, fol. 68.

22. *Ashley*, p. 88. *MRBD*, pp. 616–17. B2/8/1, fols. 7, 72v, 91v, 114, 165, 243, 244v, 270v, 282v–3, 286, 288v–9, 298v, 329. B2/13/1, 31 March 1631.

23. *MRBD*, pp 404, 426, 534, 544, 649. D 413/22/1, p. 46. B2/13/1, 2 June and 29 July 1630; 31 March 1631; 1 Aug. 1633. The apprentice he brought to Dorchester was John Torrington, Master of the Hospital in 1638.

24. B2/8/1, fols. 142v, 211, 249. Examples of abuse in fols. 325v, 332v, 340, 345.

25. B2/8/1, fols. 207v, 247, 254v.

26. B2/8/1, fol. 50v.

27. *MRBD*, p. 616. B2/8/1, fols. 3v, 111v–13, 176v, 273, 306v, 315v, 360. For Elizabeth Bull, see also above, p. 100.

28. *MRBD*, pp. 661–2. B2/8/1, fol. 247. B2/16/4, pp. 137, 214, 236, 249. B2/16/5, 28 May 1658 and 22 Nov. 1661. Bodleian, MS Gough Dorset, 14: Richard Bury's Accounts, 1642–8, fols.

18, 21, 30, 37, 109, 112. For Hannah Gifford see below, pp. 225–6.

29. B2/8/1, fols. 97v, 287v, 298v. B2/16/3, fol. 22. *MRBD*, p. 669. B2/16/4, pp. 12, 36, 42, 49.

30. *MRBD*, pp. 392, 468, 662. B2/8/1, fols. 2v–3, 60, 73, 160, 203, 242. B2/13/1, 7 Jan. 1629/30, 4 Nov. 1630. B2/16/3, fol. 22. B2/16/4, pp. 26, 39.

31. See above, p. 116.

32. B2/16/3, fol. 92. B2/16/4, pp. 19–21, 24, 28, 30, 33, 36.

33. B2/8/1, fol. 286v. Trayford was again charged with drinking while on the watch a couple of years later: ib., fol. 359.

34. Verses from the song are in B2/8/1, fols. 340, 345. Dare had often been in trouble for drinking and disorderly conduct: see ibid., fols. 34, 83v–4, 146, 179v–80, 317v.

35. Presumably the 'fore sedan' was a conveyance for taking drunks to the town lockup, though I have found no other references to its existence.

36. B2/8/1, fol. 123v. *MRBD*, pp. 616–17.

37. *MRBD*, pp. 594, 596.

38. *MRBD*, p. 656. B2/8/1, fols. 46v, 70, 80v, 83v–4, 127v, 151v, 153v, 245v.

39. B2/8/1, fols. 275–6. Notting had unwisely played at cudgels on the evening after the assault, enabling the coroner's jury to absolve Paty of any part in his death.

40. *MRBD*, pp. 59–60, 78–83, 396–400. B2/16/3, fol. 2. B2/13/1, 6 Oct. 1629. *Whiteway*, pp. 106–7, 169.

41. *Whiteway*, p. 118. See also *MRBD*, p. 405, and B2/13/1, 21 Sept. 1631.

42. *Whiteway*, p. 120. *MRBD*, pp. 565–7. D1/10,448, p. 28. B2/16/3, fols. 21, 49v–50. B2/16/4, p. 12.

43. Rose-Troup, *White*, pp. 222, 454. DNB: 'Ironside, Gilbert (1588–1671)'. Anthony Wood, *Athenae Oxon.* (3rd edn., 1817), III, 940. A.G. Matthews, *Walker Revised* (Oxford, 1948), p. 134. Ironside's *Seven Questions of the Sabbath* (Oxford, 1637), is dedicated to Laud. For Vawter, see above, pp. 23, 43. For Bradish, see Squibb, 'Dorset Incumbents', IV, *Dorset Proc.*, 73 (1952), 155.

44. PRO, PROB 11/174: 61 Goare (Vawter); 11/187: 127 Evelyn (Coke); 11/155: 45 Barrington (Margaret Chubb). For some other links, see DRO, B2/8/1, fols. 114, 165v, 168, 213v, 247, 260v, 269v, 324v; also Pope, 'Dorset Chancery Suits', VII, 4–5; and PRO, PROB 11/146: 67 Clarke (Richard Cuffe).

45. Offices from DRO, B2/8/1 and Trinity CW and OV accounts. Also B2/16/4, p. 43; B2/8/1, fol. 193v.

46. B2/8/1, fol. 187. B2/13/1, 13 Sept. 1633.

47. B2/8/1, fols. 126, 306v, 321v.

48. B2/8/1, fol. 188. B2/8/4. PRO, STAC 8/272/17: Strode v Strode, 1616. *Ashley*, pp. 29–32.

49. See Underdown, *Revel, Riot and Rebellion*, pp. 89–91, 93, 96–9.

50. *Ashley*, p. 32. DRO, PE/DO (HT) RE 1, fol. 36v. *Whiteway*, p. 103. PE/DO (HT) CW 1, 1636–7 accounts. PRO, SP 16/222, fol. 54.

51. *MRBD*, pp. 656, 669. DRO, B2/8/1, fols. 10v, 29v, 49v, 50v, 215.

52. *Ashley*, p. 92. B2/8/1, fol. 176.

53. Hutchins, II, 382–3, 398, 501, 522–7. *MRBD*, p. 559. D1/10,448, p. 1. J.M.J. Fletcher, 'Additional Notes on Two Sixteenth Century Dorset Clergymen', *Dorset Proc.*, 44 (1923), 60. The John Williams in the Antelope affray must have been one of two grandsons of Sir John: either John, son of Robert Williams of Bere Regis, or John, son of John Williams of Plumber (Hutchins, II, 524).

54. *Whiteway*, pp. 55, 65. *CSPD, 1623–5*, pp. 188, 226, 248, 261, 280, 293, 299, 314.

55. *CSPD, 1628–9*, p. 578. Rose-Troup, *White*, p. 41. *APC, 1629–30*, pp. 92, 185–6. *Whiteway*, p. 99.

56. *Whiteway*, p. 121. D1/10,448, p. 10. Hutchins, II, 386–7.

57. B2/8/1, fol. 247. B2/8/4.

58. PRO, SP 16/46, fol. 96. DRO, B2/16/3, fols. 1v–2. *MRBD*, p. 676. *SDNQ*, 12 (1910–11), 56. *Whiteway*, pp. 107–8. D 413/22/1, p. 47. John Coker [Thomas Gerard], *A Survey of Dorsetshire* (1732), pp. 69–70. W.D.

Christie, *Life of Anthony Ashley Cooper, First Earl of Shaftesbury* (1871), I, Appendix, p. xx.

59. *MRBD*, p. 669. B2/16/4, pp. 12, 30, 33, 36, 42, 49.

60. B2/8/1, fols. 100, 103, 110, 159, 199v–200, 318v, 326v. For the corrupted watchmen, see above, p. 96.

61. B2/8/1, fols. 139, 190v, 215v, 251, 257. *MRBD*, p. 653.

62. *Ashley*, p. 98. *MRBD*, p. 661. B2/8/1, fols. 99, 238, 248v, 324v, 347v. B2/16/3, fol. 8v.

63. B2/8/1, fols. 73, 77v–8. The nature of their duties made bailiffs particularly prone to involvement in violent affrays: for one at Blandford involving Roger Pouncey, Foy, and Warman, see DRO, QSOB, 1625–37; for another at

Minterne, *Ashley*, p. 116.

64. Phillimore and Nevill (eds.), *Dorset Marriages*, VII, 2. PE/DO (HT) RE 1, fols. 16v–18v. *MRBD*, pp. 361, 664. *Ashley*, p. 106. B2/8/1, fols. 47, 98v, 100v, 164v, 167v–8, 221v, 336.

65. See below, pp. 180–1.

66. B2/8/1, fols. 352v–3.

67. B2/8/1, fols. 37v, 77v, 262v. See also above, p. 162.

68. B2/8/1, fols. 2, 133v, 180–80v, 183v, 306v, 319, 322, 352. Many other examples could be given.

69. *MRBD*, p. 665, and above, p. 79, for the witchcraft incident. For references to Roger's service as a bailiff, see *Ashley*, p. 98; and B2/8/1, fols. 73, 136v, 251v.

70. B2/8/1, fols. 339, 343v, 345v. For Derrick, see *OED*.

CHAPTER SIX
DORCHESTER AND THE KINGDOM, 1600–1642

1. *Whiteway*, pp. 43–4.

2. Whiteway's version of all this, presumably derived from his father-in-law, John Parkins, who was a member, is in *Whiteway*, pp. 33–43. For the general background, see Robert Zaller, *The Parliament of 1621* (Berkeley, 1971); and Conrad Russell, *Parliaments and English Politics 1621–1629* (Oxford, 1979), chap. 2.

3. Rose-Troup, *White*, p. 44. See also above, p. 93.

4. *MRBD*, p. 394. *Whiteway*, pp. 74–6, 151–2.

5. DRO, B2/8/1, fols. 276v–7. *MRBD*, p. 677. *Whiteway*, pp. 23 – 4, 31–2.

6. *Whiteway*, pp. 33, 47. On the politicisation, see Thomas Cogswell, *The Blessed Revolution: English politics and the coming of war, 1621–1624* (Cambridge, 1989), pp. 6–12, 281–300; Richard Cust, 'News and Politics in Early Seventeenth Century England', *Past and Present*, no. 111 (1986), 60–90; and Peter Clark, 'Thomas Scott and the Growth of Urban Opposition', *Historical Journal*, 21 (1978), 40–53.

7. *Whiteway*, pp. 50–4. D 413/22/1, p. 44. PE/DO (HT) CW 1, fol. 29.

Cogswell, *Blessed Revolution*, p. 9.

8. As argued by Cressy, *Bonfires and Bells*, pp. 59–61. The payments to ringers are recorded in PE/DO (HT) CW 1.

9. *Whiteway*, pp. 116–26; Commonplace Book, fol. 43 (notes headed 1 April 1631 – the day of the fast). DRO, PE/DO (HT) CW 1, 1631 – 2 accounts. (This entry is printed in Hutchins, II, 402, as 'the King and Laud's victory', an error followed in some later accounts).

10. *Whiteway*, pp. 40–1, 145. *MRBD*, p. 667. B2/8/1, fols. 276v–7.

11. *Whiteway*, pp. 113, 128, 139, 140, 144; Commonplace Book, fol. 35. DRO, D 413/22/1, p. 48.

12. Rose-Troup, *White*, pp. 275–6. *Whiteway*, pp. 132, 135; Commonplace Book, fols. 42v–3.

13. *Whiteway*, pp. 146–7. PE/DO (HT) CW 1, 1634–5 accounts.

14. BL, Add. MS 35,331, fol. 64. Rose-Troup, *White*, chap. 23. *CSPD*, 1631–3, p. 402; 1635, pp. 104–5, 373 (and PRO, SP 16/297, fol. 177), 435, 459; 1635–6, pp. 79, 108, 116, 125, 500, 503, 513. Two Dorchester booksellers were also harassed by the High Commission: *Ibid.*, 1635–6, pp. 502,

504, 513.

15. 'The Bishop of Bristol's Speech, At the Visitation at Dorchester, September 18, 1637', in *A Few Memorials of the Right Rev. Robert Skinner, D.D.* (1866). There may have been a compromise: in 1637–8 Trinity bought a dozen yards of matting for the chancel, and a small mat 'for the minister at communion'. But nothing was spent on railings and there is no sign of the sort of upheaval that moving the communion table would have entailed: DRO, PE/DO (HT) CW 1, 1636–8 accounts. On the altar controversy, see Nicholas Tyacke, *Anti-Calvinists: The Rise of English Arminianism* (Oxford, 1987), pp. 199–209.

16. *MRBD*, pp. 406, 425, 500. *APC, 1629–30*, p. 262. B2/16/4, p. 15. *Whiteway*, pp. 136, 158.

17. B2/8/1, fols. 55, 113v, 184v, 332v. B2/16/4, pp. 21, 30. For Way, see above, p. 80.

18. White, *Sermon preached at Dorchester . . . the 7 of March, 1632*[– 3] (1648), p. 21. *Whiteway*, pp. 115, 129, 148, 158.

19. Another Dorchester man, Samuel Conduit (presumably some connection of the puritan John Conduit), was also bound over at the same Assizes at which Day's case was first heard. See *Ashley*, pp. 90–1 (and BL, Harleian MS 6715, fol. 73v); and Underdown, *Revel, Riot and Rebellion*, p. 120. For the Gillingham and other forest riots, see *Whiteway*, pp. 106, 116; *MRBD*, pp. 651–2; DRO, B2/8/1, fol. 5v; *Ashley*, p. 102; and Buchanan Sharp, *In Contempt of All Authority* (Berkeley and Los Angeles, 1980), chap. 4.

20. *Whiteway*, pp. 139–40. B2/8/1, fol. 198v. B2/16/3, fols. 32v, 91.

21. *Whiteway*, pp. 104, 150–1. *CSPD, 1628–9*, p. 43. *Ashley*, p. 110. B2/8/1, fol. 292v.

22. *Whiteway*, pp. 66, 72, 76, 89–90, 92. *CSPD, 1623–5*, pp. 396, 408, 413; *1627–8*, pp. 43, 195, 208, 300, 397; *1628–9*, p. 75.

23. PRO, SP 14/179, no. 11; SP 16/46, fols. 13, 20; SP 16/70, fol. 61; SP 16/82, fol.

41. For those named, see above, pp. 62–3, 73, 143; also DRO, B2/8/1, fols. 134v, 156, 237; B2/16/3, fol. 20; PE/DO (HT) OV 1, 1633–7 accounts.

24. PRO, SP 16/61, fol. 143. HMC, *Twelfth Report, Appendix*, I (Coke MSS), 362.

25. For Hastings, see Christie, *Shaftesbury*, I, App., pp. xiv–xvii.

26. *Whiteway*, pp. 84–5, 89. *CSPD, 1625–6*, p. 419; *1627–8*, pp. 104, 124, 148, 151.

27. *Whiteway*, pp. 87, 94. *APC, January – August 1627*, pp. 350–1. *CSPD, 1627–8*, pp. 221, 227, 482, 508–9, 568, 586; *1628–9*, pp. 2, 76. R.C. Johnson *et al.* (eds.), *Proceedings in Parliament, 1628* (New Haven, 1978–83), II, 361.

28. *Whiteway*, p. 96. *MRBD*, pp. 675–8. DRO, B2/16/3, fols. 1, 4, 7v. *CSPD, 1628–9*, pp. 75–6, 91, 101–2, 131. *APC, 1627–8*, pp. 427–8; *1629–30*, p. 220. PRO, SP 16/153, fol. 33v.

29. Dorchester subsidy returns in PRO, E 179/105/298 (1610), 306 (1624), 313, 320, and 322 (1628); E 179/245/22 (defaulters). See also *Whiteway*, p. 64.

30. *Whiteway*, pp. 31, 78, 83. *MRBD*, p. 677. PRO, E 401/2586 (Privy Seal loans, 1625–6), pp. 270, 542; SP 16/20, fol. 139.

31. DRO, D 413/22/1, p. 46. *Whiteway*, pp. 87–9. *CSPD, 1627–8*, pp. 6, 16, 21, 34, 104, 151, 492. *MRBD*, pp. 676–7. See also Richard Cust, *The Forced Loan and English Politics* (Oxford, 1987).

32. *Whiteway*, p. 87. D 53/1, p. 22.

33. *Whiteway*, pp. 104, 112, 116. PRO, E 178/5251 (Special Commissions and Returns in the Exchequer). DRO, B2/16/2, 24 Feb. 1632/3.

34. *Whiteway*, pp. 153–6. D 53/1, p. 25. *CSPD, 1635*, p. 331; *1635–6*, p. 356; *1636–7*, p. 547; *1637*, pp. 40, 75, 80, 400, 426, 504; *1637–8*, p. 169. PRO, SP 16/302, fols. 149–51; 333, fol. 171; 351, fol. 182; 370, fol. 160; 401, fol. 87v.

35. *CSPD, 1636–7*, p. 151; *1637*, p. 400. *MRBD*, pp. 706–7. PRO, E 179/272/54 (Ship Money papers): this is not a complete return for Dorset, and may

therefore under-report opposition in Dorchester. For an early rating dispute in Dorchester, see *CSPD, 1637–8*, p. 210.

36. *CSPD, 1637–8*, p. 317; *1639*, pp. 17–18; *1639–40*, p. 556; *1640*, pp. 57–8, 241, 599. PRO, SP 16/412, fol. 59; 463, fol. 146; 466, fol. 268. *MRBD*, p. 707. DRO, D 413/22/1, p. 52. B2/16/4, p. 14.

37. B2/16/4, p. 42.

38. *SDNQ*, 12 (1910–11), 56. See above, pp. 149, 158 for Williams and Maber.

39. *MRBD*, pp. 395, 425, 435. *Whiteway*, pp. 32, 57–8, 71, 79, 95.

40. *Whiteway*, p. 59. J.K. Gruenfelder, 'Dorsetshire Elections, 1604–1640', *Albion*, 10 (1978), 3–4.

41. M. Jansson and W. Bidwell (eds.), *Proceedings in Parliament, 1626* (New Haven, 1991 –), II, [11–17 February 1626]. *Whiteway*, p. 78; Commonplace Book, fols. 149–51. Whiteway gives the count as 511 for Moreton, 498 for Browne. See also Gruenfelder, 'Dorsetshire Elections', pp. 4–10.

42. *Whiteway*, pp. 58, 74, 80–2, 84, 88, 92, 98; Commonplace Book, fols. 67v–70, 153.

43. *Whiteway*, p. 96. For public celebrations of the Petition of Right, see Cressy, *Bonfires and Bells*, pp. 76, 85.

44. *Whiteway*, pp. 102, 108–9. *CSPD, 1628–9*, p. 543.

45. For all this see Thomas G. Barnes, 'County Politics and a Puritan Cause Célèbre: Somerset Churchales, 1633', *Trans. Royal Hist. Soc.*, 5th ser., IX (1959), esp. p. 115.

46. White, *A Sermon preached at Dorchester*. *Whiteway*, p. 129. See also Rose-Troup, *White*, chap. 22.

47. *MRBD*, pp. 435–6. DRO, B2/8/1, fols. 286, 298v. B2/16/4, pp. 18–21. D 413/22/1, p. 52. B2/16/3, fol. 72.

48. *CSPD, 1640*, pp. 55, 110–11, 127, 157, 217. B2/16/4, pp. 24, 26.

49. *MRBD*, p. 678. B2/16/4, p. 44. *CSPD, 1640*, pp. 316, 334–5.

50. John Aubrey, *Three Prose Works*, ed. J. Buchanan-Brown (Carbondale, Illinois, 1972), pp. 28, 222. PE/DO (HT) CW 1, fol. 66v. B2/16/4, p. 44.

51. B2/16/4, p. 48. *MRBD*, p. 535. BL, TT, E. 168 (14): *The English Post* (1641).

52. *MRBD*, p. 508.

53. *MRBD*, pp. 544–5. B2/16/4, pp. 54–6, 59. For the drift towards civil war, see Anthony Fletcher, *The Outbreak of the English Civil War* (New York, 1981).

54. B2/16/4, p. 55.

55. *MRBD*, pp. 545, 678–9. B2/16/3, fols. 35v–6.

CHAPTER SEVEN
DORCHESTER IN THE CIVIL WAR AND REVOLUTION

1. PRO, SP 16/491, fol. 278. *CSPD, 1641–3*, pp. 375–6. J.S. Cockburn (ed.), *Western Circuit Assize Orders 1629–1648* (Camden, 4th series 17, 1976), pp. 234–5.

2. Arthur Browne, *A Seminary Priest, His Confession . . . at Dorchester* (London, 25 August 1642). Elizabeth Willoughby's account of Green's execution is in Richard Challoner, *Memoirs of Missionary Priests*, ed. J.H. Pollen (London, 1924), pp. 421–8. See also Edwin H. Burton and Thomas L. Williams (eds.), *The Douay College Diaries . . . 1598–1654*, II (Catholic Record Soc., Vol. XI, 1911), 437, 477;

and Joseph Gillow, *Literary and Biographical History of the English Catholics*, III, 18–23. For Gallows Hill, see S.E.V. Filloul, 'The History of the Dorchester Gallows', *Dorset Proc.*, 32 (1911), 61–3.

3. *LJ*, V, 215, 262. *CJ*, II, 694, 701. *MRBD*, pp. 679–80. HMC, *Portland*, I, 47. Bury's accounts, fol. 89.

4. DRO, B2/16/4, p. 62.

5. *CSPD, 1641–3*, pp. 375–6.

6. Edward, Earl of Clarendon, *History of the Rebellion*, ed. W.D. Macray (Oxford, 1888), III, 127, 158. Bury's accounts, fols. 81v, 89–92.

7. BL, TT, E 115 (6): *The Examination of George Leddoze of Dorchester, Merchant* (1642); E 115 (22): *An Abstract of Some Letters sent from Dorchester* (3 Sept. 1642); E 119 (5): *The Latest Remarkable Truths* . . . (29 Sept. 1642). John Vicars, *Jehovah Jireh: God in the Mount (1644)*, pp. 136–7. A.R. Bayley, *The Great Civil War in Dorset* (Taunton, 1910), pp. 46, 48. Dorchester was one of the 'puritanical towns' to which no quarter was to be given, Lord Poulett is alleged to have told his soldiers.

8. BL, TT, E 116 (39): *Happy Newes from Sherborne* (13 Sept. 1642); the J.W., 'merchant in Dorchester', must be John Whiteway. BL, TT, E 117 (6): *A Letter written from the Right Honourable the Earle of Bedford* (15 Sept. 1642). Bury's accounts, fol. 97. For these events see also Bayley, *Civil War*, pp. 48–9; and David Underdown, *Somerset in the Civil War and Interregnum* (Newton Abbot, 1973), pp. 41–3.

9. BL, TT, E 119 (2): *Special Passages*, 7 (20–27 Sept. 1642). HMC, *Portland*, I, 64. DRO, B2/16/4, pp. 64–7. *MRBD*, pp. 681–3, 685.

10. *MRBD*, pp. 681–4. Bury's accounts, fols. 98, 110–22. Whiteway served as captain from 5 February until the town fell to the Royalists on 4 August 1643: *DSC*, p. 132.

11. PRO, SP 28/128 (Dorset: T. Sacheverell's accounts, 1642–3). Bury's accounts, fols. 116v–17. *MRBD*, pp. 683–5. Two soldiers from units unknown were buried at Holy Trinity, one in December 1642, the other in March 1643: DRO, PE/DO (HT) RE 1, fol. 66v.

12. Bury's accounts, fols. 107v–9. O. Ogle et al. (eds.), *Calendar of the Clarendon State Papers* (1869–1970), I, 239. Bayley, *Civil War*, pp. 63–7.

13. Bury's accounts, fols. 110–12. Hutchins, II, 343.

14. BL, TT, E 105 (9): *Kingdomes Weekly Intelligencer*, no. 22 (30 May–6 June 1643). HMC, *Portland*, I, 710–12. Bayley, *Civil War*, pp. 79–80.

15. *Mercurius Aulicus*, no. 34 (19–26 August 1643), quoted in Bayley, *Civil War*, p. 101.

16. *MRBD*, p. 509. Bury's accounts, fols. 113–21. BL, TT, E 59 (1), and E 62 (16): *Certaine Informations*, nos. 24 (26 June – 3 July 1643) and 28 (24–31 July). *CJ*, III, 185. DRO, B2/16/3, fol. 49v. B2/16/4, p. 113.

17. PE/DO (AS) OV 1, p. 42. Clarendon, *History of the Rebellion*, III, 127, 157–8. *SDNQ*, 12 (1910–11), 52. *DSC*, pp. 30–1, 55–6 (the ship stopped at Plymouth was used as compensation for the losses incurred by Hill and Whiteway at Weymouth).

18. Bayley, *Civil War*, pp. 100–3. BL, TT, E 65 (8) and (24): *Certaine Informations*, nos. 30 (7–14 August 1643) and 31 (14–21 August).

19. Clarendon, *History of the Rebellion*, III, 158.

20. B2/16/3, fol. 49v. M.A.E. Green (ed.), *Calendar of Proceedings of the Committee for Advance of Money* (1888), p. 1318. PRO, C8 (Mitford)/314/118: White v Galpin, 1649. SP 18/127, fols. 106–7. John Vicars, *Gods Arke Overtopping the World Waves* (1646), pp. 100–1. The newsbooks contain conflicting versions of Sydenham's raid. See also Bayley, *Civil War*, p. 120. In 1646 Coker was found not sequesterable: *DSC*, p. 303. For Fuller and the rectory, see *SDNQ*, 17 (1921–3), 188, 287.

21. *CSPD, 1644*, pp. 239–42, 271, 352, 495; *1644–5*, pp. 12–13. Vicars, *Gods Arke*, p. 286. Bayley, *Civil War*, pp. 198, 220, 240–2. *LJ*, VII, 68. *MRBD*, p. 525. DRO, B2/16/3, p. 34. I have also used newspapers for 1644–45, in BL, TT. This John Williams was not, I think, the same as the one involved in the affray in the town in 1634: see above, p. 159. Some of Essex's soldiers died in the town: PE/DO (HT) RE 1, fol. 67. For Goring's crew, see Underdown, *Somerset*, pp. 87–90.

22. Bayley, *Civil War*, pp. 251, 253, 262, 265. *Cal. Clarendon State Papers*, I, 262. Bury's accounts, fols. 23, 26–7. *CSPD, 1645–7*, pp. 180, 416. For the Clubmen see J.S. Morrill, *Revolt of the Provinces* (1976); and David Underdown,

'The Chalk and the Cheese: Contrasts among the English Clubmen', *Past and Present*, no. 85 (1979), 25–48.

23. *DSC*, passim. I think that the figures given above may, if anything, underestimate the number of serving Parliamentarians.

24. See *DSC*, esp. pp. 32, 81, 85, 181, 489–90, 559; and Bury's accounts, passim.

25. See, for example, *DSC*, pp. 31–2, 123, 128–9, 221–2, 275, 490–1. Bury's accounts, fols. 18v–19, 22v, 91–109, 113v, 122. DRO, B2/16/3, fol. 49v.

26. *MRBD*, pp. 683, 686–7. *DSC*, pp. 55, 61, 73, 84, 127, 263–4. B2/16/4, pp. 143, 209.

27. The above examples are from *DSC*, p. 15 (the book is full of claims and orders for repayment); Bury's accounts, fols. 1–2, 19; DRO, B2/16/4, p. 113; PRO, SP 18/73, fol. 173 (*CSPD, 1654*, p. 272).

28. DRO, D1/10,448, p. 10. PRO, PROB 11/194: 139 Rivers. DRO, PE/DO (AS) OV 1, 1645–6 accounts. *MRBD*, p. 547. B2/16/4, p. 199.

29. PE/DO (HT) RE 1, fols. 66–8. Hutchins, II, 387. HMC, *Portland*, I, 279. For seasonal patterns of deaths during epidemics, see Slack, *Plague*, pp. 64–73. Mortality in Trinity parish began to increase in October 1642 and maintained a slow upward movement until the following summer; but between 8 September and 6 November 1643 twenty-three people were buried, more than twice as many as in any other two-month period. The timing strongly suggests an outbreak of plague.

30. *MRBD*, p. 517. B2/16/4, p. 75. PE/DO (AS) OV 1, 1642–4 accounts. The 1644–5 accounts are missing.

31. PE/DO (AS) OV 1, 1645–6 accounts. Nathaniel Bower was often paid small sums, presumably for distribution to others.

32. White, *Troubles of Jerusalems Restauration* (1645), esp. pp. 5, 46–9, 58–60.

33. *Cal. Adv. Money*, p. 49. PE/DO (AS) OV 1, p. 55. Rose-Troup, *White*, p. 373.

DSC, pp. 71, 78. White, *Troubles of Jerusalems Restauration*, Epistle Dedicatory.

34. Fuller, *Worthies* (ed. Nuttall), III, 25. B2/16/6E, 10 March 1646/7. White, *Troubles of Jerusalems Restauration*, pp. 54–7.

35. *Sermon preached at Dorchester, 1632* (1648), Intro. by 'W.P.' Rose-Troup, *White*, pp. 289–92. *MRBD*, pp. 601–3, 628–30. *CJ*, V, 146, 390. *DSC*, pp. 155, 160, 182. B2/16/4, pp. 84, 88. B2/16/3, fol. 95v. B2/23/8. BL, Lansdowne MS 459, fols. 24v–5.

36. *MRBD*, pp. 602–6, 713. DRO, B2/16/4, p. 95. *LJ*, X, 638. For Gower, see J.M.J. Fletcher, 'A Trio of Dorchester Worthies', *Dorset Proc.*, 47 (1926); and for his long-standing hostility to separatists, Geoffrey F. Nuttall, *The Welsh Saints 1640–1660* (Cardiff, 1957), p. 11.

37. Rose-Troup, *White*, p. 413.

38. Underdown, *Revel, Riot and Rebellion*, pp. 224, 230–1. BL, TT, E 434 (5): *Mercurius Aulicus*, 2–30 March 1648. *DSC*, pp. 471, 490. Bury's accounts, fols. 49–51.

39. *MRBD*, pp. 545–7, 551. DRO, B2/16/6E, summarised in Underdown, *Revel, Riot and Rebellion*, p. 234.

40. PE/DO (HT) RE 1, fol. 70v. Hutchins, II, 392. The puritan Richard Baxter was accused of having 'preached against their days of . . . thanksgiving for victories in Scotland': Dr Williams Library, Baxter MSS 1, fol. 260. Gower's preaching in Dorchester may have been similar.

41. *MRBD*, p. 448. B2/16/3, fol. 133. The text of the Engagement is in S.R. Gardiner (ed.), *Constitutional Documents of the Puritan Revolution* (3rd edn., Oxford, 1906), p. 391. For its reception in other places, see David Underdown, *Pride's Purge* (Oxford, 1971), pp. 304–5.

42. *MRBD*, pp. 436, 445, 628–9 and n. B2/16/3, fol. 44. B2/16/4, pp. 102, 207.

43. B2/16/4, p. 220. *MRBD*, pp. 716–17.

44. PRO, ASSI 24/1 (Western Circuit Order book, 1654–77), summer 1655 to Lent 1656/7 Assizes. Yale University,

Beinecke Library, Osborn MS b 304, Strangways Commonplace Book, p. 138r. For the royalist rising, see A.H. Woolrych, *Penruddock's Rising* (Historical Association Pamphlet, G. 29, 1955); and David Underdown, *Royalist Conspiracy in England, 1649–1660* (New Haven, 1960), chap. 7.

45. Thomas Birch (ed.), *State Papers of John Thurloe* (1742), IV, 305, 320, 520. *MRBD*, pp. 645, 687 (correct date 1656), 717. B2/16/5, 7 April 1657. BL, Add. MS 34,012 (Major-Generals' returns), fols. 11v, 21, 24v, 30, 32, 41, 55, 57v.

46. *MRBD*, p. 717. DRO, B2/16/5, 19–26 June and 30 Dec. 1657; 1–18 Jan. 1657/8. Righton's poor rate assessment never exceeded 4*d*. a week before 1658, and his son was a recipient of money from Churchill's fund for poor artisans: B2/16/5, 1 April 1659.

47. *MRBD*, p. 618. B2/16/6E. At recent Gunpowder Treasons services the two upper parishes had usually contributed well in excess of £3.

48. *MRBD*, pp. 436–7. B2/16/5, 7 Jan. 1658/9 and 4 July 1659.

49. *MRBD*, pp. 606–8, 621–2. B2/16/4, pp. 114, 220. B2/16/3, fols. 37v, 45, 97v, 99–100. B2/16/5, 26 June 1657 and 5 March 1657/8. BL, Lansdowne MS 459 (Surveys of church livings), fols. 24v–5.

50. DRO, PE/DO (AS) CW 1, 1649–60 accounts. PRO, PROB 11/245: 122 Aylett.

51. DRO, PE/DO (AS) CW 1, 1649–60 accounts. PE/DO (SP) RE 1 (St Peter's Register, 1653–1723), marriages, 1655–8. Phillimore and Nevill (eds.), *Dorset Marriages*, VII, 14–16.

52. PE/DO (AS) CW 1, 1656–8 accounts.

53. *MRBD*, p. 606. *Thurloe State Papers*, VII, 138–40. *CSPD, 1656–7*, pp. 123–4.

54. *MRBD*, pp. 636–9. Matthews, *Calamy Revised*, pp. 116, 326.

55. *MRBD*, pp. 525–6. B2/16/4, pp. 80–1.

56. *MRBD*, pp. 518, 526–8, 531–2, 629, 686–7. B2/16/3, fol. 96. B2/16/4,

pp. 96, 100–8, 116, 122, 127, 130, 135, 145, 158, 169, 171, 184, 210, 236. B2/28/1 (Seaton accounts).

57. *MRBD*, pp. 517–20, 525. B2/16/4, pp. 77, 81, 149, 151, 156–7, 164, 169, 195, 213, 218, 229. B2/16/5, 25 Dec. 1658, 28 Jan. 1658/9, 16 Sept. and 15 Nov. 1659.

58. MJ/51, Napper's Almshouse accounts, 1636–53. D1/10,448, p. 3. B2/16/3, fol. 49v. B2/16/4, pp. 114, 163, 197.

59. D1/10,448, p. 10. *MRBD*, p. 555. B2/16/4, pp. 84, 95, 100–1, 129, 148, 176, 195, 231, 242. B2/16/5, 27 March 1657, 23 April 1658, 1 April 1659, 20 April 1660.

60. PE/DO (AS) OV 1, 1646–60 accounts.

61. B2/16/6E, 2 March 1648/9, 17 May 1649. B2/16/4, pp. 123, 131, 140–1. B2/16/5, 10 Dec. 1658; 21 Jan., 18 Feb., and 17 March 1658/9. *MRBD*, pp. 518, 520.

62. *MRBD*, pp. 531–2. B2/16/4, pp. 104, 126, 137, 139, 143, 154, 177, 193, 240. B2/16/5, 30 Sept. 1657; 23 April and 13 Aug. 1658; 18 Feb. 1658/9; 22 April 1659. B2/16/6E, 30 Sept. 1657.

63. B2/16/4, pp. 103, 122, 130, 135, 139, 145, 153, 155, 158, 172–3, 175, 217. B2/16/5, 21 March 1656/7. For the prewar payments, see above, p. 123.

64. B2/16/4, pp. 79, 87, 96, 141, 145, 173, 200, 203, 206, 219, 224, 240. *MRBD*, pp. 518–20.

65. PE/DO (AS) OV 1, p. 47. B2/16/4, pp. 141–2, 150, 183, 192, 208. *MRBD*, pp. 519, 687. B2/16/5, 17–18 April and 30 Oct. 1657; 21 Jan., 18 Feb. and 17 March 1658/9; 15 July, 18 Nov. and 2 Dec. 1659.

66. *MRBD*, pp. 567–74. *DSC*, pp. 85–6. B2/16/3, fols. 35, 43, 51–2, 133v. B2/16/4, pp. 122, 154, 156. For Cromelholme, see Fletcher, 'Trio of Dorchester Worthies', pp. 134–9; and Robert Latham and William Matthews (eds.), *Diary of Samuel Pepys* (1970–83), esp. III, 199–200, and VI, 53.

67. B2/16/6E, 5 Nov. entries, 1647–51. B2/16/4, pp. 169, 177, 195. PE/DO (AS) CW 1, 1651–2 accounts.

68. *MRBD*, pp. 518–19. B2/16/4, p. 164. B2/16/5, 17 Sept. and 25 Dec. 1658. For

the Galpin family, see above, pp. 135-7.

69. B2/16/5, 10 Dec. 1658; 7 Jan. and 17 March 1658/9. B2/16/6E, 5 Nov. 1646, 5 Nov. 1659. PE/DO (AS) CW 1, 1651-2 account. PE/DO (HT) RE 1, fols. 38v-42.

70. B2/16/6E, 29 Dec. 1647. B2/16/4, pp. 93, 98, 196. B2/16/5, 10 Feb. 1659/60. MRBD, pp. 406, 670. PE/DO (HT) RE 1, fols. 41-5; RE 2, 1653/ 4-60. PE/DO (SP) RE 1, 1653/4-60. PE/DO (AS) RE 1, 1653/4-60.

71. MRBD, p. 618. B2/16/4, pp. 185, 219. We might perhaps wonder why Thomas Pouncey had to appear at the Assizes in 1655: PRO, ASSI 24/1 (Western Circuit Bail Book, 1654-77).

72. PRO, PROB 11/264: 180 Ruthen

(Derby); 11/273: 85 Wootton (Parkins); 11/272: 1658/4 (Hill). See also MRBD, pp. 558-9, 578.

73. DRO, AD/DT/W/1668/12 (Gould). PRO, PROB 11/276: 257 Wootton (Cooke); 11/262: 90 Ruthen (Loder); 11/303: 1661/9 (Palfrey). DRO, B2/ 16/4, pp. 137, 172, 191, 214, 249. B2/ 16/5, 28 May 1658.

74. B2/16/6E.

75. MRBD, pp. 551-2 (with some supplementary information from B2/16/ 6E).

76. MRBD, p. 551. BL, TT, E 1073 (3): A Distinct and Faithful Accompt of all the Receipts . . . of the Moneys collected . . . for the Relief of the poor distressed Protestants . . . (1658).

77. MRBD, pp. 436-7.

CHAPTER EIGHT
THE END OF GODLY REFORMATION

1. BL, TT, E 183 (15): Mercurius Publicus, no. 20 (10-17 May 1660). MRBD, p. 407.

2. BL, TT, E 1034 (15): Gilbert Ironside, A Sermon Preached at Dorchester . . . (1660). For Sherborne, see Underdown, Revel, Riot and Rebellion, pp. 271-2; for Ironside, above, p. 153.

3. PRO, SP 29/1, fol. 55. DRO, PE/DO (AS) CW 1, 1660-1 accounts. MRBD, p. 407. B2/14/1, 1661 accounts. See also Cressy, Bonfires and Bells, pp. 64-5.

4. MRBD, pp. 715, 717. B2/16/5, 16 and 30 Nov. 1660; 1 and 8 Feb. 1660/1; 20 Dec. 1661; 14 April and 9 May 1662.

5. MRBD, pp. 443, 646. B2/16/5, 5 Oct. and 16 Nov. 1660; 20 Dec. 1661; 14 Jan. and 7 March 1661/2. See also Patricia Crawford, Denzil Holles (1979), pp. 192-7.

6. MRBD, pp. 87, 455-6. B2/16/5, 20 Dec. 1660. For Constantine, see Keeler, Long Parliament, pp. 140-1.

7. B2/16/5, 27 July 1660. MRBD, p. 437. Basil D. Henning, The House of Commons, 1660-1690 (1983), I, 215; II, 68-9. Presumably Guy's 'excise constable' was Joseph Michell, who had been both a brewer and a

parliamentarian official, but which of the other two constables (John Haysham and Thomas Bedford) was the runaway and which the penny constable it is impossible to tell. 'Runaway' is presumably an allusion to civil war cowardice.

8. Calendar of the Clarendon State Papers, V, 53. PE/DO (AS) CW 1, 1660-2 accounts, and 31 March 1662.

9. MRBD, pp. 608-9. B2/16/5, 27 July; 3-19 Oct. 1660. D1/10,448, p. 12. PE/ DO (SP) RE 1, title page. Crawford, Holles, p. 209. Matthews, Calamy Revised, pp. 26, 244-5.

10. MRBD, pp. 574, 629-30. B2/16/5, 14 March 1661/2; 30 May 1662.

11. MRBD, pp. 521, 548, 707. B2/16/5, 20 July, 3 Aug. and 3 Oct. 1660; 2 Jan. and 13 Feb. 1660/1; 19 April 1661; 7 Feb. 1661/2; 28 March and 2 May 1662. B2/16/6E, 5 Nov. 1660, and payments to Long, 1661-2.

12. B2/16/5, 6 and 20 July, and 31 Aug. 1660; 13 Feb. 1660/1; 31 May, 7 June, and 18 Sept. 1661; 15 Jan., 7 Feb., and 14 March 1661/2; 28 March, 11 and 18 April 1662. PE/DO (AS) OV 1, p. 112, 1660-1 accounts.

13. Text in J.P. Kenyon (ed.), The Stuart

Constitution (Cambridge, 1969), pp. 376–8. See also Ronald Hutton, *The Restoration* (Oxford, 1985), pp. 158–61.

14. B2/16/5, p. 140. D1/10,448, p. 19.

15. *MRBD*, pp. 574–5, 608–10, 618–19, 633 and n. BL, TT, E 195 (4): *Kingdoms Intelligencer*, 22–29 Sept. 1662. PE/DO (AS) CW 1, 1662–3 accounts. D1/10,448, pp. 12, 27. PRO, PROB 11/312: 1663/112.

16. Henry Glover, *An Exhortation to Prayer for Jerusalems Peace. In a Sermon preached at Dorchester at the Assizes . . . March 19 1662* [–3] (London, 1663). *MRBD*, p. 607. Crawford, *Holles*, p. 184.

17. For this and the following paragraph, see PRO, SP 29/98, fol. 351; 29/99, fols. 122–3; 29/106, fol. 170; 29/107, fols. 187–97; and 29/124, fols. 175–7 (*CSPD, 1663–4*, pp. 601, 613–14; *1664–5*, pp. 112, 115, 130, 431; *1665–6*, p. 53).

18. *MRBD*, pp. 443, 456, 646. DRO, B2/16/5, p. 165.

19. B2/16/5, pp. 244–5, 258–61, 272. The four were Richard Atkins, Edward Jones, Jasper Samways, and William Twisse (the last-named had been ejected in 1662).

20. Dr Williams Library, MS 89.25 (Lyon Turner MSS), p. 17. *MRBD*, pp. 643–4. DRO, PE/DO (AS) CW 1, 1665–6 accounts. *CSPD, 1664–5*, pp. 555–68. Hutton, *Restoration*, pp. 235–6. Charles II again visited Dorchester in 1672.

21. PRO, SP 29/93, fol. 14; 29/98, fol. 351; 29/99, fols. 103–10; 29/107, fols. 193–5. Matthews, *Calamy Revised*, pp. 47, 116, 156, 244–5, 317–18, 456, 482, 515.

22. Dr Williams Library, MS 89.25 (Lyon Turner MSS), pp. 18–19. PRO, SP 29/320, fols. 159–60, 227–8. *CSPD, 1671–2*, pp. 308, 337–8, 434–6, 500; *1672–3*, p. 261. *MRBD*, p. 639. See also G.J. Davies, 'Early Dorset Nonconformity', *Dorset Proc.*, 97 (1975), 24–30.

23. PRO, SP 29/321, fol. 224. DRO, B2/16/5, p. 223. PRO, PROB 11/342: 1673/65. Nonconformist mayors included

Samways (1674), Twisse (1675), John Cradock (1676), Edward Jones (1678), Richard Atkins (1679), and John Gollop (1681).

24. PRO, SP 29/114, fol. 264 (*CSPD, 1664–5*, p. 251). G. Lyon Turner (ed.), *Original Records of Early Nonconformity* (1911–14), I, 123. DRO, QS Minute Book A (1669–87), 5 July 1670; 6 Oct. 1674.

25. *MRBD*, p. 619. B2/16/5, pp. 166–7. B2/23/6 (Constables' accounts, 1673–4). DRO, N10/A15 (Quaker Sufferings), p. 7. PRO, ASSI 23/1 (W. Circuit Gaol Book, 1670–7), 1 March 1675/6; ASSI 24/1 (W. Circuit Bail Book, 1654–77), 1676. Lilly's outburst against the overseer suggests anger by an ex-Parliamentarian at someone who had deserted the cause: Hewett had fought for Parliament in the civil war.

26. PRO, PROB 11/337: 1671/120 (Bartlett); 11/341: 1673/25 (Palfrey); 11/374: 1683/121 (Bedford); 11/359: 1679/61 (Poole); 11/447: 1698/215 (Haydon); 11/386: 1687/30 (Stansby).

27. DRO, PE/DO (AS) CW 1, 1662–6 accounts. This estimate is based on the assumption that wine cost 2s. a quart (as at Holy Trinity in 1686–7) and that of the 3s. 2d., 3s. was for wine. If these assumptions are correct, they would have used one and a half quarts per communion, enough for about eighty people. From a comparison of the parish registers, the population of All Saints was about equal to that of Holy Trinity. For the 1619–20 communions at Holy Trinity, each of which consumed over six quarts, see above, p. 106.

28. *MRBD*, pp. 619, 623–34. B2/16/5, p. 187.

29. *MRBD*, p. 556; and see also B2/16/5, pp. 276, 294. There are no traces of Corporation activity by Samways after the end of his mayoralty in 1675.

30. B2/16/5, pp. 143–4, 148, 177–8, 221, 237, 250, 255, 261, 267, 288, 296. B2/14/1, 1666 account. *MRBD*, pp. 528–9. B2/1/1 (Sessions Minute Book), 21 Sept. 1682.

31. B2/16/5, pp. 144–5, 164, 168, 187,

210, 217, 219, 252. *MRBD*, pp. 522–3.

32. PE/DO (AS) CW 1, 1662–3 accounts; OV 2, 1669–83 accounts. B2/16/5, pp. 152–3, 162, 176, 183, 190, 209, 218, 225, 227, 233, 238, 247, 269, 276.

33. B2/16/5, pp. 144, 146–7, 177, 179, 235, 246. *MRBD*, pp. 521–3.

34. Most of the 5 November collections are listed in B2/16/6E. See also *MRBD*, pp. 522, 549–50; and B2/16/5, pp. 162, 221, 225, 233, 269, 276, 291.

35. *MRBD*, pp. 416, 417 and n., 521. B2/16/5, pp. 154, 157, 163, 187, 193, 195. B2/31/1 (apprentice indentures), 9 March 1663/4; 17 Aug. 1664; 3 Feb. 1664/5.

36. *MRBD*, pp. 529, 710. B2/16/5, pp. 165–7, 207, 283, 286. B2/1/1, 23 Aug. 1676; 13 July 1677; 11 April 1681; 21 Sept. 1682; 20 Aug. 1683. B2/23/6.

37. Bayley, *Civil War*, p. 15, n. DRO, QSOB, 1663–74, pp. 163, 437. *MRBD*, p. 709. B2/1/1, 23 Aug. 1676; 13 July 1677; 4 Sept. 1684. PRO, SP 29/312, fol. 327v (*CSPD, 1672*, p. 345).

38. DRO, PE/DO (AS) CW 1, 1673–80 accounts. PE/DO (HT) CW 2, 1685–8 accounts. PRO, E 101/668/33, account of Joseph Derby, 1671. DRO, QS Minute Book A (1669–87), 3 Oct. 1682. *MRBD*, pp. 710–11.

39. PRO, PROB 11/324: 1667/60 (Dashwood); 11/350: 1676/50 (Gould); 11/327: 1668/89 (W. Wade); 11/360: 1679/9 (J. Wade); 11/342: 1673/65 (Terry); 11/366: 1681/87 (Bestland).

40. *MRBD*, pp. 537, 549–50.

41. DRO, PE/DO (AS) CW 1, 1666–9 accounts. *MRBD*, pp. 550–1. B2/16/5, p. 275. PE/DO (HT) CW 2, 1687–8 accounts.

42. Bodleian, Rawlinson MS D 1350, fols. 211–13v. *Dorchester Church Records*, pp. 20, 32, 34.

43. *Dorchester Town Records*, pp. 292–3. Bodleian, Rawlinson MS D 1350, fol. 160v.

44. Clap, *Memoirs*, p. 29. Caldwell, *Puritan Conversion Narrative*, p. 70, suggests the 1680s as the date of composition.

45. PRO, SP 29/203, fol. 118 (*CSPD, 1667*, p. 152).

46. *CSPD, 1675–6*, p. 353. Henning, *House of Commons*, I, 215; II, 69, 422.

47. Henning, *House of Commons*, I, 215; II, 365–6. *MRBD*, pp. 375–6. DRO, PE/DO (AS) CW 2, 1679–85 accounts. B2/14/1, 1683–5 accounts.

48. B2/1/1, and B2/2/1, 6 Jan. 1679/80, 31 Aug. 1681.

49. *MRBD*, pp. 640–3. I am grateful to Tim Harris for his advice on the 1681 Address.

50. B2/2/1, 11 April 1681. B2/2/1, 20 Aug. 1683, 4 Sept. 1684. Bodleian, Tanner MS 129, fols. 105, 128.

51. Henning, *House of Commons*, I, 216; II, 70. For the Loders, see above, p. 218.

52. DRO, PE/DO (AS) CW 1, 1684–5 accounts. PRO, ASSI 23/2 (Western Circuit Gaol Book, 1678–85), 12 March 1684/5. W. McD. Wigfield (ed.), *The Monmouth Rebels 1685* (Somerset Record Soc., 79, 1985), pp. 19, 106, 110.

53. There are several good accounts of the rebellion and its aftermath. For the Assizes, see especially Peter Earle, *Monmouth's Rebels* (1977), pp. 170–4; Robin Clifton, *The Last Popular Rebellion* (1984); and Robert Dunning, *The Monmouth Rebellion* (Wimborne, 1984), pp. 53–5, 64. See also G.F. Nuttall (ed.), *Letters of John Pinney* (1939), pp. 28–9.

54. DRO, PE/DO (AS) RE 1, burials, 1685–7 (one of those buried was the Taunton schoolmistress, Mary Blake). PE/DO (AS) CW 1, 1685–9 accounts. DRO, QS Minute Book A (1669–87), 12 Jan. 1685/6. See also Dunning, *Monmouth Rebellion*, p. 56.

55. PE/DO (HT) CW 2, 1688–9 accounts. *MRBD*, p. 407.

56. PE/DO (HT) CW 2, 1 June 1686, and 1686–7 accounts.

EPILOGUE
ON TO CASTERBRIDGE

1. Throughout this Epilogue quotations from Thomas Hardy's *The Mayor of Casterbridge* are printed in italics.

2. DRO, PE/DO (AS) CW 1, 1683–5 and 1690–1 accounts. *Daily Courant*, 27 Oct. 1714: quoted in Kathleen Wilson, 'The Rejection of Deference: Urban Politics and Culture in England, 1715–1785' (Yale Ph.D., 1985), pp. 38–9 (I am grateful to Tim Harris for further information on the 1714 riot). Daniel Defoe, *Tour through the Whole Island of Great Britain* (Penguin edn., 1978), p. 209.

3. *MRBD*, pp. 523–4, 529. B2/8/2, 14 March 1705/6.

4. B2/3/9–17, Sessions Rolls, 1699–1707.

5. B2/8/2, 1697–1707.

6. *MRBD*, p. 584. In the nineteenth century the family produced an important and highly successful photographer, John Pouncy.

7. *MRBD*, pp. 438–42. For the MPs, see Romney Sedgwick, *The House of Commons 1715–1754* (1970), I, 233; and Sir Lewis Namier and John Brooke, *The House of Commons 1754–1790* (1964), I, 265–6.

8. See *Ashley*, pp. 36, 43, 45–9; and above, pp. 67, 69, 79.

9. The depositions about the 1707 skimmington are in B2/8/2, 25 Feb. 1706/7.

INDEX